Paris '44

Paris '44

The Shame and the Glory

PATRICK BISHOP

VIKING

an imprint of

PENGUIN BOOKS

VIKING

UK | USA | Canada | Ireland | Australia
India | New Zealand | South Africa

Viking is part of the Penguin Random House group of companies
whose addresses can be found at global.penguinrandomhouse.com.

Penguin Random House UK,
One Embassy Gardens, 8 Viaduct Gardens, London SW11 7BW

penguin.co.uk
global.penguinrandomhouse.com

First published 2024
005

Set in 12/14.75pt Bembo Book MT Pro
Typeset by Jouve (UK), Milton Keynes
Printed and bound in Great Britain by Clays Ltd, Elcograf S.p.A.

The authorized representative in the EEA is Penguin Random House Ireland,
Morrison Chambers, 32 Nassau Street, Dublin D02 YH68

A CIP catalogue record for this book is available from the British Library

HARDBACK ISBN: 978-0-241-49296-3
TRADE PAPERBACK ISBN: 978-0241-49297-0

To old friends, old comrades:

Richard, Teresa, Nina, Mark, Felicity, Keith,
Claire, Laura, Xan, Jane, Viv, James, Charles and Tina.

Contents

List of Illustrations

Images in the text

Plate sections

Maps

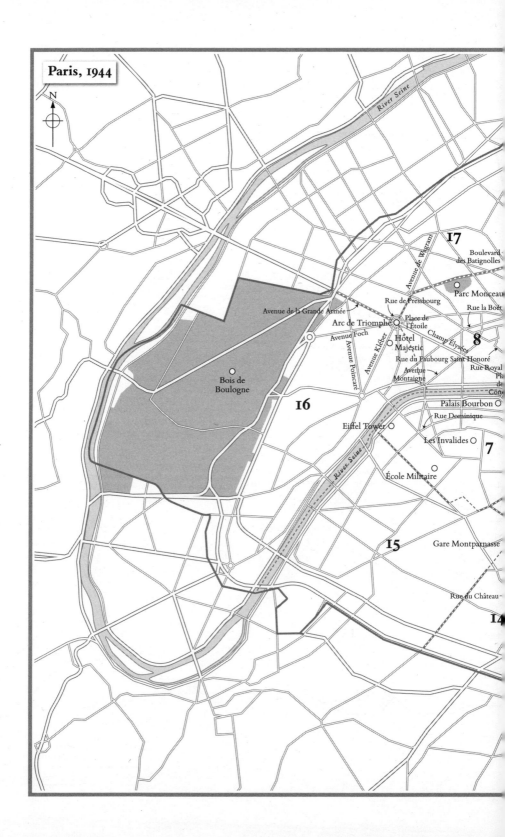

Paris, 1944

N

River Seine

17

Boulevard
des Batignolles

Rue de Pressbourg

Parc Monceau

Avenue de la Grande Armée

Rue la Boët

Arc de Triomphe

Place de
l'Étoile

Avenue Foch

Champ Elysées

8

Hôtel
Majestic

Avenue Kléber

Rue du Faubourg Saint Honoré

Rue Royal

Avenue Poincaré

Avenue
Montaigne

Pl
de
Con

Bois de
Boulogne

16

Palais Bourbon

Rue Dominique

Eiffel Tower

Les Invalides

7

École Militaire

15

Gare Montparnasse

Rue du Château -

14

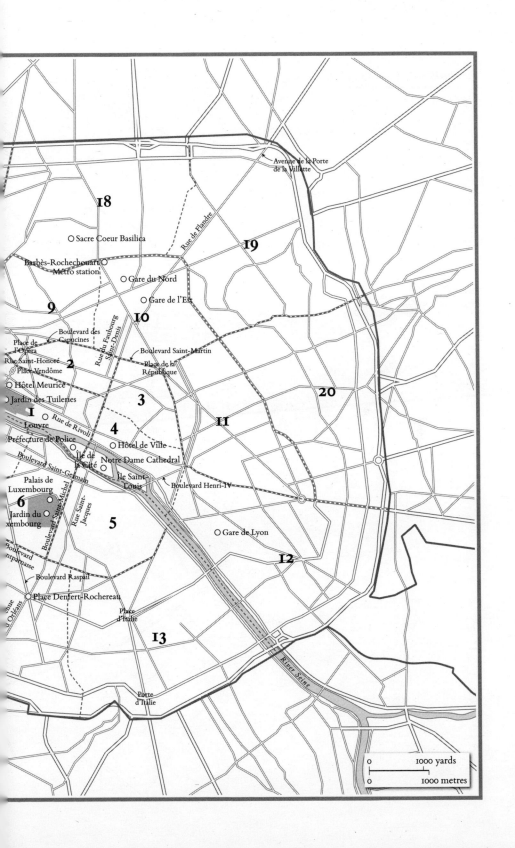

18

○ Sacre Coeur Basilica

Barbès-Rochechouart ○
Métro station

9

○ Gare du Nord

○ Gare de l'Est

10

19

Rue de Flandre

Avenue de la Porte
de la Villette

Boulevard des
Capucines
Place de
l'Opéra
Rue Saint-Honoré
2
Place Vendôme
○ Hôtel Meurice
○ Jardin des Tuileries
I
Louvre ○ Rue de Rivoli
Préfecture de Police
Boulevard Saint-Germain
Palais de
Luxembourg
6 ○
Jardin du
xembourg

Rue du Faubourg Saint-Denis

Boulevard Saint-Martin
Place de la
République

3

4
○ Hôtel de Ville
Île de ○ Notre Dame Cathedral
la Cité ○
Île Saint-
Louis
Boulevard Henri-IV

11

20

Boulevard Saint-Michel
Rue Saint-Jacques
5

Boulevard
ntparnasse
← Boulevard Raspail
○ Place Denfert-Rochereau

e d'Orléans

13

Place
d'Italie

○ Gare de Lyon

12

Porte
d'Italie

River Seine

0   1000 yards

0   1000 metres

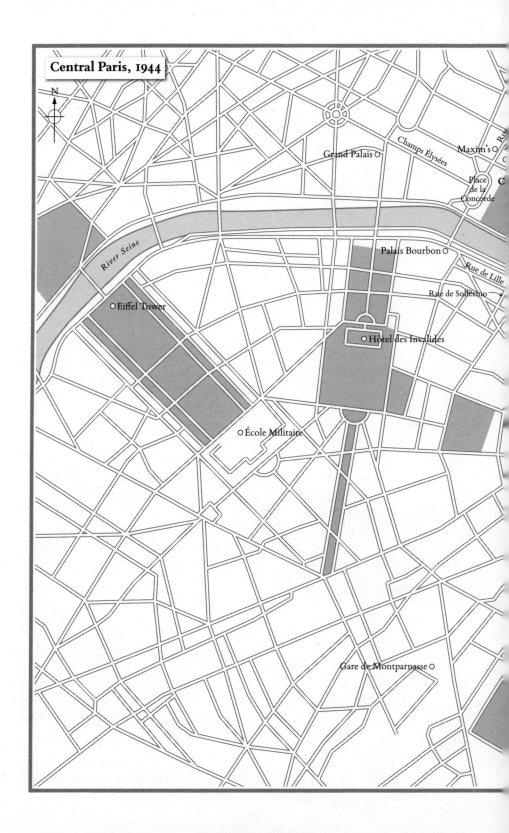

Central Paris, 1944

N

Grand Palais

Champs Élysées

Maxim's

Place de la Concorde

River Seine

Palais Bourbon

Rue de Lille

Rue de Solférino

Eiffel Tower

Hôtel des Invalides

École Militaire

Gare de Montparnasse

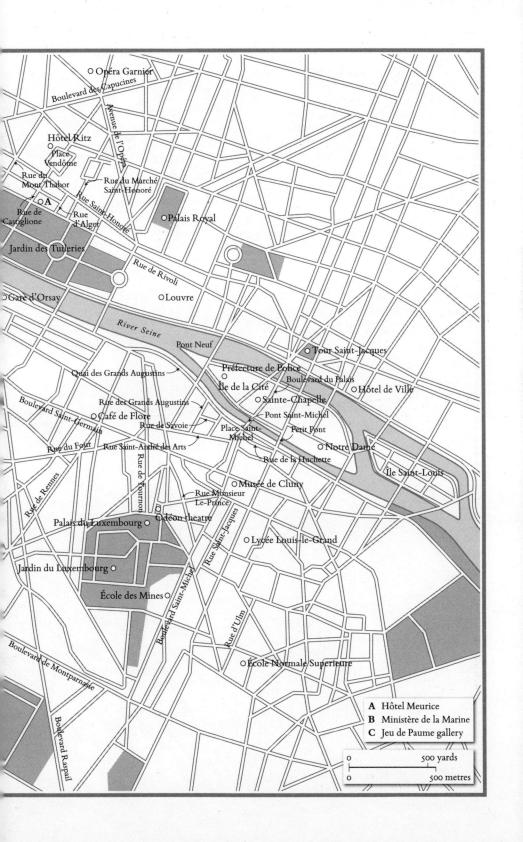

Opéra Garnier

Boulevard des Capucines

Avenue de l'Opéra

Hôtel Ritz
Place Vendôme

Rue du Mont Thabor
Rue du Marché Saint-Honoré

Rue Saint-Honoré

Rue de Castiglione

Rue d'Alger

Palais Royal

Jardin des Tuileries

Rue de Rivoli

Gare d'Orsay

Louvre

River Seine

Pont Neuf

Tour Saint-Jacques

Quai des Grands Augustins

Préfecture de Police

Île de la Cité

Boulevard du Palais

Hôtel de Ville

Rue des Grands Augustins

Sainte-Chapelle

Boulevard Saint-Germain

Café de Flore

Pont Saint-Michel

Rue de Savoie

Place Saint-Michel

Petit Pont

Rue du Four

Rue Saint-André des Arts

Rue de la Huchette

Notre Dame

Île Saint-Louis

Rue de Tournon

Musée de Cluny

Rue de Rennes

Rue Monsieur Le-Prince

Palais du Luxembourg

Odéon-theatre

Rue Saint-Jacques

Lycée Louis-le-Grand

Jardin du Luxembourg

Boulevard Saint-Michel

École des Mines

Rue d'Ulm

Boulevard de Montparnasse

École Normale Supérieure

Boulevard Raspail

A Hôtel Meurice
B Ministère de la Marine
C Jeu de Paume gallery

0   500 yards
0   500 metres

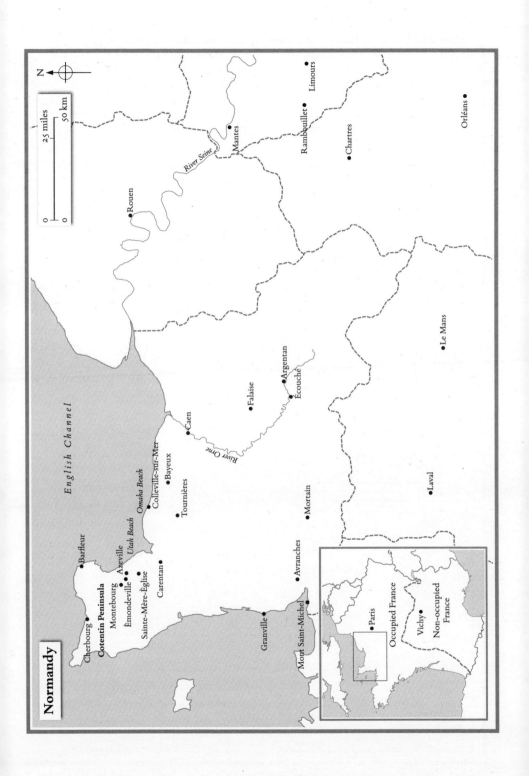

Normandy

N

25 miles
50 km

English Channel

Rouen

River Seine

Mantes

Rambouillet • Limours

Chartres

Orléans

Le Mans

Argentan
Écouché

Falaise

Caen

Coleville-sur-Mer
Omaha Beach
Bayeux
Tournières

Laval

Mortain

River Orne

Barfleur

Azeville
Utah Beach
Montebourg
Émondeville
Sainte-Mère-Église
Carentan

Cotentin Peninsula

Cherbourg

Avranches

Granville

Mont Saint-Michel

Paris

Occupied France

Vichy •

Non-occupied France

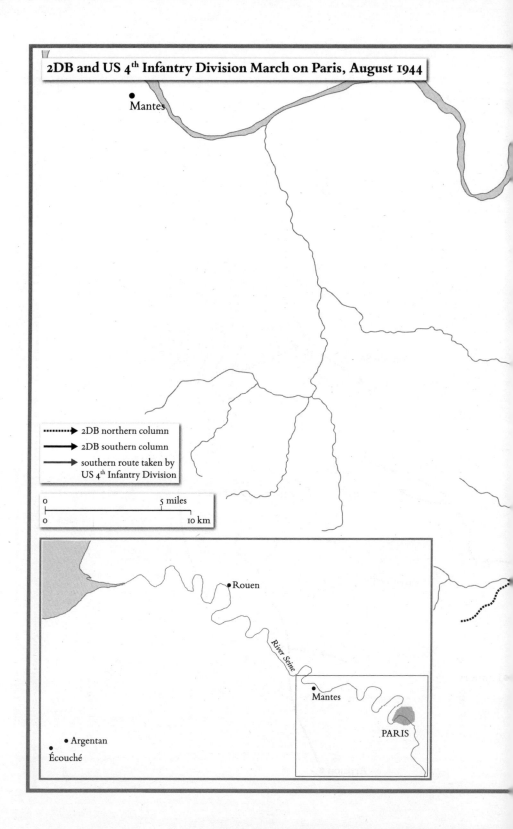

2DB and US 4th Infantry Division March on Paris, August 1944

Mantes

2DB northern column
2DB southern column
southern route taken by
US 4th Infantry Division

0   5 miles
0   10 km

Rouen

River Seine

Mantes

PARIS

Argentan
Écouché

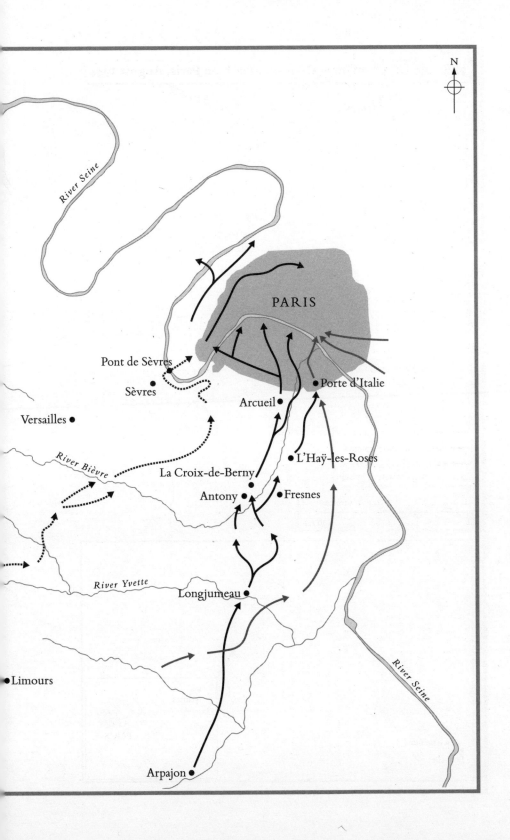

N

River Seine

PARIS

Pont de Sèvres

Sèvres

Versailles

River Bièvre

Arcueil

Porte d'Italie

La Croix-de-Berny

L'Haÿ-les-Roses

Antony

Fresnes

River Yvette

Longjumeau

River Seine

Limours

Arpajon

Introduction

In the early summer of 1945, the maternity wards of Paris were suddenly very busy. The upsurge in births was a living, breathing legacy of what had been the party of the century, that glorious Friday in August 1944 when Paris was liberated from the Germans, setting off an explosion of happiness that echoed round the world. The American war reporter Ernie Pyle arrived by jeep to witness:

> a pandemonium of surely the greatest mass joy that has ever happened . . . We all got kissed until we were literally red in face, and I must say we enjoyed it . . . when the jeep was simply swamped in human traffic and had to stop, we were swarmed over and hugged and kissed and torn at. Everybody, even beautiful girls, insisted on kissing you on both cheeks . . . the fact that I hadn't shaved for days, and was gray-bearded as well as bald-headed, made no difference.

Among the population, the longing for deliverance was so deep that some feared at first that the American uniforms in the streets must be a hallucination. 'But no, I am not dreaming,' wrote a middle-aged man of letters, Gustave-Jean Reybaz, in his diary. 'The nightmare of occupation is finally at an end and Paris has rolled away the stone of its own tomb and is reborn again.'

The eruption of exhilaration and relief reflected the unique position that Paris held in the world's affections. Its fate mattered to almost everybody. In November 1939, three months into the strange interlude of inaction before fighting erupted in the west, which the French called the *Drôle de Guerre* and the British the Phoney War, Maurice Chevalier recorded a reassuring song. 'Paris sera toujours Paris' was a message to the world that whatever Hitler threw at the place, 'Paris will always be Paris.' The verses described the boarded-up statues, taped-over windows, gas masks, rationing, air-raid sirens and blackouts now marring the beauty of everyone's favourite city. But the refrain promised:

> In spite of all the gloom and dark
> The city we all love — you'll see!
> Will never, ever lose her spark
> Paree will always be Paree
> The more they dim the lighting
> The more we'll come back fighting
> Our spirit and our humour floating free
> Paree will always be Paree!

The defiant tone struck a chord everywhere and the song was a hit, becoming a staple of Chevalier's repertoire. As prophecy it was a flop. Seven months later the German army walked into Paris unopposed, the start of more than four years of suffering, humiliation, deprivation and shame. Maurice Chevalier survived the occupation. Casimir Oberfeld, the man who composed the song, did not. He was one of 77,000 Jews sent from France to extermination camps by the German and French authorities and died in January 1945, freezing to death on a forced march just as the Russians were closing in on Auschwitz.

In 1949, four years after the end of the war, Josephine Baker recorded another song about Paris. Baker was born in America but rose to fame in France, where she lived for the rest of her life. Unlike Chevalier, who would later be accused of collaboration, Baker had an impeccable war record for which she was awarded the Resistance

Medal and the Légion d'Honneur. In 'Paris, Paris' she celebrated her adopted home town: a 'corner of paradise', 'favourite of all my loves', its 'charm and elegance / the very soul of France'. This too was a hit, signalling that after all the tribulations of the occupation the city was back to its old self. Paris was doubly lucky. It emerged from the war with both its buildings and its reputation mostly intact. The process of rehabilitation began while the party was still in full swing. The liberation morphed from historical fact to legend overnight. The story of what had happened and what it meant was shaped by the man whose presence dominated the first delirious days of freedom. 'Paris! Paris outraged! Paris broken! Paris martyred!' declared Charles de Gaulle in a carefully crafted speech delivered on his arrival on the great day. He continued triumphantly: 'But Paris liberated! Liberated by itself, liberated by its people with the help of the armies of France, with the help and assistance of the whole of France, of that France which fights, of the only France, of the true France, of the eternal France.'

De Gaulle was delivering what we might today call 'his truth', but it did not sit easily with the facts. Given the very limited scale of the uprising, could the people of Paris really be said to have liberated themselves? The 'armies of France' amounted to one armoured division, the 2ème Division Blindée (2DB), which was entirely equipped by the Americans, and the first of its troops to enter the city were mostly Spanish republicans, refugees from the civil war. The 2DB's firepower had been greatly reinforced by the presence of the American 4th Infantry Division, following close behind in case things went wrong. The 'whole of France' had played no direct part in the liberation. The one 'true', 'only' and 'eternal' France was a Gaullist invention. The nation rarely agreed on anything and the occupation had only opened another bitter chapter in a long history of discord.

But these were all mere facts and when confronting the newly minted legend they were bound to come off worse. De Gaulle had understood brilliantly the power that the city on the Seine exercised over the world's imagination. It was loved as if it was a person rather than a place. People would believe what they wanted to believe, and no one wanted to think badly of someone they cherished.

At its heart, Paris was as much an idea as a reality. Its identity had been built collectively by both its inhabitants and a multitude of outsiders, many of them artists of various kinds who had the status of honorary citizens. Among them were Ernest Hemingway and Pablo Picasso, who had done much to give the twentieth century its voice, shape and colour, and both of whom were on the star-studded guest list at the liberation party. Paris was part of who they were and a host of wannabe Hemingways and Picassos had moved to the city hoping some of its magic would rub off on them. *Paris*: the two syllables conjured a world of endless possibilities where fantasies of romance and fulfilment could come true. It was the self-proclaimed capital of freedom and tolerance, the very things the Nazis wanted to smash to pieces. When Paris fell, it was as if a great beacon had been extinguished. When it rose again, the light blazed out once more and the struggle against the forces of darkness seemed as good as won.

There was some truth in this rosy rendering of events. But the real story is more complicated and more interesting. This book is an attempt to tell it truly while never denying the power and authenticity of the myth. I write as a devotee who first hitchhiked to Paris with a friend when we were just eighteen, pitching a tent in the campsite in the Bois de Boulogne and subsisting until our money ran out on bread, cheese and red wine that came in plastic bottles. I have lived there on and off for years, yet each morning, as I step through the heavy door of the apartment block and into the bustle and show of the street, I feel the same surge of pleasure and anticipation as the first time I went there and everything was new.

I have tried, where possible, to relate events through the eyes and actions of an ensemble of those who were part of the mighty drama, both locals and foreigners. Some, like Hemingway, Picasso and J. D. Salinger, are legends. Others, like the fascist writer Robert Brasillach and the communist leader Henri Rol-Tanguy, merely well known. Then there are those you may never have heard of, though it is time that you did. They include a medic turned Resistance gunwoman, an androgynous Hungarian sculptor and a French bluestocking who quietly set about saving the nation's art treasures from the Nazi looters. All played some role, big or small, in the great events that follow.

As well as freedom, liberation brought judgement. The chaos and the ever changing odds offered opportunities for the quick-witted to dodge one fate and embrace another. No one did this more successfully than one of the story's prominent characters: the city's German military commander, General Dietrich von Choltitz of *Is Paris Burning?* fame. A man described by his captors as 'a cinema-type German officer, fat, coarse and be-monocled', who until then had been Hitler's loyal servant, was able to recast himself as the city's saviour, another myth built, as we shall see, on shaky foundations.

The lives of these men, women and teenagers converged that August in eleven days of drama, joy and bloodshed. Almost all the actors are now dead. If they could rise from their graves and tread the streets once more, they would find Paris much as they remembered it – proud and beautiful, interestingly raw and grimy behind the smooth exterior and above all, like this story, full of ambiguities.

Prologue:
The Diabolical Tourist

It was a glorious morning in June 1940 and Arno Breker was at his house in the southern suburbs of Berlin. A golden mist floated over the city and the scent of pines from the Grünewald filled the air. He had to remind himself there was a war on. The silence was broken by the ring of the telephone. It was still only 7.15. Who could be calling this early?

'Geheimstaatspolizei,' said the voice at the other end. 'You are going on a short journey. A car will be outside in an hour.' Breker tried to find out more, but the line went dead. He felt a stab of alarm. What could the Gestapo want with *him*? He steered clear of politics. It was true he was Hitler's favourite sculptor but that, he told himself, was due solely to his talent, not because he cared much for Nazi ideology.

He turned to his Greek-born wife Demetra who was hovering by his side. What could it mean? Breker's first thought was to ring his friend Albert Speer, who was Hitler's chief architect and a member of the Führer's inner circle, but then he remembered that Speer had been out of town for days. Argument with the Gestapo was futile and could only make things worse. There was nothing to do but pack a bag – and wait. An hour later the doorbell rang. Two SS officers stood outside. Breker hugged Demetra goodbye. They were both 'worried though neither of us admitted it. We knew that under a dictatorship anything was possible.'

The car sped through the Grünewald. All the sculptor's attempts at conversation were ignored. They skirted the Havel lake and turned west. They were not going into Berlin then. Soon afterwards they drew up at a small airfield: Laaken. A twin-engine Junkers Ju-52, the workhorse of the Luftwaffe, stood by the runway. Breker was told to wait while some soldiers finished loading the aircraft. They were humping baskets of vegetables and crates of assorted fruit juices. It was an odd cargo, he thought, as he waited to see what happened next.

Four hundred miles to the west, Albert Speer was kicking his heels in a small village in the Ardennes forest, just inside the Belgian border with France. He had arrived at Brûly-de-Pesche a couple of days before, ordered there by Hitler. He was used to abrupt summonses to drop everything and rush to his master's side. Often by the time he got there the reason why his presence was so urgently required had been forgotten or turned out to be a passing whim. He knew better than to complain. This, he soon learned, was not another wild-goose chase.

Hitler had spent the last few weeks directing the final phase of the Battle of France from a reinforced concrete bunker in the woods at the edge of the village. On 22 June the war in the west ended with the signing of an armistice. The site Hitler chose for the ceremony was heavy with symbolism. It took place in the same railway carriage in the same clearing in the forest of Compiègne, 50 miles north of Paris, where Germany had formally surrendered in 1918.

The Führer was in high spirits when he welcomed Speer to the headquarters, telling him: 'In a few days we are flying to Paris. I'd like you to be with us. Breker and Giesler are coming along also.' Hermann Giesler was another of Hitler's pet architects. That evening Hitler outlined his plan. The idea of a triumphal entry into the city had been considered and rejected, not least because he had been advised that the parade would be vulnerable to attack by the British Royal Air Force. Never mind. Hitler would celebrate the moment in a way that reflected his other persona, the frustrated artist and architect. The visit was to be a kind of 'art tour' and instead of a troop of generals he wanted artists at his side. Speer knew Paris well, and Breker knew it even better, having lived there for years in the late 1920s and early 1930s. Their expertise was unlikely to be needed. They were going as acolytes, to endorse the leader's judgements and observations.

Breker's nerves had calmed down a little by the time the Junkers bumped down in a forest clearing. He kept his mouth shut as he was driven through woods along empty roads and past deserted villages, cleared of their inhabitants. A sign told him he was entering Brûly – a cluster of stone and slate houses with a modest chapel in the centre. The car pulled up and Speer and Giesler appeared to meet him. 'A bit worried, were we?' asked Speer with a malicious smile.

When Hitler got round to seeing them, his good mood was intact. He apologized to Breker for dragging him away from his home without warning, but he wanted the 'old Parisian' to be at his side for the tour. The city, he admitted, was something of an obsession for him and when young he had dreamed of living there. Destiny had other plans: 'But now the gates are open to me I have no other idea in my head but to visit with my artists.' There was a practical purpose to the trip. Between them they were going to rebuild Berlin, and the monuments and avenues of Paris would inspire their plans. And there was also a political dimension: by forgoing a triumphal entry he was showing goodwill towards his new conquest. Despite the Compiègne theatricals he 'had no intention whatsoever of inflicting a humiliation on the French people after their defeat', and hoped for an end to the catastrophic enmity between the two nations and the start of a new era of Franco-German co-operation. Breker was relieved to hear this. Paris was his second home. Nonetheless, the idea of returning there at the side of its conqueror 'felt like a moral burden that I was not sure that I could shoulder'.

Departure was set for early the following morning. The artists were told to wear uniform. The greatcoat issued to Breker was much too big for him and had enough cloth left over to make a pair of trousers. When the party gathered before dinner the sight made Hitler 'burst into laughter'. They sat at a pine table in a peasant cottage. Hitler chewed a mush of vegetables, freshly arrived with Breker on the Junkers-52, and washed it down with sips of fruit juice. They were due to take off at 3 a.m. in a four-engine Focke-Wulf Condor with Hans Baur at the controls. Baur had been Hitler's personal pilot since 1933, but he was much more than a mere aerial chauffeur. The genial Bavarian was an early convert to Nazism and as loyal and obedient as a good dog. Hitler exalted him as the quintessence of German decency: simple, uncomplaining and cheerful, someone who wanted only to serve, and 'never asked anything from me'. He was also a brilliant aviator and had flown more than 600,000 miles, a comfort for the Führer, who disliked flying.

The airstrip, a few miles away over the French border, was fogged in. There could be no delay if they were to complete the crowded itinerary on time and, as the mist showed no signs of lifting, Baur took off blind, using the instruments.

They landed at Le Bourget aerodrome in the north-eastern suburbs of Paris just as the sun rose. It was a fine Sunday morning and promised to be a hot day. Hitler wore a plain lightweight greatcoat, a white shirt and dark tie and a peaked cap. Three large open-topped Mercedes staff cars were waiting to drive them into the city. Hitler sat in the front of the lead car next to the driver. Behind him were Breker and Speer. Giesler was in the back, alongside Hitler's adjutant Nicolaus von Below and Hans Baur, who would record some of the event on an 8mm movie camera. They set off at high speed, slaloming round abandoned barricades, evidence of the French rout, slowing at the German checkpoints for the barrier to lift and the sentries to salute.

It was the first time Hitler had seen the city. They entered by the Porte de la Villette and took the rue de Flandre towards the centre, down drab canyons of identical six-storey apartment blocks with leprous plaster façades. This was working-class Paris: raucous, Red-voting and chronically rebellious. It was of no interest to Hitler, who had chosen to start the tour with a homage to what he believed to be an architectural masterpiece. The Paris Opéra, which opened in 1875, was a vast confection of ornamented stone, in a neo-baroque style that was recent enough to have fallen out of fashion and not yet old enough to acquire the dignity of age. To sophisticated contemporary eyes it looked at best painfully dated, at worst hideously kitsch.

Hitler, though, was entranced. They drew up in front of the steps to the main entrance where the Paris garrison commander, Colonel Hans Speidel, was waiting with some of his men. Before entering, Hitler toured the outside, admiring it from all angles. He had boned up thoroughly for the trip. Breker and his companions were treated to a stream of praise for 'the use of the stone . . . the quality of the design, its deceptively simple functionality, the harmony of the artistic ensemble. It all seemed to fascinate him.'

Once through the doors Hitler stood, apparently awestruck, before the grand staircase that the architect Charles Garnier intended as the centrepiece of his creation. Hitler's personal photographer Heinrich Hoffmann snapped away. Every chandelier was lit up as if for a gala night featuring some star soprano. But the place was empty, apart from one blue-uniformed caretaker who watched impassively from a corner of the foyer. His name was Pierre Théodore, known to all as Glouglou, and his apparent indifference struck Breker as an omen. The idea that France and Germany would henceforth live in harmony was a fantasy and Breker 'felt for the first time the tragic gulf that now separated the occupiers from the occupied'.

The caretaker obeyed their request to be shown around, but in what Speer felt was 'a businesslike and distinctly aloof manner'. The party climbed the staircase and entered the auditorium with Hitler keeping up an incessant commentary. As he enthused about its beauty Speer saw 'his eyes glittering with an excitement that struck me as uncanny'. He was childishly keen to show off. At one point his photographic knowledge of the plans failed to match the reality in front of him: a salon which should have been there was missing. Breker was told to ask the caretaker to explain. Glouglou replied that there had indeed once been such a room but it had disappeared in some long-ago renovation. Hitler was delighted. 'You see how well I know my way about!'

The tour lasted fifty minutes. As they left, Hitler told an adjutant, Wilhelm Brückner, to thank their guide. When Brückner tried to slip him a large tip, Glouglou waved it away. Hitler noticed the exchange and asked Breker to use his French to try again. This time the refusal was curt. Once again Breker felt a twinge of disquiet. This was the first representative of the conquered France they had come across and he seemed 'unmoved and showing no sign of having been impressed'. Very soon afterwards it became clear that not everyone in Paris shared Glouglou's reserve. As they drove away, the movie camera focused on a pair of policemen patrolling along the side of the Opéra, white batons in hand. On seeing the motorcade their eyes swivelled left and they raised their hands respectfully to the peaks of their *képis*. The scene was repeated when they passed four more policemen – *les flics* in common parlance – who stood stiffly to attention and saluted as the cars entered the place de la Madeleine, half a mile away along the boulevard des Capucines. The area would normally be coming alive at this hour with waiters setting out the tables on the pavement ready for the early mass-goers to take their morning coffee. But fear had emptied the city and it looked to Breker 'like a theatre set'.

Hitler seemed to find the Madeleine a comedown after the Opéra, a mere Napoleonic knock-off of the temples of classical antiquity. The broad stone plain of the place de la Concorde however 'made a great impression'. From there the driver was ordered to proceed slowly up the Champs-Élysées so that the Führer could savour the symbolism of the ascent to the Arc de Triomphe, which now seemed more of a folly than an unanswerable statement of French power. The grandiosity of the ensemble of arch and avenue conformed to his own plan for a mighty east–west axis which would link the defining monuments of the new Berlin. As the capital of the new Europe, it would have its own triumphal arch. Speer had already made the drawings, reverently following a design done by the Führer in 1925 when he was a daydreaming nobody. It bore a remarkable resemblance to the one in Paris. As if to drown out the charge of plagiarism, the Berlin monument would be of a different order of magnitude. Napoleon's effort was 160 feet high. Hitler's creation would dwarf it, soaring to 386 feet. It too would be a memorial to the nation's war dead with the names of 1,800,000 of them chiselled into the granite. Everything, he had told Speer, would be bigger and better. The 'Champs' was 330 feet wide, but 'we'll make our avenue seventy-odd feet wider'. Architecture served the purposes of power. It should be devoid of humanity, nightmarishly vast and intimidating, creating a townscape on which the citizen makes no more impression than an ant.

For the moment though, Hitler was lost in admiration of the original. The triumph was all his. He looked down the sweep of the Champs at the city lying nakedly below, its riches and pleasures there for the taking. But this was no time to linger. He had great victories to consolidate and the timetable was tight. They climbed back into the cars and cruised down the avenues Foch and Poincaré to the esplanade of the Trocadéro, which provided the ideal platform to look across the Seine to the Eiffel Tower. They got out and like an ordinary bunch of tourists posed for pictures with the tower in the

background – except that in the resulting photographs nobody is smiling. Hitler looks straight at the photographer, the expression in his eyes overshadowed by the peak of his cap and his arms crossed protectively in front of his crotch. A pair of gloves trails from his hands. Speer's smooth, complacent face is angled left, his shrewd eyes staring neutrally into mid-distance. Breker, on the Führer's left shoulder, is weighed down with what looks like movie camera equipment while his well-cut features struggle to find an appropriate expression.

They crossed the pont d'Iéna to the Left Bank, stopping at the École Militaire and the Hôtel des Invalides. The sight en route of a statue of General Charles Mangin, who had commanded the French army of the occupation of the Rhineland in 1921, caused Hitler to stiffen in disapproval. 'We'll have to do something about reminders of this sort,' he grunted, and shortly afterwards the plinth was blown up and Mangin was melted down. The next monument commanded his respect. Beneath the dome of the Invalides, he paused in front of the gargantuan purple quartzite sarcophagus of Napoleon for a few minutes of solemn contemplation. That his own career might also end in failure and defeat seemed unimaginable on a day like this.

They remounted the staff cars and cruised slowly past the Senate and the Odéon theatre, pausing briefly to inspect the tombs of Voltaire and Victor Hugo in the chilly bowels of the Panthéon. Hitler ordered a detour to take in Montparnasse so he could see the terrace cafés where Breker had idled in his bohemian Paris days.

They were driving through a dreamscape. It was Paris as no one had ever seen it at this hour, apparently devoid of people. Then, as they were returning back up the rue de Rivoli to the Hôtel de Ville, they skirted Les Halles, the food-market district known as the Belly of Paris. Breker saw a gaggle of rotund women standing at a street corner. They were fishwives from the market, notorious for their cockiness and sharp tongues. They were 'just approaching them when the fattest one saw us, pointed at Hitler and shrieked: "It's him! It's him!"' They ran in terror, as if they had seen a monster.

The tour ended at Montmartre, looking down over the city from Sacré-Coeur. Out of the bowl of lead roofs and chimney stacks shimmering in the heat haze rose the gilded domes of the monuments they had just visited. Hitler gazed over it benevolently. 'I thank the destiny that has allowed me to see this great city which has always fascinated me,' he said. 'It is absolutely essential that this marvel of western culture that flourishes below us should be preserved intact for posterity.' And that was it. They got back into the cars and sped back to Le Bourget. It was not yet nine o'clock.

Breker had been comforted by his leader's apparent commitment to preserving a place he professed to love. But Hitler had sometimes contemplated a different fate for the city. That evening, back in Brûly, he ordered Speer to press ahead with the full-scale rebuilding of Berlin. Paris was beautiful, but the new Berlin would eclipse it. His next words were spoken 'as if he were talking about the most natural thing in the world'. Hitler told him: 'In the past I have often wondered whether we would not have to destroy Paris. But when we are finished in Berlin, Paris will only be a shadow. So why should we destroy it?'

1. City of Darkness, City of Light

Paris was where Ernest Hemingway had made his name, but by June 1940 his salad days in the city were just a memory. He was in Cuba, though his mind was in Spain, reliving the events of a few years back. The new novel had been a struggle, but he was starting to feel good about it and he had finally found the right title. Days combing through the Bible and the works of Shakespeare for inspiration produced nothing. Then John Donne came to the rescue. His exhortation to 'never send to know for whom the bell tolls – it tolls for thee' seemed to have 'the magic that a title needs to have', matching perfectly the sense of loss and human solidarity he was trying to capture. He was almost finished with it and friends with whom he shared the manuscript were telling him it was the best thing he had done. More importantly, his editor Max Perkins approved. The relief was enormous. A big success might wipe away some of the worry and uncertainty clouding his personal life.

Standing at the chest-high desk at which he worked in La Finca Vigía, his hilltop home near Havana, he looked more like a bum than the world's most famous writer. His beard was thick and his hair long, the result of a vow not to visit the barber until the book was done. He viewed the end with mixed feelings. Writing might be exhausting but it kept reality at bay, stridently represented by Martha Gellhorn, his latest partner though not yet his wife. She was about to arrive back in Cuba with her mother in tow after a month in New York. He loved her looks, especially her thick blonde hair ('like a wheatfield in the wind') and her determination to prove she was his equal in courage. But she was much less tolerant than his previous wives when it came to putting up with nights out boozing with the boys and the bullying streak which others seemed willing to accept as the price of genius.

During a break in writing, he shared with his publisher Charles Scribner his recipe for dealing with difficult women. 'You have to be

Marty and Ernest

firm with them,' he wrote. A man should say, 'sure he will take her to Havana. Then at the last minute say "Darling, things have come up so that I cannot take you to Havana. No, I cannot explain. It involves issues that are Too Big. Trust me darling as you always have . . ." ' He was joking, sort of, but if this was really how he wanted things to be with 'Marty' she was unlikely to stick around for long.

The alpha-male routine was not the only problem. Another threat to the relationship was the fact that they were in the same line of business. His first wife, Hadley Richardson, was an unsuccessful musician. His second, Hadley's best friend Pauline Pfeiffer, was a writer of sorts, a journalist for *Vogue* in Paris when he met her. But Martha was the real thing, a truth-seeking, risk-taking reporter he had met and fallen for in Madrid three years previously when they were both covering the Spanish Civil War. By then she had already published a novel and a collection of short stories, and now a second novel was about to appear. While Hemingway was reliving an old war in his imagination, Gellhorn was in the thick of the new one and had been in Helsinki in late November 1939 when the first Russian bombs landed on Finland.

Marriage was one way of asserting his dominance over Martha and he was due to wed her as soon as Pauline gave him a divorce. The process was not going well. After years of quiet submission, Pauline was pushing back. She was after him for serious money – 500 dollars a month to support their two sons, Patrick and Gregory – despite having lots of her own and was 'shelling' him 'plenty, plenty'.

Hemingway's problems were professional as well as personal. He was now the best-known novelist in the English-speaking world, the king of a new way of writing, but uneasy lay the head that wore the crown. His unique style was much copied and easy prey for parodists. It was a sort of homage but also a sign that the novelty might be fading. Upstarts and smart alecks were snapping at his ankles, convinced that his day was drawing to a close and theirs was about to dawn.

One budding contender was a sleek young New Yorker called Jerome Salinger. By his own account he was 'tall, dark, and when dressed I look either dapper or sloppy'. His personality was 'alternately cynical and Pollyanna-like, happy and morose, affectionate and indifferent'. Although success was coming very slowly, he was convinced of his own talent and free with his judgements on the big names he aspired to join. He was quick to praise – Scott Fitzgerald and William Faulkner were among his favourites – and also to disparage. As a freshman at Ursinus College in Pennsylvania in 1938 he had received with scepticism the news that Hemingway had written his first and, as it turned out, only play, set in besieged Madrid and called *The Fifth Column*. 'We hope it is worthy of him,' he declared in the college newspaper with arch concern. 'Ernest, we feel, has underworked and overdrooled ever since *The Sun Also Rises*, "The Killers", and *A Farewell to Arms*.'

The sophisticated tone was redeemed slightly by the fact that Salinger knew more about life than most privileged nineteen-year-old Americans, having just returned from a long stay in Europe, sent there by his father, who had a successful food-importing business, to learn the basics of the trade. After passing through London and Paris he spent some months in Vienna where he witnessed the Nazis' persecution of the Jews. Hemingway's domination of the literary landscape seemed to irk him. When the war came he wrote a spoof piece about the slew of macho novels he foresaw emerging from the war, entitled 'Men without Hemingway' in satirical reference to *Men without Women*, an early collection of short stories. There were plenty more budding writers like Jerry Salinger who felt the same way, but none who would have the experience of coming face to face with the object of their mockery in the most dramatic circumstances imaginable, in the city where the older man had won his spurs.

Hemingway had moved with Hadley to Paris in December 1921, nearly twenty years before. Their first choice had been Rome but on the advice of a friend, the novelist Sherwood Anderson, they swapped the Eternal City for the City of Light. It was a good move. 'What a town,' he wrote to Anderson a few days after arriving as he drank hot rum punch on the terrace of the Dôme café in Montparnasse and savoured the taste of his new life. It would be the only city he ever loved.

Fame and money had coarsened him. The youthful ebullience and enthusiasm that in the old days could be taken as a sort of innocence had dulled into braggadocio. Now that his claim to being the greatest writer of the age was widely acknowledged, he seemed unsure of what to do next. Unlike Martha. She was itching to return to the front, leaving him behind once again. The simple thing would have been to swallow his pride and follow. But that was not Hemingway's style. The next few years would be spent posturing and dithering. When at last he answered the bugle's call, it would lead him back to where he started out, with all its wistful memories of youth and hope and possibility.

Paris was a concept as much as a city, and Hemingway was one of many outsiders who had shaped its image. Hundreds of thousands visited each year. Many more admired it from afar via movies, songs, books and magazine articles, which all portrayed it as a citadel of beauty, progress, freedom and romance. When the Germans marched in, the loss felt personal. By then Warsaw, Copenhagen, Oslo, Amsterdam and Brussels were already in Hitler's hands, but the international response to these tragedies did not compare to the global gasp of dismay at the sight of a giant swastika flag flying from the

Eiffel Tower. In the United States, *Time* magazine reported the event as a historic catastrophe on a par with the fifth-century AD sack of Rome. The Germans were 'the modern version of Alaric's Visigoths', desecrating 'the city that stood as Western civilization's tallest monument to art, science, letters, liberty and love'.

Broadway and Hollywood led the mourning. Jerome Kern and Oscar Hammerstein, who wrote some of the great musicals of the age, composed a sort of requiem – 'The Last Time I Saw Paris' – which went straight to the top of the charts.

> A lady known as Paris, romantic and charming
> Has left her old companions and faded from view
> Lonely men with lonely eyes are seeking her in vain
> Her streets are where they were, but there's no sign of her
> She has left the Seine

None of the other fallen bastions of European civilization had been personified in this way. References to them were gender neutral. To the French and the non-French alike, Paris was a woman, not a real one but a confection of male fantasies. She was beautiful, sophisticated, amusing, mysterious yet available; a mistress rather than a wife or a mother. And now she was German property. It was as if she had been kidnapped and was about to be violated by sacrilegious, philistine brutes.

The catastrophe was commemorated on celluloid. In the 1942 film *Casablanca*, Hollywood director Michael Curtiz (born Manó Kaminer in Jewish Budapest) looked back yearningly at a place he idealized as a symbol of the lost world the Allies were fighting to restore. It was where Rick, the Hemingwayesque hero played by Humphrey Bogart, and beautiful, noble Elsa (Ingrid Bergman) met and fell in love. Their romance is charted in flashbacks, with the Arc de Triomphe, the Eiffel Tower, the *bateaux mouches* on the river as backdrops, a montage that evokes a place and a time when good still stood a fighting chance and evil had yet to fasten its grip.

Until the day of liberation this idea of Paris would gleam like a distant lighthouse through the gloom of war, a place of beautiful thoughts where such sins as were committed were done in the name of love and pleasure and not in the cause of the hatred and cruelty that were the guiding passions of the dark new empire. For French and foreigners alike there could be no victory until Paris was free.

This image of the city was as artificial as the Warner Bros. Studios sets in Burbank, California where Curtiz shot virtually every scene. Long before the Germans got there, Paris was the capital of an unhappy nation. When Hemingway arrived in the early 1920s, the party to celebrate the end of the worst war in history was still roaring. The euphoria of survival faded to reveal an unwelcome truth. The shared sacrifice of 1914–18 had changed nothing and many of the old divisions remained. Since 1789, France had been ruled successively by a constitutional monarchy, a republic, an oligarchy, an emperor, two more kings from different branches of the Bourbon royal house, a second republic, a second emperor and now a third republic. Each transition had been forged in violence. The latest republic emerged from the fratricidal bloodshed of 1871 when French troops crushed the uprising of the Paris proletariat and their short-lived Commune with extraordinary brutality.

No change of regime had brought real unity and the French were still unable to agree on how they should be ruled. By 1930 the Third Republic had the distinction of lasting longer than any other form of government since the Revolution. That did not mean it was stable, and respect for it was leaking away. Governments came and went, but the same faces remained at the top, rotating from one post to the next. Every year there was a new scandal, usually involving gaudy financial swindles in which politicians played a murky part. This was not what 1.4 million men had died for in the recent war, and many of the population looked on their rulers with hostility, contempt or indifference.

Try as it might, the Republic had proved unable to persuade the outlying political traditions of right and left to reconcile with the centre. Throughout the post-war years they both struggled to assert themselves as the true spirit of the nation. On one wing were royalists (even though the French had killed one king and overthrown two others since 1793, respect for the monarchy remained remarkably durable), Catholics and reactionaries who had never accepted the verdict of the Revolution. On the other were the radical proletariat and their educated supporters who took their inspiration from 1789 and the successive revolts of the nineteenth century.

The most prominent of the groups agitating for a return to the past was the Action Française movement, founded in 1899 at the height of the Dreyfus affair, a military scandal that ended up convulsing the nation. The trials of Captain Alfred Dreyfus, a quiet, unsoldierly-looking artillery officer, on trumped-up espionage charges provoked a crisis that laid bare the fault lines in French society. Conservative France seized on Dreyfus as a symbol of everything they hated, his Jewishness confirming his perceived guilt. Progressives and republicans vociferously proclaimed his innocence. Public opinion divided into pro and anti camps, and the aftershocks of the affair would rumble on well into the twentieth century.

The chief ideologue of Action Française was a poet and literary critic called Charles Maurras. He was short with a large lumpy nose, deep-set eyes, coarse goatee beard and elephantine ears. Despite profound deafness he had been a brilliant student, and in France intellectual ability, no matter how impractical, ensured respect. Maurras wanted to restore France to an imagined golden age of wise monarchs ruling under the spiritual guidance of the Catholic Church, whose culture he admired even if he had by now lost his faith. Action Française preached antipathy to foreigners – including Germans – celebration of French regional cultures and differences, violent hostility to the left and profound anti-Semitism.

Maurras' followers formed leagues, starting in 1908 with the Camelots du Roi, the 'street sellers' who hawked the royalist message in the *Action Française* newspaper and took an oath to restore the monarchy by any means. Many of them were sons of the bourgeoisie and students at the various faculties of the Latin Quarter. Their loutish behaviour carried a threat of insurrection and in the 1930s, along with other rightist youth groups, they brawled regularly with young leftists. Maurras stoked the general climate of violence, calling for the murder of Third Republic leaders.

While inspired by France's revolutionary past, the radical left also looked to the future and the example set by the Soviet Union.

The birth of the Parti Communiste Français (PCF) in 1920 further destabilized the French political landscape. Its leaders were ruthless, disciplined and two-faced. They actively participated in local and national elections and in the 1936 general election won 15 per cent of the vote, but their first loyalty was to the Soviet Union and every move they made was approved or directed by Moscow. This attitude began to be mirrored on the right. Action Française and its allies were supposed to be super-patriotic. But as the 1930s progressed, some of them would look beyond France for answers to the country's problems and find them in the doctrines of fascist Italy and Nazi Germany. So it was that Frenchmen who had faced the Germans in the trenches only a few years before were now looking upon them as brothers and even saviours.

The anger in the air ignited one cold night in early 1934 when central Paris echoed with shouts, shots and the screams of wounded men. On the morning of 6 February there was nothing to suggest that a demonstration called by far-right leagues that day would be any different from the nine that had passed off reasonably peacefully already that year. As usual, the target was the government – at that point a coalition of leftist parties known as the *cartel des gauches*. The particular grievance was the new prime minister Édouard Daladier's decision to sack Jean Chiappe, the fervently right-wing prefect of the Paris police who had gone easy on the leagues while cracking down on their socialist and communist counterparts.

The tumult on the streets was one manifestation of a generalized mood of dissatisfaction that was stoked by an incendiary press. There were many reasons to dislike the government, whatever your political affiliations. The nation had just learned of a new financial scandal that once again reached into the heart of the establishment. It involved a handsome crook called Alexandre Stavisky who seemed to spring straight from the pages of a novel by Irène Némirovsky, then enjoying great success following the appearance of *David Golder*, the tale of a poor Jewish boy who started his career selling rags in Ukraine before moving to France to become a ruthless and icy-hearted international financier.

Like Némirovsky, Stavisky was also Russian-Ukrainian by origin, born in Kiev in 1888 to Jewish parents who moved to France. Early jobs included singing in a nightclub and running a clinic which promised to provide accurate pregnancy tests using a bogus examination device. He also managed municipal pawnshops in the south-western city of Bayonne from where he sold hundreds of millions of francs' worth of valueless bonds, apparently with the help of friends in high places. Stavisky was first arrested in 1927 and put on trial for fraud, but the proceedings were continually postponed and he was granted bail some nineteen times. Late in 1933 when it seemed the game was up, he fled to a chalet in Chamonix. There, on 8 January 1934, the police found him dying from two bullet wounds to the head. The official verdict was suicide. Most believed he had been murdered by hitmen hired by his political accomplices who feared exposure at the trial.

The Stavisky affair was a propaganda gift to the right. To them, sleaze and the Republic were synonymous, and where there was sleaze, there were bound to be Jews. Their anti-Semitism was ingrained and reflexive but it also provided an excuse for the nation's multiple failings. Frenchmen alone could not have brought France so low. They had surely been corrupted by outsiders who owed loyalty to nothing except money. This view was shared by many. Even the subtle and sympathetic Némirovsky often portrayed her fellow Jews as hollow figures, whose obsessive pursuit of wealth obliterated their capacity for love or empathy.

On the afternoon of Tuesday 6 February, the centre of Paris began to fill with demonstrators. Many headed for the place de la Concorde, the broad stone and cobble expanse on the Right Bank of the Seine where Louis XVI and his queen, Marie-Antoinette, had lost their heads. It was given its name in an attempt at reconciliation but had since become a favourite venue for citizens keen to vent their anger. The demonstrators marched in under the banners of their organizations. Along with the street-fighting Camelots were the more respectable youths of the Jeunesses Patriotes. A paramilitary air was supplied by the Mouvement Franciste, admirers of Mussolini who wore blue shirts stitched with fascist-style insignia.

Directly across the river from the place de la Concorde another group congregated outside the Bourbon Palace, home of the Chamber of Deputies. They had a disciplined look and some were missing an arm or a leg. They belonged to the Croix-de-Feu, led by Colonel François de la Roque, which started life as a veterans' association, and with half a million members was by far the largest of the right-wing groups. As darkness fell, the crowd on the Right Bank tried to cross the pont de la Concorde to join up with the Croix-de-Feu but were held back by mounted police. As the evening wore on, the demonstrators grew bolder. At about 6.20 they hijacked a bus, forced the passengers off and set it on fire. When the police and fire brigade intervened they were bombarded with cobblestones, iron railings and metal chairs from the adjacent Tuileries Garden. The police charged, laying about them with the flat side of their sabres. The crowd fought back with improvised spears made from broom handles spiked with razors. The street lights were smashed, plunging the scene into darkness, lit here and there by burning vehicles and flaming torches. Some rioters had brought guns and started shooting. The police fired back. It was midnight before exhaustion set in and the violence subsided. By then, sixteen people were dead and about 2,000 injured.

The left accused the right of trying to overthrow the Third Republic, but there was little evidence of any co-ordinated plan – the Croix-de-Feu crowd which surrounded the parliament had made no attempt to break in. The violence nonetheless galvanized the republican left. Whatever its faults, the old order represented some sort of stability. The prospect of a far-right rebellion suddenly seemed real. Chronic squabbling was replaced by a closing of ranks and the communists, encouraged by Moscow, began promoting an alliance with the socialists which two years later would result in a Popular Front coalition government of anti-fascists, under a Jewish prime minister, Léon Blum, supported from the outside by the PCF. Its arrival would send shivers down the spine of conservative France.

Watching the riots that night was a twenty-year-old freelance photographer called André Friedmann. He arrived in the place de la Concorde at about 6 p.m. having been taken there by Hug Block, an older photographer who ran a small photo agency. André got to work, shinning up trees and lamp posts to capture the scale of the crowd. When things hotted up, he darted into the mob, risking the gunshots and swinging police sabres. Eventually he was restrained by Block, who told him it was not worth getting killed for frames which due to the poor light would almost certainly be unusable. But in those few hours Friedmann had discovered a taste for danger that would determine the course of his adventure-filled life.

André had been born Endre in 1913 in Budapest, where his Jewish mother and father ran a successful fashion salon for the wives and daughters of the city's officials and businessmen. He was headstrong and mischievous and shared his father Dezsö's philosophy that quick wits trumped hard graft in life, which in any case was there to be enjoyed. From his mother Julia he inherited a strong survival instinct and an ambitiousness which was easy to miss under his carefree exterior. He had thick dark hair and deep brown eyes, and a charm and sense of fun that warmed any room he was in. Beneath the *joie de vivre* ran a streak of melancholy that in adulthood would emerge at the end of long nights when drink had washed away the surface gaiety.

Endre was an anarchist by nature. At sixteen he had his first brush with trouble when he was injured by the police while taking part in a violent demonstration against the authoritarian government of Admiral Horthy. In the summer of 1931, aged eighteen, he was arrested as a suspected communist, beaten and thrown into jail. His parents called in a favour from a well-placed customer to obtain his release, but it came with the condition that he left Hungary. Endre set off for Berlin, which turned out to be not much of a refuge with Nazis and communists fighting in the streets. There he was reunited with a fellow Hungarian, Eva Besnyö, whose family lived in the same apartment block as the Friedmanns. Eva was now a professional photographer and through her he got to know the owner of Dephot, a development lab that doubled as a photographic agency. Starting out running errands he moved on to simple assignments, covering minor sports events and the like. His natural talent was obvious and the jobs soon got more prestigious. In December 1932 he was sent to Copenhagen to cover a visit by Leon Trotsky. It was his last commission for Dephot; a few months later Hitler was in power and Germany was no place for Jews or left-wingers. He returned home to Budapest briefly but by the autumn was on the move again. This time the destination was Paris.

The city was full of émigrés, many of them Jews driven west by rising anti-Semitism in Germany, Poland and Hungary. Endre thought he could make a living with his camera. He was, as usual, broke. He didn't know anyone and didn't speak French, but he trusted in his luck and picked up languages fast. He arrived in September 1933 with a childhood friend called Csiki Weisz. They found a room in a hotel in the rue Lhomond on the edge of the Latin Quarter and started hunting for contacts and employment. Endre began calling himself André in an effort to fit in. Work was scarce. The pair survived by stealing food and borrowing from the least hard up of their friends. On one occasion their landlord seized some of their clothes in an attempt to enforce payment and they had to take it in turns to go out wearing their one remaining suit. André found all this funny rather than dispiriting; at least that is how he presented things as he joked and cadged from café to café.

If he ever felt homesick there were other Hungarians around, many of them artists and bohemians. They included a thirty-one-year-old engraver and sculptor called Anton Prinner who stood out even in this unconventional company. Like André, Anton had been born and brought up in Budapest, studying at the Academy of Fine Arts before going to Paris in 1926 for what was intended to be a short recce trip but ended up becoming permanent. He too had started life with a different name. Anton was born Anna Prinner, who at art school had been famous for her beautiful hair. The hair was now cropped and instead of a skirt the artist went around in the *bleu de travail* overalls and corduroys worn by French workmen, topped by a Basque beret. Prinner's physique suited the transformation. He was slim and flat-chested with big hands. He had a high forehead and large, slightly sloping eyes set above an aquiline nose framed by high cheek bones. At first glance he looked frail and elfin. In fact he was as resilient as the nails on the soles of his heavy boots – and he needed to be. Prinner's range of work was eclectic, including the physically demanding techniques of wresting sculptures from stone and metal.

Prinner

Once seen, Anton was never forgotten. Yet far from being designed to attract attention his adopted look was more of a disguise. He was equally friendly with men and women and no one knew for sure his sexual inclinations. He was gregarious and convivial, a much liked regular at all the usual bohemian haunts of Montmartre and Montparnasse, but he never offered any serious answer when the obvious question arose as to why he had chosen to live life as a man. There were hints that, initially at least, the decision was pragmatic. During Anna Prinner's time at the Budapest fine arts academy it had started to move away from traditional teaching to embrace new trends, emanating largely from Paris.

But outside the walls of the academy Budapest was a tough place for an aspiring artist with modernist inclinations. It was even tougher if the artist was a woman. Anna apparently calculated that a move to Paris would improve her chances of success, but understood that even in the land of the avant-garde women were still second-class citizens. Soon after arriving in Paris Anna decided to change gender identity. Both decisions turned out to be permanent. Anton never returned to Hungary, and with each passing year the aura of masculinity deepened so that by the end it was hard to see in the wiry, pipe-smoking sculptor the long-haired Anna of the old days.

Prinner had also landed in Paris with nothing, and the first years were hard. Like André he too had a comrade in poverty, a fellow Hungarian painter called Árpád Szenes. They started off in Montmartre, though its reputation as the artists' quarter was being overtaken by Montparnasse on the other side of the city. They worked on their real art by day and in the evenings earned a meagre living doing quick-fire cartoons of tourists in the place du Tertre. By the time André arrived Anton was already a well-known figure in the famous haunts of Montparnasse bohemia: the Dôme, the Select and the Closerie des Lilas. Somewhere on the circuit the pair met and became friends. Once the young photographer began to pick up assignments he would sometimes use Prinner's bathroom as a makeshift darkroom to develop film.

Over the next few years their paths would diverge as André Friedmann spread his wings. He soon decided to junk his old identity entirely. He had been using a single-name byline on his pictures but 'Friedmann' risked confusion with another photographer of the same name and 'André', he decided, sounded too much like a hairdresser. He needed something glamorous and memorable. Thus was born Robert Capa, the name under which he would achieve global fame. When asked his reasons for picking it he sometimes claimed that he chose 'Robert' because people told him he looked like the American screen heartthrob Robert Taylor, and 'Capa' as a sort of homage to Hollywood director Frank Capra whose films he admired. It was as good an explanation as any. Soon Paris became less of a home than a base for foreign forays.

At the end of 1938 the influential British photojournalism magazine *Picture Post* carried an eleven-page spread of his images from Spain billing him as 'the greatest war photographer in the world'. He could go anywhere and photograph anything, but even Capa's restless soul needed somewhere to belong to and inevitably it was 'the beautiful city where I first learned to eat, drink and love'. The next war would take him down many roads. It was fated that one of them would eventually lead him back to Paris.

The clashes in the place de la Concorde of 6 February 1934 were not much more than a brawl compared to some of the great Paris street battles of yesteryear. But their effect on many who witnessed them or heard about them was much greater than the modest casualties suggested. The political atmosphere remained heavy with anxiety and uncertainty. The recent war and the millions of deaths had not brought peace. The rip-roaring capitalism of the 1920s had ended in the Great Depression. Parliamentary democracy looked worn out and ineffective. The extremes of left and right offered clear-cut solutions and a framework of thought and action with which to achieve them. The drama of that evening persuaded some that it was time to choose their side.

While Robert Capa was darting among the demonstrators, Robert Brasillach was sitting in a cinema on the avenue Montaigne, off the Champs-Élysées. Brasillach made his living writing film reviews and articles for highbrow magazines. Leaving the theatre he saw fires burning in the place de la Concorde and hurried to check what was going on. The sight of flaming vehicles and broken glass was thrilling. He wrote later that he 'felt the birth of an immense hope that stirred the blood, the hope of a national revolution'.

Brasillach was twenty-four, short and slight with olive skin and a smooth, chubby face. Thick, round spectacles made him look like an amiable owl and his personality seemed to match his appearance. He could be easy-going and generous, a lover of life's pleasures both simple and sophisticated. He was also vengeful and intellectually arrogant, and his pride and spiteful pen would lead him to some strange places. Brasillach's writings came to promote a vision of a new France based on a rose-tinted version of the old one, one that, though almost empty of practical detail, offered an exit from the perceived tawdriness of the Third Republic. His vision placed him on a collision course with partisans of the rival Utopia. There was no room for compromise in the cultural battles that raged as France counted down to the next war. For left and right, victory involved the destruction of their ideological enemies. Brasillach would come to be seen by some as a quasi-saint and by others as the distillation of the evils of the age, and when the final verdict was delivered on him it would be a matter of life or death.

Brasillach was born in Perpignan in 1909, the son of a junior army officer who was killed in 1914, not by the Germans, which might have altered his son's later political outlook, but by local insurgents in French North Africa. His mother then married an army doctor and the family moved to Sens, south-east of Paris, from where Robert won a place as a boarder at the capital's prestigious Lycée Louis-le-Grand high school in the rue Saint-Jacques in the Latin Quarter. Over the centuries it had produced an astonishing number of France's great statesmen, scientists, artists, writers and philosophers, as well as the Marquis de Sade.

Brasillach graduated to the equally illustrious École Normale Supérieure, a few hundred yards up the road in the rue d'Ulm. There were many Action Française supporters among the students of the Latin Quarter and although he had been exposed to the nationalist ideas of Charles Maurras at high school he was not yet a convert. He and his friends, he said later, were 'not liberal but tolerant . . . we were eighteen years old, a bit mixed up in our thinking, fairly disgusted with the modern world and with a distinct leaning towards anarchy'.

He was more interested in Paris than in politics. As a student he and his friend Maurice Bardèche explored the working-class districts, home to the *petites gens*, where tourists rarely ventured, intoxicated by the sights and sounds of 'Paris in the morning, the street vendors shouting their wares, the mountains of vegetables . . . the fish, grey and white on the slabs'. He would remember these days as 'the most beautiful moments of my life', visiting the theatre with friends, stopping on the way home for oysters and white wine on the slopes of Montmartre, dancing in the Latin Quarter on the evening of Bastille Day to the sound of violins and accordions in streets lit up with blue and white lanterns.

This was when French people still talked about the recent conflict as *la der des der – la dernière guerre des dernières guerres*, the war to end all wars. But as the 1920s turned to the 1930s it became ever more clear that the peace of 1918 merely marked a pause in Europe's troubles.

Slowly, relief and hope for the future drained away to be replaced by a mounting sense of dread. Faith in the ability of parties of the centre to deal with the crises was waning while the attraction of those at the political poles increased. Brasillach was among those who felt the pull. He started to believe that the *petites gens* he had idealized in his salad days had been corrupted by modern culture. He denounced 'the girly shows, the illustrated papers' which 'published the confessions of stars and launched the term "sex appeal" . . . the crowds now share all the vices and pleasures that were once reserved for the rich'.

In 1934, the year of the Stavisky scandal and the Concorde riots, he was gripped along with the rest of France by the trial of an eighteen-year-old Parisienne. Violette Nozière was the only daughter of an engine driver and a housewife who shared a small apartment in the working-class 10th arrondissement in north-central Paris. On 18 August 1933, she served her parents drinks laced with a lethal dose of barbiturates. The father, Jean-Baptiste, died; the mother, Germaine, lived. As they writhed in agony, Violette established her alibi, touring the cafés of Montmartre and drinking and dancing until dawn. When the police caught up with her she confessed straight away, claiming in her defence that her father had raped her for six years. This brought her little sympathy and instead she was denounced as a liar. The case became a cause célèbre and Violette was suddenly a cipher for the ills of the nation. She stood in the dock, chic and blank-eyed, as the prosecution painted her as a picture of depravity. Her parents had struggled to give her a decent education, enrolling her in the smart Lycée Féne-lon girls' high school in the 6th arrondissement. Much good had it done her. After leaving prematurely, she took a string of office jobs, supplementing her pay with some amateur prostitution, and spent her leisure hours hanging out with right-wing students in the Latin Quarter or with foreigners in Montmartre.

Violette provided a handy propaganda tool for both sides. To the left she was an object of some sympathy, not as a human being but as a victim of class oppression, the plaything of long-haired Action Française types. To the right she was a symbol of what happened when traditional values were abandoned, 'the scarlet idol of a cap-sized world, the flower of the evil of our age . . .' according to the

Paris-Midi newspaper. That was how Brasillach saw her. He was repelled by 'this awful little heroine, pale and haggard, and by the details of her sordid, sorry life which stumbled between cocktails and drugs . . . affluence and poverty, lived out against the backdrop of a cheap hotel'.

The tone of contempt and disgust was widespread on both sides. With it went an eagerness for drastic change. In 1930 Brasillach was a nationalist, a proponent of traditional family-based values and a defender of French culture against cultural contamination from abroad. But after 1934 he started to look to France's neighbours for answers to his own country's problems. His fluent pen made him a good living, writing for the right-wing press. His main outlet was the weekly *Je Suis Partout* whose title ('I am everywhere') reflected its focus on international affairs, though it was also heavy on art and culture. In June 1937, Brasillach took over as editor-in-chief.

He had already begun to turn his attention from literature and cinema to politics. The arrival of the Popular Front in 1936 alarmed him, particularly when Léon Blum appointed thirty-seven of his fellow Jews to prominent posts. The Jews, he complained, were getting in everywhere. The French cinema industry had 'practically closed its doors to Aryans and the radio had a Yiddish accent. Even the most peaceable people were starting to look askance at the crinkly hair and hooked noses that could be seen all around . . .' Not that he hated Jews personally, of course. His anti-Semitism, he claimed, was founded on patriotism and reason, not on emotion or blind prejudice, as a logical reaction to disproportionate Jewish wealth and influence. In February 1939, *Je Suis Partout* published a special number on the subject, the second in a year. The content was mainly the work of Lucien Rebatet, a disciple of Maurras. His polemics were illustrated with cartoons of big-nosed Jews, laden with bulging money bags, busy selling out France. Brasillach's front-page editorial was more temperate. 'First of all no persecution,' it began. 'No persecutions and no pogroms.' Nonetheless action was needed. The influence and activities of Jews in France constituted a threat to national peace and independence and were pushing the country to war. Refugees escaping Germany, Poland and Hungary should be denied French nationality. Even native-born Jews could never be properly French. Those who held citizenship should be designated as members of an official minority, 'which will protect them at the same time as it protects us'.

Hand in hand with the Jewish menace was the threat from the French Communist Party, the PCF, which in June 1936 propped up the Popular Front government from the outside. It seemed like the prelude to a Bolshevik takeover that would plunge France into a conflict like the one brewing in Spain. The paper was strongly pro-Franco and when Brasillach eventually visited Spain in 1938 he was entranced by the young Falangists he met, fighting for 'a pure nation, a pure race, never believing the promises of liberalism or in the equality of men or the will of the people'. For him, fascism was an exalted state of mind as much as a political credo, and 'the young fascist is first and foremost a joyful being'.

In September 1937 Brasillach made a flying visit to the annual Nazi rally at Nuremberg. He enthused about the 'enormous flags, some five storeys high . . . vivid under the grey sky, which complemented the ancient houses and matched the flowers on the balconies . . . historic Germany is united with the Third Reich'. The evening spectacles sparked further raptures. The crash of marching boots, the immense, adoring crowds and the Wagnerian light effects enthralled him, prompting contemptuous comparisons with the shabby scene back home.

A brief meeting with Hitler himself did cause Brasillach to wonder for a moment where all this was leading. While impressed by his 'natural grandeur' he was disquieted by his 'strange, unworldly eyes', which gave the Führer a supernatural aura. He seemed like 'the Archangel of Death' capable of descending from the heavens 'to kill his oldest and dearest companions'. Yet he left Germany thrilled by the vigour of the young Nazis and impressed by their determination to build a new Europe, while at the same time understanding the implications for France. All the marching and chanting might 'soon be the prelude to invasions'. France needed to prepare for the worst, but there could be no salvation if it was left to the traitors and incompetents of the Third Republic. The answer was for the nation to build its own version of fascism. It would be rooted in national culture and tradition but the central themes would echo those sounding in Berlin and Rome: contempt for democracy, obedience to an all-powerful man of destiny and hostility to Jews and communists. For him the path to fascism had been short but there were many at both ends of the political spectrum who were making the same sort of journey.

When Henri Tanguy heard about the Concorde riots, he too felt his blood tingle. 'I told myself that it was no longer possible to stay detached from what was going on,' he remembered. It looked as if the war of ideas was turning physical and he knew which side of the barricades he would be fighting on. He was already on the fringes of the PCF but now the danger of a 'fascist' takeover completed his conversion to communism. The times demanded clarity and direction. By nature he was a joiner, someone who sought structure and certainty. In a previous generation he might have found a natural home in the lay structures of the Catholic Church. The party provided a similar belief system with unchallengeable authority figures, clearly defined teachings and a culture of unquestioning obedience.

Henri was from Brittany, born on 12 June 1908 in Morlaix into the conservative, respectable lower-middle classes. His father, Anatole, a petty officer in the French navy, was away from the family for long stretches. Money was tight and Henri had to leave school at thirteen to start a succession of lowly jobs as a telegram delivery boy, a despatcher at a cab company and a wine bottler. If life was tough, he faced it cheerfully. He was healthy and *sportif*, mad keen on the endurance cycling that was all the rage in Europe.

In October 1923, when Henri was fifteen, his mother Mathilde suddenly packed two suitcases and whisked him and his younger brother away to Paris. She needed to get away from her husband. Anatole had left the navy in 1919 and was now working as a manager in a shipyard in the north. His home visits were not something to look forward to. Henri had been conceived during one of Anatole's absences and he took to beating the boy and calling him a 'dirty bastard'. Henri never knew the identity of his real father. Anatole's cruelty, Henri claimed, 'never gave me a complex because the memory of it was wiped out by my mother's love'.

In Paris, the close-knit Breton community helped Mathilde find a flat and a job. They settled into a tiny furnished flat in the rue du Château in the 14th arrondissement, close to the Gare Montparnasse. Later they moved to another apartment in the rue de l'Ouest, a few hundred yards away. Henri soon got taken on as an apprentice sheet-metal worker at the Talbot factory in the western suburbs. Until then he had shown no particular interest in politics, though the upheavals shaking Europe made it difficult to remain completely indifferent. Certain things he had seen in Brest impressed him. The naval dockyard was regularly disrupted by strikes as anarchists fought the layoffs that came with peace. In 1919 they came out to protest against the treatment of a naval engineer officer called André Marty, one of the leaders of a mutiny by the French fleet. The navy had been sent to the Black Sea to support White Russian forces against the Bolsheviks in the civil war that followed the 1917 revolution. The crews rebelled, partly out of sympathy for the Reds, but mostly in protest at their conditions and the slow rate of post-war demobilization. André Marty was sentenced to twenty years' hard labour. The furore that followed led in 1923 to a pardon. This son of a bourgeois Perpignan wine merchant promptly joined the Communist Party and the following year was elected to parliament.

In the Talbot factory, Henri saw the proletariat close up for the first time. He was entering the ranks of the *métallos*, skilled metal workers who took no nonsense from the bosses, who in turn treated them with wary respect. It was an early lesson in the necessity of pride and insistence on proper rights and rewards. After eight months at Talbot he left and moved from *boîte* to *boîte*, as the workers called the factories and workshops, switching jobs when a better-paid one turned up. In the spring of 1925 he arrived at Renault. He worked in the panel-beating shop, fitting shaped metal to the wooden coachwork. The pay was good but there were constant disputes with the management over piece rates and rows with the company security men who tried vainly to enforce rules like the ban on smoking on the line. The spirit of combat was contagious – and Henri enjoyed the constant clashes.

But the agitation was mainly about money. One day Henri was approached by a young stranger who asked him if he was interested in joining the Billancourt branch of the young communists. It was less impressive than it sounded. There were only ten *métallos* in the Renault cell and Henri became the treasurer. He was still at least as interested in cycling as he was in class warfare. He joined the Club Vélo International, one of the foremost in the country. He would get up before dawn to complete a 20-mile circuit that took him over the heights south-west of Paris, before finishing up at the Renault factory gates. He was regularly near the top finishers in many gruelling road races in the seasons that followed. 'Cycling for me was a fantastic education in how to build energy and physical endurance,' he remembered. 'It gave me the lungs and heart of a sportsman.' This stamina would help him greatly in trials to come, as did the friendships he forged at the club.

When Henri was called up for compulsory military service he was sent to North Africa to join the 8th Regiment of Zouaves, a light infantry unit. He turned out to be an excellent shot and was promoted to company armourer. There was a chance that he might be sent off for officer training, but the move fell through when it was decided he was too valuable where he was. In August 1930, after fifteen months of mostly exemplary service, he was discharged, a Zouave First Class, and returned to his mother's flat and a job at a works near by. It was founded by the aviation pioneer and aircraft designer Louis Breguet. The factory made a wide range of weapons and components for the armed services. Henri worked there contentedly. The pay was excellent and there was little friction between bosses and workers. Henri felt no need to rejoin either the union or the party. With his solid build and light brown hair he looked a little bit like Jean Gabin, who played stylish working-class heroes in the great romantic realism movies of the decade, such as *Quai des brumes* and *Le Jour se lève*. He dressed like one of the Gabin characters in tailor-made suits and 100-franc shoes. He picked up with his old cycling friends and they went on long road trips to Le Havre and the Channel coast.

Like all arrondissements, the 14th had its own life and you didn't have to leave it to feel the throb and pulse of Paris. Later he would recall fondly the shops, ateliers, little cabarets, bars and bistrots. There was food everywhere, especially in the morning when the street vendors returned from Les Halles with barrows laden with fruit and vegetables and began shouting their wares to the housewives doing their shopping. The intimacy created an atmosphere of mutual dependency and solidarity which in turn brought a sense of security. The Concorde riots of February 1934 persuaded Henri and many like him that this was an illusion. He might appear rather bourgeois in his natty suits but now he kept recalling 'memories of what I had seen in Brest . . . the Black Sea mutineers and the workers in the Renault factory . . . I felt an overwhelming need for action . . . from then on I threw myself into the struggle.'

He rejoined the youth branch of the PCF. On Sunday mornings they went to the rue de l'Ouest street market to sell *l'Avant-Garde*, provoking punch-ups with right-wing youths hawking their own newssheets. His new-found militancy got him sacked from Breguet, but he soon got another job up at Nessi brothers in Montrouge on the southern edge of Paris, a factory which made piping and ventilation systems. It was a 'very paternalistic shop' whose owner treated the workers like family, and few at first were willing to go along with Henri's confrontational tactics. When he approached the boss with a long list of demands, Nessi pleaded with him to be reasonable, 'rolling up his sleeve to show the scars he had received in the 14–18 War. Meanwhile I looked out of the window and whistled . . .' After seven months Henri was fired from there too.

His days as a *métallo* were over. The Communist Party was there to pick him up, arranging a senior job at the headquarters of the metal workers' union in the rue du Faubourg-Saint-Denis. In February 1937, after energetic lobbying, he was sent to Spain to join the communist-controlled International Brigades, which since the previous autumn had been fighting with the forces of the Republic.

About 30,000 young idealists travelled to Spain to take up arms against General Franco. They came from all over the world, but the majority were from Europe and in particular from France. Most were communists and socialists, prepared to shed blood fighting fascism. When Henri got there the war was nearly eight months old. The government had stopped Franco's army outside Madrid, but both sides were now locked in a slogging match on multiple fronts that neither could win without outside backing. The Republic was getting little help from the democracies of France and Britain. In London the Conservative government had embarked on a policy of appeasing Hitler and the Nazis. In Paris, the Popular Front's hold on power was shaky. Fear that open support would provoke an uprising by the now outlawed far-right leagues led the government to tread carefully. Both Britain and France signed up to a non-intervention agreement. So too did Germany, Italy and the Soviet Union. But only the democracies went any way to actually observing its terms. Germany and Italy on one side and the Soviet Union on the other filled the vacuum with arms and military advisers, and Spain became a proxy battleground.

Tanguy went to Spain expecting to fight. He spent most of his time there as a political commissar, sustaining morale and enforcing ideological orthodoxy among the *brigadistas*. He worked under his old hero André Marty, the Black Sea mutineer who was now the International Brigades' chief political commissar. Marty was constantly on the lookout for deviations from party orthodoxy. The penalty for heresy was death, and he and his henchmen seemed to put as much energy into hunting down real or imagined dissidents as they did fighting the nationalists.

Marty's eye never lingered long on Henri Tanguy, for the younger man's faith was simple and strong and he was trusted as a reliable enforcer of the official line. Eventually Henri's wish to pick up a gun was granted and when he left Spain following the final defeat of the Republic in the autumn of 1938 he had repeatedly proved his fidelity and his personal courage on the front lines. He returned to Paris with a bullet still lodged in his shoulder, ready to do whatever the party asked of him.

2. The Black Rain

On 10 May 1940 the Germans launched the war in the west. In less than a month they had invaded the Low Countries, driven the British back across the Channel, overwhelmed the French army and air force and cleared the way to Paris. Even with the enemy at the gates, the capital kept its nerve. On 9 June, five days before the Germans entered, a middle-aged writer called Pierre Audiat reported that people were 'carrying on as they normally would have done on a nice Sunday in springtime'. Columns of German tanks were reported at Forges-les-Eaux, 60 miles to the north, yet 'the atmosphere remained calm. The fighting felt far away and sightings of enemy aircraft were infrequent.' The distant rumble of artillery carried on the breeze did not disturb the crowds who packed the pavement cafés along the Champs-Élysées sipping multi-coloured aperitifs. There was no need for alarm just yet. After all, 'ministers were at their posts and the President of the Republic slept each night at the Élysée palace'.

This sangfroid persisted on the morning of Monday 10 June when the prefect of the Paris police, Roger Langeron, set off for the place Beauvau for a meeting with his boss and long-time friend, the interior minister Georges Mandel. Langeron was fifty-eight, lean and bald. His keen eyes observed the world through pince-nez spectacles. A prominent nose, bold moustache and cleft chin created an impression of intelligence, vigour and resolve. The role of prefect was political as much as administrative and he had needed all these qualities to navigate the tricky waters of pre-war state affairs in his six years in post.

En route to the rendezvous he noted the columns of refugees fleeing the fighting as the Germans swept through the north of the country, but the composure of Parisians seemed unaffected by the spectacle. All that was about to change. Mandel had dramatic news. Having assured the population that it was staying put, the government was running away, 'obliged to flee the city' for 'compelling military reasons'. Mandel was leaving Langeron in charge, along with the prefect of the Seine department, Achille Villey, 'to represent the government of France before the invader'. Langeron worried that Mandel was going to quit the government and he would lose his most valuable ally. They had first met as juniors in the Cabinet of Georges Clemenceau, whose aggressive leadership of the country in the darkest days of the previous war had earned him the nickname 'Tiger'. In recent years, as minister and official, Mandel and Langeron had formed a tight partnership against communists and Nazi sympathizers bent on undermining the Third Republic from within, an alliance that now made them both – but particularly Mandel, who was Jewish – highly vulnerable.

Mandel assured Langeron that he had no intention of resigning. Someone had to be around to stiffen the backbone of the vacillating and divided leadership. Mandel's fear was that Prime Minister Paul Reynaud, who was all for continuing to resist, would be forced out by the powerful faction pressing for an immediate armistice. The most likely replacement was a figure who enjoyed unrivalled prestige among the population. Marshal Philippe Pétain was the country's greatest military hero thanks to his role in the epic defence of Verdun in 1916. But he was now eighty-four and the fight had long gone out of him. Mandel predicted that if Pétain took over 'he will give away everything and my services will quickly be terminated'. He and Langeron shook hands and the prefect took his leave, wondering whether he would ever see his old friend again.

Langeron set off to call on Prefect Villey and to brief his senior police officers and commanders of the Republican Guard responsible for the military security of Paris. Their instructions were to stay at their posts and see that order was maintained, but under no circumstances to offer any resistance to the enemy. Before leaving, the government declared Paris an 'open city', thus gifting the capital to the invaders on the understanding that they would do no harm to people or property. That night Langeron dined at the Ritz with his wife and another couple. The main restaurant was completely empty. They ate in the garden where only one other table was occupied. The Langerons' friends were leaving town in the morning. Towards eleven o'clock they said their farewells in the deserted place Vendôme, 'all of us anxious and worried for the future of our country'.

As news broke of the government's departure, Paris woke from its trance. Over that night of 10/11 June trust in authority collapsed like the wall of a dam, and panic flooded in. The following morning hundreds of thousands of Parisians locked their apartments and looked for the quickest way out. The trains were soon overflowing and the gates of the main termini locked. By noon the roads to the south and west were choked. Langeron looked down from the window of his apartment on the boulevard du Palais behind the Préfecture de Police on the Île de la Cité and saw peasants from the north and city folk mixed together in 'an endless parade of infinite sadness: horse-drawn carts . . . baby carriages, pedestrians, cyclists, dogs and farm animals. The cars had mattresses on the roof and bags dangling from the sides stuffed with what in their haste the fugitives had deemed to be most precious or most dear . . .'

Everyone, high and low, had something they could not bear to leave behind. In the opening scene of her novel *Suite Française*, Irène Némirovsky described the scene that evening as the wealthy Péricand

Exodus

family prepared to abandon their grand home on the boulevard
Delessert in the 16th arrondissement with four of their five children
and an elderly parent in tow: 'Night was falling but the Péricands' car
was still waiting outside their door . . . They were trying in vain to cram
in all the family's bags, suitcases and overnight cases, as well as all the
baskets containing the sandwiches, the thermos flask, bottles of milk
for the children, cold chicken, ham, bread and the boxes of baby cereal
for the elder Monsieur Péricand. There was also the cat's basket . . .'

A strange phenomenon deepened the sense of apocalypse. Langeron
had woken that morning to find the city cloaked 'in a cloud of black
smoke so thick you could barely see in the streets'. Elliot Paul, an American writer living in a narrow street off the boulevard Saint-Michel, saw
it too. There was 'oil in the blackened air and soot in the rain and the
wretched city was pressed down by the lowering sky'. Some feared it
was poisonous gas. It turned out to be smog from burning fuel dumps
north of the city, but there was little comfort in this explanation. 'The
darkened skies deepened everyone's fears and doubts,' wrote Langeron.
For Paul it was a metaphor for what was about to happen, marking 'the
end of a world in which Paris was supreme, in which France was alive,
in which there was a breath of freedom'.

Those with the most to lose watched as their solid and comfortable world crumbled like a meringue. In Némirovsky's account, at
the hour of departure the social inhibitions that before forbade too
much familiarity between neighbours dissolved, and they started to
behave like ordinary people, 'gesticulating to one another, trying, at
first calmly then with increasing agitation and a mad, dizzy excitement, to get the family and all the baggage into a Renault, a saloon,
a sports car'. The stillness of the night, the sweet scent of chestnut
blossom mingled with petrol only increased the sense of impending
doom. 'You could smell the danger in the air, in the silence,' she
wrote. 'Everyone looked at their house and thought: "Tomorrow it
will be in ruins, tomorrow I will have nothing left. We haven't hurt
anyone. Why?" Then a wave of indifference washed over their souls.
"What's the difference! It's only stone, wood – nothing living! What
matters is survival." Who cared about the tragedy of their country?

Not these people. Not the people who were leaving that night.' In every street in Paris the same realization was taking hold: that now, and for the foreseeable future, there was no security to rely on but yourself, and for a few hours the most precious thing in the universe was the feel of the warm cheek and thumping heart of your parent, spouse, sibling, son or daughter as you held them close.

As the hordes fanned out from the capital the competition for resources soon dispelled the brief moment of solidarity. Life on the road became a frantic scramble for petrol, for food, for beds for the night, and the resources available went to those who could pay most. The authorities – national and local – had made no contingency plans. Without any official to turn to for help, the bounds of loyalty shrank to encompass only family or self. Of the 2.25 million who inhabited Paris, only between 700,000 and one million remained. The fugitives lived thereafter with an indelible memory of helplessness and the bitter knowledge of what happens when order is shattered. It was, recalled one refugee on the road from Paris to Tours, 'as if one was no more than a leaf, swept away in a whirlwind . . .'

Not everyone had been caught unawares. When the Germans reached Paris, the most famous artist in the world was living in a small town on the Atlantic coast. Pablo Picasso left his aristocratic town house in the rue des Grands-Augustins on the Left Bank on 16 May 1940, six days after the blitzkrieg in the west began. He took the train to Royan, a resort on the Gironde estuary, where he had already separately installed both his latest mistress Dora Maar and a previous love, Marie-Thérèse Walter, and their daughter Maya, now aged four. The two women were living unbeknown to each other in different hotels. Picasso had been coming and going since his initial departure from the capital the previous September, organizing the removal of some of his work to safe storage beyond the reach of the Germans. He had reason to fear them. Having never shown any real interest in politics he was moved to paint his first political painting by events in his home country. *Guernica*, the canvas – 25 feet by 11 feet – created in response to the Luftwaffe's terror bombing of the capital of the Basque Country in April 1937, was acclaimed around the world and made him a hero to the left. It was a very temporary departure from his habitual fixations on sex, death, magic and mythology. Nonetheless, a flag had been raised. He was now associated with the republican, anti-Franco and anti-fascist cause. It remained to be seen if his global fame was enough to shield him from the Nazis.

Picasso was a sincere anti-fascist but a reluctant propagandist. His artistic ambition pushed everything else to the edge of his vision, politics included. He was essentially a Manichean who saw the world as a perpetual battleground between the forces of good and evil. The Nazis came as no surprise to him and they were not worth getting worked up about. His main concerns were selfish. The war was fundamentally a huge nuisance. It threatened to wreck the rhythms of work and play he had spent so long harmonizing in order to set up a routine that allowed him to live entirely as he chose. The Germans had forced him to leave Paris, his studio and his friends, ruining the domestic equilibrium he had worked hard to establish and opening the door to many a potential bust-up with his various women. He summed up his feelings to his long-suffering Spanish friend and confidant Jaume Sabartés: 'If it's to annoy me that they make war they are carrying it too far, don't you think?' Yet there was also a sort of heroism in his egotism. He was as superstitious as any peasant and terrified of death, a prospect brought closer one way or another by the coming of the Germans. But when, just after the war broke out, the American embassy in Paris offered both Picasso and Henri Matisse sanctuary in the United States, both refused.

Picasso's complicated life was made more bearable by the nearby presence of a close friend and business associate. Paul Rosenberg had been the artist's dealer since 1918 and as the trust between them had grown Rosenberg had taken on the role of curator of his reputation. In 1939 he organized the first big Picasso retrospective in the United States at the Museum of Modern Art in New York. They saw each other constantly. For years they were neighbours. The apartment Picasso shared with his first wife, the Ukrainian-born ballet dancer Olga Khokhlova, was just a few doors down from the Rosenberg gallery at 21 rue La Boétie, a bourgeois street in the staid 8th arrondissement. It had opened in 1910 and soon became a showcase for adventurous new talents breaking the boundaries of art. Rosenberg liked to keep his business dealings with his artists simple by signing them up on exclusive contracts (Braque, Léger and Matisse were also on his books). Their work was shown on the ground floor. For customers who found it too daring, there was more conventional fare on the mezzanine. The profits from the latter helped Rosenberg to fund his younger protégés so they could get on with their work without worrying about money.

Unlike some wealthy French Jews who had been lulled into complacency by the belief that they enjoyed full membership of the country's elite, Rosenberg quickly grasped the meaning of Hitler's rise. In the late 1930s he began shifting some of his vast collection overseas, to the USA and London. In February 1940 he moved his family to Bordeaux, as a preliminary to leaving the country altogether if necessary, in which case they would head for America. Until then, like the rest of France, they were stuck in the waiting room of the Phoney War. After a brief stay in Tours, Paul, his wife Marguerite and their two children, Alexandre and Micheline, rented Le Castel, a nineteenth-century faux château complete with stone turret, in the village of Floirac La Souys on the eastern edge of Bordeaux. It would take Picasso less than two hours to get there from Royan in his chauffeur-driven Hispano-Suiza and he was a frequent visitor along with his friend and rival Georges Braque, who had also moved to the area.

The house filled up with Rosenberg relatives as the situation worsened. From 10 May 1940 the family heard a litany of terrible news bulletins as the German columns raced through the Low Countries and then penetrated France, sending the French army reeling back in disarray. There were constant agonized debates about what to do next. For all their sophistication and international connections, the Rosenbergs were indelibly French. Patriotism as well as the melancholy of exile, no matter how comfortable, made flight a miserable prospect. On 18 June, thanks to the help of the Portuguese consul in Bordeaux, Aristides Sousa Mendes, the family group which had now grown to seventeen received visas to enter Portugal. Two overloaded cars carried them to Hendaye near the Spanish border where they joined a multitude of refugees. In Lisbon, after many tribulations, they obtained American visas to sail on to New York and a new life in America.

Despite Rosenberg's forethought he had not been able to get all of his collection to safety. About 2,000 artworks, some of them masterpieces, remained in France. On leaving Paris he had brought with him a cache of 162 paintings. Like the work on show at the gallery it was a rich mixture of the old and the new. From the nineteenth century was a Van Gogh self-portrait, as well as canvases by Corot, Delacroix and Sisley. There were also pictures by Braque, Léger, Matisse and Picasso. The nervous watching and waiting of the Phoney War had not blunted his passion for collecting, and in the spring of 1940 he took the train from Bordeaux to Nice to visit Matisse in his studio and returned to Le Castel laden with new work. To store his treasures he rented vault No. 7 at the Banque Nationale pour le Commerce et l'Industrie in the town of Libourne, less than 15 miles away. There they sat, awaiting the day when Rosenberg could return to Paris and the life and work he loved.

On leaving France, Rosenberg was forced to say goodbye to his son. When the party reached the frontier with Spain, French border guards ordered Alexandre out of the car, along with his two first cousins, Jean and François Helft, who were travelling with the family group. The French army had ceased to fight but the armistice was not yet signed, and males over seventeen years of age were not allowed to leave the country. Alexandre was nineteen and like every young French man had been obliged to do basic military training. He was serious and scholarly and after school at the elite Paris Cours Hattemer academy had gone on to study philosophy and theology at the Sorbonne. His cousins were equally unsoldierly. They now decided that, even though the situation seemed hopeless, they would fight for France but from England where Charles de Gaulle had just raised the flag of the Free French.

They managed to get on board the Polish liner turned troopship *Batory* before it sailed from Saint-Jean-de-Luz carrying to Britain Polish troops who had fought in the Battle of France. When Alexandre turned up in London to volunteer for the Free French they were still in too much disarray to take him on. Next he tried the RAF but was rejected on the grounds of his extreme short-sightedness, which the recruiting officer suggested would mean he would be unable to locate the country he was attacking, let alone the target. On 1 July he returned to the Free French and this time was accepted and sent for officer training in Camberley, the start of a journey that would take him to West Africa, the Sahara Desert, Egypt and Normandy. It was four years before he returned to Paris for an extraordinary home-coming that would reunite him not only with his city, but with his father's art collection.

The pain of the great exodus would scar the memory of all who lived through it, but so too would the shame. Paris had fallen with con-temptible ease. Between the city and the Germans stood a combined Allied force of 135 divisions, only six fewer than the enemy. In tanks, the defenders outnumbered the attackers by a ratio of eight to five. In the air, the sides were evenly matched, though the French aircraft factories were better placed to churn out replacements for losses. Above all, France possessed the great natural advantages of a nation defending its own territory. And that territory was protected by an ultra-modern defensive barrier of steel and concrete fortifications that politicians and generals had assured the people would shield France from invasion – the Maginot Line, which stretched the length of the country's eastern frontiers from Italy northwards, though not to the Channel coast.

The truth, acknowledged openly or privately by everyone of every political stripe, was that France should at least have stemmed the German attack. That is what had happened in 1914. The war that followed endured for 1,550 days and ended in French victory. This one had lasted forty-seven days and finished in utter defeat. As many as 85,000 men had died. More than one and a half million had been taken prisoner – one in seven of French males between the ages of twenty and forty – most of whom would be sent to camps in Ger-many where they were put to work in the service of the enemy war effort, a perpetual source of guilt and embarrassment to the new French authorities.

Any comparison with the past only emphasized the totality of the failure. It was the third time in seventy years that the Germans had tried to take Paris. In the Franco-Prussian War of 1870–71 the French withstood blockade and bombardment for more than four months before surrendering. In 1914 they stopped the enemy forces on the Marne when they were only 20 miles from Notre-Dame cathedral. This time it took only thirty-five days from the start of the campaign in the west for the Germans to reach Paris. By then the French armies had more or less collapsed and all the Germans had to do was walk in. There were only four recorded instances of armed defiance, suicidal attacks in the southern and western suburbs by anonymous individuals. So it was that Paris fell for the loss of three dead Germans and six French. It would be fourteen months before another Frenchman dared to shoot at a German, and many more before redemption for the shame of defeat felt like a possibility.

The scale of the defeat and the great exodus that followed imbued events with an almost biblical profundity. They felt like acts of God, not in the sense of arbitrary strokes of misfortune, but as divine punishment. This was how Pétain rationalized it. France had had it coming, he told the nation a few days after taking over as head of the new government emerging from the ruins of the Third Republic. What had just happened was not the fault of the French army. Since the victory of 1918, he declared on 20 June, 'The spirit of pleasure has triumphed over the spirit of sacrifice. We have demanded more than we have been prepared to give and chosen the easy life. Hence the unhappiness we face today.' Many accepted the verdict, even the very young. At the end of June, Irène Némirovsky's daughter Denise concluded in a school essay: 'No doubt this humiliation will be more useful to the soul of France and to all the French people than the victory that would have made us too proud. We will benefit more from defeat.'

Pétain's stance would later be presented as treason. That implied a conscious decision to betray. But Pétain justified his actions as painful necessities, forced on him by the catastrophic failures of the Republic. He had proved himself a great leader, who Charles de Gaulle acknowledged after the war had 'showed me the gift and the art of commanding'. Having saved France once in the last war he was ready to do it again. This time, though, he was offering not action but acceptance: the shield and not the sword. It was hardly surprising. At eighty-four he had neither the energy nor the spirit to interpret his duty any other way. Most of the population agreed with him. The nation rallied to him as a reassuring symbol of a proud and confident past, a rock to cling to in a storm of fear and confusion. His passivity reflected their own dread at the thought of more bloodshed. If the hero of Verdun felt it was acceptable to stop fighting and come to an accommodation with the invaders, then so could everybody else.

Pétain was more than a warrior. His reputation was built not just on victory at Verdun but also on the role he had played in quelling the large-scale mutinies and desertions that broke out in the army in 1917 after one pointless 'big push' too many. The mutinies were on a scale to threaten a total Allied collapse on the Western Front. He restored order by a combination of firmness and compassion, showing himself everywhere on the front, disciplining commanders as well as men, but also tasting the soldiers' soup to ensure it was up to scratch and awarding generous stretches of leave. He had no children of his own, but with this mix of common sense and humanity he became a father figure in the minds of hundreds of thousands of soldiers and their families. Their loyalty would prove very durable.

In the summer of 1940 Pétain seemed the only man capable of leading France out of despair. The very fact that he was staying put confirmed his prestige and authority. In the panicky debates before the surrender there had been talk of the government fleeing to French North Africa to continue the fight from there. The marshal was having none of it. He told the Cabinet on 13 June that 'to form a government in exile outside mainland France would simply be to abandon the country to the invaders'. He was remaining 'among the French people, to share their sorrows and miseries'. It was a pledge that he would make many times over the coming years, fashioning himself as a sacrificial figure willing 'to make a gift of myself to France to alleviate her sufferings'. All the acts – and failures to act – of his government were legitimized by the fact of their physical presence. Conversely, all those who left could be portrayed as traitors and cowards, and chief among them was Pétain's former admiring protégé de Gaulle, who very soon would be court-martialled *in absentia* and sentenced to death.

As it was, after the armistice only nineteen deputies and three senators chose to sail for Algeria aboard the transatlantic liner *Massilia* to keep the struggle alive. Among them were Georges Mandel and Édouard Daladier. Mandel's anti-fascist credentials were impeccable. Daladier had been three times prime minister and had signed the Munich agreement alongside Neville Chamberlain, but he had no illusions about Hitler and tried to accelerate rearmament before what he knew was an inevitable war. Together they might have formed the core of an overseas Resistance movement, one with far more immediate authority than that which gathered around de Gaulle in London. They never got the chance. On arrival in Morocco they were arrested by the French authorities and with the other *Massilia* fugitives sent back to prison in France.

The armistice signed on 22 June at Compiègne carved the country into several sectors. The Germans took control of the north and the western seaboard down to the Pyrenees, facing Britain on one side and its Atlantic sea routes to America on the other. This was the Occupied Zone, which made up about 55 per cent of the country. The rest would, for the time being at least, be free of German troops. The two were separated by an arbitrary demarcation line. The new government would technically retain sovereignty over the whole country as well as over France's colonial empire. However, it was made clear in the provisions of the armistice that officials in the Occupied Zone were to do Germany's bidding and in a key undertaking the government pledged to 'immediately direct all officials and administrators of the occupied territory to comply with the regulations of, and to collaborate fully with, the German military authorities'. France was allowed a token 'armistice army' of 100,000 men and to keep its powerful, modern fleet as long as it stayed in port. German efforts to get France to formally join the Axis alliance with Italy and Japan were met with a mixture of guile and evasion by Pétain and, in theory at least, the country remained neutral.

On 10 July 1940, a total of 846 French deputies and senators gathered in the Grand Casino in Vichy to agree a political structure to deal with the new reality. There was little resistance to the proposals. They amounted to a wholesale rejection of the past. The representatives – all of them men as women did not yet have the franchise in the land of Liberty, Equality and Fraternity – voted to dissolve the Republic they had been elected to serve. They now handed all governmental authority to Philippe Pétain. As *chef* or head of what was called simply 'the French State' he now had complete executive and legislative power and the right to draw up a new constitution. Of the 846 gathered, only eighty voted against, almost all of them socialists and radicals. (A further twenty abstained.)

A headline in the next day's paper announced: 'The Fate of France is in the hands of Marshal Pétain.' The expectation was that he would immediately start drawing up a new constitution. Pétain decided that this could wait until a proper peace treaty was signed with Germany. That depended on Hitler, who was unwilling to agree a broad settlement in the west until Britain had been defeated. Neither a peace agreement nor the new constitution would ever come to pass. Not that there was any clamour to return to pre-war politics. Invasion by an old enemy might have been expected to cement national cohesion. The French tragedy created little solidarity among the victims. On the right it only sharpened the hatred that had flourished in the inter-war years. Some felt less hostility towards the German invaders than they did towards their fellow countrymen whose attitudes and policies they blamed for hollowing out the nation until it was no longer capable of defending itself. The assortment of politicians, technocrats and opportunists shaping the new state decided it should above all be a repudiation of everything the Third Republic had come to represent.

France was told that the pain of defeat would be eased by the advent of a 'National Revolution' that would heal all the harm done by the Revolution of 1789. In the place of messy democracy would be authority, invested in a single figure, the stern but benevolent Philippe Pétain, the one man everyone could trust. The get-rich-quick ethos and lax morality of the 1930s would give way to the pre-revolutionary values enshrined in the new national motto of 'Work, Family, Homeland'.

The programme marked the triumph of the spirit displayed in the

place de la Concorde in February 1934. It was drafted for Pétain by a
group of acolytes led by an Action Française-supporting deputy
called Raphaël Alibert. Alibert was a fervent Catholic and follower
of Charles Maurras and would have restored the Bourbon monarchy
if he could. Instead, he had to make do with the marshal. The political preparations for Pétain's accession were in the hands of Pierre
Laval, a deft political operator who had already twice been prime
minister. He started his career as a left-leaning lawyer. His many
enemies disparaged him as a shifty horse trader of the type supposedly
found in his native Auvergne, although the white silk tie he wore for
luck made him look more like a Chicago mobster, as well as highlighting the nicotine stains on his teeth. Laval's unscrupulousness had
become his strength. He declared before the debate in the Vichy
casino that 'parliamentary democracy has lost [France] the war. It
must disappear and give way to an authoritarian, hierarchical,
national and social regime.' Naturally he would have a place at the
summit and, though his fortunes fluctuated, Laval would remain at
the centre of events until the end.

After fleeing Paris, the government passed through several way
stations before settling in Vichy. It arrived there by accident rather
than choice. Other possibilities had been raised and discarded – the
Germans vetoed Marseilles as it was too close to French North Africa,
where despite Pétain's assurances they still feared he might decide to
decamp. Vichy was, above all, convenient. It was a spa town, full of
comfortable and fairly modern hotels and had an excellent telephone
system. The thousands of rooms could easily be turned into living
quarters and offices to house the 40,000 bureaucrats who displaced
those taking the waters.

The move was supposed to be temporary. The Germans agreed at
the outset that the new government could set up shop in Paris. Vichy
was a provisional capital, just as the armistice was a provisional peace
deal. Both were destined to last. Soon this small town on the banks of
the Allier river, known as the gateway to the mountainous Auvergne,
seemed to be a fitting seat for the new political entity. Even in peacetime it had an air of unreality. It was a toytown that filled up in the
summer with comfortably off pleasure seekers who soaked them-

selves in the healing baths, walked the shaded paths of the central park, gambled in the casinos and watched the variety shows in the theatres. In the autumn it emptied and became a draughty and depressing ghost town. Vichy was as shallow as the new state conjured up in its casino, but it also served as a handy metaphor. People went there, after all, as a sort of act of atonement for the sins of the flesh. And, as some literary-minded inhabitant noted, the waters of the springs were tinged 'with the salty taste of tears'.

In many ways it was the antithesis of Paris, but that – in the eyes of Pétain – was part of the attraction. He came from what the English would call yeoman stock, people who farmed in the Pas de Calais, and the capital symbolized everything that he and his circle now rejected. It was where the Third Republic had been born and the breeding ground for all the corrupt ideas and attitudes that had led to its downfall and France's defeat. It gave a warm welcome to every dangerous new trend, from communism to short skirts and jazz, and had come up with many dubious innovations of its own. Its stylish decadence was the enemy of family solidity. In short, it stood for the world that the National Revolution proposed to overthrow.

Vichy suited Pétain very well. Government HQ was established in the stucco-fronted, balconied, five-storey Hôtel du Parc, built like most of the place at the turn of the century, which overlooked the trees in the square at the heart of the town. He had an office and bedroom in a corner suite on the third floor with his prime minister Laval on the floor below. The Pavillon Sévigné, a mansion on the banks of the Allier, was requisitioned as his official residence, but Pétain made limited use of it. The soldierly simplicity of room 35 at the Hôtel du Parc set an example of austerity, as well as matching his tastes.

His daily routines had a choreographed feel that reflected the regal character of the regime and, like monarchs of old, much of it was lived out in public. The marshal got up at 7.30, glanced at the newspapers, then had a *café au lait* and a slice of bread, butter and jam with his stout and homely wife, a divorcee called Eugénie. They had married in 1920, though he would have many mistresses and claimed to have bedded his last woman at the age of eighty-six.

The morning was spent meeting his ministers and signing decrees.

At 12.30 he took a constitutional, walking the paths of the central park with his young medical adviser Dr Bernard Ménétrel and aide Captain Bonhomme, followed closely by four policemen. Pétain acknowledged the greetings of his fellow promenaders and patted their children on the head. Then it was back to the hotel for a simple but substantial lunch with a dozen or so of his entourage. His diet was dictated by Ménétrel. A typical menu consisted of cold hake with tartare sauce, followed by salt pork and cabbage, salad, cheese and stewed pears and no more than a glass or two of wine. In the afternoon were more meetings, and audiences with visitors, and in the evening an official dinner or trip to the theatre, with the Pétains carefully paying for their own seats. Every Sunday morning at 11.15 he went to mass at the church of Saint-Louis, not so much to pray as to set an example.

He looked the picture of health. He didn't smoke and his clear blue eyes had no need for glasses. His blood pressure was that of a man half his age and the cane he carried was a prop rather than a necessity. The old soldier knew the value of appearances. But those who saw him up close soon realized that his mental capacity did not match his physical vigour. The pace of business depended on whether he was having one of his good days or one of his bad ones. When the new American ambassador Admiral William D. Leahy went to present his credentials to the marshal in January 1941 (for the US, along with the USSR, Canada and many other states, had chosen to recognize Vichy), he was instantly impressed by his 'energy and force of character'. Meeting him again the following afternoon he saw instead an old man, 'tired and discouraged'. In private, the public serenity often gave way to crotchetiness. Pétain's compassion was reserved for the abstraction of 'the people'. He was mostly indifferent to the misfortunes of individuals and could be cold and cutting, particularly to politicians.

He was celebrated in an unofficial new anthem – the Germans banned the 'Marseillaise' in the Occupied Zone along with the tricolour flag: 'Maréchal, nous voilà!' exalted Pétain as the embodiment of France and proclaimed the nation's gratitude and obedience. The tune was plagiarized from a pre-war ditty called 'La Margoton du bataillon', which celebrated a garrison-town good-time girl. Equally incongruous was the fact that the tune was composed by a Jew, who would die as a result of the new regime's policies. Casimir Oberfeld was born in Poland but moved to France where his film scores and songs – among them 'Paris sera toujours Paris' – provided much of the popular musical soundtrack for the 1920s and 1930s. When Paris fell he took refuge in Nice in the Unoccupied Zone, only to be rounded up when the Germans arrived, ending up in Auschwitz.

One verse of the anthem ran: 'In giving us your life / your genius and your faith / you are saving the fatherland / for the second time.' The comparison to Jesus Christ verged on the blasphemous, but there were few complaints from the Catholic Church as most of the senior clergy welcomed the National Revolution.

Its message was summed up in a ubiquitous propaganda poster. The images and typeface mimicked posters of the early nineteenth century. In the foreground stands a moustachioed peasant holding a fishing rod and creel. His wife is seated next to him on a stool wearing a headscarf, with three toddlers at her side and the latest addition in a cradle at her feet. Cows browse in front of a church tower while a blacksmith hammers away in his smithy. Behind, in the mid-distance, a row of factory chimneys makes a nod to modern reality. It is only far off, tucked away on the right-hand edge, that the Eiffel Tower makes a grudging appearance.

At the centre is a portrait of the marshal above a Gallic double-headed axe symbol fixed to a marshal's baton and known as the *francisque*, which was Vichy's answer to the Italian *fasces*. Apologists for Vichy subsequently claimed that this was not a fascist enterprise, even though it might look like one with its cult of personality, its emphasis on authority, its slogans and its iconography. For one thing, it never tried to build a single, all-powerful party structure, as in Italy and Germany. Vichy lacked a coherent ideology like Nazism or fascism. There had not been time to design one. The only 'ism' that Pierre Laval proved faithful to was opportunism, and he never took the National Revolution seriously. Others, the 'technocrats', pre-war industrialists like Pierre Pucheu, Jean Bichelonne and François Lehideux, went along with the Ruritanian elements only because they saw an opportunity to build a rational, materialistic future for France based on ever more efficient factories, which ran headlong into the marshal's vision. How sincerely did he himself believe in it? No one knew for sure.

In so far as Vichy had a philosophy it was based on rejection and revenge. Under the guise of uniting the nation it shrank the definition of Frenchness, casting out communists, freemasons, Jews and foreigners whose very identity made their loyalty suspect. It was in part the institutionalization of the ideas of Charles Maurras and movements like Action Française. Even so, many former adherents rejected the new order, and staunch right-wingers of the pre-war period were well represented in the small band who first rallied to de Gaulle in London.

But many more saw Vichy as a golden opportunity to pursue their old agenda. Maurras himself welcomed Pétain as a 'divine surprise'. The government expended much energy on settling old scores. One of its first acts was to outlaw freemasonry. The Vichy mindset was conspiratorial. The masons, with their secret ceremonies and global reach, had long been denounced as intrinsically anti-French and accused of being at the heart of much of the dirty business of the Third Republic. Naturally, they were in league with the Jews. The

Dreyfus affair had revealed the extent to which anti-Semitism permeated all levels of conservative France, ranging from mild dislike to pathological hatred.

Pétain was not an obvious anti-Semite. He had stayed out of the Dreyfus controversy and had Jewish friends. He nonetheless took an active part in framing the first tranche of anti-Semitic legislation enacted in October 1940. This adopted Nazi-style definitions of Jewishness and excluded those who fell within them from army and state posts, important economic positions and key professions and any job that influenced public opinion. All foreign Jews were now subject to arrest and internment, and by the beginning of 1941 some 40,000 had been rounded up and put into camps.

This was the start of a stream of edicts designed to humiliate and impoverish French Jews living in France and the overseas territories, and to clear the way for the deportation of non-French Jews. The policy was an entirely French initiative and Pétain was under no pressure from the Germans to enact it. This came as a pleasant surprise to the occupiers, who now knew that they would have few difficulties in imposing their own racial programmes. Before long the persecution of all Jews had become a joint Franco-German enterprise.

The sudden transformation from democracy to authoritarianism was matched by a radical re-evaluation of French interests. France and Britain had fought side by side against the Germans twice so far that century. Even so, the relationship had often been fractious, the result of suspicion and hostility built up over hundreds of years of enmity. Vichy harboured many Anglophobes, including Pétain himself. From August, cinema audiences learned from Vichy propaganda newsreels that their former allies were now their enemies, and their recent enemies their friends. One film showed huge fires burning at an industrial facility on the Atlantic coast and steel-helmeted soldiers wielding hosepipes. The voice-over explained: 'During their retreat, the English set fire to the oil storage depot at Lorient thereby harming their former allies. It was only thanks to the intervention of numerous teams of German firefighters that a million litres of fuel were saved.' The invaders' benevolence did not stop there. According to the commentary, overlaid with images of cheerful Franco-German co-operation, they had taken the lead in clearing away the debris of war, restoring the railway system and delivering humanitarian aid to returning refugees with 'the ladies of the German Red Cross at work everywhere'.

Vichy's propagandists were up against a deep and widespread French antipathy towards Germany and Germans. The light touch that the invaders showed in the early months of the occupation came as a relief to all. Pétain's message that France must take its punishment and get on with things was widely accepted, but that did not mean you had to like your conquerors. However correct their behaviour, for most ordinary French men, women and children (despite what they were being told from on high) the Germans were still, in the end, the enemy. When they talked about them in private they used the old pejorative nicknames from the last war: they were the Fridolins, the Frisés, the Chleuhs, the Boche. As the war progressed and the Germans' behaviour worsened, the idea that occupiers and occupied could be friends became a fantasy that only Franco-fascists could entertain. And despite the best efforts of the collaborationist press, the Allied bombs that increasingly fell on innocent French civilians would never arouse any significant anger against the British and Americans.

Even so, British actions following the armistice gave a helping hand to the Vichy narrative. On 3 July 1940, the Royal Navy bombarded the French fleet at anchor in the Algerian port of Mers-el-Kébir in order to stop it falling into German hands, killing 1,400 sailors. Two months later, the British launched a failed amphibious attack with Free French troops led by de Gaulle on the French port of Dakar in French West Africa. These incidents shored up Vichy's message that 'perfidious Albion' was still the real enemy and, despite having fought three wars in the last seventy years, France and Germany were natural allies. This war was over now, leaving a 'middle way' between defeat and subjugation and an opportunity to go forward as associates in a shared enterprise to rebuild Europe, forming a common front against the Bolsheviks, the Jews and the 'Anglo-Saxons'.

This was the hope sustaining Pétain when he travelled to a provincial railway station in the Loire valley on 24 October 1940 for his first and last meeting with Hitler. The Führer was returning from Hendaye near the Spanish border where he had tried unsuccessfully to persuade General Franco to join the Axis. The little town of Montoire was conveniently en route. Both men wore uniform for the encounter. The photograph of them shaking hands looked to the outside world like evidence of criminal complicity. The Vichy propagandists presented it as simply two old soldiers settling their differences and concluding a decent peace. Six days later, over the radio, Pétain told the nation what he had agreed: 'It is in a spirit of honour, and in order to preserve the unity of France . . . within the New European Order which is being built, that I today embark on the path of collaboration.'

The word sounded innocuous enough. It would be a while before it became synonymous with shame and dishonour. That there could be principled collaboration with the Nazis was an illusion that Pétain was slow to abandon. Germany's interests would always come first, second and third. Whatever leverage the marshal imagined he might wield was heavily outweighed by the presence of the huge number of French men who were to remain prisoners in Germany until a final peace agreement was signed. Their plight ensured that Vichy's compliance was always, in the end, guaranteed.

In November 1942, the French suffered a second military humiliation that destroyed any lingering fiction of independence. An Anglo-American force invaded French North Africa. To face the new threat from the Mediterranean, the Wehrmacht marched south to take over the Unoccupied Zone. Henceforth there could be no fantasies about middle ways and if Germany and France were 'partners' it was only as partners in crime.

3. *Deutsches Paris*

Robert Brasillach returned to Paris in April 1941 after nine months in a German prisoner-of-war camp to find the city had undergone a complete Nazi makeover. The gigantic swastika flags he had so admired in Nuremberg now drooped from every major building, hanging so low that they seemed almost to brush the street. The pavements were as crowded as ever. Reassured by the Germans' apparent commitment to 'correct' behaviour, most of those who had fled had by now returned home and the population was back at its pre-war level of about two and a half million. The roads were quieter. The difficulties of running a car meant they were now full of 'bizarre contraptions hitched to a bicycle or a tandem' – the *vélo-taxis* powered by human legs that had taken the place of motorized cabs.

Brasillach headed to the Left Bank and the Latin Quarter where he had passed his blissful teens and twenties. Spring was in the air and in happier days Parisiennes would have dressed up to welcome it. The women he passed seemed to have abandoned their old elegance in favour of practicality. Their legs were sheathed in thick woollen stockings and they wore capes with monklike cowls, a relic of cold winter months in barely heated apartments. They clumped along on shoes with thick wooden platform soles, a new fashion born of necessity. The occupiers were requisitioning the bulk of the leather supply to send to the army and there was little to spare for civilian footwear. It was part of a ruthless policy of appropriation and exploitation. Under the terms of the armistice, France had agreed to pay the costs of the occupation at a daily rate of 160 million euros in today's money, and the conquerors got first pick of the produce of its factories, fields, pastures, vineyards and orchards, leaving the vanquished to scrabble for what was left.

The crossroads bristled with signs in heavy Gothic script directing the garrison troops to this or that command post, office or barracks.

Some of the cinemas in which Brasillach had passed many hours in his days as a film reviewer were now designated *Soldatenkino* and reserved for Germans only. Nonetheless, the sight of Notre-Dame and the Seine flowing beneath quays lined with the tin stalls of the second-hand booksellers filled him with sweet nostalgia. Even the taste of his first *café au lait*, an acrid travesty brewed from roasted barley as there were no more coffee beans to be had, could not dispel the feeling that 'this would always be my very own Paris, no matter how difficult life might be'.

His last visit had been just days before the fall. Brasillach was serving as a lieutenant in an infantry unit guarding a sector of the Maginot Line when a summons arrived, calling him to appear before a tribunal in the capital. Georges Mandel had ordered a judicial investigation into *Je Suis Partout*, the latest round in a long-running feud with the newspaper sparked by an editorial in January 1939 calling for the interior minister to be arraigned for treason because of his 'warmongering' attitude towards Germany. The paper was subsequently banned but the row rumbled on and, as editor-in-chief, Brasillach was right in the legal firing line. By then the Germans were closing in on the city and after two days in police custody he returned to his unit, just as they were ordered to lay down their arms. They had not fired a single shot.

Brasillach saw himself as a patriot and the 'frightful defeat' hit him as hard as it did most Frenchmen. It also brought a certain bitter satisfaction. For years he and the *Je Suis Partout* polemicists had been warning that the Republic would be the ruin of France and calling for its replacement by 'a French fascism, suffused with the strong and joyful dreams of youth'. Now it was too late and they had watched 'the collapse of our nation and our desires'.

What was left was summed up by Brasillach's friend and colleague Lucien Rebatet in a single word: *décombres* (rubble) – the title of his bestselling polemic on the debacle. But once the dust had settled, Brasillach found that things did not look quite so bad. With endless hours in which to read and write and to chat and philosophize with fellow prisoners, life in the officers-only Oflag VIA in Soest, just east of Dortmund, was rather like his student days at the École Normale Supérieure. The news arriving from Vichy encouraged him to think that France's shattering defeat might be a blessing in disguise. The proposed National

Revolution seemed to match some of his own ideas. Like most of the Soest prisoners he rapidly became a fervent supporter of the marshal and his letters home were full of praise for the Vichy project.

Brasillach did not remain a prisoner for long. To the new government and the German occupiers, Brasillach's detestation of the old order and enthusiasm for the new Germany made him a valuable propaganda asset. He wasn't just a journalist, he was a serious literary figure whose last novel, *The Seven Colours*, had been shortlisted for the prestigious Prix Goncourt. Both the German embassy in Paris and the French authorities pressed for his release. The Vichy initiative came from the top. Admiral François Darlan, a smooth operator who had spent far more time at headquarters than he ever had at sea, was now prime minister following a spectacular but temporary falling out between Pétain and Pierre Laval. He wanted Brasillach to head up the government's film service. It was an important post. The cinema was a powerful arm of propaganda, and Brasillach was a reasonable pick, having written a highly regarded history of the cinema with his old school chum Maurice Bardèche, who had since married Brasillach's sister Suzanne. The Germans had other plans, however, and the job came to nothing. Still, there were no hard feelings: in March 1941 he was released and free to return to Paris and *Je Suis Partout*.

The tables had been resoundingly turned since the days of 1940 when the government tried to have the senior staff editors jailed. Now it was their arch-enemy Mandel who was in prison and the paper was back on the streets with circulation touching new heights. Brasillach's old colleagues were glad to see him and he settled again into the editor's chair. There were some ideological disagreements among them, but then there always were. The hot air arising from passionate debate is what kept such journals aloft. The main disagreement was over Pétain. Brasillach was staunchly loyal to him. He endorsed Pétain's verdict that those who stayed behind to try to shield France from the invader were the real patriots, unlike the 'traitor' de Gaulle. 'The unity of France', he declared, 'is not centred on London or Jerusalem or New York.' The choice was between 'on one side England, English gold, the ignoble [French] émigrés, the Jews and the crazies. On the other, we have the *maréchal*.' The more radical elements, led by the pathologically anti-Semitic Rebatet, were hostile to the new leader. It seemed to them that Vichy looked very much like the Third Republic in disguise and they doubted the National Revolution would lead to their goal of full-blooded collaboration with the Nazis. It would be a few years before these differences widened into a rift.

In the meantime Brasillach was happy. Like many writers he craved attention and *Je Suis Partout* was soon the biggest-selling weekly in the Occupied Zone with a circulation of a quarter of a million and turning a healthy profit. Many of its readers were young – a fact that pleased Brasillach, who was now in his early thirties and determined to hang on to his youthful optimism and energy. Germany seemed certain to win the war. While the going was good he was able to convince himself that a distinctively French fascism could blossom under the conditions of the occupation. He saw what he wanted to see. His way of dealing with the crimes of Vichy and the Germans that gave the lie to his claims that they were on the side of civilization was to look away. If not, he blamed the victims for bringing punishment on themselves. The power of words is what Brasillach ultimately believed in. And they could be used to explain away anything, including his own behaviour.

At first it appeared that Vichy policy was putting into practice much of what he had long been advocating. The October 1940 law on the status of Jews seemed to enact the very thing he had called for in his *Je Suis Partout* editorial in February 1939. The statute and the forty-nine anti-Semitic laws and decrees that followed launched a devastating assault on the position, wealth and dignity of all Jews in France. The order allowing prefects to intern foreign Jews at will meant that they could also be taken to camps prior to expulsion. However, the opening words of the *Je Suis Partout* leader had firmly specified 'first, no persecution'. What was this if not systematic oppression?

Brasillach said nothing. There was no comment either when at the end of May 1942 a German order made it compulsory for all Jews over six years old in the Occupied Zone to wear a yellow Star of David. He also kept quiet when a few weeks later, and with Vichy's blessing, French police carried out mass arrests of foreign and stateless Jews, ostensibly for deportation to German work camps in the east. The most notorious operation took place in Paris on 16 and 17 July when

Jewish women wearing the Star of David

9,000 *flics* swooped in what became known as *la Grande Rafle* – 'the Big Round-Up'. More than 13,000 Jews, including 3,900 children, were bussed to the Vélodrome d'Hiver, a sports stadium near the Eiffel Tower, and held for days without adequate food, water or sanitation. They were then moved to transit camps at Drancy, a former housing estate in the north-east suburbs, and Pithiviers and Beaune-la-Rolande, in the Loiret department south of Paris. There they were packed into cattle trucks bound for Auschwitz. Many died en route of thirst and starvation. Those who made it went to the gas chambers.

It took Brasillach two months to make a public comment about the *rafle* and when he did, it was buried deep in an editorial. Some children had been separated from their parents in the round-up, apparently to maintain the pretence that the adults were to serve as labourers for the Reich. The Catholic archbishop of Toulouse, Monsignor Saliège, among others, had protested that the splitting of families was inhumane. Brasillach seemed to agree. It was better that children should be sent off with their parents, he wrote, and 'in this case humanity is in accord with wisdom'. It sounded like an expression of decency, but his readers would have been in no doubt as to what he really meant. Even if at this stage of the war the suspicion that the Germans were engaged in a mass extermination programme in the east was too appalling to entertain, only a fool could believe that anything other than suffering and hunger awaited the deportees. Brasillach showed no curiosity about what happened to the Jews when they reached the end of the line. Friends and followers would later try to excuse him as a naïf, blind to the evil that his literary gifts were inadvertently promoting. The truth was that under his direction *Je Suis Partout* peddled hate. He thirsted for revenge against the leading figures of the Third Republic, in particular Léon Blum, Paul Reynaud and the paper's arch-enemy Georges Mandel. When, in early 1942, five former ministers went on trial in the Auvergne town of Riom charged with betrayal of their duties and bringing about defeat, Brasillach was delighted. He was dismayed when the Vichy case collapsed after the evidence suggested that the blame lay with the army high command instead. In his weekly front-page editorial he fantasized about rounding up all the old gang and sending them to a Pacific island, saving just two 'for annihilation'. In making the choice, he mused, 'I don't think we would hesitate: Mandel and Reynaud must be hanged first.' Each week the paper carried a column called 'Partout & ailleurs' ('Everywhere & elsewhere') gleefully revealing the identities and locations of Jews who had changed their names and gone into hiding, as well as pointing out Gaullists and communists.

Occasionally Brasillach's enthusiasm faltered. He was with Rebatet at the printing works putting the paper to bed when the news broke that Hitler had invaded the Soviet Union. Rebatet rejoiced but Brasillach felt a twinge of alarm, asking doubtfully: 'It's awfully big Russia, isn't it? How do you think it's going to turn out?' He quickly recovered. 'Germany has taken up arms to defend the whole of European civilisation . . . against Bolshevism,' he trumpeted soon afterwards. Henceforth he would praise the stormtroopers as modern Siegfrieds fighting 'for French civilisation as well as for that of Germany, Italy and Spain'.

When the ultra-nationalists Marcel Déat and Jacques Doriot founded the French Legion of Volunteers against Bolshevism to take their place alongside the Germans on the Eastern Front, Brasillach applauded. It showed the world that the French were not a defeated nation but partners with the Nazis in defending the west from the 'barbarians'. As late as July 1943 he went on a German-organized propaganda trip to the Eastern Front in a party that included Doriot, who was wearing the Legion's SS-style uniform. They were taken to recently discovered mass graves in Katyń forest where many of the 21,857 Polish officers and members of the Polish intelligentsia murdered by the Soviets in 1940 were buried. Brasillach did his bit, speaking briefly on French radio and writing up the massacre as further proof of the necessity for France and Germany to unite against the Red menace. He claimed later that he had been present not as a Nazi mouthpiece but as an investigative reporter. However, he showed no inclination to pursue the many similar atrocities committed by his patrons.

Brasillach's support for Germany was based on the delusional assumption that when the Nazis achieved their victory Hitler would grant France a privileged place in the new European order. In his mind they had been on the same side all along. 'Anti-Semitism isn't a German invention,' he once argued. 'It's a French tradition.' His fatal weakness was his vanity, accepting the attention and flattery heaped on him by the occupiers as no more than his due and imagining that, far from manipulating him, the Germans were simply paying him the respect owed to a great intellectual who had chosen to stand with them on the right side of history. As time passed it would get harder and harder to maintain this fantasy, though his pride would never allow him to admit his mistake. This stubbornness would cost Robert Brasillach very dearly.

There was a grain of truth, however, in Brasillach's delusions: Hitler did look on France differently compared to his other conquests. The flying tour with his artist friends had been a gesture of respect. Of the French themselves he knew nothing. The closest he had come to them was in his days as a 'front fighter'. As was often the case with combatants in the Great War, the experience had created more sympathy than hatred. The French were therefore to be treated with a degree of courtesy unthinkable in the case of the Poles or Russians and the occupation would be framed to take some account of the feelings of the losers. On 18 June he ordered his troops in France to be 'an example of the German military spirit in terms of their rectitude, good humour and manliness in all situations'. That meant 'behaving in a correct manner with the Parisians'.

This would prove to be a sentimental indulgence, to be dropped instantly as soon as it became inconvenient. Practical considerations came first. Hitler's plan for eastward expansion meant Germany had to use its manpower sparingly. By putting the entire French civil service at the occupiers' disposal, Pétain had lifted an enormous weight from the Germans' shoulders. But for things to run smoothly the Germans needed the acquiescence of the population at large and that meant using the carrot as well as the stick. The aim was to co-opt the French, not to crush them, starting with those who influenced the way the public thought and behaved.

The man appointed to win them over had ideal qualifications for the job. Otto Abetz was thirty-eight years old, tall, blond and cultured. He looked like everyone's idea of a Teutonic aristo but came from a modest background, the son of an estate manager in Baden-Württemberg who died when Otto was in his early teens. He started out as a social democrat and defender of the Weimar Republic. In 1931 he joined the Nazi Party, attracted by the ostensibly anti-capitalist elements in its manifesto. He was too young to have fought in the war but was gripped by the conviction that the future lay in German–French reconciliation and co-operation. There were many like him in France, including the journalist Jean Luchaire. Abetz joined with Luchaire to found the Franco-German Committee which organized camping and skiing trips for the youth of both nations. He also married Luchaire's secretary, a Frenchwoman called Susanne de Bruyker.

Abetz caught the eye of the Nazi foreign minister Joachim von Ribbentrop and in 1937 joined the German foreign service. The following year Ribbentrop sent him to Paris with a mission to charm the capital's elite. He made many conquests but his eagerness got him into trouble. A few months before the war broke out he was expelled following allegations that he had bribed newspaper editors to publish pro-German articles. Abetz loved France and its culture, but there was no doubt where his loyalties lay. He set out his views in a memo to Ribbentrop which stated: 'Germany's interests demand, on the one hand, that France be maintained in a state of internal weakness and, on the other, that France be kept at a distance from foreign powers hostile to the Reich.' This policy was approved by Hitler when the two met in the Führer's Bavarian Alpine retreat near Berchtesgaden in August 1940. As a result he was given responsibility for political dealings with the French, as well as control of newspapers, publishing, radio, film and theatre.

Abetz set about building a cultural alliance. It would be a lopsided arrangement in which French artistic life would be tolerated only if it conformed to the Reich's agenda. He opened the Deutsches Institut in the Hôtel Sagan, a light-filled mini-palace that had been the Polish embassy in the rue Talleyrand, near the Invalides, where French artists and scientists could rub shoulders with their German counterparts. Humbler Parisians could go there for free German lessons. Some 5,000 took up the offer.

The staff knew their business. The associate director, Karl Heinz Bremer, taught at the École Normale Supérieure before the war. He was tall and blond and Robert Brasillach was soon entranced by him. At the end of 1941 Bremer invited him, along with the novelist Pierre Drieu La Rochelle and the poet and novelist Abel Bonnard, to a 'congress of European writers' in Weimar, the home of Goethe. They were taken to concerts and banquets, and Brasillach enthused predictably about the 'vitality and youth of the country'. They met Arno Breker, whose work was showcased by the Institut. In May 1942 his musclebound sculptures were put on display at the Orangerie gallery in the Tuileries Garden, in what became the cultural event of the year. At the opening, the naughty boy of pre-war French literature Jean Cocteau lauded Breker as Germany's Michelangelo.

Abetz also created the Informations-Abteilung or News Department to control the output of press, publishing and radio, abetted by his pre-war comrade Jean Luchaire, a sleek, corrupt opportunist. Luchaire had the backing of Vichy and soon became the king of the collaborationist press, editing both *Le Matin* and *Les Nouveaux Temps*, two of the biggest-selling daily papers in the Occupied Zone.

The pair's patronage guaranteed well-paid work in widely read publications. Just as important, it brought invitations to the best parties. These were things that mattered, and many of the big names of the intellectual right, as well as the politically uncategorizable Cocteau and numerous show business celebrities, were happy to accept them. Before the summer of 1940 was out the soirées and entertainments laid on by the embassy and its outposts were crammed with *le tout Paris*.

Watching the scene with cool detachment was a hero of the 1914–18 war who was now one of Germany's most famous writers. Captain Ernst Jünger arrived in Paris in the summer of 1941. Forty-seven, slim and handsome with a full head of greying hair, Jünger worked out of the Hôtel Majestic. This was the headquarters of the Militärbefehlshaber in Frankreich, the German military commander for the whole of France, and a stone's throw from the Arc de Triomphe. Jünger's multiple duties ranged from intelligence work monitoring the literary crowd to once having to supervise the execution by firing squad of a deserter. None was very taxing and he had plenty of time to enjoy the Paris social and cultural scene. The commander was Otto von Stülpnagel, a cadaverous dandy who wore patent-leather jackboots and gold buttons on his uniform. Jünger found him painstakingly courteous but also 'wooden and melancholy'. Stülpnagel's permanent state of anxiety was evidence of his ongoing struggle with Nazi rivals from the SS and Gestapo, who were suspicious of his lack of zeal in hunting down Jews and communists. By early 1942, he had had enough and resigned, to be replaced by his cousin Carl-Heinrich von Stülpnagel, who was unreliable in a different way. During his service on the Eastern Front Carl-Heinrich had shown no qualms about shooting hostages or deporting Jews. As commander of the Seventeenth Army in Russia and Ukraine he ordered mass executions in reprisal for partisan attacks and supported the operations of the *SS-Einsatzgruppen* extermination squads. He was not, however, a Nazi. He had been engaged in plotting against Hitler since before the war and would continue to do so from his base at the Majestic.

Jünger observed the intrigues with the philosophical detachment he brought to everything. One of the many aphorisms which studded his journal stated: 'In moments of inescapable chaos individuals

must proclaim their allegiance, like a battleship hoisting its colours.'
He faced many moral dilemmas in his time in Paris. On 6 March 1942,
he recorded rumours related to him by a visitor from the Eastern
Front about the mass slaughter of Jews and perceived enemies of the
Reich that had been going on since the German invasion of the Soviet
Union in June the previous year. 'Butchers' were operating 'charnel
houses' in frontier states like Poland and had 'single-handedly killed
enough people to populate a middle-sized city'. But his qualms were
confined to his diary and far from hoisting his colours he stayed neutral. When he had the chance to join the second Stülpnagel's
anti-Hitler plotting, Jünger held back. He preferred to use the abundant downtime wandering around town, socializing with fellow
intellectuals and wining and dining his French girlfriend, a married
physician called Sophie Ravoux, while his wife Gretha and two sons
endured hardship and Allied bombs back home in Germany.

The picture Jünger painted of occupied Paris showed that many of
the upper crust had adjusted fairly easily to their new circumstances.
They operated in a climate of moral laissez-faire, refraining from
judging in order not to be judged themselves, and the only luxury not
available was that of having a conscience. One summer's day in 1942
he called on the Comtesse de Cargouët, a young French noblewoman.
They 'talked about the end of the war and she said she was betting on
the Germans. Then we discussed English society and Churchill whom
she met a few times. She said all the whisky he drank was preserving
him like plums in brandy.' At lunch with Vichy's representative to the
German high command in Paris, Fernand de Brinon, he sat next to the
actress Arletty. 'Just the word *cocu* [cheated-on husband] is enough to
make her laugh,' he noted, 'which means that in this country she is
almost always in a state of merriment.' Arletty's career was booming.
With German support the French film industry was churning out
more movies than before the war and she was currently starring in
Madame Sans-Gêne. The title meant 'shameless lady', a role she would
play just as well off screen when she took a Luftwaffe officer as her
lover. Jünger was amused by another guest, Sacha Guitry. The actor
and dramatist's immense output had barely faltered since the occupation and Jünger would see him often at social gatherings in the years

ahead, always ready to turn whatever twist events had taken into an ironic joke.

Arletty and Guitry were beneficiaries of the German policy of pretending that despite the occupation Paris was still Paris. That meant that the theatres, music halls and nightclubs which had made it the entertainment capital of the world could not stay dark for long. Encouraged by their new masters, the big names hurried back to resume their pre-war careers. Stars who exemplified Frenchness like Edith Piaf, the Belleville street urchin who became famous as the pale, pinched face of working-class Paris, the 'Singing Fool' Charles Trenet and the twinkly-eyed Maurice Chevalier in his boater and bow tie were soon delighting occupiers and occupied alike at the Folies Bergère and the Gaîté de Paris. The clubs which had made Paris a jazz mecca before the war reopened cautiously. Nazi ideology classified the music as degenerate, but the occupation authorities turned a blind eye. There were plenty of jazz fans in field-grey uniform and they took their place alongside the long-haired bohemian *zazous* and their girls in the basement dives of the Left Bank where pre-war legends like Django Reinhardt could be found playing most nights.

The city's renowned restaurants like Fouquet's, Le Grand Véfour and La Tour d'Argent barely missed a beat in adapting to the new clientele. Arrangements with the leading black marketeers ensured that standards were maintained and at Maxim's the head waiter, Albert Blaser, led Field Marshal Göring to his table with the same respectful solemnity as he had shown to the presidents and prime ministers of the Third Republic. Business boomed at the famous brothels. Fabienne Jamet, the madame of 122 on the rue de Provence, would sigh later that she had 'never been so happy' as when the Germans were in town. The streetwalkers at the lower end of the market were equally content. Their soldier clients could pay them in kind as well as cash, offering powdered eggs, soap and occasionally oranges and bananas which could be bartered or sold on in the city's seething black economy.

Pablo Picasso's comfortable existence was a testament to the sincerity of the Germans' live-and-let-live policy when it came to the artistic *prominente*. As someone whose paintings had featured in the notorious 'Entartete Kunst' ('Degenerate Art') exhibition put on by the Nazis in Munich in the summer of 1937, he was not allowed to show his work. Otherwise he was left alone. People who practised mass murder without a second thought were wary of the damage to their reputations should they be seen to molest a world icon. Sophisticates like Abetz were fans. So too was Arno Breker, who had known Picasso in his inter-war years in Paris. Picasso was polite when he encountered them, without going in for too much public socializing of the sort that would later taint the names of less cautious artists like Cocteau and Guitry.

Nonetheless, it was useful to have friends in high places when, as Picasso sometimes did, he sailed close to the wind. It was money not politics that caused the problems. Picasso was keen to hang on to his wealth, not least to make sure he had the materials to keep up the relentless output which was his way of drowning out the clamour of war. While most of Paris often went without food, fuel and soap, his connections meant he could get his hands on the vital commodities of life, and he ate most days at Le Catalan, a black-market restaurant near his house. Marie-Thérèse Walter, his earthy muse and mother to his daughter Maya, was not so lucky. One day he showed her a cupboard where stacks of gold ingots were hidden under tablets of Marseilles soap, telling her that were anything to happen to him the gold was hers. At that moment soap meant more to her than bullion and she asked if she could have some. Picasso prevaricated – a favourite tactic when anyone asked a direct favour – and she left empty-handed. However, he did provide Marie-Thérèse with a regular supply of coal, wrapped up in 5-kilo parcels which she had to collect from his house and hump home on the Métro.

Once or twice he stepped over the mark and had to rely on German admirers to get him out of trouble. His dealings on the currency markets brought him to the attention of the authorities, going as high as General Heinrich Müller, right-hand man of the chief of the SS Heinrich Himmler. Abetz explained the problem to Breker who boldly intervened, telling Müller: 'If you lay a hand on Picasso, the world's press will create such an uproar your head will spin.' It was a measure of the artist's mystique and reputation that men who had the blood of thousands on their hands thought it wise to leave him alone.

Picasso's decision to stay on in Paris under the rule of those who hated everything he appeared to stand for seemed baffling. It could be interpreted as a display of heroic stoicism and, in its way, a form of resistance. Picasso was honest enough with himself to see it differently. When his girlfriend Françoise Gilot asked him why he had not taken up the invitation to go to America, he replied: 'It isn't really an act of courage. It's just a form of inertia. I suppose it's simply that I prefer to be here.' His life was as ordered as a monk's. He lived in a large studio-apartment housed in an aristocratic mansion at 7 rue des Grands-Augustins and rose most mornings around midday. There he was looked after by a live-in housekeeper, Inès Sassier, a young woman he had met when she was waitressing in a restaurant during one of his pre-war visits to Mougins in the South of France, and her husband Gustave. The only other permanent resident was his dog Kazbek. The mistresses were installed at a safe distance from each other. Marie-Thérèse Walter lived with Maya in a flat in the boulevard Henri-IV on the other side of the Seine near the Bastille. Dora Maar, once a model of progressive independent womanhood but now his doormat, was closer to hand, just round the corner in the rue de Savoie.

As he prepared for the day, visitors who had been invited to drop by or been bold enough to invite themselves gathered in an outer room to hear whether or not they would be granted an audience. The gatekeeper was his faithful and much abused secretary and friend from his salad days in Barcelona, Jaume Sabartés. The routine had the feel of a royal levee and Sabartés was alert to signs of *lèse-majesté*, such as anyone uttering anything less than rapturous approval of any works on display. Not that there was much danger of that. As one visitor observed, Picasso 'could have shit on the floor and they would have admired it'.

Inevitably, he and Jünger met. They came together at a party given by Florence Gould, who was born to French parents in the US, married the son of a Wall Street banker, then moved with her husband to Paris to build a hotel and casino empire. She seemed to have been genetically programmed to prosper in the moral chaos of the occupation, sleeping with everyone and pimping for senior German officers, while hosting lavish parties. On 22 July 1942 Jünger decided to pay Picasso a call. He rang and the door was opened by the master himself, 'a short man in a simple worker's smock'. Jünger 'had the impression I was looking at a magician, an impression that was only intensified by the little green pointed hat he wore'. Picasso was content to play the role of wizard, telling his visitor that 'My pictures would have the same effect if, after they were finished, I were to wrap them up and seal them without showing them to anyone.' He seemed to find Jünger unusually empathetic, telling him, 'Both of us sitting here together would be able to negotiate peace over the course of this afternoon. In the evening people would be able to turn their lights on again.' Jünger quoted the remark approvingly in his diary. It was nonsense, but Picasso was right about one thing: the soldier-philosopher and painter-alchemist were quite alike, wrapped up in their own metaphysical preoccupations, aloof from the madness that had set the world around them on fire.

Lest anyone should think that relations were too cosy, Picasso liked to recount small acts of rebellion. When the Germans started to make an inventory of all French art assets, he was obliged to show them the paintings he had stashed in a strongroom in the boulevard Haussmann. At one point an official noticed a photograph of *Guernica* – the original was now in the care of the Museum of Modern Art in New York. 'Did you do that?' the German asked. 'No, you did,' Picasso quipped – or at least that is what he told his cronies at one of their regular evening gatherings at the Café de Flore.

The German inventory was an ominous development for all those who owned works of art. Like everything else in France, they were now a resource to be plundered. Within weeks of the occupation an organization called the Einsatzstab Reichsleiter Rosenberg (ERR) arrived in Paris. It was part of a huge operation, overseen initially by the Nazis' chief ideologue Alfred Rosenberg, to seize all major cultural artefacts in the Nazis' new domains. His taskforce was set to work combing the national museums and galleries and private collections, listing their contents, then seizing the best pieces to be crated up and carted off to Germany. Jewish-owned collections were to be confiscated wholesale. The intention was to send the pick of the plunder to the planned

Führermuseum in Hitler's Austrian home town of Linz, where he himself was expected to take a hand in curating the contents. Everything from medieval illuminated manuscripts to Impressionist paintings was seen as spoils of war. 'Degenerate' paintings by modern artists would have no place in the new gallery. However, they would help to pay for it, and the propaganda minister Joseph Goebbels set up a special agency authorizing German dealers to sell off stolen *entartete Kunst* on the world art market in Switzerland.

Much of the finest modern work was in the hands of the big Paris collectors, many of them Jewish. Among them was Picasso's dealer and close friend Paul Rosenberg. The Germans had not been in the city a month when raiding parties descended on the leading galleries. When they turned up at Rosenberg's establishment at 21 rue La Boétie they found it empty. The premises were requisitioned and in May 1941 reopened with much fanfare as the Institut d'Étude des Questions Juives, a pseudo-academic centre, French-staffed but under Gestapo control, which pumped out anti-Semitic propaganda.

The officers of the ERR did not give up easily. They wore Wehrmacht uniforms and pursued their duties with military rigour. They now had a very hard taskmaster in the sizeable form of Hermann Göring, perhaps the most powerful man in Germany after Hitler, who had pushed Alfred Rosenberg aside. With the ERR at his disposal, Göring could now start to satisfy his craving to grab Europe's finest art for himself.

On 5 September 1941, acting on a tip-off, a Nazi squad turned up in the pretty town of Libourne perched on the edge of the Gironde river and headed for the Banque Nationale pour le Commerce et l'Industrie. In vault No. 7 they found 162 paintings that Paul Rosenberg had been forced to leave behind when he departed for Portugal and then New York. They were crated up and despatched to Paris to join the mighty treasure trove of stolen art piling up in a tall, rectangular, high-windowed stone building which stood in the north-western corner of the Tuileries Garden. The Jeu de Paume had started life in 1861 as a traditional tennis court but was later transformed into an exhibition space. It was a handy place to sort and stack the ERR's loot ready for Göring to come and pick it over. A special room, nicknamed the *salle des martyrs*, was reserved for modern work that might not be to his taste but would serve as currency for barter or sale to fund the expansion of his collection. It was here that Rosenberg's Libourne cache was stored to await whatever Göring had in mind for it.

For the 20,000 or so Germans who administered the occupation from the capital, Paris was a dreamscape, a playground where they could do all the things that money or convention prevented them from doing at home. Their ranks were swollen by soldiers, sailors and airmen on leave from active service. A fortnightly publication appeared, *Der Deutsche Wegleiter*, packed with information on where to eat, drink, watch movies, buy watches and cameras for themselves, and perfume, fur coats and underwear for their wives and girlfriends back home. It looked just like a pre-war visitor guide, except that these tourists had no intention of departing. Why would they when the natives were so apparently welcoming? The 1–15 November 1941 issue has a picture on the title page of a lance corporal and private sitting on stools outside an old church, one painting, the other sketching. Two young boys look over the painter's shoulder at his work. Underneath are the words 'Art and Art Supervisors!' and the caption 'Off-duty you can capture memories'.

Once the war in the east began, a posting to Paris was the difference between heaven and hell. While the bulk of the Wehrmacht were freezing and dying on the steppes of Russia, the lucky few were having the time of their lives. The *Wegleiter* listed fifty-two cabarets where you could drink, dine and watch a saucy show, paying for the fun at a grotesquely favourable exchange rate. German women were as keen as the men to take advantage of the Reich's new playground. There were plenty of jobs on offer and at any time about one in ten of the German strength were *Wehrmachtshelferinnen*, female auxiliaries who worked as support staff for the military. To the French they were the *souris grises*, the 'grey mice', on account of their uniforms. Many were from humble homes, grateful for the chance of adventure and an escape from the traditional roles of childbearing and housekeeping idealized by the Nazis. Upper-class women also took the chance. Twenty-one-year-old Ursula Rüdt von Collenberg arrived in Paris in April 1942 at the invitation of her Luftwaffe general uncle to work in the archive service and was installed in a 'wonderful and huge room with a bath and a telephone' at the Hôtel d'Orsay on the Right Bank. She lunched in the German embassy in the rue de Lille and had finished her duties by four or five o'clock, when she was free to go to the opera or theatre to see the likes of Sacha Guitry and Jean-Louis Barrault. Her uncle gave 'fantastic dinner parties' at his Neuilly villa, formerly the home of a wealthy Jewish woman, 'with all the right French guests: Marquis So-and-so and Comte Tra-la-la . . . we had a young Frenchman come to give us language lessons. There was lovely material to be bought for clothes and I found a little White Russian dress maker. Fantastic deals were being transacted all around on the sly, for wines, food, shoes, what have you. We could buy what we wanted, much more than the French.' Years later she remembered without shame her eighteen months in the city as 'the most wonderful and unforgettable time of my youth'.

For a while the likes of Collenberg could cling to the fiction that the population looked on them in much the same way as they did the tourists who flocked there before the war and that the jewellers, furriers, nightclub owners and brothel keepers were as happy to have their custom as anyone else's. There were others who realized that the life they enjoyed bore little resemblance to the one endured by most of the city's inhabitants. Walter Dreizner was sent to Paris in October 1942. He was thirty-four and had been a telephone engineer in his home town of Halle in central Germany when he was called up for service in a signals unit. Dreizner was a keen photographer and spent his spare time wandering the city with his French girlfriend Raymonde, taking pictures of the sights and in time becoming friendly with prominent local photographers. Some of his shots were artistic studies of the Eiffel Tower and the sunworshippers at the Piscine Deligny floating swimming pool moored on the Seine. But he was an honest chronicler and many of his photos record the misery of everyday life as it went on at the periphery of the occupiers' vision. One shows a youngish woman bundled in what was once an expensive coat, delving with her bare hands through a rubbish bin in search of scraps of food. In another a shabby old lady pushes a pram loaded with precious firewood.

Hunger and cold were real afflictions for most Parisians from the start. Since the Prussian siege of 1870–71 the city had forgotten what it was like to starve. Within a few months of the occupation food, and where to find it, became a daily obsession. For all the talk of partnership, there was little left after the conquerors had helped themselves and each year between half and three-quarters of French livestock and crops ended up in German bellies. In September 1940, rationing was introduced. Each inhabitant was allotted a food allowance according to age and occupation, obtainable only on production of a 'ticket' issued by the local *mairie*. An adult was entitled to 350 grams (12 oz) of bread a day, 350 grams of meat a week and 500 grams of sugar, 300 grams of coffee and 140 grams of cheese a month. The bread ration was quite generous – more than an average baguette's worth a day. The coffee ration would cover a daily cup, but soon it was a parody of the real thing, only 10 per cent coffee beans and the rest made from ground-up chicory and acorns. The meat ration translated into a couple of modest steaks or chops or half a chicken a week, but your ticket was useless if the butchers' shops were empty. And the monthly cheese ration amounted to two meagre mouthfuls.

In time rice, noodles, butter, fish, chocolate and wine were added to the list. So too were soap, textiles and tobacco. In pre-war Paris even those on modest wages could eat well, dress in some style and wash and smoke as much as they liked. Now malnutrition was rife and it would leave its mark on the rising generation. By the end of the war adolescent girls and boys were on average 11 centimetres and 7 centimetres shorter than they had been in 1935 and as often as not their smiles would reveal teeth that were missing or black with decay. Life for those at the bottom was a perpetual struggle against hunger and disease, and in the winter months bitter cold. Coal was a weapon of war and most of the output from the mines was shipped straight to Germany. The hospitals overflowed with the victims of diet deficiencies who occupied a low place on the list of priorities and were given over to the care of the student doctors. Madeleine Riffaud, on secondment from the Sorbonne medical school, recalled a procession of worn-out women, 'underfed, with wrinkled cheeks and sallow skin, reeking of poverty'. Some had resorted to selling their bodies to the Germans to stay alive.

One day when she was in charge of admissions a young, very pregnant girl walked in. She took the patient through the questionnaire: 'Marital status? Single. Who to contact in case of emergency? No one. Name of father? "I couldn't tell you, mademoiselle. All I did was feel the buttons of his uniform."'

For rich and poor alike, survival meant doing something that in peacetime would have made them feel guilty, embarrassed or outright ashamed. It was hard to live on rations alone and even the most respectable were sometimes forced to buy on the black market. Everything could be found if you knew the right people and had enough money. If you were without either, you had to rely on 'Système D' – D for *débrouiller*, meaning to sort out, get on with or make the most of a difficult situation. Bartering became a way of life. A doctor would treat a plumber and be paid with a chicken acquired when the plumber fixed the drains of someone who kept poultry in their back yard.

Many Parisians had family in the countryside, where cream, eggs, cheese were still available and relations who had not been visited for years suddenly found themselves very popular. But ingenuity and enterprise alone could not fill the gap. The mealtimes that Parisians

Hunger

had observed with quasi-religious reverence before the war were often reduced to pit stops to fill up on whatever fodder could be scraped together. In peacetime 'rutabagas' (swedes) were what you gave to pigs and horses. Now they were more than acceptable fare. In a guide to how to live elegantly under the occupation, the novelist Colette provided a recipe for *tarte aux rutabagas*. She claimed that their juice was also good for smoothing away wrinkles. To combat the cold she advised spending the greater part of the day in bed, as she herself did when unable to find any coal or kerosene to heat her grand flat in the Palais-Royal.

Françoise Girardet, a well-brought-up eighteen-year-old, lived with her parents in a nice apartment in the posh suburb of Neuilly, but in winter there was 'no means of heating other than one open fireplace in the drawing room'. Her father 'used to bring home old telephone directories from his office and we burned them as slowly as possible'. Damp soon invaded the walls and she was forced to 'cover my bed with newspapers to try and keep my bedclothes dry but I [still] suffered from chilblains on my hands and feet'. The *vélo* became an indispensable tool of life. There were two million in Paris, one for virtually every inhabitant, of which 750,000 were new and each cost almost as much as a pre-war car. Theft was a constant problem, as was the extreme difficulty of finding replacement inner tubes. When that became impossible, there was always Système D. Françoise Girardet and her friends 'invented a replacement system . . . using wire which was threaded through old corks which were inserted instead of the tube. Not very comfortable but it did the trick.'

As time passed, the occupiers found it ever harder to convince them-selves that the city had accepted its fate. One summer day in 1942 Ernst Jünger was walking back to his office in the Majestic when he dropped into a shop in the avenue Wagram to buy some stationery. He noticed the young woman behind the counter 'was staring at me with deep hatred. The pupils of her light blue eyes were like pinpoints. She met my gaze quite openly, with a kind of relish – a relish with which the scorpion pierces his prey with the barb of his tail.' By then the numb-ness of defeat and occupation was wearing off. Paris was biting back.

4. First Blood

At eight o'clock on the morning of 21 August 1941, a smart young German naval officer called Alfons Moser climbed the steps to Barbès–Rochechouart station on the elevated section of Line 4 of the Paris Métro and took his place on the south-bound platform in the direction of Porte d'Orléans. When the train arrived, he got into the first-class carriage, followed by two young men whose shabby clothes looked out of place among the suits and briefcases. Just before the doors slid shut, one pulled out a pistol, two explosions split the air and Moser collapsed. The pair fled, jumping over the ticket barrier and barrelling down the steps to the busy street. By the time the police and Métro guards got Moser to the nearby Lariboisière hospital he was dead, having bled out from the two bullet wounds in his back.

In a few noisy seconds everything had changed. The phoney calm of the preceding fourteen months was shattered, to be replaced by a cycle of attack and reprisal. The occupiers could no longer count on a docile, submissive Paris. And Parisians could no longer tell themselves that the well-behaved Germans they saw lounging on the café terraces and posing for snaps in front of the Opéra were any different from those terrorizing Hitler's new domains in the east.

On one side in the struggle that followed were French communists like the man who had killed Moser, reinforced by a cadre of foreign immigrants, many of them Jewish. In time, they would form a loose alliance with an array of other resisters who defied simple ideological categorization. Some were rightists, Action Française supporters before the war who had chosen the opposite path to the likes of Robert Brasillach. Others were leftists unwilling to submit to the blind obedience demanded by Moscow. Many had no firm political convictions at all but were inspired by a variety of motives including patriotism, the defence of fundamental human values and a simple determination that evil could not be allowed to go unchallenged.

This tiny, ill-assorted and pitifully armed band were pitting themselves against a hugely more powerful enemy. On their own the Gestapo and the SS intelligence service, the SD, had nothing like the numbers to do a thorough job, but they were massively reinforced by the security services of the French state, plus a large number of local employees – at least 32,000 according to German figures. The resisters were fighting their fellow countrymen as much as they were the Germans and the struggle that followed would have many of the elements of a civil war, with all the hatred and savagery that went with it. For most of the time it would pose no military threat to the occupation. Its very existence, though, was enough to give substance to the claim, propagated by de Gaulle from London, that the real France had never been defeated.

Moser's killer was a twenty-one-year-old Parisian called Pierre Georges, a baker's son who trained as a metal worker, joined the Communist Party and in October 1936, aged just seventeen, went off to fight in Spain. A police mugshot dating from December 1939 shows a good-looking young tough in a leather jacket and raggedy woollen scarf; he has a straight nose, square chin and deep-set eyes burning with defiance and determination, his dark wavy hair rising in ridges from a high forehead. His companion was Gilbert Brustlein, twenty-two years old, a pale young man with a faint moustache smudging his upper lip. His father, a Protestant from Alsace, had died shortly after the last war and he had been brought up in poverty in Paris by his mother.

The assassination was in part an act of vengeance for the deaths of two comrades, Samuel 'Titi' Tyszelman and Henri Gautherot, executed two days earlier. Titi was a Polish Jew, Henri another Parisian *métallo*. Both had been arrested during a communist-organized anti-German demonstration on 13 August when a crowd of about a hundred young men and women marched down the boulevard de Strasbourg shouting 'Vive la France!' and 'Down with Hitler!' German troops opened fire and the French police moved in to make arrests. Titi was wounded and soon run to ground by the police. Henri was discovered in the concierge's lodge of a building in the boulevard Saint-Martin. The following day, the military governor of France Otto von Stülpnagel announced that henceforth anyone taking part in a demonstration would be charged with aiding the enemy – a capital offence. The pair were put before a military tribunal, sentenced to death and executed by firing squad.

Both were members of newly formed units that came to be known as the Bataillons de la Jeunesse (Youth Battalions), made up of young communists from the working-class east of Paris. The executions accelerated their plan to target senior German officers, shooting them down whenever they got the chance. It was Georges' bad luck that, despite Moser's smart uniform, he was a mere midshipman and commanded nothing more than a clothing depot in Montrouge. Nonetheless, a German was a German. As they slipped into the crowd on the avenue Barbès, Pierre murmured to Gilbert, 'Well, now we've avenged Titi.' So they had, but the consequences would be savage.

The shooting signalled that the French Communist Party had at last thrown its weight behind the Resistance. What had been a motley alliance now had a hard and disciplined core. As always, the PCF had taken its lead from Moscow. Eight weeks before the Barbès attack, Germany had invaded Russia, changing the entire dynamic of the war. Mastery of Europe was not enough. Hitler had made his bid for world domination, an epic gamble which to some of the cooler heads among his generals seemed as likely to end in disaster as in triumph. The Nazi–Soviet partnership was shattered. Hundreds of thousands of men and thousands of tanks smashed through the Red Army, killing and capturing on a vast scale and destroying enormous quantities of equipment. The PCF's Moscow-directed strategic ambivalence towards the occupiers turned instantly to outright hostility. French communists were now a fifth column, assigned to undermining the enemy in the rear.

Like many in the party, Henri Tanguy welcomed the news. His loyalty had often been tested in the year between the occupation and the German attack. He was now thirty-three, a married man with a three-month-old daughter. By joining the underground fight he would be exchanging a relatively secure existence for a life that would in all probability be dangerous and short. But at least the fog of moral confusion had lifted. The enemy stood before him clearly, and by resisting the occupation he would be doing his duty both as a communist and as a Frenchman.

Cécile

He was fortunate to have a strong woman to support him in the dangerous days ahead. Henri met Cécile Le Bihan when he got back from Spain at the end of 1938 to take up a job at the Paris headquarters of the communist-controlled metal workers' union, where she worked as a typist. Cécile was Breton-born like himself, clever and serious. At school she excelled in English and maths and would have gone into teaching had the family finances allowed. Henri was more than ten years her senior but she was pleased when he asked her out to the cinema. Their first date was not a success. She had to work late that evening and by the time she arrived at the rendezvous he had gone off in a huff. The following day they tried again. This time things went better and on their next outing he took her home to meet his mother.

Whatever the Communist Party said about female equality, their relationship was constructed on traditional French lines, with Henri making the important decisions. Early on he warned her that his commitment to the cause and the likelihood that he would soon be off to another war ruled out any immediate thoughts of marriage and children. But when Cécile told him she was pregnant he relented, and in April 1939 they tied the knot in the 20th arrondissement *mairie* near her home.

Cécile understood Henri's reluctance. She grew up in a politically charged household and her electrician father François was one of the founders of the PCF. The family flat in the rue Louis-Ganne was a safe house for foreign comrades from all parts of the globe on their way to and from Moscow. She joined the female branch of the young communists, the Union des Jeunes Filles de France, while a teenager, and in the years ahead would prove herself as steadfast and brave as her husband.

She shared Henri's obedience to Moscow, but the events of the previous few years had involved some painful and bewildering ideological somersaults. The Soviet non-aggression pact with Germany in August 1939 had stunned the world and sickened many inside the PCF. Moscow was now effectively on the same side as the fascists whom many young comrades had gone off to Spain to fight. Thousands of French communists tore up their party cards. Henri and Cécile chose to swallow Moscow's line that it had been forced to make a deal with Hitler after the British and French refused to join the Soviet Union in an anti-Nazi front.

French communists were seen by their own compatriots as doubly treacherous, loyal not only to Stalin but also by extension to Hitler. The Popular Front had fallen apart when the communists abandoned their backing in protest at Léon Blum's failure to give more vigorous support to the Spanish Republic. It was replaced by a centrist coalition which turned on the communists after the Hitler–Stalin alliance. The PCF leader Maurice Thorez fled to Moscow and the newspaper *L'Humanité*, which told the faithful what to think, was banned. The new party line presented the war as a clash between rival blocks of imperialists, with the proletariat the inevitable victims. The workers' duty was to carry on the class struggle. Ravaged by arrests and persecution, the PCF could do little more than distribute anti-war literature and wait for the situation to clarify.

Tanguy had been away during the ideological upheavals, called back to the army when France mobilized. He returned willingly to resume his old military trade of armourer with an anti-tank unit on the Maginot Line. Not long before he had been a senior officer in the International Brigades. Now he was just an ordinary soldier, accepting orders from his class enemies. There was little resentment; like everyone he felt a deep respect for the military, earned by the sacrifices of 1914–18. He was a communist but he was also a Frenchman. Marxist internationalism had to struggle when faced by the patriotism drummed into every French schoolchild from the first moment they sat down in a classroom. In the end, the PCF had given up and belatedly encouraged members to celebrate their national identity and history – in particular the revolutionary tradition. Henri liked soldiering and admired soldierly qualities. When, during the Nazi–Soviet marriage of convenience, communist propaganda portrayed de Gaulle as a villain, an upper-class warmonger and adventurer, Tanguy resisted the caricature and on hearing de Gaulle broadcasting from London remembered him as a forward-thinking military professional who had tried to get the army into a fit state to wage a modern war.

France's military weaknesses were all too clear to Henri when he arrived on the Maginot Line. Communications trenches were shoddily constructed and collapsed when it rained, but no one seemed to care. The winter was harsh and the meat and wine froze solid. In the ablutions block, you had to crack the ice to wash, so many didn't bother. Just as in his national service in North Africa, Henri impressed his superiors. His colonel wondered out loud why he had not been recommended for officer training. Henri thought he knew the answer: a note on his file, recording his political allegiance. By the time the fighting began he had been transferred to a unit in the Pyrenees. When the army fell to pieces many threw away their weapons and returned home. Henri stayed at his post, despite a tragedy at home. Just before the fall of Paris, the Tanguys' seven-month-old daughter Françoise had fallen ill with diarrhoea and Cécile hurried her to hospital. The city was covered in the mysterious pall of burning smoke that heralded the Germans' arrival and she wondered if 'that was what had made my baby ill'. She left her in the hospital overnight and 'When I went back the next day, there was another baby in her bed.'

Henri got back on 18 August 1940 to find the streets full of Germans and the party organization in complete disarray. Vichy's hatred of the communists was unabated, but to Otto Abetz, Hitler's ambassador to France, they were merely a potential nuisance, who 'were not to be destroyed but . . . carefully watched so that when the moment came they could be put out of harm's way with a single blow'. The Gestapo agreed and, for the time being, preferred surveillance to mass arrests. Not that there was much to see. The clandestine editions of *L'Humanité*, now in circulation again, made no mention of opposing the invaders. Far from shooting Germans, the paper encouraged its readers to buy them a drink, for were the Wehrmacht rank and file not proletarians too? An early editorial enthused: 'It is particularly comforting in these unhappy times to see so many Parisian workers engage in friendly relations with German soldiers, whether it be in the street or the neighbourhood bar. Good work, comrades! Keep it up, even if that upsets certain members of our bourgeoisie, who are as stupid as they are spiteful.'

When signs of non-violent resistance first stirred in Paris, the communist leadership was not involved. On Armistice Day 1940, the 11 November national holiday to commemorate the 1914–18 dead, about 3,000 high school and university students gathered around the Arc de Triomphe and the Tomb of the Unknown Warrior to demonstrate against the occupation. German army field police units and the Paris police moved in and made more than a hundred arrests. The young men and women were from all quarters of the political compass and were there of their own volition with no direction from the PCF, though that did not stop the party from subsequently claiming a share of the glory. The truth was that, until Hitler turned his armies on the Soviet Union, the party leaders had looked on the sufferings and humiliations of the masses they claimed to champion and done nothing.

The communist about-face meant old enemies were now friends, and old friends became enemies. The rubbishing of Charles de Gaulle stopped overnight. He was now on the side of right and in September 1941 the Soviets stopped recognizing Vichy and accepted him as the leader of the Free French. French communists were no longer to shun bourgeois resisters and were to form alliances with other groups. The communists were entering this new phase weakened and demoralized by the shame of the Nazi–Soviet pact. Numbers had fallen sharply due to desertions and arrests by the French police. The few thousand who remained fell into two rough groups. There were the older comrades like Henri Tanguy, trade union veterans of the industrial battles of the 1930s who had been hardened by real combat in the Spanish Civil War. They remained in the party because, whatever their doubts, they accepted orders and explanations from above. This discipline went hand in hand with strict observance of security procedures, an attitude that had enabled them to survive. Then there were the Youth Battalions who in Henri's description were 'contemptuous of danger, generous-spirited and eager for action'. When the party went on the offensive, it was this group in the vanguard.

The campaign that followed was messy, incoherent and costly, and the German reaction was brutal. Immediately after the Barbès shooting, Stülpnagel issued a decree stating that 'any French person arrested, whether by the German authorities or by the French authorities on behalf of the Germans, will be considered a hostage'. If there were any further attacks on German personnel, 'a number of hostages will be shot', the number depending on the gravity of the act. There were already plenty of political prisoners on hand to provide the victims.

The warning was no deterrent. In October Gilbert Brustlein, together with the Italian-born Spartaco Guisco, who had fought alongside Henri Tanguy in Spain, arrived in Nantes in search of targets. 'Spartaco elbowed me,' Brustlein recalled later. 'There in front of us, two superbly dressed officers were walking across the square.' They closed up behind them and fired at point-blank range. Guisco's 7.65mm revolver jammed, but Brustlein's 6.35mm did not and he could hardly miss. One German went down, emitting 'inhuman, terrifying screams'. The pair jumped on a tram and escaped, leaving Lieutenant-Colonel Karl Hotz dead on the pavement. Though they did not know it, they had struck lucky. Hotz was a real prize, the military commander of the city. The same day, another team claimed a second impressive scalp in Bordeaux, shooting dead a military adviser called Hans Reimers.

Stülpnagel had already made good on his reprisal threat. He ordered the execution of three hostages after the Barbès shooting and a further ten on 16 September in response to a flurry of non-fatal attacks on military personnel. This was not enough for Berlin. Hitler had decreed that fifty to a hundred hostages were to die for every German killed. But Stülpnagel's willingness to take harsh measures was starting to falter. For one thing he feared the damage they might do to Franco-German collaboration, telling Ernst Jünger that 'the industries would produce more the better this matter was managed'. According to Jünger, 'things had affected [the general's] nerves and shaken him to the core', and he began suppressing the number of Resistance attacks he reported back to the high command in Berlin, to ease the pressure for reprisals. He had decided they were counter-productive and 'doing the *résistance* the greatest favour . . . with a single revolver shot, a terrorist could incite a powerful ripple effect of hatred'. However, Stülpnagel was even more worried by the 'allegations of weakness and unreliability' levelled at him by his Nazi Party enemies.

His concern about the effect on public opinion was shared by the Vichy leaders, although they accepted that some reprisals were inevitable. The former industrialist, now interior minister, Pierre Pucheu suggested the executions would go down better if all the victims were communists and provided a list of candidates, who came handily supplied with retrospective death penalties imposed by a French court. On 20 September, after a German officer was shot and wounded in central Paris, a further twelve hostages were shot.

Whatever his misgivings, Stülpnagel recognized that the Nantes and Bordeaux assassinations required a spectacular display of ruthlessness if he was to keep Berlin off his back. Two days after the killing of Hotz, twenty-seven left-wing and trade unionist prisoners were taken from the Châteaubriant internment camp north of Nantes, which was under French control and guarded by gendarmes. The local prefect was ordered to draw up a list of victims, but he refused, and the names were supplied instead by the Paris police. SS troops took the men away in two trucks to a quarry at La Sablière where they were shot. The youngest to die was seventeen-year-old Guy Moquet, the son of a communist deputy. He left behind a desperately moving letter to his parents, which would become one of the great texts of the Resistance. 'Of course I want to live,' he wrote. 'But what I want with my whole heart is that my death serves a purpose . . . Those of you who remain, be worthy of us.' Another twenty-one were shot from a pool of prisoners in Nantes prison. In Bordeaux, fifty more were executed for the death of Reimers.

Many of the victims were local men, yet it was clear that the assassinations were the work of outsiders and, though no one claimed

responsibility for the attacks, few were in any doubt as to the perpetrators. In an article in *Je Suis Partout* headlined 'The Crimes Bear a
Signature' Robert Brasillach declared: 'Even the stupidest person must
see it . . . every French person knows that apart from a few minor incidents the country has remained calm for a year.' However, once the
Soviet Union entered the war 'everything changed . . . and using the
classic techniques of the schools of sabotage, the crimes have begun'.

Despite Stülpnagel's fears, popular sympathy for communist
gunmen was initially very limited. Following Moser's killing, an elderly literary journalist called Paul Léautaud wrote in his diary: 'The
truth is these attacks have nothing to do with patriotism. They are
murders pure and simple.' But as the number of reprisal killings
mounted, attitudes began to change. The shootings were announced
on yellow posters stamped with heavy, black Gothic script. The victims were described as 'cowardly assassins in the pay of England and
Moscow'.

Twelve-year-old Raymond Ruffin was leaving his school in Vincennes in the east of Paris with his friends when they saw a crowd
gathered round a large street-corner billboard where official notices
were displayed. They were reading the newly posted announcements
of the executions following the Nantes and Bordeaux attacks. 'Most
of the people seemed impassive,' he wrote in his diary. 'Some were
shaking their heads but no one dared to make any comment. Once
they finished reading they hurried away, as if their consciences were
troubling them.' One of his schoolmates, Robert, whose father had
been killed during the Battle of France, burst out: 'It's disgusting!'
He was quickly told to shut up by an older boy. 'Are you crazy?' he
demanded. 'Shooting your mouth off like that could get you taken
away.'

Despite the dreadful ratio of attack to reprisal, the campaign of
shootings, bombings and sabotage, none of which did the slightest
damage to the machinery of occupation, continued. A further 841
hostages would be killed in reprisals before the policy was suspended,
in order to avoid inflaming the anti-German feeling generated by a
new compulsory labour law. In September 1942, under German pressure, Vichy introduced Service du Travail Obligatoire, which sent

hundreds of thousands of Frenchmen to work for the German war effort. About 200,000 went into hiding, many of whom joined the Resistance. By then the Youth Battalions had long since fallen apart. They collapsed after being betrayed to the police by an informer seeking revenge after his girlfriend took up with one of the group, resulting in the arrest and execution of almost everyone involved. Brustlein escaped the net, eventually reaching England. Georges also lived to fight another day, fleeing Paris to organize resistance in eastern France. Their campaign had been reckless and amateurish, displaying an almost total disregard for basic security measures.

Yet there had also been something magnificent about it. Every young man and woman involved knew that once they had taken the plunge they had, in all likelihood, only a few months to live. This knowledge created bonds of love and selflessness that only a cynic could dismiss. The last letters of the Nantes hostages had crossed Jünger's desk. 'Reading them has given me strength,' he wrote. 'When faced with imminent death, man seems to emerge from his blind will and realize that love is the most intimate of all connections.' When sighting his gun on a German in this first phase of rebellion, the assassin knew that the shot that followed would condemn to death a captured comrade. But he did it just the same, knowing that if they had been in his place they would have urged him to pull the trigger. No doubt it would be his turn soon enough. It was a sacrifice that these young and mostly working-class boys and girls had weighed and thought worth while. And in the shabby and compromised world of their elders, their strange honour shone out like the evening star.

Henri Tanguy and the old guard knew the recklessness could not continue. Discipline was essential if the Resistance was to survive. Vichy had matched the Germans' measures with catch-all laws against 'anti-nationalist acts', giving the police free rein to imprison anyone deemed hostile to the occupiers' interests, as well as arranging compliant judges to sentence them to death. The police set up Brigades Spéciales tasked with tracking down 'internal enemies', which worked out of the Paris prefecture in close partnership with the Germans. Resisters of any stripe were facing all the formidable combined resources that the state and the occupiers could bring to bear and could expect no more mercy from the *flics* than they could from the Fridolins.

Even before the crackdown Henri and Cécile had decided it was too dangerous to carry on living together. She moved in with his mother in the rue de l'Ouest. He entered the world of *clandestinité*, never spending more than a few nights in the same apartment. Many of those who sheltered him were not party sympathizers but mates from his old cycling days with the Club Vélo International who, scorning the grave risk to themselves, put him up without question. When Cécile gave birth to a daughter, Hélène, at the end of May, Henri could not chance going with her to the clinic. Cécile's reticence as to the whereabouts of the father prompted one of the staff to advise her to register at the town hall for social benefits as 'an abandoned mother'. Joy at the birth was overshadowed by the arrest of Cécile's father. François Le Bihan was working as a commercial representative at the Soviet trade delegation when Hitler invaded Russia. Within hours of the news, he was arrested and taken to the Royallieu-Compiègne internment camp north of Paris. François was murdered at Auschwitz on 19 September 1942.

In the autumn of 1941 party discipline hardened. The PCF was led by a triumvirate, with Jacques Duclos the overall leader responsible for political direction and Benoît Frachon overseeing union activity. Command of the military campaign was given to Charles Tillon, yet another former *métallo* who had opposed the passive party line against the Germans. In mid-July, Henri was summoned to a rendezvous with Danielle Casanova, a thirty-two-year-old Corsican-born dentist, whom Henri and Cécile had known before the war. She had been closely involved in French and international party organizations and had since gone underground. Danielle was now responsible for setting up the military command structure for the Paris area. She and Henri met in front of the Closerie des Lilas on the boulevard Montparnasse, which in happier times had been one of bohemia's favourite landmarks. Casanova wanted first to know if Tanguy was in or out. He understood that by engaging in the armed struggle he was probably signing his own death warrant but his answer was unequivocal. 'I immediately said yes,' he recalled. Casanova told him he would be

controlling operations in the Paris area alongside two seasoned comrades, both veterans of the Spanish Civil War. They were starting
almost from scratch, with a substantial pool of potential recruits but
an almost complete lack of arms and explosives. They were fighting
for communism but they were also fighting for France. In order to
win they would have to join forces with people their faith had taught
them hitherto to regard as their eternal class enemies.

Jacques Delmas was brought up in a wealthy, artistic family 'bathed in
an unconditional love of France which left an indelible mark on me'.
When very young his mother Georgette told him: 'I am your mother
and I love you so much, but remember that your mother is also France
and your duty is to serve her.' Many French men and women from all
regions and backgrounds and political outlooks had been raised to
think this way. In the summer of 1940 they were all faced with the
same stark question: were they willing to translate these values into
action? And if the answer was yes, how were they going to go about it?

By then Jacques was twenty-five, athletic, good-looking and
smart, and had the world not gone mad around him he would have
been anticipating a glittering future. If Henri Tanguy put people in
mind of the husky actor Jean Gabin, Delmas resembled some great
sporting heroes of the era. The 'Four Musketeers' – Jean Borotra,
Jacques Brugnon, Henri Cochet and René Lacoste – had put French
tennis on the map, dominating the game in the late 1920s and early
1930s. Delmas was a gifted amateur player and seemed like a compos-
ite of the quartet as he cruised the capital's classier tennis clubs in his
immaculate whites, charming the ladies and networking the men.

His childhood had not been easy. He was often ill and his adored
mother was overprotective, another cause of friction between her and
his 'handsome, refined, highly strung, artistic and angry' father who,
when he wasn't chasing women, made a good living inventing gadgets
for the automobile industry. They divorced when Jacques was twelve.
Bad health and the storms of a failing marriage disrupted his education and he moved from school to school. Stability was restored when
he settled down at the distinguished Lycée Lakanal in the south Paris
suburbs and his mother got married again to a kindly furniture dealer

called Maurice Legendre, who had been a fighter pilot in the last war. From him Delmas got another lesson: 'There is nothing in the world that can resist the might of courage combined with generosity.' To that could be added willpower. By the time he was eighteen, thanks to all the time he spent on the tennis court and rugby pitch, he had transformed himself from chronic sickliness into 'rude good health'.

Delmas was all set for university when the Great Depression of the early 1930s crossed the Atlantic and there was no money for further education. For a nasty moment it seemed he would have to go to work as a salesman in his stepfather's furniture shop. But Jacques had already learned to make his own luck and through the father of a girl he met at the tennis club got a job with a financial newspaper. Journalism would merely be the day job though. Jacques was cocky, impatient and ambitious. In his spare time he attended the prestigious École Libre des Sciences Politiques and was soon selected for training as an *inspecteur des finances*. What sounded like the pathway to a crashingly dull bureaucratic career was in fact a much contested rung on the golden ladder leading to the upper reaches of the French state. If this was not enough, he also wrangled a commission in the army reserve and was sent off not to the military school at Saint-Maixent 'like everyone else' but to the far more illustrious Saint-Cyr. Drive like his was not a recipe for popularity, but Jacques was good at making and keeping friends. For all his ambition there was something trusting, almost naive, about his enthusiasm. And as he said himself, he was filled with 'an incurable optimism when it came to human nature'. It was a quality that he was going to need in the dark years ahead.

When the French armies collapsed, he was serving in an Alpine unit in the hills above Nice. The surrender 'felt like the end of the world . . . in a single blow, everything, my way of thinking, the values I held dear had been annihilated'. If France was indeed his mother then she had been 'betrayed, violated, and reduced to slavery'. Those who felt like Delmas were never going to accept the occupation. He was just as clever, educated and ambitious as Robert Brasillach, who was busy promoting the idea that the German occupation was actually a good thing. For Jacques there could be no accommodation, only revenge and the restoration of France's honour. The conviction overwhelmed him, as if it was 'a chemical reaction', uninfluenced by any discussion with friend or comrade. He was going to 'mobilize my entire being to continue the fight'.

The question, though, was how? After demobilization in July 1940 he retreated to a small hotel in Nice with Odile, whom he had married the previous year, and their five-month-old daughter Clotilde. In the search for help he started, as usual, at the top, going to see Nice's mayor, Jean Médecin, only to be told, 'The war is over! Pick up your old life, raise your family and good luck!' The hotel was starting to get on his nerves, especially when each night at nine o'clock exactly little Clotilde was being woken up by strange noises coming from the house next door. One evening he went to complain and was pulled inside by the owner who explained: 'It's the interference on the signal from London.' That night he listened for the first time to *Les Français parlent aux Français* – 'The French Speak to the French' – coming over the airwaves from the BBC and the voice of General Charles de Gaulle, a man he had never heard of, calling on the French people to rally behind him.

At that time de Gaulle was only a symbol. Powered by his enormous self-belief he had set out to transform himself into the incarnation of the unconquered spirit of France. He was very fortunate to have found sanctuary in a country whose leader shared his grandiose romanticism and could glimpse in the tall, austere and preposterously proud and touchy general the outlines of greatness. Churchill's almost immediate recognition of de Gaulle's claim to leadership gave an incalculable boost to his fortunes, though he would never properly acknowledge the debt. For the next few years, de Gaulle's energies would be devoted primarily to building his position with the British, the Americans and the Soviets. The campaign involved almost continuous clashes as an obscure general, devoid of political authority and almost entirely lacking in military resources, tried to assert himself as an equal. The effort left little time to devote to the nascent Resistance movement back home, even if he had wanted to encourage it. His interest was strictly limited and for him its importance was primarily the propaganda value it brought to the claim that France had never truly surrendered. Once

activity began in earnest, he would be quick to claim moral and political ownership of the struggle.

The voice coming over the wireless from the BBC gave patriotic
French men and women a flag to gather round. It spurred Delmas to
return to Paris in order to find people who could help him join de
Gaulle in London. What he saw there appalled him. The Germans
were marching daily down the Champs-Élysées, lounging on the
brasserie terraces and gawping in the windows of the smart shops.
They had even imposed their own peculiar smell, a mixture of 'rancid
leather, synthetic fabric, boot grease and sweat'. He 'boiled with
anger and sorrow', but outwardly at least none of the inhabitants
seemed to mind. Paris had been 'morally disembowelled'. It was as if
'an intruder had kicked in your door, slept in your bed, raided your
fridge, smoked your cigars, drunk your wine and read your books.
And this with the approval of certain members of your family who
would tell you it was all your fault and you deserved it.'

None of his Paris contacts were able to put Delmas in touch with
a representative of de Gaulle. He decided to seek the help of his old
commandant at Saint-Cyr, Colonel Groussard, who he felt he could
trust despite the fact that he was now serving under Pétain in Vichy.
After sneaking across the demarcation line he finally tracked him
down, only to be advised by Groussard to return to Paris and report
to a friend and old Saint-Cyr classmate Colonel Alfred Heurtaux,
who had intelligence links with the Gaullists in London. When they
eventually met, Heurtaux refused his request to go to Britain. He
was more valuable to the cause remaining in his post in Paris – an
excellent place to gather economic intelligence. Delmas accepted the
decision: 'Instead of fighting in broad daylight I was being enlisted in
the army of shadows – and that thanks to the good graces of an anti-
Nazi at the heart of the Vichy set-up.' As he was finding out, in the
strange world he was stepping into 'nothing was simple'.

Long afterwards, Delmas would reflect that the Resistance movement
was really a 'youth uprising'. By that he meant the young in spirit, for
the occupation had fostered a climate of timidity and he came across
many who were 'old men at twenty'. And resistance could take many

forms. Rose Valland was not young and her defiance had nothing to do with guns or bombs. When the Germans arrived, she was forty-one and working at the Jeu de Paume state art gallery, tucked in the corner of the Tuileries Garden and the place de la Concorde. She did not fit the conventional idea of a Parisienne. She seemed uninterested in men, wore round, wire-framed glasses and her hair was scraped back over her high forehead in a bun. Nor did she come from the same middle-class background as most of her colleagues. Rose was a black-smith's daughter from a village near Grenoble, but thanks to the French education system her early talent had been recognized and encouraged. She studied art history and shone in competitive exams, winning a place at the august École Supérieure des Beaux-Arts on the banks of the Seine, before going on to the École du Louvre in 1931. She specialized in contemporary art and her eye was as sharp as any dealer's. Later she became a volunteer assistant curator in the conservation department at the Jeu de Paume. Official enlightenment only went so far. Despite all Rose's diplomas, her status as a woman disqualified her from a salaried job there and she had to support her voluntary work by teaching.

She was still working at the Jeu de Paume when it was requisitioned by the Nazis' Einsatzstab Rosenberg art-looting taskforce.

Rose

The works stolen from Paul Rosenberg and the city's other great Jewish art dealers had first been stored in the German embassy in the rue de Lille and in the Louvre, but space was getting tight and the gallery made a handy warehouse. On 31 October 1940, a convoy of lorries rattled up to the entrance and men in Luftwaffe uniform began unloading packing cases, passing them rapidly from hand to hand to be piled up against the walls. There were at least 400 of them. As the crates were wrenched open, Rose's job was to list the contents, as agreed by the Germans in an initial meeting with her bosses. Despite having no help or office to work in she carried on 'drawing up lists as full and precise as possible, to show to the Germans that a French-woman also knew how to obey orders'. It was a brilliant pose. Soon she would become invisible to them, just another lackey who could be relied on to do their bidding.

Three days later, Hermann Göring arrived on the first of numer-ous visits he made to pick over the merchandise. His preference was for German old masters, which were sent to Carinhall, the hunting lodge he had built in the forests of northern Brandenburg to com-memorate Carin Fock, his Swedish first wife who had died ten years before. Other conventional work was destined for Hitler's planned gallery in Linz, while the despised modern stuff could be turned into ready cash via the Swiss art dealers of Zurich and Lucerne.

In overall charge of French national museums was a fine-featured senior civil servant called Jacques Jaujard, whose motto was 'To lead is to anticipate'. He had already lived up to it, moving 4,000 of the Lou-vre's greatest treasures including the *Venus de Milo* and the *Mona Lisa* to safety in various far-flung châteaux, so that when the Germans arrived they found the gallery virtually empty. Although unable to protect what remained, he could at least attempt to document the vast programme of cultural despoliation. The Jeu de Paume was the major collection point for the Jewish-owned loot and it was essential to have someone on the inside. But the Germans soon decided they would carry out the cataloguing themselves and fired most of the French staff. As a lowly conservationist, Rose escaped the cull. Jaujard now had a spy on the inside and, as it turned out, a very efficient one. Almost every day for the next four years she turned up at the museum, humble, discreet and obliging, while all the time logging the pieces as they went in and out, as well as the comings and goings of the staff. Some nights she took negatives of photographed artworks home to copy, returning them in the morning. The penalty for discovery would almost certainly have been deportation to the women's camp at Ravensbrück, from which she would have been very lucky to return. Occasionally the Germans' antennae twitched. She spoke their language suspiciously well, the result of a study course in Germany in the 1930s and would chat casually to the lower-ranking staff to find out where the artworks were being sent.

Sometimes, when something seemed amiss, she was called in for Nazi-style questioning, an experience she would remember with characteristic understatement as 'very disagreeable'. But nothing deterred her from each time returning to her secret work. She also had a keen ear for office gossip. Much of it centred round the chief of the ERR in Paris, Colonel Kurt von Behr, a fifty-something early convert to Nazism who was married to a rapacious Englishwoman called Joy Clarke. He was tall and swaggering, and Rose noted acidly that he wore his cap 'so that it shaded his face . . . which had the great advantage of hiding his glass eye'. In the early days it seemed 'he didn't lack charm and spoke French well'. This was the time when the conquerors 'were still euphoric with victory and wanted to show their good side in the hope of persuading us that they weren't savages'. They were never going to fool Rose.

Madeleine Riffaud made up her mind to join the Resistance one chilly autumn morning at Amiens railway station. She had left home when the Germans invaded, escorting her sick grandfather to stay with relatives in the south. Now they were returning. On arrival at Amiens she set off to find a stretcher for the old man, who was clearly dying. The station was full of troops. 'They were camped there, waiting to go who knows where and I had to walk through them, stepping over them,' she remembered. She felt an 'instinctive, animal fear'. The sight of a young girl in a thin skirt with hair down to her shoulders delighted them. They 'wanted to have some fun, like all soldiers do'. They 'joked, grinned . . . one pulled my skirt. Some others touched my behind.' An officer put a stop to it but then turned on Madeleine and gave her a sharp kick in the backside which sent her sprawling. As she got to her feet and dusted herself down Madeleine made up her mind. She would 'seek out those who refused to accept humiliation and occupation . . . I had no idea where they were but with a bit of time and a bit of luck I was going to find them. And that was it.'

Madeleine was brought up in the Somme where the flat landscape was patched with cemeteries full of the dead of the recent war and the fields were seeded with unexploded shells. Her parents were both school teachers. Her Catholic mother and pacifist father had given her a strong sense of right and wrong. She was petite with a lively, heart-shaped face. She loved her grandpa, a sturdy patriot who took her duck hunting in the marshes. Madeleine turned out to be a very good shot, once bringing down a brace with left and right barrels. She was also questioning and argumentative – what the British called 'bolshie'.

It was years before she was able to fulfil her promise to herself. In the bitter winter of 1942 she went down with tuberculosis and was sent to a sanatorium near Grenoble. There she fell in love with another patient, called Marcel Gagliardi. He confided that he had contacts with the Resistance back in Paris. On being discharged they went to Paris together, she to study midwifery. After a long wait, Marcel introduced her to his network and she began to be given tasks. At first it was restricted to 'liaison', delivering messages and fixing meetings for the men. But before long she would take her place in the ranks of the fighters.

It was not until the end of 1943 that the Resistance was sufficiently organized and equipped to have the potential to become anything more than a nuisance to its enemies. The very different groups opposing the occupation were by now acting in reasonable harmony. They had been pulled together in an extraordinary feat of organization that was largely the work of one man, sent to France by de Gaulle for the purpose.

Jean Moulin was handsome and magnetic, a career civil servant who rose rapidly to become prefect, or regional administrator, of Eure-et-Loir based in Chartres. When the Germans arrived, he was arrested for refusing to sign a statement falsely claiming that civilians killed in a bombing raid had been murdered by Black Senegalese troops. He was tortured, and tried to kill himself by slashing his throat, but survived. The Germans were still in their conciliatory phase and they allowed him back to work, only for Vichy to sack him for his left-wing sympathies. He eventually escaped to London to join de Gaulle, who sent him back to France in January 1942 with a mission to unify the disparate anti-occupation elements springing up around the country. Moulin's progressive political record helped gain the trust of the left while his association with de Gaulle secured the respect of the right. Nonetheless he had a hard task ahead. For the next year he went from meeting to meeting, cajoling and reasoning with individuals whose temperament and experience inclined them to cling to their independence. He lived constantly under the threat of capture or betrayal. After a brief return to London in early 1943 he arrived back in March.

On 27 May, in a first-floor apartment at 48 rue du Four in the 6th arrondissement, the groups voted unanimously to come together in a coalition called the Conseil National de la Résistance, the National Resistance Council, which would work against the occupation under de Gaulle's leadership. It was made up of eight organizations: six old political parties from the Third Republic which were now banned, and two outlawed trade unions. Their politics ranged from the deep conservatives of the Organisation Civile et Militaire, the association of soldiers and civil servants to which Jacques Delmas belonged, to the Moscow-directed communists of the Parti Communiste Français. It was a phenomenal piece of clandestine diplomacy that assured Moulin an eternal place in France's history. Less than two months after this great achievement he was tortured to death after being betrayed to the Gestapo.

By the start of 1944 Moulin's work was paying off. The Germans were facing a disciplined coalition from across the political spectrum which had buried its differences for the time being to form a united front. The people of Paris looked on the Resistance no longer with alarm and incomprehension but with increasing respect and hope. Vichy's National Revolution had delivered few of its promises. The government was split by feuding factions. From the start it had been a ramshackle coalition of opportunists, deluded patriots and Franco-fascists and now the ultra-collaborators had the upper hand, demanding ever closer association with the Nazi cause and hunting down and killing their internal enemies. The old marshal was a shrunken figure, largely confined to his toytown capital, his authority steadily draining away. Instead the French now looked to the king over the water, to Charles de Gaulle, the upstart whom Vichy had sentenced to death.

The resisters' goals, which had once seemed infinitely distant, were getting closer with every month that passed. In 1940 the Germans looked invincible and the conquest of Britain only a matter of time. At the start of 1944 they were on the defensive everywhere. In the east, the Red Army was surging forward and the German invaders were retreating from their vast early conquests leaving millions of dead or captured comrades behind them. In the south, the Americans and the British and their allies had long since retaken North Africa and were pushing north from Italy. Hitler's war aims were now unachievable and the dream of world domination fading fast in everyone's mind but his own. How it would all end, however, was difficult to discern. Resisters and collaborators alike referred to the passive mass of French people as *attentistes*, or those who wait, holding back from committing themselves until they could be sure which side was going to win. By the spring of 1944 it seemed that the waiting was almost over. Britain was full of American troops and the opening of the long-awaited Second Front, somewhere in northern France, was surely close at hand. Even the optimists knew better than to get their hopes up. The Germans had been preparing for the invasion for years and were likely to fight to the bitter end. The prospect of victory was real. Achieving it could only be difficult and bloody.

5.   Countdown

Tiverton lay in a fold in the damp green hills of Devon. It had a couple of pubs, a cinema and a tea room and that was about all. It was a long way from New York City and sometimes Jerry Salinger felt nostalgic for his home town. As he joked in a letter to his old teacher Whit Burnett in May 1944: 'I wish I were back in your class at Columbia . . . Can you arrange it?' The future was uncertain and perhaps very brief. He lived in a tent with six cots and a pot-bellied stove and had done his best to adjust to military life, but the truth was, 'My mind is never really with these people . . . I've been a short-story writer since I was seventeen.'

Salinger arrived in England with the US 4th Infantry Division in February 1944, crossing the Atlantic in the liner *Mauretania*. He served in a counter-intelligence unit attached to the division's 12th Infantry Regiment. There had been a lot of chopping, changing and hanging about during his two years in uniform. But although nothing had been said officially, it was clear that the 'Ivy' – as the 4th called itself after its roman numerals – would be going into action very soon.

He was twenty-five years old, six feet two inches tall, dark-haired and slim. He had been in love twice, or thought he had, and was beginning to know what success felt like, though getting it in your hands and fixing a solid grip on it were proving to be two different things. He worked very hard and believed he was destined for greatness. If he had picked any business other than writing, he would surely have been further along his chosen path by now, given the advantages that life had bestowed on him.

Salinger was born in Manhattan on 1 January 1919. His father Sol was the son of a rabbi and ran a successful food business. His mother, Marie Jillich, was a mixture of German, Scottish and Irish. 'Sunny', as the family called him, was a lucky child, cosseted by his mom and sister, Doris, seven years his senior, who shielded him from Sol's kindly attempts to impose paternal authority. Life in their large apartment on the corner of East 91st Street and Park Avenue was secure, prosperous and conventional.

Young Jerome was sent off to McBurney, a prep school for middle-class kids, on the opposite side of Central Park. He enjoyed acting and fencing, but academic work didn't much interest him. His grades were often poor and when he was fifteen the school said they didn't want him back. Sol decided the time had come to impose some real discipline and arranged his son's entry to the Valley Forge Military Academy in Wayne, Pennsylvania in the hope it would set him on the straight and narrow. Salinger disliked and mistrusted the hearty values the place was supposed to inculcate and he could be sarcastic with the staff and fellow cadets, though he felt affection for the misfits. He was still a mediocre student, but an enthusiastic member of the aviation club, French club and glee club as well as literary editor and prolific contributor to the school yearbook, *Crossed Sabres*. Jerome became 'Jerry' and was popular with his peers while always standing slightly apart. At night in the dorm, after the bugler had sounded 'taps', he scribbled away at his stories by torchlight. In an article predicting what the future held for his fellow cadets, his prophecy for himself was that he would write a great play. It was a joke of course, at least for the time being.

When most of his classmates headed off to university or to begin military careers, Jerry returned to the city and in the autumn of 1936 started a Bachelor of Arts degree at New York University. The following year he dropped out after a dismal exam performance. Sol stepped in again, deciding that it was time Jerry got a taste of his world and sent him to Europe to learn German and the basics of the meat-packing business. The journey took him via London and Paris to Vienna. He arrived in September and lodged for four months in the top-floor flat of 10 Gregor-Mendel-Strasse in a wealthy part of the city with Hermann Safir, one of Sol's business associates, and his family. Salinger enjoyed himself, despite the darkening political landscape. He learned the language, made friends with the Safirs' nineteen-year-old son Leo, bought a green felt Tyrolean hat and went ice skating with a young Englishman called Donald Hartog. He would say later that it had been a happy period when he 'felt a real sense of freedom for the first time in his life'.

At the end of 1937 he was sent off to Bydgoszcz in the north of Poland to work in a slaughterhouse and canning factory that belonged to Oskar Robinson, another of Sol's contacts. Robinson, aka the 'King of Bacon', was not there to mentor him, having recently dropped dead at the roulette tables of the Casino Baden outside Vienna. The apprenticeship was a rude shock after the fun and excitement of Vienna. It was deep winter in Bydgoszcz and the Vistula river often cloaked the city in freezing fog. Each morning he went to the slaughterhouse where pigs were transformed into tinned ham for the American market. The experience convinced him he was not cut out for the family business. On 9 March 1938 he boarded the luxury liner *Île de France* at Cherbourg and sailed back to New York. While Jerry was at sea Austria was swallowed up by Nazi Germany. When Hitler's troops entered Vienna on 12 March, they were greeted by cheering crowds. The persecution of the city's many Jews started immediately, sparking a scramble to leave. The Safirs were among the lucky ones who made it to the US.

The *Anschluss* joining Austria to Germany was preceded by months of political ferment with Austrian Nazis roaming the streets bullying and intimidating their enemies. It was impossible for any visitor not to feel the danger in the air. Salinger had spent several months of his short life in an electric political atmosphere, charged with the explosive ideologies that were powering the war in Spain. He had seen it all up close, and it seemed to his family that, although he had enjoyed Vienna, it left an indelible imprint on him. What he learned about people, power, politics and the individual versus the group, the dishonesty and the betrayals, would stay with him for the rest of his life and the understanding it gave him of human nature would form the fabric of his work.

Sol's plan had evidently failed and that autumn Jerry resumed his education, this time at Ursinus College, a small university in Pennsylvania, to study English literature and French. Most of the students were of Dutch Protestant stock, and compared to them he cut a sophisticated figure in his black velvet-collared Chesterfield coat and with his tales of abroad.

Once again, he failed to stay the course and quit Ursinus after a semester, returning to Manhattan where he drifted from Greenwich Village coffee house to fashionable mid-town bar. While marking time he met the sister of an old Valley Forge friend, a thirtyish married lady with intellectual tastes called Elizabeth Murray who got him interested in F. Scott Fitzgerald. The reading public tended to choose a camp when it came to America's two most prominent writers. You were either a fan of Hemingway or a fan of Fitzgerald, but not often both.

Salinger was a Fitzgerald man. Reading and brooding, smoking and talking for hours with Elizabeth, a more solid idea of the future he wanted for himself began to take shape. He was going to be a professional writer, and initially at least a writer of short stories. At the time they were all the rage, regarded both as a valid art form and as commercial entertainment. Short stories were a staple ingredient in America's bestselling weekly magazines, like *Collier's*, the *Saturday Evening Post* and, most prestigious of all, the *New Yorker*. Getting a piece published in any of these was to plant a foot on the nursery slopes of literary success. The market was tough, with many hopefuls competing with established writers for limited space. But behind the dilettante camouflage Salinger was dedicated, determined and hard-working.

He decided that to learn the craft properly he would have to return, yet again, to school. In January 1939, he enrolled at Columbia University in New York and joined the short-story writing class of Whit Burnett, a literary entrepreneur who as well as teaching owned and edited *Story* magazine. It was more experimental – and much less lucrative – than the established outlets but a useful shop window for young writers. In Burnett's class Salinger at last found discipline and a teacher whose opinion he trusted. He was grateful for the encouragement he got from Burnett, and in the coming years would often turn to him for advice which Whit was happy to give, garnished with rough affection.

Early in 1940 *Story* published Salinger's first piece of fiction. 'The Young Folks' described an encounter between a bored young man

1. The rue de Rivoli, almost empty of vehicles, looking east with the Meurice on the left and the Tuileries on the right. The giant flags left no doubt about who were the masters now.

2. The face of Vichy: Pétain (*left*) and Laval.

3. Soldiers were promised 'Jeder einmal in Paris' ('everyone gets to see Paris once').

4. Ernst Jünger (*left*) and comrade on the roof of the Majestic.

5. Tandem vélo-taxi taking punters to the Longchamp races.

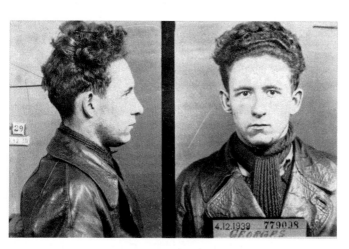

6. Pierre Georges – aka Colonel Fabien, who fought from first to last.

7. War tourist: Robert Brasillach, second from right, with French LVF volunteers in German uniform on a trip to the Eastern Front.

8. Von Choltitz calls it a day.

9. Leclerc and the 2DB being welcomed ashore at Utah Beach by Americans on 1 August 1944.

10. Ernest von Clausewitz: Papa in military strategist mode.

11. 'Six-feet-two of muscle and typewriter ribbon' – J. D. Salinger in his beloved jeep.

12. Moment of decision: De Gaulle explains to Ike why the plan has to change.

13. Béatrice Briand, undisputed boss of her rue de la Huchette barricade.

14. Fifis.

and a glib young woman at a party in Manhattan, the dialogue interspersed with much lighting and stubbing-out of cigarettes. Nothing much happens. It was reminiscent of a Fitzgerald story, inviting the reader to find depth and truth in the apparently inconsequential. Jerry was ecstatic to have made it into print. 'I can't think,' he wrote in a thank-you letter to the magazine's staff. 'Magnesia-white feathers fluffing around in my stomach. But I'm terribly pleased and grateful to you.' It was a long time before he repeated the trick; every story he submitted to magazines that year was rejected. He was good at appearing to shrug off the setbacks as part of the game but inevitably there were moments of self-doubt. In the spring of 1941 he tried to join the military, even though America was not yet in the war. No reasons for this surprising decision were ever offered. To his mother's joy he was rejected when the army doctors detected that he had a slight heart problem.

He returned to the dispiriting business of writing stories for an invisible readership, and as the year progressed magazine editors started to pick them up. In July 1941 *Collier's* published 'The Hang of It', a short tale of army life written just before he tried to enlist. The tale was sentimental with a cute ending. On the other hand, the magazine had a circulation of four million and attracted top writers like Damon Runyon, whose name was now alongside Salinger's on the contents page.

The story was a departure from Salinger's usual subject matter, which was drawn directly from the world he moved in. He looked upon his own milieu disapprovingly. The well-heeled young people drifting pointlessly from one entertainment to the next were by and large 'phoney', the most damning judgement he could deliver. Yet, on the face of it, Salinger was as phoney as any of them. Through Elizabeth Murray he met a trio of girls who moved in the smartest New York circles. One, called Oona, was the sixteen-year-old daughter of the famous playwright Eugene O'Neill. Jerry was instantly smitten and bombarded her with declarations of love. During a brief separation while he worked as an entertainer on a luxury cruise ship in the Caribbean, he realized he may have come on too strong. 'Oona, de luna,' he wrote. 'I've seen the folly of my ways and never again will

I shovel heavy amo[u]r into your pretty ear. In the future [I] shall be gay. I shall ride up and down Park Avenue on a white horse, throwing bottles of champagne at blind beggars.' He signed off: 'Cordially, Thiero Santi Winslow'. When Oona left for Hollywood to try and break into films, Jerry's long-distance eloquence was powerless. Her acting career went nowhere but she caught the eye of Charlie Chaplin, who was thirty-six years her senior. To Jerry's dismay the couple got married in 1943 as soon as she turned eighteen.

By then Salinger was settling into a new life in uniform. Following America's entry into the war medical requirements were lowered and in April 1942 he was called up. Soldiering, whatever its drawbacks, was anything but phoney. Military routine brought discipline and a level of contentment. He wanted to be an officer but was knocked back by the selection board. The plus side of remaining in the ranks was that it gave him more time to write, and he went on submitting to the big magazines, achieving a respectable success rate. The big prize was an appearance in the *New Yorker*, which would have marked his debut as a serious author. The magazine had accepted a story called 'Slight Rebellion off Madison' in October 1941 and intended to run it in the December issue. It was about a troubled prep-school boy, home for the Christmas holidays. He walks out on his girlfriend when she refuses to run away with him, then gets drunk in a bar while periodically telephoning the girl's home and making a nuisance of himself. The character's name was Holden Caulfield.

After Pearl Harbor in December 1941, the *New Yorker*'s publishing schedule was thrown into confusion. Jerry's editors pulled the story, promising that it would be published very soon. By the time he arrived in England, more than two years later, it had still not appeared. In the meantime, the magazine had rejected several other offerings, causing him to complain to Whit Burnett that the publication was only interested in derivative material by a 'crowd of little Hemingways'.

Such frustrations seemed less important as final preparations for the Allied invasion of France began. The imminence of action and the prospect of death had a strangely mellowing effect. He would be inclined, he told Burnett, to be calmer and kinder in future, both to others and to his characters. He had learned something from his enforced association with men who came from an America that was very different to his own. He would tell his son Matt many years later that discovering the 'native intelligence' of many of his comrades who had come up without the education or opportunities he had enjoyed was 'one of the few deeply pleasant surprises of the war for him'.

He arrived in England as part of a sixty-man cohort of counter-intelligence specialists and it struck him later that compared with the gregarious GIs in the infantry units 'there wasn't one good mixer in the bunch. We were all essentially letter-writing types . . .' He shared a six-man tent in the grounds of Collipriest House, an eighteenth-century country mansion outside Tiverton where the Ivy Division was headquartered. Among them was John Keenan, of New York Irish stock, who had been a rookie cop when he was called up. The two met during a stopover in London on the way to Devon. While the others went off to tour the bars, John got tickets to the theatre and bumped into Jerry in the foyer. They hit it off and remained friends for life. John was easy-going. His seven months in the NYPD had been a good preparation for the frequent idiocies of army life and taught him how best to handle annoying superiors. Jerry never learned and 'was not too tolerant of people he thought were fools'.

Off duty they hung out together sampling Tiverton's small pleasures. 'We got along very well,' John remembered. 'We went into town when we could, went to the pub and had a warm beer. He went to Mass with me a couple of times. He wasn't a Catholic but he said it can't do me any harm. It was something to do . . .' Neither spent much time discussing the merits of the war. 'You were there because you had to be . . . Everyone was involved in the war. Everyone thought the war was right. Everyone thought they had to be doing something.'

Salinger had laid out his feelings in a speech delivered by one of his characters, Technical Sergeant John 'Babe' Gladwaller, in 'The Last Day of the Last Furlough', one of three stories he sold to the *Saturday Evening Post* before shipping out to England. Gladwaller too is about to go overseas and on the eve of departure has dinner with his parents, his little sister and a close friend, also now in uniform, called Vincent Caulfield whose younger brother Holden has just been reported missing. During the meal, his father holds forth about the trials he and his comrades had endured in 'the last one', prompting Babe to reply: 'Daddy, I don't mean to sound pontifical, but sometimes you talk about the last war – all you fellas do – as if it had been some kind of rugged, sordid game by which society of your day weeded out the men from the boys. I don't mean to be tiresome, but you men from the last war, you all agree that war is hell, but – I don't know – you all seem to think yourselves a little superior for having been participants in it.'

That did not mean that Babe would shirk his duty. He went on: 'I believe in this war . . . I believe in killing Nazis and Fascists and Japs, because there's no other way that I know of. But I believe, as I've never believed in anything else before, that it's the moral duty of all the men who have fought and will fight in this war to keep our mouths shut, once it's over, never again to mention it in any way. It's time we let the dead die in vain. It's never worked the other way, God knows.'

While Salinger was getting ready for battle in Devon, Robert Capa was in London, planning a party. It was late May 1944. He had already seen plenty of action in North Africa and Italy and the capital was the obvious place to wait for the big one – the Allied invasion of France which could come at any moment. He had found himself a steady girlfriend, Elaine Parker, whom he called 'Pinky' on account of the unusual tint of her hair and the strawberry taste he detected on her skin. Pinky had saved ten bottles of Scotch and eight of gin from her alcohol ration while Bob was away. They also rustled up a case of champagne and some brandy at twenty-five shillings a bottle and a box of fresh peaches. The latter they placed in a goldfish bowl, before pouring in the brandy, then topping up with champagne. The resulting rocket fuel would supercharge what promised to be one of the liveliest parties in London that spring.

Their largesse was sure to be appreciated by the guest of honour. Ernest Hemingway was in town and Capa wanted to give him a proper welcome. They had known each other since meeting during the Spanish Civil War. The photographer had arrived there two and a half weeks after the outbreak with a girl in tow. This, he told his friends, was no mere fling but the woman he had long been waiting for. Like

Gerda and Bob

Capa she had changed her name. Born Gerda Pohorylle she now wanted to be known as Gerda Taro, which had a Gipsyish ring to it that suited her personality. She was twenty-four, just over five feet tall and slender with grey-green eyes and fair hair which she hennaed to give it a foxy tint. She was the daughter of a Leipzig businessman and her Jewish blood and left-wing beliefs made Germany a dangerous place for her when Hitler came to power. She left for Paris where she met Capa when he came to photograph her girlfriend to illustrate an insurance brochure. It took a year before they got together, following a holiday with friends in the South of France. Capa wrote to his Hungarian photograper friend André Kertész: 'Never before in my life have I been so happy. Now only pick and spade could separate Gerda from me.' They moved in together and began working as a team, with her writing the captions for his pictures. Then he taught her how to handle a Leica and she started taking pictures for herself.

When the Spanish Civil War broke out in July 1936 they went to Barcelona, making frequent risky trips to the front lines and capturing pictures that fixed the war in the minds of millions. Over the next year, as they went back and forth between the comforts of Paris and the hazards of Spain, their relationship changed. Gerda was headstrong, avid for fame, and she scared Robert with her recklessness. She was tiring of being his protégée and starting to find his devotion cloying.

In April 1937 they were in Madrid and staying in the Florida Hotel, the headquarters of the international press. Among the journalists was a cluster of celebrity writers including Ernest Hemingway. He was then thirty-seven and back in a world that he knew and loved. His 1926 bestselling novel *The Sun Also Rises* drew on a trip with companions from Paris for the Pamplona bull-running festival. When the civil war began, he was working on a novel – *To Have and Have Not* – but abandoned it for a while to return to his old trade of journalism, arriving in Madrid as special correspondent for the North American Newspaper Alliance syndicate. Progress on the novel had been fitful and Spain promised adventure and inspiration as well as the opportunity to reinvent himself. The new Hemingway was a paradigm of the intellectual *engagé* whose commitment to social justice equalled his devotion to his art, and he dressed for the part in wire-rimmed glasses, beret and bushy moustache.

As well as reporting he was making a documentary film called *Spanish Earth* with fellow writer John Dos Passos and Belgian director Joris Ivens which presented the war as a struggle between cruel and exploitative traditionalists on the one hand and crusaders for a just and decent future on the other. It was how most of the writers who flocked to observe events saw things and blind eyes were often turned to republican atrocities. They also trod carefully when reporting the role of the Soviet Union. Moscow demanded a high price for its support. The Spanish government's entire gold reserves were shipped off to Odessa as payment for arms supplies. Political commissars and the NKVD secret police sought out dissidents inside the ranks of the left, regardless of nationality, and murdered them. Their victims included an outspoken left-wing Spanish writer and friend of both Hemingway and Dos Passos called José Robles. The circumstances of his disappearance in 1937 were disputed but there was no doubt that a Soviet agent was behind it. The murder of Robles turned Dos Passos against communism for ever. Hemingway dismissed his fate as one of the harsh injustices that happen in war. It was the end of their friendship.

Another of Hemingway's roles was as master of the revels at the Florida. When Capa arrived with Gerda, the two men recognized each other as kindred spirits, sharing a fondness for boozy camaraderie, self-dramatization and women. Robert happily joined the writer's court, addressing him, as did everyone, as 'Papa' – the patriarchal nickname that Hemingway had awarded himself back in Paris. He would later claim that he had 'adopted him like a father'. Robert's affection was always tinged with cynical amusement at Hemingway's macho pretensions, even though he had helped to burnish the image, photographing him swigging from a whisky bottle and poring over maps before setting off from Valencia for a day at the front.

Capa's work in Spain, and one photograph in particular, would make his name for ever. It was taken in early September 1936 when he and Gerda were near Cerro Muriano, north of Toledo, on their way to cover the exodus of civilians fleeing insurgent air raids. They ran into militiamen from the anarcho-syndicalist Confederación Nacional del Trabajo. Their battle was over but Capa persuaded them to pose for pictures. One showed a man apparently at the moment of death having been hit by a bullet. As Capa would prove over and over again, he was perfectly willing to risk the danger inherent in getting such a shot, but this – his most famous photograph – was in fact posed. The message it conveyed was authentic enough. The falling soldier, his sunburned worker's arm flung out as his rifle flies from his hand, brilliantly captured the eternal struggle between the weak and the powerful, and between the idealist and the cynic.

In December 1938, a new and influential British magazine called *Picture Post* carried a spread of pictures from the thick of a battle on the River Segre. Readers were introduced to the man who took them as 'The Greatest War Photographer in the World – Robert Capa'. By then he was back in Paris and recovering from what he admitted to his mother was 'a total breakdown'. He had won fame if not fortune, but he had lost the woman he loved. Gerda was killed in July 1937 while covering the fighting at Brunete near Madrid while Robert was in Paris. She was struck not by a bomb or a bullet but by a tank which reversed into a moving car while she was standing on the running board.

Capa drank and wept, sinking into a grief so deep that friends feared he would kill himself. For a while he carried dozens of copies of a portrait he had taken of Gerda in Spain, handing them out to strangers and telling them that she had been his wife and that he had been there when she died. In time he seemed to recover. The carefree image he had cultivated demanded it. But those who knew him best sensed that something fundamental had changed, and all the partying and womanizing was a vain attempt to relieve the pain within.

As always, work was the best therapy, and with the coming of war there would be plenty of it. At first, he intended to stay in Paris, but a request to the French Foreign Ministry for accreditation was turned down and he departed for America. When Paris fell, he was thousands of miles from the action, covering an election in Mexico for *Life* magazine. When he heard the news, he told his brother Cornell: 'It depresses me very much. The world was never as sad as it is now.'

The big party in London would be the first time Capa had seen Hemingway in two and a half years. The last had been in September 1941 when *Life* sent him to the Sun Valley hunting resort in Idaho to photograph Hemingway and Martha Gellhorn, more than a year into what was turning out to be a very fractious marriage. Since moving to London, Capa had been busy recording many facets of the war, from the daily life of the Gibbs family in working-class Lambeth to flying in a B-17 Flying Fortress on a bombing mission over Sicily.

Hemingway had thus far steered clear of the conflict, spending much of his time in Cuba. According to his version of events, his leisurely existence of writing interspersed with angling expeditions on his boat *Pilar* was actually a front. He and his fishing companions might look as if they were merely having fun but they were in fact engaged in 'secret work for the government' hunting down German U-boats. It was news to the director of the FBI, J. Edgar Hoover, who was of the opinion that 'Hemingway is the last man . . . to be used in any such capacity,' especially if 'his sobriety is the same as it was some years ago'. Martha had left for London in the autumn of 1943 to report for *Collier's*. Shortly after arriving she wrote urging him to give up his 'shaming and silly life' in Cuba and come and join her. Everyone she met told her what a hero her husband was. Now, surely, it was time to live up to his reputation. Hemingway took the scolding badly, muttering that she was trying to get him killed. Despite everything, Martha still felt some love for him and in the softer passages of her letters looked forward to a future when they would 'write books and see the autumns together and walk around the cornfields waiting for the pheasants'. In the meantime, there was a war there for them both to report on – and it was about to reach a crucial moment. 'I would give anything to be part of the invasion and see Paris right at the beginning and watch the peace,' she wrote in December 1943.

Three months later she was missing her husband and flew home. He was not in a welcoming mood. She recalled how he woke her when she was trying to sleep, to 'bully, snarl, mock. My crime really was to have been at war when he was not, but that was not how he put it. I was supposedly insane. I only wanted excitement and danger. I had no responsibility to anyone.' With his endless self-mythologizing, Hemingway had created a trap for himself. If he wanted to carry on being 'Papa' he would have to go to war. But it was Martha he blamed for the dilemma and he took pains to make sure she was punished. He would go to London to report for *Collier's*, which until now had been using Gellhorn's services. Places to cover the invasion were tight and official accreditation was limited to one correspondent per publication. That meant she would have to scratch around to find another sponsor if she was to get up front with the action. Hemingway had a further humiliation in store for her. When the pair arrived in New York in April 1944 to make the journey to England, he told her there was no room for her on the flight he had wangled on a Pan Am transatlantic clipper as 'they didn't take women'. She had to make the dangerous crossing on a cargo ship laden with explosives. He arrived in England on Wednesday 17 May and photographers recorded him standing at the top of the aircraft steps. They were there not just for him but for another famous passenger. Gertrude Lawrence, the renowned actress, was returning from Hollywood after a long absence, to do her bit for Britain. It seemed that women were allowed on the flight after all.

Hemingway had never before been to what he nonetheless insisted on calling 'dear old London town', but he wasted no time in making himself at home, checking into the Dorchester Hotel, which was much in demand because of its supposedly impregnable basement bomb shelter. He paid an early visit to the White Tower, a restaurant in bohemian Fitzrovia, also one of Capa's favourites and a social hub for journalists and their military minders. There he spotted an acquaintance, a New York playwright and screenwriter called Irwin Shaw, now in uniform as a private soldier in the service of the US Army Signal Corps film unit known as the 'Hollywood Irregulars'. It was not Shaw he was interested in so much as his companion. She was petite and sharp-featured with brown curly hair and highly visible breasts and her name was Mary Welsh. The dynamic thirty-six-year-old had propelled herself from small-town Minnesota to the centre of the wartime social scene in London, where she worked as a journalist for *Time* magazine. She was also Shaw's girlfriend – or rather he was her latest boyfriend. Though married, she invariably had a lover in tow, usually better connected and more socially elevated than Jewish, Brooklyn-born Shaw.

His meal finished, Hemingway strolled over to the couple. After being introduced to Mary he immediately invited her to lunch. To Shaw's chagrin, she accepted at once – enchanted, she claimed later, by the 'beautiful eyes' above the 'great, bushy, brindled beard'. They met once again at the White Tower. The weather was warm and the owner favoured the couple with a table on the pavement. The gesture backfired when conversation was drowned out by the din from the traffic. It didn't matter. Hemingway was entranced. Mary had checked in to the Dorchester as a precaution in case the German bombers which had just attacked the capital returned, and a few days later he knocked on her door. She was lying on the bed chatting with a visitor, a British journalist and socialist activist called Michael Foot. Without preamble the writer launched into a long account of his upbringing in Chicago. Then he abruptly declared: 'Mary, I do not know you, but I want to marry you.' Mary told him he was being silly, but a seed had been sown.

Papa did not cut a very dignified figure when, on the evening of 24 May, he made his entrance at the party laid on for him by Capa and Pinkie at their expensive penthouse flat in Belgrave Square. The beard he had grown to cover the cancerous patches inflicted on his face by the Cuban sun and to compensate for his thinning hair looked outlandish among the smart uniforms and spruce barbering of the other male guests. Decades of heroic drinking had blotched his skin with broken veins and he seemed a lot older than his forty-four years. But he still glowed with the aura of celebrity and, once through the door, all eyes were on him.

The place was packed. As Capa noted: 'The attraction of free booze, combined with Mr. Hemingway, proved irresistible. Everyone was in London for the invasion and they all showed up at the party.' Papa was in high spirits and brimming with bonhomie towards the men and gallantry towards the ladies as he gulped the high-octane concoction brewed in his honour. On being introduced to Pinkie he told her, 'You are a treasure. You are the kind we seek. You are something beyond words,' to which Capa responded, 'Get your own girl!'

The air was thick with cigarette smoke and the scent of the coming battle. Many of those present would soon be going into action, among them Bill Walton, a friend and colleague of Mary Welsh, who had given up war corresponding and retrained as a paratrooper with the 82nd Airborne Division and would jump into the landing zone when D-Day finally arrived. In such company Hemingway was anxious to demonstrate his macho credentials. Another guest was the writer's adoring kid brother Leicester, sixteen years his junior, another member of the army documentary film unit. They engaged in some mock sparring and Leicester was invited to punch Ernest in the stomach. The challenge was extended to an English doctor friend of Capa's called Peter Gorer. After expressing admiration for the writer's iron abdomen, Gorer was treated to a lengthy account of Papa's skin problems. At about 4 a.m., as Capa recalled, 'we reached the peaches. The bottles were empty, the fish bowl dry and the guests began to trickle away.' Dr Gorer offered to give Hemingway a lift back to the Dorchester. Capa 'ate the peaches and went to sleep'.

At 7 a.m. he was woken by the telephone. 'They said something about a Mr. Hemingway and asked me to come down to the emergency room. There, on an operating table, I found 215 pounds of

Papa. His skull was split wide open and his beard was full of blood. The doctors were about to give him an anesthetic and sew his head together.' Driving the short distance back to the hotel in the black-out, somewhat the worse for drink, Gorer had run into a solid steel water tank. Hemingway's head smashed into the windscreen and his knees into the dashboard. It took the doctors at St George's Hospital on Hyde Park Corner two and a half hours to put in the fifty-seven stitches needed to close the head wound.

One of the first to reach his bedside was Mary Welsh. Hemingway assured her he would be back in action in a day or two, despite his splitting headache and crocked knees. A less welcome visitor was Martha Gellhorn. Her ship had finally docked at Liverpool where reporters told her of the crash. On reaching London she dropped her bags at the Dorchester and hurried the few hundred yards to the hospital. Her concern soon evaporated at the sight of her husband propped up in bed, his head swathed in bandages, surrounded by empty bottles. In the ensuing row she told him that she had had enough of his 'bullying' and 'play-acting'. This time, it seemed, they were really through. When Hemingway was discharged from the hospital – hobbling, plagued with headaches and minus his third wife – the invasion was less than a fortnight away. It was not a good start to Papa's war.

Britain was also experiencing an invasion. Out-of-the-way places that had rarely seen a stranger were flooded with foreigners. In May the countryside of Yorkshire began filling up with sunburned men who wore American uniforms but spoke French and carried the Cross of Lorraine on their tunics. They belonged to the French 2nd Armoured Division, the 2ème Division Blindée (2DB). It would become better known as the 'Leclerc Division', after its commander, whose energy and vision had done so much to bring it into being.

Philippe Leclerc was forty-two and stick thin with the profile of a raptor. He radiated austerity, barely drank and in all the years of separation remained faithful to his wife. He was something of a prig and easier to respect than to like, though many by the end had come to regard him with affection. A riding accident left him with a limp and the Malacca cane he carried seemed an extension of his personality,

twitching irritably to express his frequent moods of dissatisfaction or impatience. His relations with his superiors were often difficult and the only authority he unquestionably accepted was that of his God.

The story of Philippe Leclerc illustrated the difficulty of predicting where a Frenchman's loyalties would lie when faced with the great moral dilemmas posed by defeat and occupation. He was born Philippe de Hauteclocque into a Catholic aristocratic family from Picardy who lived their lives as if the French Revolution had never happened. Philippe inherited their deep conservatism. He read the *Action Française* paper and went to mass daily. Too young to fight in the previous war, he entered the Saint-Cyr military academy in 1921 where he was assessed as 'remarkably intelligent . . . a soldier to his soul'. When the Germans attacked in the west on 10 May 1940, he was chief of staff of the 4ème Division d'Infanterie. The unit was surrounded in the German advance, but he managed to escape through enemy lines. After returning to the fight he was wounded in the head in an air attack and captured on 15 June. He escaped again, jumping through a window.

With his background and outlook, de Hauteclocque was the sort of person that Vichy's message of a return to traditional values was aimed at. Yet on hearing that Pétain had agreed the armistice he felt only disgust and a burning determination to carry on the fight. After saying goodbye to his wife and six children he crossed into Spain under a false ID card in the name of Philippe Leclerc and took a boat to London to join de Gaulle. He kept the new name to shield his family from reprisals and it was only after D-Day that his real identity was known in France.

In August 1940, de Gaulle sent Leclerc to Central Africa with a handful of men to rally the colonies to Free France. Cameroon came over swiftly, but when the authorities in the neighbouring territory of Gabon resisted he led a force of Foreign Legion and local troops against them and after a month-long battle seized the capital Libreville. Leclerc then moved north to Chad and set up his headquarters at Fort Lamy. From there he made a series of raids in support of the Allied forces fighting in the Western Desert. In early 1941 after a month-long siege, they captured from the Italians the important oasis staging post of Kufra in southern Libya. At the end of the battle Leclerc and his men took a vow that became known as the *Serment de Koufra* ('Oath of Kufra'), swearing 'never to lay down arms until the day when our beautiful colours float again above Strasbourg Cathedral'. It would take three years and eight months of hard fighting before this solemn promise was honoured.

By the autumn of 1943, Leclerc's initial band of French *colons* and locally raised troops, feebly armed with outdated weaponry and equipment, had grown into the 2ème Division Blindée. Thanks to the largesse of the Americans, the 2DB was now equipped with 160 M4 Sherman tanks and 280 armoured M3 half-tracks. The division was about 15,000 strong, including 3,600 Moroccans and Algerians. The Black Africans who had supported the Free French valiantly from the outset were cut loose. The division would be under American operational command and the racist policies of the US military excluded Blacks from combat units. Under Leclerc's authority the 2DB restored tattered French pride on the battlefields of North Africa. Now, much strengthened, its men were lining up for the great adventure that was about to begin and preparing to take their place in history.

Among the more exotic arrivals in Yorkshire that spring were a unit that set up camp around the small market town of Pocklington. They trundled around the lanes in armoured half-tracks, with far-off place names painted on the side: 'Guadalajara', 'Brunete', 'Teruel'. The shoulder flashes on their tunics identified them as members of the French Régiment de Marche du Tchad (RMT). But many of the men were Spanish and the names on their vehicles commemorated battles of the civil war. After the final defeat they fled over the Pyrenees and into France, where the authorities locked them up in disease-ridden camps and prisons. They were offered asylum on condition they joined either the French army or 'labour battalions'. Some chose to enlist in the Foreign Legion. Others were shipped off to North Africa and put to work in fields, on construction projects or in factories, where conditions were often atrocious. The dreadful treatment they received gave them few reasons to love the French. But they had even more cause to hate the fascists. When, following the Anglo-American invasion of North Africa in November 1942, the Free French raised their standard, a number deserted and joined what was called the Corps Francs d'Afrique. In August 1943 it was incorporated into the newly formed Leclerc Division.

The RMT's 3rd Battalion, where many of the division's Spaniards ended up, was commanded by Lieutenant-Colonel Joseph Putz. He was lean, chisel-faced, a veteran of the 1914–18 war who had fought in the Spanish Civil War and commanded the mostly French 15th International Brigade (La Marseillaise). In 1939 he was working as an official in the Algerian colonial administration. With the arrival of Vichy, there was no room for a man like Putz. Fearing arrest, he departed for southern Morocco, but when the Americans and British invaded North Africa he joined the Free French. Since then he had led his battalion through the grim fighting to dislodge the Axis armies from North Africa and earned the respect and trust of his men. 'Putz was not really your typical soldier,' judged one of his officers, 'though he was a real warrior. He was also very human, open, smiling and sympathetic and exactly the right man to lead a such a unit.'

Of all the companies in the battalion, the 9th was the most Spanish and was consequently known as 'La Nueve'. Among the members were communists, anarchists, socialists and moderate republicans. There was a danger that the factionalism that had hampered the loyalist cause in the war would undermine the company's discipline. Command was therefore handed to an officer who was a Frenchman and above the ideological fray.

Captain Raymond Dronne was a man the Spanish could respect. Like Putz he had been an official in the colonial service in French Cameroon when the armistice was signed and Frenchmen overseas had to choose between Vichy and de Gaulle. He had unhesitatingly chosen the general, even though he had little idea who he was. Dronne was a stocky thirty-six-year-old, and still moved stiffly as a result of being hit in the elbow, hip and foot by machine-gun bullets from a German aircraft during the Battle of Ksar Ghilane in Tunisia fourteen months before. He came from a farming family in the Sarthe region of western France and growing up wanted to be a lawyer or a journalist, certainly not a soldier. After leaving school in Le Mans he studied at Leipzig and Berlin universities where he formed the 'juvenile ambition to work for Franco-German reconciliation, being convinced that it was in the common interest of our two countries to put an end to their old rivalries and start listening to one another'.

Dronne's politics were moderately left wing, which put him at odds with the many Camelots du Roi at the Sorbonne. Returning to his digs in the Latin Quarter late one evening he felt an urgent need for a leak. While thus engaged, he was set upon by half-a-dozen walking-stick-wielding students who knocked him to the pavement shouting, 'This is from the king!' When he got up, he realized he had inadvertently been urinating against an Action Française poster. The following day, still in pain, he bought a heavy walking stick 'and proceeded to give a good hiding to the Camelots whenever the opportunity arose'.

Before shipping out from Oran to Greenock on the Clyde to join the Allied forces massing for the invasion, Captain Dronne had given the men of La Nueve a stern talking to. The well-publicized atrocities committed by all sides in the civil war meant that Spanish republicans had a dubious image in Britain. This was a chance to restore their reputation. He urged them: 'For the honour of the French army and the honour of Spain, your behaviour and your turnout must be impeccable.' The folk of Pocklington had nothing to fear. La Nueve were warmly received, especially by the local girls, who, the Spanish were pleased to note, seemed to prefer them to their French comrades, not least because they were better dancers.

By now Dronne had got the measure of his men and they of him. On his appointment in 1943 Leclerc had told him: 'Everyone's terrified of them but they're good soldiers and you're going to sort them out.' Dronne knew some Spanish, but his main qualification was that he was an ardent republican just like his men and, unlike many in the ranks of the 2DB, he had been a Free Frenchman from the first hour. They began preparations for the move to England in the last months of 1943 in a flea-infested Beau Geste-style fort at Skhirat between Casablanca and Rabat on the Atlantic coast of Morocco. Their American instructors showed them how to assemble and operate the M3 armoured personnel carriers they would be fighting from. They had wheels at the front and tracks at the back, on which sat an open-topped armoured steel box that could carry a dozen soldiers, mounted with a machine gun. The half-tracks soon acquired names. While some commemorated civil war battles, Dronne chose a simple sentiment for his command jeep: 'Mort aux Cons' or 'Death to Idiots'. They also got their hands on new weapons – light and heavy machine guns, mortars and anti-tank bazookas. By the time they set sail for Britain in April the division had shaken down into a cohesive fighting machine in which La Nueve served as a sturdy and reliable cog.

Their efficiency was as dependent on mutual respect as it was on military skill. The chemistry of the unit was complicated. Dronne needed a second in command. The obvious choice seemed to be Lieutenant Antonio van Baumberghen, his Flemish name reflecting his family's ties to Spain's Habsburg monarchs who historically had ruled the Low Countries. It was too much of a mouthful for most of the troops and he was known simply as 'Bamba'.

Although the ordinary soldiers and NCOs got on well enough, whatever their political tribe, Dronne found that 'many of the Spanish had a lot of trouble obeying Spanish officers'. Having shaken off the yoke of deference during the years of the Republic, they were not going to like taking orders from a cultured patrician. Dronne liked Bamba. He was intelligent and good fun, but the rougher elements in the company saw him simply as a class enemy. Dronne was warned that there was talk of shooting him on the battlefield when an opportunity arose. If Dronne was killed or put out of action Bamba would automatically take over command, with potentially disastrous results.

Dronne discussed the problem with Putz, who solved it by assigning Bamba to a non-combatant unit and sending a spare lieutenant as a replacement. Amado Granell was from a very different background. He was the son of a woodcutter from Burriana near Valencia on the Mediterranean coast who had gone into the military and reached the rank of sergeant before the death of his father forced him to quit and return home to fend for the family. He was running a motorcycle shop when the civil war broke out. He volunteered to defend the Republic and ended up commanding a brigade. When resistance finally collapsed, he boarded a British merchant ship crammed with refugees bound for Oran. There the French put him to work in a labour camp, until the Anglo-American landings freed him to return to the struggle, eventually as a lieutenant in the RMT.

Granell was even-tempered and conciliatory. Despite his working-class origins he was no revolutionary and hoped that one day a restoration of the monarchy would reconcile Spain's warring elements. His steady authority would reinforce Dronne's efforts to maintain discipline and effectiveness in the company. They were an extraordinarily assorted crew. Platoon sergeant Ramon David went under the pseudonym of 'Fabregas'. Like many of them he used a *nom de guerre* to protect his family back in Spain from persecution. He was the son of a rich Catalan industrialist who sent him to school in Britain. He put his fluent English at the disposal of his comrades and after departing Pocklington composed elegant love letters on their behalf to the lasses they left behind. Fabregas was at ease with everyone, high and low. On the cloudless night before his death he enthralled everyone, identifying the constellations glittering overhead. Some of the company could have walked out of the pages of *For Whom the Bell Tolls*. Sergeant Martín Bernal was a former *torero* who fought under the name 'Larita Segundo'. There was the one they called 'El Gitano', a pure-blooded Gipsy, 'brave and swashbuckling' in Dronne's admiring words, who never learned a word of French.

The ranks of La Nueve were home to some surprising non-Spaniards as well. The commander of the third section, Johann Reiter, was German. His father, a former officer in the Kaiser's army, was murdered in 1934 for his anti-Nazi views. Reiter had just graduated from the Munich military academy and decided to continue his career in the French Foreign Legion. The legion attracted many Germans, among them some ardent Nazis who kidnapped him and dragged him back to Germany. After being jailed in Bavaria he escaped and got back to Spain where he fought for the government, commanding a machine-gun unit. German, Gipsy, rich man, poor man, saint and sinner. They were brothers in arms now, and all their differences would be washed away by the blood and sweat of battle.

The Leclerc Division spread out among the rolling Yorkshire Wolds and waited for the order to move south. Everyone in the 2DB had a story. Few serving in 1944 would have dreamed in their earlier life that this is how they would end up. Alexandre Rosenberg certainly made an unlikely warrior, and his parents thought so too. When his art-dealer father Paul and mother Margot finally reached sanctuary in New York they began trying to persuade him to abandon the Free French forces and join them. Since signing up in London in July 1940 he had been bombarded with letters begging him to get the next transatlantic boat. After a while Alexandre stopped opening them and they took to sending telegrams, the combined cost of which, the joke went, would have paid for the purchase of a tank. His first posting was to a fort overlooking the Atlantic at Pointe-Noire in the French Congo. His subsequent adventures took him to Chad and across the Sahara to Cairo and Egypt. By the time he reached England with the 2DB he was a lieutenant and a specialist artillery spotter in the 3ème Régiment d'Artillerie Coloniale.

The formation included an all-female ambulance unit staffed by volunteers. It was founded by Florence Conrad, an American resident in France for many years who returned to the US in 1941 determined to do her bit to liberate her adopted home. The unit took the name of 'Rochambeau' after a French general who had fought on the American side against the British in the Revolutionary War. Before long they were nicknamed the 'Rochambelles', and fifty women would serve with the 2DB in the course of the war.

The Leclerc Division was proof of de Gaulle's extraordinary ability to unite individuals of disparate views and backgrounds. Within its ranks were passionate Gaullists and some who, until recently, had been ardent Pétainists. There were Catholics, Protestants, Jews, Muslims and atheists. There were rugged, sunburned colonial settlers who had never set foot in Paris and metropolitan sophisticates for whom Nice was as far south as they were prepared to go. War had uprooted them from their favoured routines and thrown them into trials and adventures they could never have foreseen and which were now about to begin in earnest.

Down in Devon things were stirring. In the middle of May the Ivy Division started to pack up its base in Tiverton and move to forming-up areas in the countryside behind the ports of Dartmouth, Torquay and Exmouth. The soldiers' new homes were oblong tented camps surrounded by wire and covered with camouflage netting that they nicknamed 'sausages'. After all the intensive training of the previous months, the sudden inactivity felt unsettling. The planners laid on plenty of entertainments and distractions. Makeshift cinemas showed the latest Hollywood movies – *Mr. Lucky*, a tale of unlikely romance between a gambler and a socialite starring Cary Grant and Laraine Day, and *Going My Way* with Bing Crosby playing an unconventional priest in a tough New York parish. Alcohol was now banned and such escapist fare was one way to take the minds of the boys off what lay ahead. The pranking and banter endemic in military routine had died away. Instead the officers absorbed themselves in endless rereading of their orders while the soldiers tried to lose themselves in card playing, letter writing and reading. The meals they ate as they waited were ominously good – steaks, pork chops, lemon meringue pie and ice cream. Each one felt like the last supper.

On 31 May the division started to load on to its landing ships, moored in their hundreds in the waters off the little Devon harbours. There they sat for days until the evening of 5 June when one by one they slipped anchor and butted out into the grey waters of the Channel. The men were told to keep their equipment down to a weight of 44 pounds but most were carrying extra items that added to the load. Some took a Bible, others extra cartons of cigarettes. Stowed in Sergeant Jerry Salinger's pack were the manuscripts of six stories featuring the character who now loomed large in his imagination: Holden Caulfield. 'All of them I like very much,' he told Whit Burnett in a letter just before he left Tiverton. He didn't want him to publish them yet but 'to save for the book on him I'm doing for you'.

6.   Bouillon

The French leaned on the same proverb as the rest of the world to comfort themselves when life was grim: *L'heure la plus sombre est juste avant l'aube*. In the spring of 1944 the nights were black and the dawn felt a long way off. The invasion was coming, there could be no doubt of that. But when?

In the meantime, the Germans were growing nervous and vengeful and Paris was hungrier than ever. In the Tuileries, the flower beds were planted with swedes. The flow of food from the rural areas had dwindled to a trickle. Once the Germans and black-marketeers were done there was barely anything left for ordinary folk, and the generosity of country cousins had withered as they stockpiled for an uncertain future. Over the rooftops the once all but vacant skies were streaked with the contrails of small, high-flying aircraft. The sight of them brought excitement and also a frisson of dread. The feathery lines, like chalk on a blackboard, were sketched by reconnaissance planes busy photographing targets for the Allied bombers. They raised expectations that salvation might be just around the corner. But with hope came the fear that death might come sooner than liberation.

For much of the occupation the Allied air forces left Paris alone. It was twenty months before the city was hit by bombing. On the night of 3/4 March 1942 the RAF launched a large raid on the sprawling Renault factory in the south-western suburb of Boulogne-Billancourt where 16,000 French workers churned out lorries for the German military. About 300 bombs hit the target, destroying 40 per cent of the works and putting them out of action for four weeks. The cost in innocent lives was equally devastating. Inevitably, bombs tumbled into the apartment blocks that sat cheek by jowl with the factory. Nearly 400 French civilians were killed, more than double the death toll of any RAF raid on a German city to date. Vichy portrayed it as a Churchill-inspired act of terror and an attempt to appease Stalin, who for months had been railing against his Anglo-American allies' failure to take the pressure off his armies by opening a Second Front in the west.

The RAF returned to drop leaflets declaring that the factories' importance to the German war effort made them a legitimate target, adding the hope that ultimate victory over the Nazis would bring 'a measure of consolation' to the families of the dead. Many Parisians seemed to accept the justification.

By early 1944, Parisian stoicism was being tested to the limit. In April the Allied bombing campaign began in earnest. War factories were no longer the objective. Now it was the synapses of the French rail network where its lines met in and around the capital. You did not have to be a military expert to understand the purpose: it was to cripple the Germans' ability to move men and materiel around to counter-attack an invasion force. On the night of 18/19 April, mass fleets of British bombers struck railway yards at Juvisy, just south of Paris, and Noisy-le-Sec on its eastern edge. Juvisy once boasted that it was 'the biggest railway station in the world' and controlled routes south and west of the capital. Noisy sat on the lines leading back to Germany, which funnelled war exports and deportees to the death camps in one direction and German troops and equipment in the other. Both attacks were counted successes by the RAF, but the collateral damage was enormous, with the Noisy operation killing 464 French civilians.

The following night the raiders were back and this time they struck the city. The target was the marshalling yards at La Chapelle in the heart of the 18th arrondissement, where thick skeins of track flowed away from the Gare du Nord and the Gare de l'Est. The RAF post-operational report claimed that the bombs were 'extremely concentrated', but many landed in surrounding low-rent housing blocks, killing 670 people. In the aftermath, children from nearby schools were drafted in to help with the rescue work. Among them was the inquisitive and perceptive Paris schoolboy Raymond Ruffin, now fourteen, who was 'gripped by the apocalyptic scene in front of me, truly a field of smoking ruins'. There was 'no trace of streets, avenues or alleyways. Everywhere a thick carpet of rubble on which floated the reek of gas, burnt explosive and the overflow from the

sewers.' In the middle of the chaos he noticed 'a lone tree left stand-ing, and clinging to the end of its branches some strips of cloth and net curtains and even a single bicycle wheel'.

Paris had received its first real taste of being blitzed, and the casual attitude many had shown to the howl of the air-raid sirens quickly vanished. A middle-aged journalist called Jean Galtier-Boissière noted that in Batignolles and Montmartre as soon as the first note sounded 'everyone rushes to the depths of the Métro, carrying little suitcases containing their most precious possessions. On the boule-vards, the big cinemas stay open to welcome weeping families.' Others preferred to take their chances in the open air, spending their nights on the park benches in the square des Batignolles.

The bombs brought a faded figure back to the centre of the national stage. In all his time as head of the Vichy state Philippe Pétain had not once set foot in its *de jure* capital. His refusal to move there was intended as a little show of defiance, but now he felt that Parisians needed him and he was finally coming to show sympathy and solidarity. For a while now the marshal had taken little part in decision making and Vichy policy was largely directed by Pierre Laval, who after being briefly removed from power by Pétain for being too pro-German was now back as prime minister at the occupiers' insistence. He had returned the favour by intensifying his loyalty to them, telling French males it was their duty to volunteer to fight for the Nazis on the Eastern Front.

Despite his shrinking prestige, the marshal had his uses. When the Allied air campaign started, the Germans arranged for him to visit areas in the north where most of the bombs were falling, in the hope that he would stoke popular anti-Allied feeling. So far he had been welcomed warmly, but after such a long absence no one knew for sure how he would be received in Paris. On the morning of 26 April, he went to Notre-Dame for a memorial mass for the victims of the bombing. From there he was driven across the pont d'Arcole to the Hôtel de Ville. A huge crowd had gathered. Among them was Raymond Ruffin, who while shopping with his friends for scarce school supplies in the Bazar de l'Hôtel de Ville department store near by had heard the marshal was coming.

There was barely a German in sight as Pétain climbed the steps to a specially built platform in front of the city hall. High on the tower above the central façade someone had run up the French tricolour, which the Germans had banned since 1940. As he came into view 'an immense clamour rose from the sea of humans, interspersed with interminable clapping'. The marshal 'took a long look around him, his eyes resting on the multitude of young people and kids gathered at the foot of the stage'. He stood upright and immobile as the ovation went on and on, his baton in one hand and gloves in the other, and Ruffin 'had difficulty convincing myself that this dashing and debonair old boy, the very image of the venerable grandfather, could be the same person who allowed all the terrible things that had been done by the regime over which he was supposed to preside'. The speech that followed was short and vague. Pétain declared that he 'could not visit Paris without coming to see you', and that he was there 'to recall myself to your memory' and to 'comfort you for all the sufferings bearing down on Paris'. It was a 'little visit of thanks' to those of whom he thought often. He finished with the promise, 'As soon as I can I will come back,' this time 'officially'. He then set off to visit survivors of the bombing in a hospital in the north of the city.

The square rocked with cheers as Pétain was driven away. Some of the crowd started singing the unofficial Vichy anthem 'Maréchal, nous voilà!' but it was quickly drowned out by the strains of the 'Marseillaise', also forbidden by the Germans. The competing choruses revealed the confused loyalties of the crowd – and of Paris. Ruffin had 'never imagined that the man of Vichy was so popular'. Many of the crowd were probably members of ultra-collaborationist groups and the school children in the front rows had been taken there by their teachers. But there were also 'hundreds and hundreds who had gone out of their way to be there', driven by a mixture of curiosity and residual respect. As the crowd ebbed away, Ruffin 'suddenly understood that more or less everybody there was applauding not the head of the French state which was so compromised and treasonous' but the sight of the tricolour and a man in the uniform of a French *maréchal*, symbols 'of a nation that refused to die'.

Pétain's banal but heartfelt words were open to interpretation and some present thought their true meaning lay in what he *didn't* say. He had been full of sympathy for the victims of the air raids but there was no condemnation of the perpetrators. His reference to 'sufferings' in the plural could be taken as an allusion to the miseries of the occupation, and the promise to make an early 'official' return seemed to hint that he would soon be restored to real power, once the Allied armies arrived.

By the time Pétain's speech was published in the press it had been rewritten by the German censors to form a standard denunciation of the Allies. In a telling passage he was made to beseech the French 'in my name and in the name of [Prime Minister] Laval, to do nothing which could jeopardize . . . the future of France'. This was a clear instruction to have nothing to do with the many armed Resistance groups that were now fighting the occupation.

It was Pétain's last feeble show of defiance. Like some feisty care-home patient making a bid for freedom, only to be intercepted by security at the front door, he returned to Vichy, from where two days after his Paris adventure he addressed the nation over the radio. This time he repeated his lines obediently, urging listeners 'to adopt a correct and loyal attitude towards the occupying forces' and promising: 'When the present tragedy is over and when, thanks to Germany's defence of the continent . . . our civilization is finally safe from the danger of bolshevism, it will be time for France to rediscover and affirm her rightful place.'

A few days after the marshal's visit, Jacques Delmas bounded up the stairs to the first-floor dining room at Lasserre, a new and expensive restaurant near the Champs-Élysées. Waiting for him was a fellow resister called Lorrain Cruse. They were expecting a third, whom they knew only by her codename, 'Jocelyne'. It was she who transmitted their messages by radio to the Free French intelligence service, the Bureau Central de Renseignements et d'Action in London, and decoded the signals they sent back. When Jocelyne arrived, she told the head waiter to bring champagne. 'Champagne? You're mad!' whispered Jacques. 'No, no,' protested Jocelyne. 'I've got some news.' So she had. The message she carried from London appointed Delmas de Gaulle's military delegate for the whole of France. With the job came promotion to the rank of brigadier-general. And 'for good measure' he had been made a Chevalier of the Légion d'Honneur, a lofty state award. These tidings gave a welcome lift to his spirits. His habitual optimism had been tested to the limit over the autumn and winter following a series of appalling blows to all elements of the Resistance. They had barely survived the battering and were only now starting to recover.

The spirit of resistance was expressed most forcefully by killing Germans. In 1943 it was the communists who were spilling most of the blood. By now they had a fully formed military wing in the shape of the Francs-Tireurs et Partisans (FTP), the 'irregulars and partisans' founded in the summer of 1942 to wage urban guerrilla warfare. It was made up of several elements, of which the most active was the Main-d'Oeuvre Immigrée organization (MOI) founded by foreign-born workers, many of them Jewish, and some veterans of the Spanish Civil War. In the summer of 1943 they were led by Missak Manouchian, a charismatic poet with thick wavy hair and soulful deep-set eyes. He had been brought up in an orphanage in French-administered Lebanon after his parents were killed by the Turks in the Armenian genocide. In 1925, when he was nineteen years old, he moved to France and settled in Paris, where he worked for a while as a lathe operator at Citroën and eventually became a communist. His passion for literature was as great as his interest in politics. He wrote powerful verse in Armenian and had co-edited literary magazines.

Under his command the MOI struck the biggest blow the Resistance had landed on the Germans to date. On the morning of 28 September 1943 a team shot dead Colonel Julius Ritter as he left his home in the 16th arrondissement. Ritter was the local head of the hated Service du Travail Obligatoire, set up to force French men to work in German industries. Its introduction had driven many uncommitted males into the arms of the regional Resistance, joining the bands of guerrillas operating in the countryside known as the Maquis, and Ritter's assassination was a real coup. It was one of nearly thirty MOI attacks that autumn and brought a savage response from the Germans and the French police. There were now more French collaborators dedicated to hunting down resisters than there were Germans. From the beginning of 1943 the Resistance faced the added menace of the paramilitary Milice (militia), founded by Joseph Darnand, a First World War hero turned copy-cat fascist complete with Hitler moustache. Its 25,000 or so members, who wore black uniforms and floppy berets, joined for a wide variety of reasons ranging from ideological conviction to the lure of regular pay and rations. Others abused their newly acquired authority to settle scores with neighbours. Their existence deepened the fear that liberation from the Germans might bring with it the dreadful prospect of a civil war.

The regular police routinely did what the Germans ordered, supplying the manpower for arrests and round-ups, and specialist units pursued communists and resisters with as much zeal as the Nazis. Under the leadership of Commissaire Fernand David, the Special Brigades of the Paris police were among the resisters' most vicious opponents and worked hand in glove with the German military's secret police organization, the Geheime Feldpolizei, and the Gestapo. The Brigades were tireless, dedicated and remarkably efficient, following suspects for weeks until they had identified all the members of a network and only then striking.

They led the campaign to destroy the Manouchian organization and in mid-November captured twenty-three members. Among them was Manouchian himself, and after being tortured he was handed over to the Germans. Torture was an essential part of the Brigades' procedure, and their methods included extracting confessions with the use of lead-tipped whips. Once someone was captured it was assumed that sooner or later they would talk and all their contacts, safe houses and meeting places were henceforth blown. Agents sent in from London were given a rubber-coated cyanide capsule to be bitten on *in extremis*.

The French and German organizations hunting the resisters also had subtler methods, offering captives the choice of turning traitor. Among those who co-operated was Joseph Davidovitch, a Polish-born Jew and long-time communist activist who became political head of the Manouchian group in the Paris region. After being arrested by the Special Brigades in October 1943 he was allowed to 'escape' and rejoin his comrades. His reappearance aroused suspicions and he was forced to confess, and executed in December. There were many who felt that the French communist leadership shared some of the guilt for Manouchian's downfall. Even when it was clear that the police and Germans were closing in, no attempt was made to smuggle him and his men out of the country. The bitter conclusion of those who survived was that the French communists had decided that the foreign-born comrades, though useful as long as they were killing Germans, were ultimately expendable.

The Gaullist groups had also been hit badly over the winter. The Germans' most spectacular success came with the arrest of Pierre Brossolette, a headstrong, passionately socialist journalist and budding politician from the Parisian upper bourgeoisie who in the early years of the occupation gathered intelligence and co-ordinated the emerging Resistance networks. In 1942 he escaped to London where he impressed de Gaulle, who put him to work building his political prestige with the Allies. Brossolette was a frequent voice on the BBC broadcasting to France. He also did much to carry the message of the French Resistance to the outside world, speaking at big public meetings in London and creating an unforgettable image of an 'army of the shadows', anonymous, self-sacrificing and astoundingly courageous.

Brossolette knew far too much to be risked on operations, yet he was allowed to return to France late in 1943 to try and repair the damage done by the arrests of the autumn. When weather delayed his departure by air, he and another Resistance leader, Émile Bollaert, who had replaced Jean Moulin, tried to leave by boat from Brittany. They were captured after being betrayed by a local woman but it took weeks before their identities were established. In March 1944 Brossolette was taken to an apartment block at 84 avenue Foch where the SS counter-intelligence service had their headquarters and tortured for two and a half days. He was unable to take his cyanide pill and when his captors left him alone for a few minutes in a sixth-floor maid's room he climbed through the window and jumped, dying later of his injuries.

The randomness with which disaster could strike could induce a mood of fatalism. Jacques Delmas believed in luck. His own experiences in life had taught him its importance. But he was also convinced you could tweak the odds in your favour, and he followed security procedures scrupulously. His job in the Ministry of Economics and Finance provided excellent cover not only for gathering intelligence but also to explain his frequent travels outside Paris. It was essential to seal the different compartments of your life as tightly as possible. Even his wife, now living in the Dordogne with his parents, was kept in the dark for her own safety. Outwardly he was every inch the correct civil servant, 'in a smart suit, complete with breast pocket handkerchief', a rising bureaucratic star. In his leisure time he pursued his pre-war routines, playing tennis and turning out every winter weekend for rugby. But 'in the shadows', he noted, '[I] followed my activities as a spy and a soldier by always covering my tracks'. For two years he moved apartments every few months. In the same period he rented 'a good thirty rooms to which I alone had the key, chosen because they had easy exits via back doors, service staircases or skylights'. To reduce the threat of being followed he developed tradecraft which after the war would be standard operational procedure in a thousand spy movies. His 'rule in the Métro was to get into the carriage at the very last minute and dart out again just as the doors slid shut'. Despite all these precautions, there were moments when he had no choice but to take a potentially fatal leap in the dark. Once, in desperate need of an alibi to cover his tracks, he had to ask his boss to back up his story if the Gestapo or Special Brigades came to check. It turned out that his superior was 'one of us' and became a valuable ally. But if he hadn't been, and it had seemed that he was liable to betray him, Delmas was quite prepared to have him killed or 'to eliminate him myself'.

By the spring of 1944 the German and French security services were learning that ruthlessness brought mixed results. After three months of torture and interrogation the Manouchian group were put on trial in the Hôtel Continental near the place Vendôme in a blaze of publicity. The proceedings lasted just a day and at the end all twenty-three defendants, including Manouchian, were duly found guilty. All but one were then taken to the Mont-Valérien fortress in western Paris, tied to stakes and shot. Hours before his death the poet wrote a last letter to his wife. 'Today it is sunny. I look at the sun and the beauty of the natural world that I so loved, as I bid farewell to life and you all, my beloved wife and dear friends.' The sole woman on trial, the Jewish-Romanian Olga Bancic, was spared death temporarily thanks to a French law forbidding the execution of females by firing squad. She was later transported to Stuttgart and, on her thirty-second birthday, beheaded with an axe.

That spring the authorities plastered Paris with copies of a red-inked poster, which became notorious as *l'Affiche Rouge*. It was illustrated with mugshots of ten members of the Manouchian 'gang', portraying them as wild-looking desperados and highlighting the Jewishness of seven of those pictured. 'Liberators?' asked the headline. If so, it was 'Liberation by the Army of Crime'. The propaganda backfired. To many, these long-haired, raggedy young men looked like heroes, unbowed, glowing with conviction and contemptuous of death.

Every week, the ranks of the Resistance strengthened. The Germans and their French allies had left anyone with a spark of spirit with few honourable choices. The situation was summed up in an editorial in a widely circulated underground newspaper, *Défense de la France*. It told its readers that all it wanted for them was 'a peaceful and happy life in which we create, build and love. But those who want to stop us from living must die. Our duty is clear: we must kill. Kill the German to cleanse our territory, kill him because he kills our own people, kill him to be free. Kill the traitors, kill those who betray, those who aid the enemy. Kill the policeman who has in any way helped arrest patriots. Kill the men of the Milice, exterminate them . . .' It finished with a simple question: 'French men, French women, look into your hearts and answer this: *Do you want to live or die?*'

Madeleine Riffaud saw *l'Affiche Rouge* one morning on the Métro. To her it looked like 'a roll of honour' and she was ready to take her place on it. She had given up her studies at the Paris medical faculty to devote herself to the FTP. Until now she had been ferrying arms, distributing leaflets and running messages. She had also tried her hand at the activity known as *prendre la parole*, meaning the delivery of quick, fiery speeches to Sorbonne students in lecture halls or to housewives queuing outside shops then disappearing before a German or one of the *miliciens*, who now roamed the street looking for 'traitors', intervened. She soon gave up after discovering she got stage fright. Haranguing crowds was not what she had joined for. She wanted action and her bosses agreed.

But real action was severely limited by the lack of guns. The British Special Operations Executive was supposed to provide the hardware to mount operations, but the difficulties of dropping arms to urban areas and political reluctance to put large stocks of weaponry in the hands of communists meant deliveries were strictly limited. Allied policy preferred sabotage over military action, so priority was given to plastic explosive – *plastique* – and detonators. Madeleine's group had just two pistols in their armoury. The *plastique* 'looked like modelling clay and smelled of almonds'. All it needed was to insert a 'time pencil' detonator into a ball the size of an apple and you had a very handy bomb.

Her new activities meant increased danger but also satisfaction and exhilaration. Action 'left very little room for melancholy', and she had personal reasons for feeling low. Marcel Gagliardi, the young man she had met in the sanatorium in the Vosges who introduced her to the Resistance, was now very ill. Madeleine had recovered from tuberculosis. He had not, and had been told his breathlessness meant he was no longer fit for active service. Marcel accepted the decision and Madeleine would have to carry on alone. That spring, the group's activities got ever bolder and more risky. Their orders were to do 'everything possible to weaken and demoralize the Germans'. One evening, she went with three male comrades, 'Paul', 'Manuel' and 'Janson', to the place d'Italie in the 13th arrondissement where, they were told, a convoy of German trucks was parked up. When they arrived, the drivers were in the back of one of the vehicles playing cards. The plan was for Madeleine and Paul to stick balls of *plastique* on the lorries' fuel tanks, then break the detonator pencil releasing the acid which would slowly drip down to spark the explosion, leaving them enough time to get clear. Janson was to act as lookout while Manuel stood near by with a pistol in his pocket to cover them until the job was done.

Madeleine and Paul had planted two bombs and snapped the detonator pencils when they heard shouts. The Germans had noticed Janson loitering suspiciously and got down from their lorry, machine guns at the ready, to investigate. The square was crowded and Janson slipped away. Manuel calculated that there were too many people around to risk firing his gun. Madeleine and Paul froze as the Germans turned their attention towards them. Then Paul wrapped his arms around her and began kissing her passionately. Seconds passed.

She heard the Germans laughing: 'Those French! They're always at it!' They walked calmly away and a few minutes later heard the satisfying thud of their bombs exploding.

For Germans in Paris, their old playground had become a place of fear. After two years working as a signals technician, Private Walter Dreizner was sent home to Halle on leave. The journey opened his eyes. When he left Germany, its cities had been intact and total victory seemed only a matter of time. Now it looked like a nation on the edge of ruin. The return train took him through Leipzig, which was still recovering from the battering it had taken from mass British and American raids on successive nights in February. He arrived back in Paris on May Day to see the city 'out celebrating, all of Paris wearing lilies-of-the-valley . . . hundreds of pretty women race through the street on their pretty bicycles, flimsy dresses fluttering behind them like flags. Crowds flood the boulevards and out of the open doors of the cafés comes the sound of "Je suis seule ce soir", which is the hit of the hour.' There seemed to be something more than simple gaiety behind the fun. It was as if the crowds were asserting their ownership of the city. Dreizner knew he could no longer wander freely with his Leica and his girlfriend by his side, dropping in on French photographer and artist acquaintances and being treated as if he was a friend. The charming old streets and squares now reeked of menace. 'Paris is increasingly becoming a trap for us Germans,' he wrote. 'Those of us in uniform are in danger everywhere. Our enemies are invisible. They're lurking, waiting to ambush.'

The nervous mood was noted by eighteen-year-old Françoise Girardet. The occupiers now seemed 'more and more worried, hostile and aggressive . . . their attitude towards the Parisians became very disturbing and unpredictable'. One day she was strolling through the Printemps department store, looking at the expensive goods still on sale but which only Germans and black-market tycoons could afford. Suddenly 'shots rang out, the doors were closed and shouts were heard'. A German officer had been gunned down inside the shop, apparently by the Resistance. Françoise ran for the exit to find it locked. She guessed the German security men would arrive any second and start taking hostages. She looked around, trying not to panic. She was near the fur department and suddenly had the brainwave of hiding inside one of the long coats. She 'stayed there for what felt like half the day, hardly daring to breathe and listening to the shouts'. She heard footsteps approaching and German voices and stiffened with fear as they passed. Then the footsteps grew louder again and she 'stopped breathing, but no, they passed me and went away'. By now she was 'drenched with sweat and exhausted'. Then 'slowly and very carefully I crept out and peered over the banisters'. She saw a sales assistant approaching who told her, 'You did well to hide . . . they took ten people randomly from every floor.' The assassin meanwhile had got away.

For all the seething *bouillon* of danger on the streets and the prospect of invasion, Ernst Jünger retained his habitual detachment. 'The landing is on everyone's minds,' he noted airily in his diary on 8 May. 'The German command as well as the French believe it will happen in the next few days.' When it failed to materialize he noted disapprovingly that some senior staff officers were nonetheless still showing signs of anxiety, 'retreating to their rooms late at night with thick folders full of documents'. Jünger greatly admired his chief, the military commander for France Carl-Heinrich von Stülpnagel, known as 'Blondie' or 'Red' to distinguish him from his dark-haired cousin Otto, whom he had replaced in the role. He appreciated his 'princely qualities', which included a love of 'peace and quiet, of leisure and of the company of a small intellectual circle', which naturally included himself.

Yet even Stülpnagel, it seemed, was starting to feel the strain of the occupation. On 31 May Jünger noticed 'clearly, from one of his repeated gestures, that he is tired: with his left hand he tends to rub his back, as if supporting it, or keeping his posture erect. At the same time his face wears a worried expression.' His anxiety may have had as much to do with the progress of the conspiracy in which he was a key player as it did with the prospect of the Allied invasion. Though he had been willing to massacre civilians and co-operate with the Nazi extermination programme in his time on the Eastern Front, he had, as Jünger knew, 'been an opponent of [Hitler] since the very beginning'. With catastrophe looming for Germany, Stülpnagel had joined the circle of senior officers plotting to kill the Führer. When the moment came, he was going to order his men to join the coup and turn on the Nazi organization in France.

At every level, in every quarter, people were having to choose – or change – sides. As their situation worsened some arch-collaborators doubled down on a German victory. Those in control in Vichy seemed no longer to make any distinction between France's interests and those of the occupier. Hitler had taken to making government appointments himself. When he let it be known that he wanted Marcel Déat as labour minister, Pétain's objections were ignored and the socialist turned fascist began hatching plans to force yet more Frenchmen to work in German war factories. The interior minister and de facto Milice leader Joseph Darnand made the ultimate gesture of devotion to the Franco-German alliance, joining the Waffen-SS, swearing an oath of loyalty to Hitler and going off to fight on the Eastern Front. Out of conviction or calculation, most of the Nazis' most prominent French cheerleaders continued to denounce the Allies and praise the Germans. Two or three times a day Radio Paris shrilled with the voice of Philippe Henriot, who as well as serving as minister for information and propaganda had won a reputation as the 'the French Goebbels', heaping hate and abuse on Jews, communists and the Resistance.

Even Robert Brasillach's faith in German victory was slipping away. His ability to see only what he wanted to was deserting him. He now realized that with the Germans everywhere in retreat there would be no new Europe founded on Franco-German brotherhood. Pride, and his ironclad self-regard, prevented him from admitting he had backed the wrong side. The future now looked dangerous. But perhaps there was time to edge quietly back from the abyss before it engulfed him. Personal tragedy and professional troubles had clouded the previous year and a half. In 1942, his dear friend from the Deutsches Institut Karl Heinz Bremer was uprooted from Paris, put into uniform and sent to the Eastern Front where he was soon killed. Brasillach was devastated. He wrote a eulogy recalling the 'plans we made together

when peace came ... we wanted to go walking, go camping ...'
Their relationship had seemed to him like a physical manifestation of
the Franco-German national consummation he yearned for.

Bremer's death ended one dream. Events brought about the slow
demise of the other. By the summer of 1943 Brasillach could no longer
summon the will to pretend in print that all was well. The divisions
among the editorial staff at *Je Suis Partout* had widened, with the zealots led by Lucien Rebatet in the ascendant. Brasillach's tone grew
wistful and nostalgic. He still wrote affectionately about Pétain,
whom the hardliners despised, and lamented the failure of the National
Revolution to deliver a distinctly French version of fascism. The
crunch came in late July 1943 when, following the Allied invasion of
Sicily, Mussolini was abandoned by his fellow fascists and arrested.
When Brasillach's readers opened the next issue of the weekly to see
his thoughts on the drama they were surprised to find he had devoted
his column to a book review. Polemicizing was now a tricky and
potentially dangerous activity and Brasillach tried to persuade his colleagues that their paper should drop politics and recast itself as a
literary review. To the hardliners this was simply a betrayal. Brasillach
was branded a *dégonflé*, a real term of abuse in the ultras' vocabulary
signifying a faintheart who had shrivelled like a leaky balloon when
the going got tough. There was no way he could stay.

A week or two later, his name disappeared from the masthead
and the editorship passed to the fanatical collaborator Pierre Cous-
teau, brother of the oceanographer Jacques. The paper's diehard
stance did no harm to sales, which climbed to 350,000 and made the
shareholders richer. Brasillach's account of the episode was vague
enough to give his supporters grounds for later claiming that the
Germans had got him fired as punishment for his waning enthusiasm for the cause. In fact the occupiers continued to regard him as
a reliable ally. His services as a journalist and novelist were still in
demand and his articles now appeared in the Vichyite *Révolution
Nationale*. The censors liked what they saw. Following a piece on
the familiar theme of the 'collaboration of hearts' between France
and Germany a propaganda staff report noted he had 'resumed his
valuable political work'.

Even as he parted company with his old paper he was privately preparing his future defence. In the midst of the break-up he sent a letter to Rebatet, defining his position. 'I am Germanophile and French,' he wrote. 'French more than National Socialist really . . . I don't want to be more German than French.' Vanity would not allow him to admit the extent of the turnaround. In a damning and contradictory proviso, he stressed that he 'still had faith in the Wehrmacht and in Adolf's patriotism'. But it was already too late to change his tune. He knew that sooner rather than later, if he was to be sure of saving his skin, he would have to run away.

Social chameleons like Jean Cocteau had been happy to drink the invaders' champagne. For a while the playwright's willingness to mix with the top brass of the occupation had seemed more like vanity than treason. He could not be expected to pass up the best invitations in town just because the host was German. Now there was little time for parties and, if there had been, French guests would have thought hard before attending. Before long there would be some explaining to do. In the meantime, it was as well to have some good deeds in the bank for when the awkward questions started.

Cocteau had shown himself willing from time to time to intercede with the Germans on behalf of buddies in trouble. In March, one of his oldest friends suffered a catastrophe. Max Jacob had been a fixture of the Paris artistic scene from the early years of the century. Picasso met him soon after his arrival in Paris in 1901. Jacob helped him to learn French, shared a room with him and introduced him to fellow artists. Jacob was Jewish, but had converted to Catholicism and, long before the war, exiled himself to the small town of Saint-Benoît-sur-Loire about 90 miles south of Paris. There he led an austere existence, going to mass and doing the stations of the cross daily in the ancient Benedictine basilica. He wrote frequently to his friends, letters which revealed both deep spirituality and a shrewd strategic awareness. In January 1941 he was already predicting that the war would end with the arrival of the Americans, then a very distant prospect. Ultimately, though, he saw the struggle in simple terms. Hitler and Stalin looked 'very like the Antichrist. These are my sole political convictions.'

When the Germans arrived, someone tipped them off that the devout old gentleman who haunted the basilica was a Jew.

It was not until 24 February 1944 that the net closed around him in a routine round-up of the last remaining Jews in the area. He was taken to the military prison in nearby Orleans where he shared a cell with sixty others, sleeping on stinking mattresses. On the train to the Drancy transit camp the escorting gendarmes agreed to get letters to his friends, in which he asked for their help. Cocteau responded bravely, quickly rallying a band of high-profile supporters like Sacha Guitry to lobby their German contacts to intervene to spare the life of a man who, they asserted, was one of the great artists of the century. Max had specifically asked that 'Picasso . . . do something for me'. After years of silence, Picasso had rekindled their old friendship, making a rare trip from Paris to see him in Saint-Benoît in January the previous year. But when two emissaries tracked down Picasso in Le Catalan to ask him to intervene with the authorities, he turned them down. 'Max is an angel,' he said. 'He doesn't need our help to fly away from his prison.' Cocteau's efforts appeared to have paid off when an official at the German embassy who admired Jacob's work promised to help. On 5 March 1944, he told Cocteau that he had managed to get the Gestapo to agree to his release. Cocteau and a few companions jumped in a car and hurried to Drancy. It was too late. Max Jacob had died the day before of pneumonia. Two weeks afterwards, his friends gathered in the baroque church of Saint-Roch on the rue Saint-Honoré for a memorial service. Picasso had told the Abbé Morel, who conducted the service, that he would not be coming as 'everyone who turned up would be arrested'. He later thought better of it, for he was spotted hovering outside the church, apparently wanting to register his presence but unwilling to go in.

For Picasso, as for many others, passivity was no longer a prudent stance. As judgement day approached, it was necessary to put markers down indicating where your true loyalties lay. Early on in the occupation he had fallen ill for three days and spent the time writing. The result was a play called *Desire Caught by the Tail*, which revealed glimpses of his attitude both to life and to the war. It was not until 19 March 1944 that he decided to arrange its first performance, an informal affair, staged in the rue Monceau apartment of the surrealist writer and ethnographer Michel Leiris and his art-dealer wife Louise, where overflow stock from the gallery downstairs jostled on the walls. The parts were taken by the writers Raymond Queneau, Jean-Paul Sartre and Simone de Beauvoir, by Picasso himself and his mistress Dora Maar, and the piece was directed by Albert Camus. The audience was filled with the leading lights of the Paris intelligentsia including the poets Paul Éluard and Pierre Reverdy. Almost everyone there was either a communist of some description or a surrealist, or both. Camus and Reverdy were active members of the Resistance. Picasso was none of these things, though the play's lack of plot and its impenetrability to interpretation allowed it to be labelled as an exercise in surrealism.

The general tone of the work was nihilistic. Love is portrayed as a form of humiliation and humans are powerless in the face of the tidal wave of wickedness swamping the world. The final words, spoken by Big Foot, the Picasso-like protagonist, are: 'Light all the lanterns. With all our strength throw flights of doves against the bullets and lock the doors tight in the houses demolished by bombs.' It was not much of a play, but it summed up Picasso's fatalism and solipsism which together had made him unwilling to do anything that would risk upsetting his comfortable routines. His record under the occupation was hardly heroic. But the performance had gathered together some of the leading lights of the intellectual Resistance in his honour, and, when the time came, that could be very useful.

For de Gaulle, trying to shape events from afar, expelling the Germans was only the first step. The big prize was control of what came after. This was the thought that dominated his calculations as he at last turned his attention to the Resistance. The London broadcasts had been aimed at the French people as a whole and securing the loyalty of the disparate elements of the underground had been left to subordinates. Men who had risked everything to carry on the struggle in France were sometimes taken aback when they finally came face to face with the man they looked up to as their leader. Jacques Lecompte-Boinet, founder of the Ceux de la Résistance group, dined with de Gaulle and his wife Yvonne one evening in November 1943 in Algiers. After Madame de Gaulle had gone to bed, the general settled back and let rip with a long rant about the treachery of the Americans and British that lasted until well after midnight. 'While he was talking, I thought about how different he was from the idea that my Resistance comrades and I had developed about him,' Lecompte-Boinet recalled. 'Nothing about us resisters. Not a word of thanks . . . he affects not to have any need of us.'

Now he did. The Resistance had become a real factor in the story, offering both threat and opportunity. The biggest danger came from the communists. Having done more and suffered more than any other group, they would naturally be expecting a share of the post-victory spoils. There were already signs that the left generally had strong ideas about what the new France should look like. On 15 March 1944, the National Resistance Council representing all the groups adopted an egalitarian manifesto for the future, informally and optimistically known as 'The Happy Days'. It revived pre-war visions of a proletarian paradise with workers' co-operatives running everything. This was not what de Gaulle and his more conservative followers had in mind. There was an even more alarming possibility. As the old saying went, whoever controlled Paris controlled France. What if the communists used the mounting chaos to rise up and seize the city, just as their Communard forebears had done in 1871? Two years before, de Gaulle had unwisely declared that 'national insurrection' would be 'inseparable' from national liberation. It was a tactical declaration aimed at pleasing his Soviet supporters. Whether or not the French communists would take his words literally depended largely on Moscow.

De Gaulle had been on surprisingly good terms with the Soviets, ever since the USSR recognized him as the legitimate leader of France back in September 1941. The relationship was entirely cynical and pragmatic. Stalin used the Free French to prod the consciences of the Allies when demanding that they open a Second Front in Europe. De Gaulle flirted with Stalin in the hope of extracting concessions from the 'Anglo-Saxons', and at one low point in his relationship with Churchill even talked about moving Free French headquarters to the Soviet capital. If you believed the noises from Moscow, there was no danger of the PCF mounting a coup. They would not act without instructions from above and in January 1944 their leader Maurice Thorez, who had been exiled in Russia since the start of the war, declared that French communists were 'not thinking of taking power now or after the liberation'. This made sense. From Stalin's point of view, a putsch would be counter-productive. His prime interest was in winning the war and he had no wish to endanger relations with the Allies by meddling in France.

Naturally, de Gaulle was distrustful of communist assurances. His difficulty was he needed the communist Resistance for his strategy for the liberation to work. Some sort of uprising was necessary if France and in particular Paris could claim to have played a major part in their own salvation. However, revolt risked death and destruction on a massive scale and the political chaos it might unleash would be difficult if not impossible to control. What was needed was a spectacle, not a full-blooded insurgency. So it was that de Gaulle found himself on the same strategic page as the Americans and British when they discussed the role of the Resistance in the upcoming invasion. All agreed that there should be no national uprising to coincide with the landings and that activities should be limited to supporting the Allied armies by sabotage and intelligence gathering.

De Gaulle needed to tighten his control on the ground. As the Allied invasion approached, his disciples began to prepare France for his coming. In a move designed to impose order on the armed struggle, the French intelligence service in London divided the country into twelve regions and appointed a 'military delegate' who would oversee operations and co-ordinate with the Allied forces when they arrived. They were overseen by the national military delegate, Jacques Delmas. Delmas would now be working closely with Alexandre Parodi, a former senior civil servant living secretly in Paris whom de Gaulle had appointed as the representative of the provisional government. In February, all the fighting groups had been amalgamated into the Forces Françaises de l'Intérieur (FFI), the biggest element of which was the communists of the Francs-Tireurs et Partisans (FTP). In April, the FFI were placed under the orders of General Pierre

Koenig, commander of the Free French army standing by to join the invasion.

These arrangements were bound to lead to friction. The communists had been the boldest in confronting the Germans and had suffered the biggest losses. Whatever Moscow said, the local fighters had their own ideas of what an uprising meant. Now they would be increasingly told what to do by men with a different agenda and whose calculations would probably prescribe caution. Accepting the authority of de Gaulle was one thing. Ceding their hard-won place in the coming struggle was another. The arrest in May 1944 of Pierre Dejussieu, a career army officer who was chief of the FFI in the Paris region, triggered an early test of strength. Dejussieu was a Gaullist and the Gaullists wanted one of their own to replace him. There were endless arguments and debates before the matter was settled. On 1 June Henri Tanguy became leader of the FFI for the Paris region and the surrounding departments of the Île-de-France. That day he issued his first order, calling for 'an intensification of action'. It was signed 'Rol', his new *nom de guerre*, a homage to an old friend from Spain, Théo Rol, who had commanded the 'Commune de Paris' International Brigade and been killed in the fighting at Sierra de Caballos in September 1938. That was where the struggle against fascism had started. Now it was reaching its climax, and everything Rol-Tanguy had learned was about to be put to the test.

7. Ashore

On the morning of 6 June 1944 Jerry Salinger stood on board a landing craft butting through the choppy Channel waters towards the dunes of Utah beach. The coastline was grey and flat and flickered with flame. The air was filled with competing noises: the slap of the sea against the hull, the retching of seasick men and the clap of naval guns followed by the whoosh of big shells spinning towards the Germans. There had been a certain distance between Salinger and his comrades. As he joked to Whit Burnett, they had him tagged as 'a Quiet Intelligent Guy with one of them dry sense of humours'. Now they were all the same, stripped of distinctions and facing death as equals.

The bow grated over the sand and the door went down. The men on board revved their jeeps and drove down the ramp and into the shallow water, praying that all the hours they had spent waterproofing the engine would get them to dry land. Salinger was arriving with the rest of his small unit in the second wave of landings. They belonged to the Counter-Intelligence Corps, and their job was to follow in the wake of the advancing Ivy Division infantry, interrogating prisoners and gathering information. That did not mean they were safe. As they slithered up the fine sand of the tracks exiting the dunes, bombs from the German mortars kicked up dirty black plumes and the air was full of the snap and buzz of sniper and machine-gun fire.

Utah beach was at the north-western end of the D-Day landing zone, halfway up the Cotentin peninsula, the thumb of lush pasture-land which pokes north into the Channel from lower Normandy. While the Allied forces on the eastern flank pushed inland, the Ivy's three battalions – the 8th, 12th and 22nd – were tasked with swinging right to capture the vital port of Cherbourg on the northern tip of the peninsula. Once secured, men and materiel could funnel through it into the bridgehead.

The defenders had flooded large areas of the marshlands behind the shoreline, forcing the invaders to advance along routes that were well covered with guns. Nonetheless, the 12th Regiment to which Salinger's unit was attached, managed to move 5 miles inland by the end of D-Day. The landscape heavily favoured the Germans. The Americans relied on tanks to support the infantry. But the Shermans weighed 40 tons and were more than 8 feet wide. They were designed to sweep over wide plains, not crawl through the narrow sunken lanes criss-crossing the small fields and thick hedgerows that covered the Cotentin.

The Ivy's first objective was the town of Montebourg and the high ground behind it, a dozen miles distant and just under halfway along the road to Cherbourg. As the division pushed north, it ran into a well-designed German blocking line dominating the main road. It took seven days to capture Montebourg, during which, as the regimental history stated, 'Every yard gained was bitterly contested and dearly paid for.' The battle was terrifying, exhausting and bloody, and the contrasting tranquillity of the landscape gave it the quality of a nightmare. Picturesque stone villages that had never known war were ripped apart by shellfire and the fields filled up with slaughtered cattle, which lay, bloated and stinking, with their legs sticking surreally skywards. Many German positions had escaped the aerial reconnaissance cameras and were only revealed by the spurt of flame and smoke when an artillery piece or machine gun opened up. Each one had to be suppressed before the advance could continue.

Often it took repeated charges by small groups of GIs with rifles and grenades to clear them out. Each little victory brought no respite. German soldiers were drilled to counter-attack whenever a position fell. In the first weeks of the campaign the tempo never faltered. By the end of June, of the nearly 3,100 men who had come ashore with the 12th fewer than 1,000 remained. The fighting men made a distinction between themselves, who were 'soldiers', and the headquarters and rear echelon staff, who were merely 'in the army'. Jerry Salinger's counter-intelligence duties put him in the 'army' category, but in the narrow space of the battlefield everyone was in the firing line.

The regiment was held up for two days at the village of Émonde-ville on the road to Cherbourg. On the slopes behind Azeville, the

Germans had built an elaborate gun battery with multiple casemates which could hit everything to seaward and landward. In the years waiting for the invasion they had made themselves comfortable, and the facilities included a large 'casino' where they relaxed and held Saturday-night dances, bussing in girls from Cherbourg for their overnight entertainment. Much of the fighting took place around a waterlogged hollow at the entrance to Émondeville. It is clearly the scene of a Salinger short story called 'The Magic Foxhole', which recounts the descent into 'battle fatigue' of an educated misfit. Jerry remained true to Babe Gladwaller's admonition in 'The Last Day of the Last Furlough' that the participants should 'keep our mouths shut' about their experiences, for although the story contains only incidental mention of combat he chose never to publish it.

Jerry shared a jeep with John Keenan, the former New York rookie cop. They were sergeants and worked alongside three or four other non-coms under two officers. Salinger took an instant dislike to the bad-tempered captain in charge, who came from the East Coast upper classes and like to drink. Keenan remembered that although 'it wasn't our function to fight the enemy we were always under fire. We were always the subject of artillery, mortars and whatnot – it was constant.'

Bocage

It meant frequent dashes to take cover. 'I'm still scared,' Salinger wrote to Whit Burnett on 28 June. 'I'll tell you this: you never saw six-feet-two of muscle and typewriter ribbon get out of a jeep and into a ditch as fast as this baby can . . . No use in being foolhardy, I always say.' Keenan recalled one sticky moment when the two were separated and Jerry 'was with another fellow and came back raging . . . He said that son of a bitch. They were being shelled and under machine-gun fire. There was a ditch and they both jumped into the ditch . . . and he tried to push Jerry out . . . he never got along with him after that.'

The unit's job was to follow close behind the assault troops and when German positions fell to seize any records and maps and question prisoners. The German that Salinger had learned in Austria had been bolstered by two intensive army language courses and was very fluent and his French was well up to questioning locals about enemy dispositions and the identity of collaborators. Once, they found themselves intervening to spare their enemies. 'Paratroopers had taken some prisoners and they were ready to shoot them,' Keenan remembered. 'And we said, you really shouldn't . . . we tried to talk them out of it and eventually we did and we wound up taking the prisoners to the compound ourselves. But the soldiers were understandably furious because they had killed their people.'

There was the odd moment of respite from the noise, dead bodies, discomfort and exhaustion. Jerry and John were the first to drive into Barfleur, a pretty fishing village south of Cherbourg. They were hungry and knocked on the door of a closed-up café. The owner let them in and served up a meal. Soon afterwards they were joined by Barfleur's mayor, who sat down with them, proclaimed the town officially liberated and produced a bottle of the local Calvados apple brandy. Years later, talking to his son, Salinger had many gripes about the tedium of army life, the queuing up, the cold and the lousy food. But he told Matt that it was only when he got to Paris that he really felt frightened, and it was an incident involving a French mob, not German soldiers, that triggered it.

The invasion had been minutely planned and massed enormous resources. Three weeks after the landing, there were a million men ashore supported by thousands of tanks, and the fighters and bombers of the Allied air forces ruled the skies. However, as the overall commander Dwight D. Eisenhower knew well, 'unless you can put a battalion [about 600 fighting men] against a squad [nine to twelve men], nothing is certain in war'. Estimates of how far and how fast the Allies could expand the beachhead soon proved optimistic. The original scheme was for the British and Canadians to push forward from the eastern landing beaches to anchor the left side of the Allied line at Caen. They were then to move south to capture Falaise, a small town 30 miles to the south. Having taken Cherbourg, the Americans were to head south down the Cotentin to Avranches at the base of the peninsula.

The line established would then begin an enormous wheel eastwards, pushing the Germans back over the Seine. But the wheel could not turn until the obstacle of Caen had been removed and the Germans threw everything into a fierce defence of the city. An objective that the British general Bernard Montgomery predicted would be in his hands within forty-eight hours of D-Day did not fall completely until 19 July, by which time the medieval city had been reduced to ruins. Along the rest of the front the Battle of the Beachhead soon turned into what Eisenhower described as 'dogged "doughboy" fighting at its worst', evoking memories of the trenches of the last war. The planners' timetable was in tatters and it was not until D-Day plus 50 that the Allies held the line they had expected to reach on D-Day plus 5.

As Salinger was going ashore at Utah, Ernest Hemingway was watching the assault on Omaha beach, 30 miles to the east. Papa was not in great shape. His head still hurt from the car smash a fortnight before. His legs were shaky and it had required a bosun's chair to swing him across to the *Empire Anvil*, the infantry landing ship from which landing craft would ferry troops ashore. The authorities had decreed that the world's most famous novelist was not to hit the beach with them. Hemingway was brave or foolhardy enough to do so had he been allowed. As it was, he was spared the high risk of death or injury. Omaha would turn out to be the most lethal of the five landing beaches. By the end of the day 2,400 American troops were dead or wounded. However, he managed to get pretty close, trundling in on a 36-foot-long 'coffin-shaped' landing craft with a party of combat engineers and their equipment before withdrawing. In the account he wrote for *Collier's* magazine, he assigned himself a central role in the proceedings. As the skipper scanned the shoreline trying to identify Colleville-sur-Mer, codenamed 'Fox Green' beach, where the troops were to be put ashore, Hemingway related how he had spotted the landmark church tower through his 'old miniature Zeiss glasses'. As they moved closer, it was he who had seen that something was badly wrong and that the first waves of infantry were pinned down, unable to get on to the high ground behind.

The captain of the landing craft, a 'handsome, hollow-cheeked boy with a lot of style and a sort of easy petulance', a Virginian called Lieutenant Robert Anderson, obeyed readily when Papa advised that they 'coast along' to find a less perilous spot. At one point they came under heavy fire rescuing survivors from a half-sunk landing craft. After much confusion and delay they finally began their run in to the shore where Hemingway saw 'three tanks coming along the beach, barely moving they were advancing so slowly. The Germans let them cross the open space where the valley opened onto the beach and it was absolutely flat with a perfect field of fire.' The lead tank was hit and two men managed to scramble out but no more, and it 'began to blaze up and burn fiercely'. The survivors were taken aboard, then a second tank caught fire. As they reversed engines and backed away towards safety, the destroyers offshore rained shells down on the concrete machine-gun emplacements overlooking the beach. Hemingway told his readers he saw 'a piece of German about three foot long with an arm on it sail high up into the air in the fountaining of one shell burst'. It reminded him 'of a scene in [the ballet] Petroushka'. Eventually the troops were put ashore, the landing craft reversed to safety 'and that was that'.

That night Hemingway was back in London in the Dorchester Hotel, where a party of British pressmen were waiting, drinks in hand, to hear his account, a more dramatic tale than the rather flat and overly

detailed story he laid out in *Collier's*. By now he was claiming to have
actually made it ashore and told how he had jolted a young lieutenant into action, kicking him 'squarely in the butt' when he seemed
not to hear his instruction to get off the beach before the Germans
zeroed in on him. As the stories rippled outwards, Hemingway's D-
Day heroics multiplied. In later versions, one of which found its way
into print, he took command of a group of GIs huddled under murderous machine-gun fire and ordered them to dig in until the tanks
arrived.

The myth-making was part of the Hemingway performance and
was received by his listeners with varying degrees of indulgence. He
was fun when he wanted to be and the professional military men who
encountered him often enjoyed his company. They were impressed
by his celebrity, appreciated his generosity and had no doubt about
his physical courage. After his return from Normandy a veteran pilot,
Group Captain Peter Wykeham-Barnes, took him on a night sortie in
his Mosquito to observe the V-1 flying bombs that had started to rain
down on London and the south-east. When they spotted an incoming 'doodlebug' Hemingway urged him to close in to deal with it.
Wykeham-Barnes refused at first, wary of getting shot down by
friendly fire from the Portsmouth anti-aircraft batteries, but soon
gave in. His caution was justified and the aircraft 'danced around like
a leaf in a whirlwind' when caught in an explosion as some unseen
night fighter downed the V-1. When they landed, 'Ernest seemed to
have loved every moment.' The problem was his unstoppable urge to
show off, even in front of men who had seen twenty times more of
war than he had. To Wykeham-Barnes and the other squadron pilots
'he had a great deal to say on . . . courage and fear, traditional Hemingway topics, and though he was as intelligent as one might expect,
he tended to take a tougher and brawnier line than that acceptable to
us worn-out old veterans'.

Sometimes Papa's boasting seemed aimed at convincing himself as
much as anyone else. Flight Lieutenant John Pudney was a peacetime
poet and journalist, serving as a press officer in the RAF and assigned
to look after Hemingway when he went on a trip to a southern England airbase housing aircraft supporting the invasion. Pudney had

admired him from afar but up close found his egotism and bragging 'shameful'. It seemed 'he was a fellow obsessed with playing the part of Ernest Hemingway and hamming it to boot: a sentimental nineteenth-century actor called upon to act the part of a twentieth-century tough guy'. If so, the invasion had given him a vast new stage to play on, though he seemed in no great hurry to leave England and get back to Normandy.

The Martha Gellhorn period was over. Robbed of the *Collier's* assignment by her own husband, she had managed to make her own way across the Channel on D-Day on a hospital ship, returning with a cargo of wounded. She sent him a note saying she was pleased he had got back unharmed from his own trip and announced that she was off to war again, to the now overlooked Italian front. This was welcome news. It meant there would be no professional competition in Normandy from Mrs Hemingway and no chance of running into her in London as he squired his new love Mary Welsh around town. But it would not do for Papa to be seen to be too far from the action for too long. After a brief, boozy trip to Cherbourg, on 18 July he flew back to France, and this time he stayed.

Bayeux was the only town of any size captured by the Allies in the first few days of the invasion. Early seizure saved it from the fate of many others. While they were bombed and shelled to ruins, Bayeux cathedral and the fine old stone houses around it survived intact. It was there, eight days after D-Day, that Charles de Gaulle arrived back on French soil. The return was everything he could have wished for. When he left, he was unknown. Now the crowds greeted him warmly, even though none of the troops who had freed them were French and de Gaulle had had to rely on the Americans to get him there. It did not matter. With his visit, he was starting to take ownership of the invasion and establish the right of the Free French to represent the future of France.

The question of what to do with de Gaulle once the troops were firmly ashore was a tricky one for the Allies. Despite having grudgingly accepted his authority, President Roosevelt was reluctant to give him any more recognition until the internal situation in France clarified. Less than two weeks before D-Day, the Committee of National Liberation in Algiers declared itself the provisional government of the French republic with de Gaulle at its head. All along, Roosevelt's worry had been that de Gaulle would seek to impose the virtual state he had created in exile and his own authoritarian rule on the French people without them having a say in the matter. He believed that, until that was done, France should be treated like Italy and come under the control of the Allied Military Government in Occupied Territories. In the meantime, he continued to hope that de Gaulle would be put back in his box, opining as late as 15 June that 'other parties will spring up as the Liberation goes on and . . . de Gaulle will become a very little figure'. There was little chance of that. De Gaulle's stature as the legitimate embodiment of the nation was growing by the hour and as Churchill had wryly pointed out to Roosevelt at the time the provisional government was declared, 'it is very difficult to cut the French out of the liberation of France'.

De Gaulle's strength lay in his inflexibility. His strategy from the outset was to demand the impossible, and he decided at the beginning of this crusade that he 'had to climb to the heights and never look down'. Churchill had seen the point of him immediately, even though he knew almost nothing about him. Roosevelt would never be convinced. But de Gaulle had a champion whose support could cancel out the presidential antipathy. This was Dwight D. Eisenhower, supreme Allied commander, who had the military and political wherewithal to get de Gaulle much of what he wanted.

'Ike' had the rare distinction of being fond of the general. It helped that he was a Francophile, having served in Paris for fourteen months from July 1928 when he worked on the Battle Monuments Commission tasked with commemorating the US military's role in the Great War. He and his wife Mamie and son John loved their 'nice life and nice group of friends' and lived in unaccustomed luxury in the 16th arrondissement in an apartment overlooking the Seine. His Paris was not the film-set bohemia of cafés and *bals musette* enjoyed by Americans like Hemingway, drawn there by the creative atmospherics and wonderfully advantageous dollar exchange rate. Unlike them he had a real understanding of what was going on behind the gay façade. His downtime was spent socializing in the grand Cercle de l'Union Inter-alliée club on the rue du Faubourg-Saint-Honoré where he met the French military and governmental hierarchy. He spoke competent if heavily accented French and took a serious interest in politics. This gave him an insight and sympathy rare among senior Allied com-manders when it came to understanding the complex problems facing de Gaulle as he tried to find a formula to impose his authority on a difficult nation.

They had first engaged professionally in North Africa. Before the Free French established their authority there, Eisenhower had been forced to deal with the former Vichy duo of Admiral François Darlan and General Henri Giraud. He found Giraud 'a terrible blow to our expectations'. Darlan was notoriously slippery, a man whose ideo-logical flexibility had allowed him to serve as head of the navy in Léon Blum's Popular Front government and, briefly, as prime minis-ter to Pétain, before defecting to the Allies. But he was no longer a problem, having been conveniently assassinated by a royalist fanatic in Algiers in December 1942, with a gun which, it turned out much later, had been provided by the local representative of the US Office of Strategic Services, the forerunner of the CIA. De Gaulle and the Free French were a great improvement and the two men got on well, though inevitably a certain distance remained. As Eisenhower recalled: 'He and I were never Charles and Ike . . . But there was always a good feeling, not only of respect and admiration, but a very measurable degree of affection.'

Ike had an unusual ability to appreciate the perspectives of others. He had an equal talent for inspiring trust. He admired de Gaulle's solitary devotion to duty and his courage in the face of the vast task he had set himself. He broadly agreed with his mission, and was pre-pared to do what he could to help him achieve it, even if this meant some difficult moments with the White House and State Depart-ment. De Gaulle unbent with Eisenhower in a way that he did with no other Allied leader. He even trusted him. The two forged a crucial understanding in Algiers as 1943 drew to a close and the new year, with all its promise and dangers, dawned. Eisenhower was just about to head to Washington prior to going on to London to take up

supreme command of the invasion and asked de Gaulle to call on him
in his office. There he deftly made it seem that it was the Free French
who were doing him a favour, rather than the other way round, telling him: 'For the coming battle I shall need not only the co-operation
of your forces, but still more the assistance of your officials and the
moral support of the French people.' De Gaulle was delighted and
took it as an apology for all the previous snubs he had suffered at the
hands of the Americans. 'Splendid!' he said. 'You are a man, for you
know how to say, "I was wrong."' The meeting, said Ike later, turned
into 'a love feast'. When they parted company two crucial points had
been agreed. Eisenhower pledged that whatever 'theoretical position'
Washington might take, 'as far as I am concerned, I will recognize no
French Power in France other than your own'. He also agreed that
when the time came Paris would be liberated by French troops. To
that end a French division would be sent to England as soon as possible, under the command of General Philippe Leclerc, to join the
invasion forces.

Eisenhower believed that, once ashore, de Gaulle 'would represent
the only authority that could produce any kind of French co-
ordination and unification'. Two days before the D-Day landing, he
gave him a personal briefing at his field headquarters near Portsmouth,
flattering him by asking him for his advice on whether he should hold
off on launching the attack until the weather improved. At the meeting it was agreed that, once battle was joined, the Resistance bands
grouped together in the French Forces of the Interior the week before
D-Day would be meshed with the conventional Free French forces
and come under the overall command of their leader, General Pierre
Koenig. Ike had already done de Gaulle a huge service by settling for
all practical purposes the argument about who controlled the liberated territories once the troops were ashore. In a directive issued on 25
May he told American and British commanders: 'Military government will *not* be established in liberated France ... the French
themselves will conduct all aspects of civil administration in their
country, even in areas of military operations.'

On 15 June in Bayeux those words became a reality. The town itself
was in a state of limbo. The local prefect was a Vichy man but moved

quickly to ingratiate himself with the British military authorities controlling the sector. The Free French had appointed a representative but he was stuck behind enemy lines, so when de Gaulle arrived on the morning after a rough sea crossing there was no one from his own organization to greet him. He was still a mysterious presence, 'Général Micro' as the collaborationist press mockingly called him, a voice on the radio rather than a creature of flesh and blood. As the jeep carrying him approached the town some people on the road mistook one of the accompanying officers for the great man himself. Even de Gaulle must have felt a flicker of doubt as they entered the town and drove up the slope to where the great cathedral loomed over the rooftops. In fact, the reception he got was reassuringly normal. The locals took the apparition in their stride and, according to one in the general's party, displayed 'warm and sympathetic enthusiasm, but in no way delirious and curiously natural – men in their bourgeois clothes, women in their summer dresses, a few gendarmes . . . it was rather as if a very esteemed and popular Republican dignitary had come one Sunday in peacetime to inaugurate a local fair'. The impression of continuity was exactly what de Gaulle was hoping to create. When he departed, he left behind an aide called François Coulet to assume power in the town on his behalf. For a while Bayeux would be the capital of the new France. But it would be some weeks yet before French people saw the first French soldiers.

At 1.30 on the afternoon of 4 August – two long months after D-Day – the moment that Captain Raymond Dronne had been fantasizing about for four years finally arrived. He was standing on the soil of France – or, to be more exact, on the beach of the Madeleine on the east coast of the Cotentin – and he felt 'my heart tighten and my eyes get rather damp'. He brushed the sand with his fingertips, as 'throwing myself flat to kiss the land of my birth was strictly the stuff of novels'. Then it was on with the business of overseeing the disembarkation of the 9ème Compagnie of the Régiment de Marche du Tchad, known to all as La Nueve. They had gone ashore with the rest of Leclerc's 2ème Division Blindée to at last join the Battle of Normandy. Dronne had no knowledge of the agreement reached in

Algiers between de Gaulle and Eisenhower that the 2DB was to liberate Paris. But 'for all of us that was our dream . . . everyone knew that whoever had Paris had France'.

In a way it was a strange ambition. There were a handful of Frenchmen among the 160-strong ranks of La Nueve, some of them *pieds noirs* from Algeria who had never set foot in France except when called on to go to war. The great majority of the soldiers, though, were Spaniards. Dronne had come to love them. As he watched them on the boat taking them across the Channel, playing cards with deadly seriousness, knives and pistols on the table, he felt a surge of pride. They were defiant, unruly and 'totally lacking in military spirit'. But that did not stop them being 'magnificent soldiers, brave and experienced warriors', as they had proved many times in the fighting in North Africa. This wasn't their war. After escaping to France following Franco's victory they had been locked up, starved and worked half to death by the very people they were now about to shed their blood for. But they 'had committed themselves to us, they had spontaneously and voluntarily espoused our cause – because it was the cause of liberty and they were fighters in the cause of freedom'.

By mid-afternoon, most of the company strength, seventeen US-supplied M3 half-tracks, anti-tank weapons and heavy and light machine guns were off the ship. They mounted up and headed west to their first bivouac, a village on the west side of the Cotentin. The landscape they moved through reminded Dronne of pictures of ruined villages in the last war. The roads rumbled with supply trucks and aircraft criss-crossed the sky, seemingly unconcerned about the Luftwaffe. Dronne went in search of news from the Americans. It was good. General George S. Patton's Third Army had broken through the German defences at Avranches, opening the way to the Brittany peninsula. It seemed they had arrived just as the battle was moving into a decisive phase.

That evening Dronne and a few of the men came across a tall, thin peasant woman who looked like a witch in a cartoon, standing in front of her house. Some of the Spaniards tried to talk to her, asking where her husband was, to be told he was a prisoner in Germany. Their cheery assurance that he would be home soon seemed to leave her unmoved.

They persisted, saying she 'must be glad to see the back of the Germans!' She raised her head and replied slowly: 'The German gentlemen were very nice. They paid top prices for the butter.' With that she went back indoors and shut the door behind her. The Spaniards were glum as they walked away. 'If all the French are like that,' said one, 'we might as well have stayed where we were.' Their disappointment was equalled by their surprise at conditions in the countryside. In England they had been told the French were starving. In Normandy at least, the locals appeared remarkably well fed. Next morning, when the 'witch' went down to the henhouse she found it was empty. Strangely, her pig had also disappeared. La Nueve were nowhere to be seen, having struck camp and headed off towards the action.

By the time the 2DB arrived in early August, the Allies' situation had improved greatly. With the capture of Caen the British and Canadians, together with a division of Poles, were able at last to move southwards to their next objective: Falaise. On the western flank, on 17 July, the American First Army had cracked the main focus of German resistance at Saint-Lô. This opened the way for the US Third Army under the energetic command of General Patton to strike southwards to Avranches and on into Brittany. The Germans' best option in the struggle to contain the Allies was to withdraw the surviving troops and equipment to a new line of defence on the eastern bank of the Seine, which is what the supreme commander in the west, Field Marshal Günther von Kluge, proposed. He was overruled by Hitler, who ordered him to withdraw valuable Panzer divisions from around Caen, where they were continuing to severely hamper Anglo-Canadian operations, and throw them into a counter-attack to cut off the American advance.

It was the equivalent of a gambler trying to recoup heavy losses by heaping all his chips on one spin of the roulette wheel. Hitler's intended 'masterstroke' was launched on 6 August from Mortain and aimed at Avranches 20 miles to the west. Its slim chances of success were further undermined by the Allies' foreknowledge of the operation from decoded Ultra intercepts. The thrust was halted and the German armour destroyed. Everything was in place for a great Allied coup. The German armies were now in danger of being enveloped as the American forces swung east and north to hook up with the British, Canadians and Poles. The encirclement that followed was called the Battle of the Falaise Pocket and, in the words of the American ground forces chief General Omar Bradley, it offered an opportunity for total annihilation of an enemy force that comes an army commander's way 'once every hundred years'.

The 2DB and the Ivy were both in the thick of the new phase of the battle. Leclerc's men were new to tank warfare, but after some inevitable initial mix-ups under the testy eye of their commander they got the hang of it. Leclerc was supposed to go nowhere without his personal protection squad, but he frequently gave them the slip, racing off in his jeep to supervise the front-line action and exposing himself to enemy fire. These excursions earned him the respect of his men and deepened the division's sense of identity. Leclerc became *le Patron* or; on account of his ever present walking stick, *Père la Canne*.

The action was observed by Ernest Hemingway, who after a late start had attached himself to the Ivy and was having, as he wrote to Mary Welsh, 'a tough, fine time'. Papa had quickly won over the division's commander General Raymond 'Tubby' Barton. Barton assigned him to the 22nd Infantry Regiment and the care of its commanding officer Colonel Charles Trueman Lanham. 'Buck' Lanham was short, touchy and tough-talking, a career soldier who also wrote stories and poetry. The pair were around the same age and took to each other instantly, forging a lifelong friendship. Hemingway had been an ambulance driver in the First World War and in Spain was essentially a scribbler. He had never done a day's military training. In the company of professional soldiers he showed due respect, especially if, like Barton and Lanham, they listened politely to his tall tales and freely offered situation reports and advice. In tight corners, Hemingway was good company, capable of creating a party wherever there was an open bottle and a potential audience. Amid the doubt and the fear, it was good to have people like Papa around.

As the regiment pushed southwards then joined the wheel east, Hemingway followed close behind. For nine days he puttered about

the front crammed into the sidecar of a motorcycle combination captured from the Germans and driven by a red-headed private from
upstate New York called Archie Pelkey, nicknamed 'Red'. It was the
realization of an enduring fantasy in which he was not an onlooker
but a man of action. He wrote as if he was a participant ('This is the
8th day we have been attacking all the time . . .') and in his letters to
Mary made it clear that he was thoroughly happy and fulfilled. He
was leading, he told her, 'a very jolly and gay life, full of deads [sic],
German loot, much shooting, much fighting, hedges, small hills, dusty
roads, metalled roads, green country, wheat fields, dead cows . . . dead
horses, tanks . . .'

On 5 August Hemingway asked Barton for permission to bring an
old friend over to join him. Robert Capa was only a dozen miles away
in Granville, which had been liberated six days before, and soon the
pair were back in harness reliving the old days in Spain. Unlike Hemingway, Capa had gone ashore on D-Day, landing in the first wave
with troops from the 1st Division, a terrifying experience which as he
freely admitted had left him trembling with fear. Having got his
film back to England, he took the next ship to France and since then
had stayed the course, witnessing the liberation of Cherbourg and following Patton's tanks on the drive south. When Hemingway sent a
captured German staff saloon to collect him he was somewhat unwilling to answer his summons, but the pull of their old comradeship
prevailed. Capa was well used to the older man's capers and recorded
wryly how Papa had lost no time in letting him know that among the
men of the Ivy 'he was as widely respected for his guts and military
knowledge as he was for his writing'. In a letter to Mary, Hemingway
hinted that a decoration for valour might be in the pipeline, claiming
that he 'had been cited for something moderately impressive but probably nothing [will] ever come of it because of irregularity of actions'.
This was pure fantasy. None of his 'actions' had any military worth.
They were, though, certainly irregular. He described to Mary with
adolescent glee how he had set off on the motorbike with some companions to watch Ivy troops attack an enemy-held village. While
'ahead of the infantry' he had been 'knocked down by a tank shell and
then fired on by tank machine gun and two people with machine

pistols on each side of the road. Had to pretend to be dead until quite a while later and could hear Germans talking on other side of hedge at about 10 feet. They spoke very disrespectfully of your big friend who they considered dead.'

Capa was with him and corroborated much of the story. According to his account, when Hemingway told him he planned to take a shortcut to get to the village, 'I didn't like it at all. Papa looked at me with disgust and said I could stay behind. I couldn't do anything but follow him, but I made it clear that I was going under protest. I told him that Hungarian strategy consisted of going behind a good number of soldiers, and never of taking lonely shortcuts through no-man's-land.' Approaching the village there was no sound of shooting to indicate that the Americans were ahead of them and Capa 'began to feel very uncomfortable. Papa pooh-poohed me, and I followed under even more protest.' As they rounded a curve in the path with Hemingway in the lead, a shell landed ten yards away from him and he was 'thrown into the air and landed in a ditch'. Capa and the rest of the crew were safe but 'not so Papa . . . the ditch was shallow, and his behind stuck out at least an inch. Tracer bullets were hitting the dirt just above his head, and the popping, which came from a light German tank at the entrance to the village, continued without a let up.' He was pinned down for two hours until the Germans were distracted by the belated arrival of the American troops.

When Hemingway emerged from the ditch to rejoin them 'he was furious', Capa reported, 'not so much at the Germans as at me, and accused me of standing by during his crisis so that I might take the first picture of the famous writer's dead body'. That evening 'relations were somewhat strained between the strategist and the Hungarian military expert'. In Normandy, Capa had proved himself no less courageous than Hemingway, but he was wiser and more gracious, and understood something that Papa did not – they were observers, not warriors, and that for all the incidental dangers their experience was very different from that of the infantry who lived in the open, eating monotonous rations out of mess tins, always dirty, exhausted and scared. Even the many reporters who did not share Hemingway's urge to prove themselves under fire took big risks. But at the end of the day they could pull back to headquarters for decent food and wine and a good night's sleep.

Jerry Salinger was in the middle of the battles that Hemingway was watching. Both men were now in the same sector, in the area around Mortain, where on 12 August Hitler lost his gamble and the German counter-offensive petered out. His unit had shared the fighting but Jerry still found time to write home. One letter, dated 7 August, was a reply to an earlier letter from a girl he had known at Ursinus College called Frances Glassmoyer. In it he reminisced about student days, calling up memories of amateur dramatics and half-remembered crushes that must have brought comfort in the middle of the dust, heat and death. It felt like half a lifetime ago since he had left America, about 1918 to be precise, 'in the year, I believe, when Wilson delivered his fourteen points' – a facetious reference to the American president's famous plan for peace. He said little about his daily life except that he dug 'foxholes down to a cowardly depth and [I] am scared stiff constantly and can't remember ever having been a civilian'. Even now he could never forget that he was a writer. He had brought his typewriter with him, stowed in the trailer towed behind the jeep in which he and John Keenan travelled, and whenever things quietened down would tap away anywhere he could, even in the middle of a field, using a wooden crate or whatever was handy as a desk.

He was disappointed that Frances had not yet seen the 15 July issue

of the *Saturday Evening Post*, which carried 'The Last Day of the Last Furlough', of which he was clearly very proud. In a throwaway line he revealed some surprising news. Apparently Jerry had run into Papa on one his forays around the front line, and the pair had hit it off immediately. 'Over here I met and have had a couple of long talks with Ernest Hemingway,' he wrote. 'He's extremely nice and completely unpatriotic. He's here for *Collier's*.'

Before their meeting Hemingway had been an icon, remote, unreal and probably ripe for knocking down. Jerry had been rude about him in print on occasion and Hemingway's strong, silent men of action seemed the antithesis of the sensitive, reflective types like Holden Caulfield whom Salinger had created to try to make sense of the world. But at the same time in a letter to Burnett he had defended him from attacks by lesser talents. Hemingway had 'worked too hard and given too much satisfaction' for inferior critics to 'take a swing' at him. In the flesh Hemingway came as a pleasant surprise, warm and uncondescending. And for all his fascination with war, he was free of any illusions about its glorious nature. It was this side of Hemingway that led emotionally intelligent people like Capa to never quite give up on him when the boastful or mean-spirited traits were in the ascendant. Salinger would see it and be warmed by it again soon, when both had emerged safely on the other side of the battlefield.

The Germans' failure at Mortain was the end of their attempt to stem the invasion. The Allies moved in to finish them off, kettling 50,000 troops into a vast killing field around Falaise. There they were strafed and bombed from the air and pounded by artillery. Even then they refused to surrender and launched numerous attempts to try to punch their way out of the encirclement. On 12 August the men of La Nueve were sent to block the line around the village of Écouché, south of Falaise. Over the next few days they repelled several counter-attacks, inflicting heavy losses and taking more than 200 prisoners. Towards the end of the afternoon of 17 August, a section posted to the north of the village near the banks of the Orne river saw about sixty Germans trying to creep past their position. The section commander ordered his men to charge the much larger enemy force, supported by fire from their half-tracks. The Germans abandoned their heavy kit and packs and swam across the river. As they climbed the bank, they were cut down by the half-tracks' machine guns, 'collapsing like puppets with their strings cut and turning the water red'. When they searched the dead, they found they belonged to the SS 'Das Reich' Division. It would be the source of much satisfaction later when they learned that these were the same men who two months earlier had murdered 633 civilian men, women and children in the Haute-Vienne village of Oradour-sur-Glane.

The Battle of the Falaise Pocket had eviscerated the German army in northern France. Visiting the battlefield Eisenhower reported that it was 'literally possible to walk for hundreds of yards at a time, stepping on nothing but dead and decaying flesh'. Many Germans nonetheless managed to escape but they left behind their heavy equipment and would struggle to regroup or offer lasting resistance to the Allies as they swept eastwards. The way was now clear to Belgium and the Franco-German border. It was also open to Paris.

'I pissed in the Seine this morning,' George Patton informed his chief Omar Bradley on 19 August. Patton and his men were now just 30 miles west of Paris. Despite this tantalizing proximity, neither Patton nor Bradley nor Eisenhower had any intention of diverting from their line of march to free the city. Paris had never loomed large in the invasion plan. From the beginning, Eisenhower's intention once the breakout began was to send his armies north and south of the capital and drive on to the Low Countries and Germany as fast as their supply lines would allow. On the way, they would join up with the Allied forces coming up from the south following the invasion on the French Mediterranean coast successfully launched on 15 August. The campaign was throbbing with the accumulated momentum of success and this was no time to change the conception. Liberating the city risked sucking them into a street battle that could last for weeks. The population was hungry and the occupiers' intentions were unpredictable, but there were much bigger considerations in play. The Germans were on the run at last, and suddenly it once again felt possible that peace might arrive in 1944. That was the real prize. Paris could wait.

8.   Reveille

Paris watched the progress of the invasion and held its breath. It was three weeks after D-Day before the city began to stir. On 1 July, a column of young men and women gathered outside the Saint-Martin Métro station then streamed down the boulevard towards the place de la République. Employees from the area's garment and leather work-shops came out to swell the numbers. Then housewives queuing to buy what food was still available joined in. As they walked they chanted: 'Down with Pétain!', 'Laval to the firing squad!', 'Death to Darnand!' and 'Milk for our children!' Young men appeared out of nowhere, a few of them with guns in their hands, and formed a cordon around the marchers. It was not much protection, but their presence raised the crowd's spirits and sharpened the mood of defiance. When the demonstration reached the square, the German military police moved in, driving trucks into the crowd and on to the pavements and sending demonstrators flying.

French police vans were also parked up around the square, but instead of piling out to reinforce the Germans the *flics* watched from the sidelines. No one could miss the significance of their decision to sit this one out. Since the first *gardien de la paix* had raised his hand in salute to Hitler's motorcade in June 1940, the city's police had done the Germans' bidding, rounding up Jews and resisters and delivering them to deportation and death without a murmur of protest. Now, it seemed, their commitment to collaboration was cooling.

That impression was reinforced a fortnight later. The 1 July demonstration was an impromptu affair involving at most a few thousand. The Fourteenth of July was Bastille Day. Until 1940 it had been a public holiday when the nation celebrated the overthrow of tyranny and the birth of democracy, but since then it had been banned by the Germans. This year it had been reinstated as a holiday, but public celebrations remained illegal. As the anniversary approached,

the communists and the clandestine trade union organizations saw a
chance to rouse the city in a massive popular protest against the
occupation and support for the Resistance. The conservative elements of the leadership were more cautious. What if the appeal fell
flat? Or worse, it was a great success inviting terrible reprisals from
the Germans and the Milice? There was another threat that worried
all wings of the Resistance. With the people waking from their long
sleep, there was a real danger that, if protests on the streets now set
the pace, the Resistance would be left behind. In an effort to seize
the initiative the leadership called on the population to mark the
holiday with mass demonstrations. Whether in direct response or of
their own volition, Parisians came out en masse in the biggest show
of defiance since the Germans arrived. Up to 150,000 men, women
and children, dressed in blue, white and red, promenading arm in
arm and singing the 'Marseillaise', filled the streets and squares of
the working-class areas. The Germans broke up some gatherings,
shooting in the air and making arrests. But once again, despite being
under orders to intervene, the French police did little or nothing
and, in the place de la Contrescarpe in the Latin Quarter, even joined
in the singing.

As at many times in the city's history, there was electricity in the
air that presaged the coming storm. All the risks and sacrifices made
by the Resistance had been in preparation for this hour, but now
that it was upon them leaders were uncertain what to do next. The
great challenge of the preceding years had been simply to stay in
existence and huge energy had gone into building structures that
pulled together the multiple outlooks and ideologies within the
ranks. The French loved committees and the result was a bewildering array of acronyms. The foundation organization was the
National Resistance Council (CNR), Jean Moulin's great creation,
which since 1942 had grouped together nine resistance movements,
five pre-war political parties and two trade unions. It oversaw the
Military Action Committee (COMAC), which in theory directed
the activities of the armed groups. Since February 1944, these had
been combined into the French Forces of the Interior, the FFI. To
complicate things, Paris also had its own, communist-dominated

Committee for the Liberation of Paris (CPL). Beneath lay a multitude of subsets.

For all the theoretical perfection of the Resistance organizational model, its successful working would depend on the qualities of those who operated it. The decision to resist had made comrades of men and women who before the war might well have despised each other. Shared danger and suffering had engendered mutual respect and affection. The resisters were united by a single overwhelming desire: to free France from the Germans. Now that liberation was in sight, their willingness to subordinate their political agendas to the greater good was about to be tested.

The potential for trouble was apparent in the contrasting backgrounds and outlooks of two figures at the heart of the coming struggle. The FFI in Paris was under the control of a proud communist proletarian, thirty-six-year-old Henri Tanguy, his chosen pseudonym 'Rol' honouring a comrade who had died in Spain. In his two stints of national service, he had never risen higher than private, but he now held the rank of colonel.

He was working under Jacques Delmas, twenty-nine, smooth, handsome and highly educated, a man whose conservatism ran as deep as his tennis-club tan. He too had a *nom de guerre* – 'Chaban'. But his was taken from a dilapidated château he had stumbled across during his clandestine travels in the Dordogne, which he fancied as a symbol of the ancient values of his sort of France. Chaban-Delmas, once a second lieutenant in the reserve, was now a brigadier-general and since April the Free French national military delegate and the link between General Koenig and all the areas where the Resistance was operating. Before the war the two would have glared at each other across the ideological barricades. Now they were on the same side, united in love of their country but divided as to how it should be ruled. Rol-Tanguy was a risk taker, even if he was careful to calculate the odds. Chaban-Delmas believed in luck but also in hedging his bets. Their impulses were mirrored in the attitudes of those who stood behind them, and the potential for conflict was great.

★

If there was one fundamental everyone agreed upon, it was the need for Paris to play a part in its own liberation, but how, and when, would become the focus of fierce and continuous arguments. As soon as Rol-Tanguy heard that the Allies had landed he issued a report stressing the 'vital necessity to go on the offensive and to arm ourselves'. Rome had been liberated the previous day and the Red Army was on the move, having finally pushed the Germans out of Ukraine. The more the enemy could be weakened behind its lines, the quicker total victory would come.

The job now was to 'arm and to organize the masses' in order to 'bring about the real liberation and independence of the country'. Rol-Tanguy was also a realist, 'completely opposed to any romantic idea of the people throwing themselves into the struggle armed only with their bare fists'. This was only a slight exaggeration. A survey of resources in the Paris region conducted in April revealed that while there were plenty of volunteers – maybe 35,000–60,000 in the city and surrounding departments – there were only enough guns for 300 of them. And despite desperate pleas for more *parachutage* arms drops, the Allies were still reluctant, held back by the difficulties of delivering supplies to urban areas but also by their unwillingness to put weapons in the hands of communists. When General Koenig tried to arrange a delivery of 40,000 Sten guns to Paris the British Foreign Office had vetoed it on the grounds they might 'be put to mischievous uses should political passions be inflamed when the war is over'.

For Chaban-Delmas the question was complicated. It was like 'being asked to square the circle. In the eyes of the world, Paris had to be seen to liberate itself. But it also had to avoid being wiped from the map.' If the uprising failed, mass reprisals would surely follow. From 1 August, everyone knew what that could mean. On that day, the Polish underground in Warsaw rose up against the occupiers. News soon filtered through that the Germans were now slaughtering civilians by the thousand and systematically destroying the city. Who was to say the Germans would not do the same to Paris? Even if they showed more restraint, rising up too soon might actually delay the occupiers' departure. No one, including the Germans themselves, knew yet when and how they would take their leave. Would they simply pull out to help defend Germany's frontiers? Or would they choose to make a stand? If the latter, the consequences would surely be catastrophic. The fight they had put up in Normandy demonstrated what they were capable of, even with diminished morale and resources. It had taken huge effort and Allied lives to dislodge them from Caen, all but destroying the city and killing about 15,000 civilians. There was a further consideration troubling the conservatives. For the likes of Chaban-Delmas, insurrections were events to be feared, ushering in anarchy and bloodshed. The 1871 Paris Commune, when revolutionaries had overthrown the government and sparked a mini civil war, was still within living memory. The Communards' heirs were sitting alongside him in the councils of the Resistance. Could they be trusted not to take advantage of the situation to repeat the experiment?

De Gaulle was anxious to discourage such dreaming. In a message to the Resistance in the spring he stated that 'there must be no national insurrection except on my orders'. His D-Day speech was a florid rhetorical masterpiece that could have come from the mouth of his resented patron Winston Churchill, but it was only a tepid call to arms. 'The supreme battle has been joined,' he proclaimed. 'From behind the cloud so heavy with our blood and our tears, the sun of our greatness is now reappearing.' It was the 'sacred duty' of the sons of France to 'fight the enemy by every means in their power'. But he went on to emphasize that 'the orders given by the French government and by the leaders it has recognized must be followed precisely'.

It was not until the Allied breakout had become unstoppable that de Gaulle gave any practical instructions. The tone was remarkably cautious and anaemic. Directives issued on 11 August for Paris and the big cities urged the population 'not do any tasks useful to the enemy', and if the Germans tried to force people back to the factories they were to go on strike. This hardly felt like the fulfilment of a 'sacred duty' or the overture to a national uprising. De Gaulle might insist that it was he and General Koenig who would be calling the shots. But in Paris Rol-Tanguy had already reserved the right to take key decisions for himself, and anyway events soon took on a momentum that neither he nor Chaban-Delmas nor de Gaulle nor all the multiple committees of the Resistance could do much to control.

Ernst Jünger watched things fall apart with philosophical detachment. Impending disaster did not stop him doing the rounds of his French friends. He even found time to make a trip to Giverny to see Monet's famous garden. The atmosphere in the various headquarters was of studied confidence and calm. He noted with amusement the faith that some of his colleagues appeared to put in the V-1 flying bombs falling on London. If they were so effective, he wondered, why were they not being used against the Allied beachhead? The military commander for France Carl-Heinrich von Stülpnagel was preparing the ground for an orderly withdrawal and his staff had identified the town of Saint-Dié near Strasbourg as a place to fall back on if the situation required it. On 21 July, Stülpnagel's HQ was thrown into chaos. That morning, the news of Colonel Claus von Stauffenberg's failed attempt on Hitler's life at the Wolf's Lair at Rastenburg in East Prussia reached Paris. Stülpnagel was an important member of the conspiracy and had assured his fellow plotters that once it had succeeded he would bring his men over and turn on the SS and Gestapo. He had certainly done his part. When a signal reached Stülpnagel that Hitler was dead, he swung into action, ordering the commandant of Greater Paris, General Hans von Boineburg-Lengsfeld, to arrest all 15,000 members of the Nazi security apparatus in the city, including the senior SS chief and commander of all German police forces in France, General Carl Oberg. When he learned that Hitler was very much alive, the order was rescinded and Boineburg-Lengsfeld set off to tell Oberg he was free again.

Stülpnagel waited stoically for the inevitable call from Berlin summoning him to death. On the way back to Germany, somewhere near Verdun, he asked for the car to stop so he could stretch his legs. A few minutes later his escorts heard a shot and rushed to find the general sinking into the waters of the Canal de l'Est. He was still alive but blinded by the self-inflicted gunshot. He survived long enough to be arraigned before the People's Court in Berlin on 30 August and hanged the same day. Jünger recorded his demise with sorrow. He had admired

his chief, a cultivated man whose mind ranged beyond military matters to science and philosophy. Such were his manners that he had
even found the time to cancel a dinner date with Jünger before he was
hauled off to Germany. 'Oh, how the victims are dying here, and
especially in the smallest circles of the last chivalric men,' he lamented.

Neither these high-level convulsions nor the bad news coming
from Normandy deflected the SS and Gestapo from their murderous
missions. Alois Brunner, the Austrian SS captain who commanded
the Drancy deportation centre just north of Paris, pressed on with
the round-up of the city's Jews. On 21 and 22 July he ordered raids on
Jewish orphanages in the city centre which netted 250 children. They
were taken to Drancy and on the last day of the month loaded into
the cattle trucks of Convoy 77 with more than a thousand others. For
all his zeal, it had been clear for weeks that the days of impunity were
coming to a close for German and collaborator alike.

Early on the morning of 28 June, Philippe Henriot was in bed with his
wife in their flat in the Ministry of Information in the rue de Solférino
on the Left Bank. Henriot was a devout Catholic, a poet, journalist
and traditionalist who before the war was a parliamentary deputy for
the Gironde department together with Georges Mandel. The pair
were on friendly terms. When the war began he was strongly anti-
German. But in 1940, when many of his ilk went off to join de Gaulle,
he remained at home to embrace Pétain and collaboration, becoming
increasingly convinced as the months passed that only the Nazis could
save western civilization from Bolshevik barbarism. He regarded himself as a devoted patriot, the Free French as traitors and the Resistance
as a rabble of communists and Jews. In 1944 he was Vichy's minister of
information and propaganda, a member of the Milice and a star com-
mentator, pouring out invective twice a day over Radio Paris in a
battle of the airwaves with the Free French broadcasters in London.

That morning he was woken by an insistent knocking on the door.
On returning with his wife from the cinema the evening before he
had sent his bodyguard home, concerned that he had not yet had his
supper, so it was Henriot, in his pyjamas, who answered. The callers
told him through the door they were a Milice protection squad, come

to protect him from a Resistance team who were on their way to kidnap him. His wife Marie-Jeanne warned him not to open up. He ignored her. Standing there were three or four men armed with Sten guns. 'Ah, it is you then,' he said resignedly. One burst of fire cut him down. The second finished him off.

The men were part of a seventeen-man team sent with COMAC approval to capture Henriot and whisk him away to a landing zone outside the city to be flown to Algiers where he would be put on trial. If he resisted, he was to be shot. The team was led by Charles Gonard, son of a prosperous Lyons businessman and a member of Combat, a long-established group of non-communist resisters. The violent death of a symbol of fanatical collaboration probably made for better propaganda than a show trial, and no one minded that the operation had not gone entirely according to plan.

Posters appeared all over Paris with Henriot's portrait superimposed over a tricolour background declaring: 'He told the truth. They killed him!' On 2 July Henriot was given a state funeral, an honour previously reserved for statesmen and the likes of Victor Hugo. The event showed there were still loyal Vichyites left in the city. Bourgeois families in their hundreds, dressed in their Sunday best, filed past the coffin laid on a catafalque overnight in front of the Hôtel de Ville. A lavish requiem mass followed in Notre-Dame, presided over by the

Parisiennes use their compact mirrors to view Henriot's funeral

Archbishop of Paris, Cardinal Suhard. Prime Minister Laval led the Vichy mourners, alongside many of the German top brass.

Five days later the Milice avenged Henriot's death with a wave of killings. At the top of their list was Henriot's old colleague Georges Mandel, the former interior minister who in 1940 had stood up against Pétain and the defeatists. He was taken from prison to the forest of Fontainebleau and machine-gunned to death.

These acts simply guaranteed a bloody response from the Resistance. For the communist hardliners of the FTP, vengeance was official policy. On 10 July a four-man squad drove in a Citroën *traction avant* to Puteaux, a north-western suburb of Paris. They parked the car near the town hall, facing downhill as the starter motor was unreliable, and waited for the mayor to arrive. Georges Barthélémy was a former socialist turned arch-collaborator. The man assigned to kill him was André Calvès, the twenty-four-year-old son of a merchant navy officer from Brest and a hardened member of the FTP's Saint-Just Compagny, based in the 19th arrondissement and specializing in assassinations of *collabos* and *miliciens*. He recalled later how he approached the mayor and drew his gun. To make sure he was shooting the right man he asked him if he was Monsieur Barthélémy. '"No," he said. He was very pale. I cursed myself for an idiot. Of course he was going to say that.' Calvès asked for his papers. Another mistake. What if he pulled a gun? As he reached inside his jacket Calvès opened fire. 'Without really noticing, I emptied the magazine into him before he hit the ground.'

Calvès had been an idealistic young man and a pacifist before the war. He was still an ardent communist (though a Trotskyite heretic), but as a result of his experiences high-mindedness now struggled with ruthlessness and cynicism. The trouble was that the nature of his work made it hard to remain impersonal, and the longer you were in the company of your victim the easier it was to see them as an actual human being. One day he was with the company adjutant Jo Guell and some other comrades when they ambushed two *miliciens* after spotting them leaving the Pasteur Métro station. 'They began babbling, claiming they were just support staff and had nothing to do with any anti-Resistance operations.' Guell was all for killing them on the spot, but the elder of the two begged Calvès to listen. 'It sounded like something he had read by Drieu La Rochelle: "We may not have the same notion of our country but we all love France."' Calvès replied: 'But we're not patriots. We're Bolshevik internationalists. Not good, eh?' The *milicien* began to plead and Calvès felt 'a sadistic joy' at having made him beg for his life. 'Normally we should have killed them – those were our orders – but it was difficult now that we had spoken to them.' His companions agreed and they contented themselves with taking their revolvers, papers and berets and sending them on their way.

There was something in what the *milicien* said. The young men hunting each other down shared youth, danger and often a sense of idealism, perverted or misguided though it might be. They had taken violently opposed stances, but the line between the two was not impenetrable and Calvès discovered that it was possible to change the enemy's mind. The following day he was with his comrade Guy Dramard when they saw a *milicien* selling black-market cigarettes. They confronted him but he pleaded he had enlisted only because he was hungry, and before long he had agreed to defect. His name was Branton and he brought with him two grenades and a uniform that would make a useful disguise. Eight days later Branton was with them in a restaurant when two *miliciens* arrived. One came over and asked to talk to Calvès. They went outside while one of the comrades stood by in case of trouble. The *milicien* was called Max and he told André he had made a big mistake in persuading Branton to desert. He replied, 'Well, let's see which of us hangs first.' This set the tone for a conversation which ended with Max deciding to defect. He was seventeen years old and admitted he had joined the Milice only to annoy his parents.

There were plenty of reasons for resisters to harden their hearts. In the hunt for weapons, Madeleine Riffaud's group like many others had taken to robbing soldiers and *miliciens*, using one gun to obtain another. By July the understanding was that once you grabbed the weapon you killed your man. On such a mission 'Picpus', one of her dearest comrades, a twenty-seven-year-old medical student whose real name was Charles Martini, relieved a German of his rifle but, like André Calvès, couldn't bring himself to gun him down. 'He was just some poor guy and he really had the wind up,' he told Madeleine afterwards. His soft-heartedness got him into trouble with the group leader, another medic, codenamed 'Paul', who ordered him to go into hiding in case he was recognized. It was a sensible decision which Picpus disobeyed. A few days later, he arranged a meeting with a comrade to pass on a key to a locker at the Tarnier hospital where guns were hidden. On his way to the rendezvous near the Bastille a German lorry pulled up. A soldier jumped out, the same man whose life Picpus had spared. There would be no mercy for the Frenchman and the German shot him down, wounding him badly but not killing him. Picpus was taken to a room at the Saint-Antoine hospital near by and a guard put on the door. The news of his whereabouts soon reached Madeleine from friends on the medical staff. Risking her life she went to see him, telling the guards she was his fiancée. He managed to slip her the key to the arms cache, and as she left she swore to herself that the shooting would be avenged.

Her resolve was only strengthened when soon afterwards she read in the *Lettres Françaises* newssheet of the killings at Oradour-sur-Glane. The atrocity had happened a month before but the details were only now circulating in the underground press. For the 'Das Reich' Division which did the killings, the event was unremarkable as the SS and the Wehrmacht had carried out hundreds of similar massacres in the east. Such horrors were new to France and the story of how everyone in the village, regardless of age or sex, was herded into the church and surrounding barns, shot down with machine guns and then immolated as the buildings were set on fire marked a new depth of German sadism and savagery towards the French.

At lunchtime on Sunday 23 July, Madeleine was in her tiny hotel room in the Latin Quarter. She went downstairs to call a comrade and was told that Picpus had died. She decided then that 'the same evening there would be one less German in Paris'. She arranged to meet her comrade Manuel in front of Notre-Dame and asked him for the loan of his pistol and bike, telling him to meet her later when she would return them. If she failed to show, he should raise the alarm. She rode along the Left Bank *quais* westwards to where the rue de Solférino runs down to the Seine. It was a beautiful day and the pavements were

Madeleine

crowded with families enjoying the sunshine. A German soldier, not an officer by the look of him, had decided to break the rules and go for a stroll alone. He was gazing down at the river as Madeleine approached. After that everything happened very quickly. She got off the bike, pulled the gun from her handbag and shot him at close range in the temple. The German 'went down like a sack of wheat'. In that moment, Madeleine felt 'a great silence inside my head'.

As she pedalled away, she noticed a policeman watching her. He waved her past, pretending he had seen nothing, and for a few moments she thought she was free. Then she heard the sound of a car racing up behind. It rammed her rear tyre, flinging her onto the road. As her handbag hit the ground the pistol spilled out. She looked up to see a big man looming over her, shouting 'Terrorist! Bitch! . . . you're going to pay for this!' Her captor was the head of the Versailles Milice who happened to be out for a Sunday drive with his girlfriend. He took her first to the local police station where her identity was established. Then it was on to the Gestapo centre in the rue des Saussaies. As she was led up

the stairs she caught sight of herself in a mirror, bloodied and bedrag-
gled from her fall, and thought to herself: 'I am going to die.'

Madeleine was not the only Parisian to kill a German that day. The
same afternoon, in the upper-class suburb of Neuilly, Jean Maspero
and Jean-Pierre Mulotte, both young members of the FFI, were cycling along the boulevard du Château. They too had heard about
Oradour and were out for revenge. When they saw a German soldier
on the pavement they dismounted and Maspero shot him. He got
away. Mulotte did not. He was from a respectable, bourgeois family,
a student at the Lycée Janson de Sailly, and was just seventeen years
old though he looked five years younger. He too was taken to the rue
des Saussaies and tortured. Three days later his body was discovered
at dawn, near where the German had been gunned down. It was riddled with bullets and next to it was a cardboard sign which read: 'It
was here that I assassinated a German soldier. For that I was shot.'

These reprisals no longer felt like the iron fist of a confident master but
were more like flailing acts of desperation. There were signs of collapse
everywhere. Convoys of lorries, covered in foliage to camouflage them
from Allied aircraft, trundled into the city from the west, laden with
wounded. From 9 August, other convoys began heading east. All
around the city, offices were emptied of files and furniture and loaded
on to trucks to be carted away. In dribs and drabs, non-essential bureaucrats and technicians started heading back to their devastated homeland.
Among the first to go were the female support staff that the Parisians
had nicknamed the *souris grises*. A bus filled with young women in field
grey was seen passing Maxim's in the rue Royale. Their faces were
pressed to the windows and they waved white handkerchiefs in farewell to the city that had given them the time of their lives. Ernst
Jünger's services were no longer needed. Before departing he walked
up to Sacré-Coeur and 'cast a last glance over the great city'. He
'watched the stones quiver in the hot sun as if in expectation of new
historical embraces'. Inevitably the sight prompted a last aphorism:
'Cities are feminine and only smile on the victor.'

★

Looting got a high priority in the evacuation timetable. On 1 August a line of lorries arrived outside the Jeu de Paume gallery and a squad of Luftwaffe soldiers started crating up the remaining artworks that had not yet been despatched to Nazi collectors or sent for sale in Switzerland. There were plenty left, among them major works by Cézanne, Matisse, Braque, Dufy and Picasso. Many had been seized from the caches left behind by Paul Rosenberg when he sailed for New York with most of his family in the summer of 1940. The soldiers were too busy to notice one of the French administrative workers as she sidled over to see what was going on. To the Germans, Rose Valland was part of the furniture – dowdy and conscientious and no threat at all to their industrial-scale art-looting enterprise. Since their arrival, she had worked as a clerk under the supervision of the ERR as it organized the wholesale theft of French art treasures; she was keeping track of everything that passed through its hands. This included details of the artwork's original ownership, when it was seized, what it was valued at and the name of the new recipient. This data she secretly copied and handed over to the director of National Museums, Jacques Jaujard, who she had met in her pre-war life as an art historian and curator. Who knew when or if the departed treasures would ever return? But that morning she saw a chance to save a large tranche before it left France. The removal operation taking place was the biggest she had yet witnessed. It seemed to her that this was a final clear-out before the Germans departed for good.

Rose counted 148 crates, some stamped with the names of the world's best-known modern artists, being piled into trucks. Others had been brought over from storage in the Louvre near by. In all, there were 1,200 paintings. She smiled as the lorries drove off. She understood German and from the soldiers' chat she had learned that the cargo was being taken to a railway station. That was good. Road traffic out of the capital was still running reasonably smoothly. If the trucks were heading straight off to the east, the paintings might be lost for ever. The railways, though, were a mess, thanks to continuous Allied bombardments and Resistance sabotage and the trains were chronically disrupted. With luck, things could be arranged so that the crates never left Paris at all. Further gentle enquiries revealed that the trucks were bound for the Gare du Nord where they were sealed in five wagons overseen by armed guards.

Rose contacted Jaujard and passed on the information as well as the numbers of the wagons, discovered on the paperwork drawn up for the despatch. Jaujard had good connections inside the Resistance, among them a senior official in the SNCF state railway company. The rail workers of France, the *cheminots*, were a tough and bloody-minded bunch and from the outset had done their best to make life difficult for the occupiers. For months they had been slowing down rail movements and the information Jaujard gave them was fairly easy to act on. The train was soon located, sitting in the sidings of the Gare du Nord ready to haul away forty-seven wagons being loaded up with stolen furs, furniture and all kinds of luxury goods, taken from storage in a warehouse in central Paris. It took eleven days to complete the operation. Colonel Kurt von Behr, the ERR chief, oversaw the work, flanked by the armed guard that was now thought necessary to protect him from assassination, shouting at the rail workers to hurry up. The train at last wheezed out of the station heading for Abbeville in the north. Behr could relax. An hour later he was informed that it had come to a halt, just 5 miles away at Le Bourget. As Rose noted wryly: 'The colonel should have foreseen that there were bound to be technical problems with such a heavily loaded train.' The railwaymen had bought time for the precious cargo. But was it enough?

The Germans' proverbial discipline was breaking down. Around town, checkpoints sprang up, manned by soldiers who robbed passers-by of their bicycles, watches and cameras. They flogged off anything they could not take with them. In an impromptu auction in the Luxembourg Garden, rabbits and chickens were on sale, as well as four cows which went for 300 francs each. The withdrawing units looked nothing like the Aryan supermen who had marched in, drums pounding and standards flying. In the search for transport, anything on wheels was pressed into service. Mixed in with the lorries were lines of cars and vans, as well as horse-drawn buggies and carts. The lower ranks had been doing their own share of pillaging and the vehicles were piled with beds, mattresses, armchairs, radio sets, tins of food, typewriters – anything that might have a value down the road. Parisians looked on with bitter satisfaction. It reminded them of their own humiliations as they poured out of the city in the dark summer of 1940.

Each day the exodus accelerated and the sound of gunfire was heard more frequently. The threat of a bullet in the back had blown away the last shreds of German 'correctness'. The women were just as likely to be out to kill you as the men. Madame Reboul, the forty-year-old wife of a well-known lawyer, was walking down the rue des Écoles in the Latin Quarter having just bought a tricolour rosette from a street vendor doing a brisk business selling his wares from an upturned umbrella outside the Maubert–Mutualité Métro station. She pinned it proudly to her blouse. Outside the École Polytechnique, a German officer was coming along the pavement towards her. When he saw her, he stopped dead, drew his pistol and pulled back the slide to cock it. For a long moment he looked at her. Then he walked on, leaving her ashen and trembling.

Madame Reboul's tricolour was another sign that the Parisians were growing bolder. When passing a German they no longer lowered their eyes. Instead they looked on eagerly as the occupiers packed their bags, noting details to feed into the gossip mill that whirred night and day, scattering fantasy and fact indiscriminately around the city. The tattle was invariably prefaced by the words *on dit* – they're saying – as though the intelligence was of cast-iron authenticity, emanating from some impeccable source. It covered all aspects of the immediate future: de Gaulle and Pétain were joining forces; Paris was to be declared an open city – another echo of 1940 – following a conference held at the Crillon, or was it the Majestic? The final German withdrawal was going to start tomorrow. No, it had been put off until the day after.

The Germans could not mistake the vindictive glint in the onlookers' eyes. The more sentimental among them had kidded themselves that their presence was tolerated. Now it was clear that they had been hated all along. Walter Dreizner had no illusions now about the city he had come to love. On Sunday 13 August it was 'hotter than hot'. A lorry was taking him from the centre to a command post in

Saint-Cloud to the west of the city to carry out some technical work. He looked out on 'a real Parisian Sunday, all Paris out on the streets, along the Seine and in the gardens'. The German rumour mill was churning too: 'Some said the Americans were in Chartres. Others that they had already moved beyond it.' It was the hottest day he could remember. He had never seen so many people thronging the Seine. A sight that a few months before would have delighted him now filled him with fear. 'This weather is dangerous,' he wrote in his diary that night. 'It could well mark the point where the Parisians turn on us. If you know the cruel history of this city you can easily believe it. It's like a thunderstorm waiting to break.'

Dreizner was right. There was a feverish edge to the new vivaciousness. It was born not just out of hope but also out of hunger. In a picture he had taken of sunbathers at the Deligny floating swimming pool, the corrugated ribs of the young men and women stuck out painfully from their swimsuits. That was back in June. Since then food shortages had become even more acute. However well fed they might be in Normandy, in Paris the bellies of all but the wealthiest and best connected were constantly rumbling. Young Raymond Ruffin came from a comfortable middle-class home, but on 4 July he noted that 'It has become impossible to put together a meal, since even the vegetables that aren't rationed (like swedes, Jerusalem artichokes, broccoli and turnips) have disappeared from the markets.' Even if you were able to find food, you then had to cook it. The disruption to the railways meant little coal was reaching the city's power stations and gas and electricity were strictly rationed, with power coming on for only half an hour once a day. According to Raymond's friend Robert, Paris 'was about to see the same hard times that it endured in the siege of 1870' when people were forced to eat cats and rats. 'What a joyful outlook!' remarked Ruffin.

Robert's prediction was not far from the mark. Dr Jean-Marie Musy, the senior Red Cross representative in Paris, reported in early August that meat supplies were only 20 per cent of what they had been five years earlier, milk 12 per cent and vegetables 10 per cent. Even bread consumption was down by 40 per cent. 'The capital is threatened with famine,' he wrote. So when a new German commander arrived on 9 August to take over as military governor of the city he inherited not only a rapidly deteriorating military situation but a city that was dark, near-starving and throbbing with hostility and burgeoning violence.

General of the Infantry Dietrich von Choltitz looked, in the words of a British intelligence report, 'like a cinema-type German officer, fat, coarse and be-monocled and inflated with a tremendous sense of his own importance'. This view seemed to be shared by his peers when their verdicts on him – delivered once he was out of the room – were secretly recorded at the senior officers' prisoner-of-war camp in which he ended up. According to them, Choltitz was a show-off and at the dinner table always had to be 'the clever one of the party'. He was a smooth bureaucratic operator 'but as a soldier, a dud'. Above all he was two-faced, a chameleon who coloured his views to blend in with the company he was keeping and told people what he thought they wanted to hear. General von Schleiben, captured when Cherbourg fell, judged him 'very crafty'. When the going was good he was 'very Third Reich but he's said to have become quite different in the meantime'. He concluded: 'He knows which side his bread is buttered on, if you know what I mean.'

In the circumstances, Hitler seemed to be taking a risk by choosing Choltitz to command a city that was about to find itself on the front line. He was a proud member of the aristocratic officer caste, whose members had just tried to kill their Führer. Almost all the twenty-six generals and 700 officers involved were called von Here or von There. The man he was replacing as Paris commandant, General von Boineburg-Lengsfeld, was suspected of association with the plotters, though even the Nazis' judicial processes required something more than mere suspicion to justify such a relatively high-level execution and he had been allowed to move on to a scheduled new posting.

Nonetheless, Choltitz's reputation as a man who unquestioningly did what he was told trumped his blue-blood background. It was this that led the chief of army personnel General Burgdorf to put his name forward to the Führer with the admiring observation that he 'never questioned an order, no matter how harsh it was'. Choltitz confirmed the judgement in a taped conversation at the facility where the captured German brass were held, at Trent Park, just north of London. He told the most distinguished of his fellow prisoners, General Wilhelm von Thoma: 'The worst job I ever carried out – which however I carried out with great consistency – was the liquidation of the Jews. I carried out this order to the very last detail.'

This admission was apparently a reference to his time serving on the Eastern Front commanding the 16th Air Landing Regiment in Erich von Manstein's Eleventh Army. It arrived in the Crimea in the autumn of 1941 alongside the SS-Einsatzgruppe D extermination unit. Manstein issued an order in September stating that it was 'unworthy of an officer to participate in the execution of Jews . . . what the SS is doing is dirty work, but we know that it must be done. We'll not stop it and generally support it. Our people must, however, be prevented from observing the executions.'

So it was that the army helped the death squads by cordoning off areas to prevent the Jews escaping and also by providing trucks and escorts to take them off to pre-prepared killing grounds where the SS killers took over. They were extremely efficient. With the aid of Manstein's army, between mid-November 1941 and mid-January 1942 the 500 or so men of Einsatzgruppe D machine-gunned to death the great majority of Crimean Jewry. Choltitz's regiment was in the Evpatoria and Feodosia areas at the end of 1941 when two mass killings took place. It was also present when Manstein finally took Sebastopol after an extended siege in July 1942. The capture was followed by the massacre of the city's 4,200 Jews.

Choltitz was commanding the 84th Army Corps in Normandy when he was summoned to Hitler's HQ near Rastenburg in East Prussia. His experience of the Battle of Normandy convinced him that the military situation in the west was desperate and probably hopeless. By the time he set off for the Wolf's Lair his divisions had lost half their men and all movements in daylight were menaced by the ever prowling Allied aircraft. Army headquarters at home refused to accept reality, making absurd demands and interfering in battlefield decisions. The most dire intervention would come from the very top – Hitler's insistence on the Panzer counter-attack at Mortain whose failure knocked the last prop out from the German defences. Choltitz and his fellow commanders were having to fight Berlin as well as the Allies. Like most of his peers he came from a long line of soldiers and belonged to a caste 'whose lives had been rooted in obedience'. Nonetheless, in order to give themselves a chance in the fight, that obedience was starting to fray, and Choltitz and the others had taken to falsifying reports and camouflaging their decisions when reporting back to base. With these deceptions Choltitz was breaking the habit of a lifetime and, having disobeyed once, he would find it easier to do so again.

His journey east only deepened the sense of approaching doom. The disruption to the railways meant he was driven much of the way. A stopover in Berlin revealed the damage left by numerous RAF raids. The news from the east was terrible. The German line was disintegrating under the weight of a massive Soviet assault, Operation Bagration, launched to coincide with the Allied landings in Normandy. It had been clear since Stalingrad that Hitler's grand plan to add vast swathes of the east to his empire had collapsed. It remained to be seen whether anything could be salvaged from the wreckage. A sober assessment would conclude that the likeliest outcome for Germany was nothing other than total defeat.

Choltitz had been as excited as anyone by the stunning initial German victories on all fronts, and like many of his ilk was prepared to accept that Hitler might after all be, as he claimed, a military genius. Those days were long gone. Whatever respect he once felt had faded, and after the 7 August meeting at Rastenburg it would disappear. The encounter would become Choltitz's party piece. The British eavesdroppers heard him tell the story many times to the inmates of Trent Park, complete with 'hilarious' Führer impersonations.

Following the 20 July assassination attempt, security at the Wolf's Lair was very tight and 'there was an SS man behind every tree, one might almost say behind every flower'. Choltitz had seen Hitler once before at a large military gathering but had never met him. The figure in front of him now came as a dreadful shock. He saw 'an old man, stooped and flabby with grey thinning hair . . . a trembling physical ruin'. He had been warned not to grip his leader's hand too firmly as it was still painful from a wound sustained from Stauffenberg's bomb. His gentle handshake was rewarded with a 'kindly look' – the only one he got in the bizarre hour that followed. As usual, Hitler talked and his guest listened. The Führer started off with a rambling account of the early days of the Nazi Party before finally turning to the war and events in Normandy. Choltitz tried to bring him up to date with news hot from the front but was silenced with a wave of the hand and a curt assurance that he was 'perfectly aware' of the situation and the promise that the counter-offensive he had just ordered at Mortain would 'at a stroke, hurl the enemy back into the sea'.

Then Hitler launched into a rant about the recent attempt on his life and Choltitz witnessed 'the explosion of a soul filled with hate'. His lips were strung with spittle, he was soaked in sweat and his body trembled so violently that he had to grip the table. Choltitz felt that he was 'face to face with a madman'. At last the ranting subsided and Hitler sank into his chair. There was a long pause before he told Choltitz why he had been summoned. 'General, you are going to Paris,' he said. 'You will have the greatest powers that a general could receive . . .'

Later that day Choltitz got his detailed orders. Paris was no longer a cushy posting where 'the only fighting going on is over a seat in the officers' mess' and would henceforth become a bulwark in the German defensive line. Anyone not doing vital support duties was to be sent to the front. Choltitz would have full powers to bring about the transformation. He would have command of all army and SS fighting units and party organizations in the greater Paris area and anyone who objected would have to answer to Hitler. At the same time the region was to be 'protected from all acts of rebellion, subversion and sabotage'. Paris itself was to become 'a fortress'.

Hitler's earlier evaluation of the military situation seemed totally at odds with what Choltitz was now being told to do. If the invaders were about to be thrown into the sea, why turn Paris into a stronghold? Hitler's talk of repelling the Allies seemed 'simply words in the air to delude those around him and himself'. The truth was that Hitler intended his troops to make a stand in the city and Choltitz would be directing the defence.

He had no desire to burn in the flames of the looming *Götterdäm-merung*. But nor did he dare to show any hint of disloyalty and share the fate of the 20 July plotters. He wasn't even fifty yet, with a wife and three children. The dilemma was how to stay alive and at the same time keep his military honour intact. Choltitz's noted ability to be all things to all men was about to face its sternest test. From now on, every decision would be calculated for its effect on an audience that included the Nazi security services, his brother officers, the German people and, as time passed, the opinion of the world at large.

Choltitz's anxieties were deepened by a chance encounter on the train back to Paris. He ran into a senior Nazi official, Robert Ley, who told him of a new law. From now on, a general's family was to be held accountable for his actions and could be executed if he was thought to have committed treason. The punishment would be enforced even if he personally escaped Nazi justice through being taken prisoner by the enemy. Choltitz tossed and turned in his sleeping compartment that night. A diversion to see his wife Umberta and three young children in the family refuge in Baden-Baden only reminded him of what he stood to lose.

He reached Paris on the evening of 9 August. He dined with Boineburg-Lengsfeld and a select group of his staff at his town house at 26 boulevard Raspail. Paris was known to be full of disillusioned elements, but Choltitz watched his words. It was only when a smaller group settled down for brandy and cigars that the conversation loosened up. Everyone in the little circle shared the same fears about how events would play out. As the level of the brandy bottle fell, the feeling of complicity deepened. Cautiously, they one by one agreed that they could see no point in mounting a defence of Paris that would only finish in defeat and the ruination of the city. By the end of the evening, Choltitz felt Boineburg-Lengsfeld was leaving him with allies on whom he could rely if the point was reached when he would have to disobey orders. As he left, he told his host he would not be taking up his offer to move into his grand residence. He would set up his headquarters in the Hôtel Meurice on the rue de Rivoli, in the heart of a city that was about to descend into chaos.

9. *Chacun son Boche!*

The following day, Thursday 10 August, the machinery of the city started to seize up. That morning, the illegal General Confederation of Labour union called an all-out strike of rail workers in the Paris region. The organizers' goal was 'not a train for Hitler!' That also meant no trains for Parisians. It no longer seemed to matter much. Tuning into the BBC the following night, the fifteen-year-old Raymond Ruffin heard with excitement 'the announcement of the liberation of Chartres. It's only fifty-six kilometres from Paris!' The Germans had heard it too. 'They are getting nervous,' he wrote in his diary. 'This evening they were shooting at any windows which weren't blacked out.'

With the rail strike, the Resistance factions were flexing their muscles. Rol-Tanguy and most of the FFI believed that now the Allies had the Germans on the run in Normandy, the time had come for action inside the city, but the dire shortage of arms and Gaullist caution were holding things back. Jacques Chaban-Delmas in particular was dead against 'premature' action, citing once again the dire shortage of weapons. But as organizing arms supplies via London was meant to be one of his responsibilities, this observation only added to FFI suspicions that he was dragging his feet. His hesitation was the product of deep concern about what the Germans could do in the window of time between the Resistance rising up and the arrival of the Allied armies. Every day new details reached Paris of the terrible price Warsaw was paying for its rebellion. On the Vistula the Germans were killing civilians by the thousands and those who were not being shot were starving. France had so far been treated far less harshly than Poland, but these were desperate times and the massacre at Oradour-sur-Glane two months previously showed what, *in extremis*, the occupiers were capable of.

Chaban-Delmas now had a political counterpart, Alexandre Parodi, chief representative of the provisional government. Together the two

would make up what was referred to as 'the delegation'. Parodi was the son of a philosopher and a solid member of the intellectual upper class. He was forty-three, slight, thinning on top, and looked every inch the senior civil servant he had been before Vichy sacked him. De Gaulle's special envoy Jean Moulin picked him out to start secret planning for the post-war administration of France. He had been living in Paris throughout the war as a Gaullist sleeper, lying low and awaiting the call.

Parodi's apparent deep-dyed conservatism made him and Chaban-Delmas seem like an ideal team who could be relied on to support each other in promoting de Gaulle's authority and reining in Rol-Tanguy and the communists. Parodi would turn out to be more appreciative of the left's contribution than his young colleague and saw the justice – and necessity – of giving them a proper share of control as events unfolded. His diplomatic touch helped counter Chaban-Delmas' sometimes grating self-assurance, reduce friction and maintain the unity of the Resistance, on which success utterly depended.

One of his first acts was to endorse Rol-Tanguy's appointment as FFI Paris region chief, assuring Algiers that, communist or not, he was the right man for the job. Rol-Tanguy reciprocated by confirming that his acceptance of de Gaulle's leadership was sincere and not some tactical deception. In Spain he had never strayed from the party line, nor since the war began had he baulked at the ideological contortions forced on the communists by Stalin's strategic U-turns. But when forced to choose, his patriotism outweighed his communism.

Hardliners like Charles Tillon of the FTP, the Francs-Tireurs et Partisans, tried to get him to incorporate the wishes of the party leadership into his plans, but he made it clear that this was a collective enterprise and the PCF would not be calling the shots.

Parodi's inclusive attitude reflected reality. Most FFI volunteers were communists. They were much more likely to take direction from a comrade than from a Gaullist blow-in. It was already hard enough for Rol-Tanguy to hold his people back, and freelance shootings and bombings were now a daily event. He reacted to the thirst for action through a series of directives raising the tempo. On 8 August he issued an order calling for attacks on rail and road targets to 'harass the enemy' as German forces fell back from Normandy.

This was just the sort of thing to alarm Chaban-Delmas. He was already deeply worried by intelligence received from London that the Allied armies in Normandy had no plans to immediately relieve Paris once their victory was complete. Instead they intended to bypass the city in the expectation that the Germans would abandon it once they found they were being cut off. It would be the first half of September at the earliest before Paris could hope to be free. This was bad news for everyone inside. None of the inhabitants could share the Allies' insouciance. By the time they were finally liberated, the four and a half million living in the region might well be starving to death, and there was no telling how the Germans would react to their defeat. Chaban-Delmas decided that drastic action was needed to persuade the Allies to get a move on. 'We could feel the uprising was not far off,' he wrote. 'We knew that the FTP and the Communists were getting very worked up and we would not be able to hold them back, certainly not until September or October.' He decided he would go to London himself with the message and he would deliver it to Winston Churchill in person.

The Free French intelligence service arranged a pick-up at a landing zone outside Lyons. Arriving at an RAF base near London on 11 August, Chaban-Delmas was delighted to find that breakfast in the mess came with 'milk, butter, jam and white bread, things I had not seen for a very long time'. He was to impress on Churchill 'that it was vital that the Allies speed up the march on the capital if they wanted to save it'. He rushed to Downing Street only to be told that the great man was having his post-lunch nap and there was absolutely no question of interrupting it for the sake of an obscure emissary from Paris. Chaban-Delmas passed on his message to Churchill's chief military adviser, General Hastings Ismay, who listened to him politely for an hour and promised to make sure it would reach the prime minister's ears. That was some consolation, but Ismay made it clear that the fate of Paris was not a pressing concern for the Allied high command and they were very unlikely to change their plans on the basis of his intelligence. Delmas relieved his feelings in a long and passionate telegram to de Gaulle in Algiers, warning that 'Paris was practically doomed to fire and destruction and Parisians, in their tens of thousands, to death.' He then made a tortuous return via Normandy, crossing the front lines on a bicycle disguised as an innocent sportsman in tennis whites, arriving back in the capital on 16 August having achieved nothing.

There was no good news waiting to improve Choltitz's mood as he began work at the Hôtel Meurice on 10 August. The rail strike called that morning looked like the start of more trouble which would almost certainly involve increased attacks on his troops. Reports from the front were ominous. The Hitler-inspired counter-attack at Mortain was going nowhere and seemed the prelude to a total collapse. Ignorant of the Allies' plans, he had to assume that Paris would soon be on the front line. According to his orders from Hitler, he was expected to turn the city into a fortress. But how was he to do that given the meagre resources available?

He had no feel for the place, having spent only three days there earlier in the war. His initial feeling was that the Allies would never attack Paris directly for fear of the resulting destruction. If, however, they did, he would be forced into a fight on two fronts: one against the enemy forces in front of the city, the other a counter-insurgency operation inside its walls. Hitler's promise that all troops currently in the capital would be at his disposal was not to be relied on. The Luftwaffe and Stülpnagel's replacement as military commander, General Karl Kitzinger, swiftly grabbed 6,000 men for their own uses. That left Choltitz with a force of two very depleted infantry divisions, the 48th and the 338th, which were deployed along the Seine to defend the western approaches to the city. The best they could hope for was to delay the Allied advance for a few days before the inevitable breakthrough.

Then he would be relying on eighteen heavy flak batteries which his orders from Hitler had assured him would provide 'an impregnable defence ring'. This he knew to be nonsense. The 88mm anti-aircraft gun was a fearsome weapon, as good against armour as it was against aircraft, but thirty-six pieces could not be expected to cover the 65-kilometre arc from where the Allied attack would likely come. After that it would be down to the 17,000 or so garrison troops to fend off the battle-hardened attackers. Many of his troops in the city were 'old daddies', clerks and orderlies, bureaucrats and bottle-washers, with little combat training and no experience. The equipment situation was no better. Boineburg-Lengsfeld had left him fourteen tanks, a mix of captured French Panhards and pre-war-model Panzers, and eighteen armoured cars. There were also 220 assorted light cannon which might come in useful. Choltitz had been in enough tight corners to be philosophical. 'So with this band of heroes I set about defending Paris,' he recalled.

He was even optimistic. The situation was fluid. Some of the units retreating from the west could surely be diverted to help out. Despite the unpromising situation his pride as a professional soldier encouraged him to believe he could 'turn the city into a nucleus of resistance . . . use the sewers to move troops around . . . punish without mercy any subversive activity and hold out for long enough in the ruins', forcing the Allies to divert at least three armoured divisions away from the march on Germany. He could even, if he wanted, 'turn Paris into another Warsaw'.

On Monday 14 August he was called to the Saint-Germain-en-Laye HQ of the supreme commander in the western theatre, Field Marshal Günther von Kluge, to discuss plans for Paris. The consciences of Hitler's generals were curious things, their workings impenetrable to those born outside the German military caste. Men who were capable of murdering innocents without thinking twice agonized over their perverse code of honour, the rules of which were equally difficult to discern. So it was that when captured senior officers were discussing the 20 July plot, there was much indignation about the method chosen to execute the perpetrators. As officers, shooting was acceptable, 'but it isn't nice to be hanged'.

Kluge was a troubled soul. He had lost faith in his Führer and had known about the 20 July plot, even though he had not participated. Nonetheless, he still felt bound to carry on faithfully doing Hitler's bidding. He did not question the proposals to prepare the defence of Paris, even though they involved a great deal of physical destruction. They were laid out at the meeting by his operations officer, General Günther Blumentritt. He explained to the gathering the strategic necessity 'of smashing the city's infrastructure to smithereens'. The idea was to hold Paris for as long as possible so as to slow the enemy advance. Factories would be blown up to prevent their output being used against Germany. Destroying the waterworks and the gas and electricity systems would paralyse the city and restoring services would cause the Allies further delay. Choltitz was sceptical. Surely the moment to do all this was when they were finally pulling out, he argued, otherwise the programme was likely to drive the population into the hands of the Resistance. And, as he pointed out, 'German soldiers drink water too.'

The respite was short. Soon after the meeting he received an order over the radio from Kluge's headquarters to blow up all but a few of the sixty-five bridges in and around the city. Choltitz claimed later that this sounded to him like idiocy, a fair enough conclusion in the circumstances. With many of the bridges across the Seine north and south of the city destroyed, the ones in Paris would surely be vital to the Normandy evacuation. They were certainly essential to move his own men and equipment around. If the city fell it would take no time at all for the Allies to patch them up. In any case, there were no specialist engineers to carry out the demolitions. When Choltitz pointed this out, a team was rapidly assigned to him – commanded, it turned out, by a Captain Werner Ebernach whom he had known before the war. The two had been on an exercise which involved blowing up two bridges across the Mulde river. According to Choltitz's post-war account, when Ebernach arrived he told him: 'Go ahead with the preparations but do not detonate anything without my personal approval. The Seine is not the Mulde . . . we have the whole world watching us here . . .' They then proceeded 'with commendable zeal' to make the preparations necessary 'to be able at zero hour to blow up everything'. A massive supply of explosives was already available in the shape of hundreds of torpedoes the Kriegsmarine had stored in a railway tunnel at Saint-Cloud.

The idea that Paris had been thoroughly rigged for demolition and all Choltitz had to do was ram down the plunger would prove extremely useful in the story he later spun about his part in the drama. According to this account, his prevarications were conditioned not just by practical military calculations but also by humanitarian considerations. 'What a barbaric act was being asked of me!' he lamented. 'What a thing to do to this city which, despite harbouring feelings of bitterness, had for four years put up with the German occupation with prudence and calm.' It was not a compliment that many Parisians would have appreciated.

Choltitz would make much of his lonely mission to do everything he could to spare the 'magnificent city which was Paris and its people' in defiance of orders from above. He asked himself, 'What right had I to cause huge distress to several million people by fixing my defence in the city centre when it would do nothing to alter the course of events?' He claimed that on top of that he 'was thinking of future relations between our two great neighbouring peoples . . . I felt it a sacred duty, in the middle of an inevitable defeat, to keep the door open to the future, and to do that I would interpret the orders I received as broadly as possible and not follow them to the letter.'

Any hesitancy certainly courted big risks. The old army elite were now under intense scrutiny from the Nazi security services. The day after the Saint-Germain-en-Laye conference, Kluge's car had been caught in an Allied air attack and he was incommunicado for several hours. This immediately aroused suspicions that he had snuck off for secret talks with the Americans. When contact was resumed, he was ordered to Berlin to see Hitler. Kluge believed the summons was connected to his passive support for the 20 July plot. There was little doubt about how the story would end and he hastened the inevitable by swallowing cyanide.

Choltitz's patience with the Parisians was immediately tested by the growing truculence of a population whose 'prudence and calm' were wearing thin. The railway strike was followed by the Métro workers walking out. It seemed to him that 'this had little military significance and it was the civilian population who would suffer the most'. Then, on the morning of 15 August, he heard some much more serious news. The police had also gone on strike. Throughout the occupation they had been a vital resource in the machinery of repression and control, working hand in hand with the Germans. The Gestapo and SS security services were already packing their bags. Who would keep order in the city now that the *flics* were deserting the sinking ship?

The police were a byword for cynicism in Parisian folklore. Their highly developed talent for self-preservation made them the most reliable of weathervanes if you wanted to know which way the winds of power were blowing. For months they had been shifting their stance, to the point where there were now three well-supported clandestine groups operating inside the 15,000-strong Paris force. They lined up with the main Resistance groupings. Honneur de la Police (Honour of the Police) were Gaullist in outlook, with 400-odd members including some from the highest ranks. Police et Patrie (Police and Homeland) were socialists, made up of 250 officers and 400 non-uniformed staff. The biggest, with 800, was the communist-sympathizing Front National de la Police (National Front of the Police). The decision to strike followed a move by the Germans on Sunday 13 August to relieve the police in the suburbs of Gennevilliers, Montreuil and Saint-Denis of their weapons. The news reached a meeting of the National Front which assumed it was the start of an operation to disarm the entire force and neutralize them in the coming struggle. The following day, all three groups met to decide how to react. The Front had invited Rol-Tanguy, who saw an opportunity to turn the former arch-enemies of the FFI into allies – and allies with guns. Between them, the police, gendarmerie and Republican Guard responsible for securing state property in the city had about 20,000 rifles and light machine guns. If things went well, large numbers of policemen might be drafted into the ranks of the Resistance, massively increasing their firepower and becoming 'a precious trump card for the FFI in the Paris region'. But that was some way off. The first thing was to persuade the police to come out on strike.

The proposal got a mixed reception. Predictably, the Gaullists were lukewarm and the communists enthusiastic, but thanks to Rol-Tanguy's arguments all three groups eventually voted unanimously to cease all duties the following day. With characteristic modesty Rol-Tanguy claimed later that the police had been moving in this direction since their inaction on Bastille Day and he had merely delivered a rhetorical final push. The new alliance might provoke some rumblings among the hardliners who regarded the police with well-merited mistrust and contempt. But the police would not now be an obstacle to an uprising, and might well be a huge asset.

Tuesday 15 August was in peacetime a holiday, the Feast of the Assumption, celebrating the Blessed Virgin Mary's ascent to heaven. Parisians woke that morning to find the *gardiens de la paix*, as familiar a sight in their *képis* and long capes as the street-corner *pissoir*, had vanished. 'In the avenues, the crossroads, in front of the *mairies*, the consulates, the banks, the railway stations, not a single cop,' noted a journalist, Georges Le Fèvre. The German exodus was now in full flood as Choltitz had issued Hitler's order that anyone unable to wield a gun was to clear out. Le Fèvre reported that without the French police to direct the traffic the exit routes clogged up with 'interpreters, cooks, mess waiters, Gestapo grasses, mechanics . . . thousands of girls in uniform weeping hot tears at the pain at having to return to the motherland'. Young Raymond Ruffin was queuing outside a bakery when he heard about the strike. 'It scarcely seemed credible,' he wrote in his diary. 'Suddenly the air was charged with electricity and everyone was tense and nervous. We felt cut off from everything; no more buses, Métro, mail . . . as for gas and electricity, that had packed up long ago.'

There was another astounding development that Assumption Day. Parisians heard over the BBC of a second Allied landing in France, this one in the south, along a hundred-mile front of the Mediterranean coast. Salvation was now approaching from two directions. At a service in Notre-Dame cathedral that afternoon, Cardinal Suhard, who only six weeks before had officiated at the requiem for the assassinated collaborator Philippe Henriot, interrupted mass to deliver a patriotic sermon encouraging the worshippers to hang on for 'one last test' in the 'decisive days' ahead and to implore the protection of Saint Joan of Arc and Saint Geneviève, the latter being the city's fifth-century patron saint whom the pious prayed to when Paris was in distress.

No help would be forthcoming from Pétain, the 'shield' of his people, or any of the other Vichy chiefs. Pierre Laval had tried one last stratagem not only to save his skin but also to secure himself a leading place in the country's future. He turned up in the capital on 9 August seeking to inveigle the seventy-two-year-old former prime minister of the Third Republic Édouard Herriot, who had been living under house arrest, into a scheme to revive the National Assembly, form a transitional government and thwart de Gaulle. Laval's lucky white tie was no longer working. The Germans squashed the initiative and Herriot anyway turned him down. Eight days later the Germans drove Laval to Belfort near the Swiss border, where he was reunited with Pétain, and the pair set off into exile together with Vichy's ambassador to Paris Fernand de Brinon and the ultra-*collabo* 'three Ds': Déat, Darnard and Doriot.

The last of the pro-Nazi intellectual *prominente* were also taking their leave of Paris. The exodus had started shortly after D-Day. The half-mad Louis-Ferdinand Céline was one of the first to run. Drieu La Rochelle sought a more dramatic departure by attempting, but failing, to poison himself. On 9 August the director of the Vichy press Jean Luchaire arranged cars to carry the chief propagandists and their families eastwards. Robert Brasillach's old colleague and friend Lucien Rebatet was among those who seized the lifeline, and according to the joke doing the rounds, the collaborationist bible *Je Suis Partout* had been renamed *Je Suis Parti* ('I've left'). Rebatet would end up joining the seedy remnants of the *ancien régime* corralled under German house arrest in the Hohenzollern castle at Sigmaringen on the banks of the Danube.

Rebatet had consistently outdone his old friend in his enthusiasm for the occupation and had turned on Brasillach when his loyalty to the Nazis appeared to falter. Now he knew that if he didn't get out fast 'all I can expect is a fucking bullet in the head'. Brasillach, however, chose to stay, cocooned in dreamy complacency, telling himself that he had done nothing wrong and that his finely wrought arguments would prevail over the rage starting to bubble in the streets. Even with the end in sight, he was not prepared to deny his old friends. One August night he was invited to a 'farewell dinner, very intimate', in the garden of the Deutsches Institut by its director Karl Epting. The place brought back memories of Karl Heinz Bremer, long dead on the Eastern Front, whose 'sweet shadow I sensed roaming under the trees'. It was a beautiful evening and they 'lingered for a long time talking in the garden under the sweet-smelling trees, about what had been and what might have been'. Epting tried to persuade him to leave for Germany, but Brasillach resisted. There would be no regrets. He 'intended to deny nothing'. Collaboration in the form it had been tried had failed 'for all sorts of reasons', but 'it had been a noble enough ideal, one that we had to return to'.

On 17 August he had a night out with his brother-in-law Maurice Bardèche. Surprisingly, the theatres were still open, though they would go dark later that night. The play chimed ominously with his circumstances. It was *Huis clos* ('No Exit') by Jean-Paul Sartre. Two days later, Brasillach filled some suitcases and climbed the stairs to a maid's room under the eaves of 16 rue de Tournon, just down from the Senate. It had been prepared for him by a female friend who without being given the slightest encouragement had for years forlornly held a torch for him. From an attic window he would watch the transformation of the city and the approach of nemesis.

Brasillach had shown courage by living in the open for as long as he did. With the police off the streets, their place was now taken by young men wearing FFI brassards and carrying guns who would have killed him if they had known who he was. Since 13 August, the sound of distant gunfire could be heard in the city, and every day it was growing a little louder. In the restless ranks of the FFI, the rumbling of the Allied artillery sharpened the thirst for German blood. Inside the Resistance, the police strike increased tensions between the eager and the wary. Rol-Tanguy had already decided it was time to start to 'move out of the shadows'.

On 14 August he left the family hideaway at Antony in the southern suburbs for a new temporary HQ closer to the centre, in the avenue Verdier at Montrouge. Cécile joined him the following afternoon. She set off wheeling her bike, with her mother Germaine pushing baby Jean in his pram while daughter Hélène skipped alongside. Hidden underneath the pram's coverlet was Henri's submachine gun and the typewriter on which Cécile tapped out orders and communiqués. 'At Croix-de-Berny there was a German checkpoint which we knew about,' she remembered. 'We went through as if we were out for a family stroll with no problems at all.' When they reached a quiet spot, she transferred the hidden items – which would have got her shot if discovered – to the bicycle panniers. Germaine returned with the children to Antony and Cécile pedalled away, taking a detour when she spotted another German post ahead. She reached the new HQ without incident 'but very happy to have arrived'.

In their eagerness to get their hands on weaponry, resisters had made themselves an easy target for the security forces, who even at this late hour were still hungry for victims. It was the Nazis' way of saying goodbye. A French turncoat working for the Gestapo called Guy Glèbe d'Eu posed as a resister to lure thirty-four young men to La Cascade, near a lake in the Bois de Boulogne on the promise of supplying them with arms. At the rendezvous the SS were waiting. They mowed them down with machine guns then tossed grenades to finish off those who were still breathing. Altogether, 123 resisters were executed in the week of 10–17 August. Everyone was now vulnerable. The occupiers vented their rage at the Parisians' ill-concealed delight in the change of German fortunes with random, pointless acts of violence. On the evening of Thursday 17 August the stifling heat lifted and crowds went into the boulevard Bonne-Nouvelle to take the air. At around 9.30 soldiers appeared and threw incendiary grenades into a shop and a café. They then started shooting at strollers, killing Samuel Blitz, aged seventy-three, Adeline Poyard, forty-six, and Léon Garcelon, thirty-two. That afternoon, a soldier sitting on the back of the last lorry in an east-bound convoy passing through Nogent-sur-Marne had opened fire on a group of onlookers, killing three men and a woman. Such murderous spite only heightened the appetite for revenge.

Choltitz had been given authority to draft the Gestapo and SS security personnel into the defence of the city, but when they decided it was time to depart he made no attempt to stop them. At their sinister headquarters around the city, smoke from burning files plumed from the chimneys, and on 18 August most of the secret policemen disappeared.

On the morning of Thursday 17 August, Rol-Tanguy raised the temperature. A proclamation was issued to the people of the city signed in his name calling on every able-bodied citizen to join the FFI. He urged them to 'group together by house and by quarter' to 'knock out the Boches and grab their guns' and 'liberate greater Paris, the cradle of France'. There was to be 'no quarter for the murderers'. The order of the day for one and all was deadly simple: 'Chacun son Boche!' Henceforth, it was the duty of every French man and woman to kill his Kraut. Given the lack of guns the slogan was more a statement of intent than a practical instruction, but it set the tone for what was to come.

Rol-Tanguy had taken the initiative without going through the laborious consultations that would inevitably follow if he involved the bureaucratic machinery of the Resistance. Nevertheless, for the sake of harmony, some *ex post facto* approval would have to be obtained. That morning, at meetings of the Committee for the Liberation of Paris (CPL) and the National Resistance Council (CNR), the argument raged back and forth. The debate took its familiar form. As always, everyone agreed that there had to be an uprising. As always, no one could agree on when the uprising should begin, and as usual resources were at the heart of the matter. Rol-Tanguy reckoned there were around 23,000 men and women in the Paris area ready to fight. He was supported by the FFI commander for the city proper, an aristocratic army officer called Colonel Jean Teissier de Marguerittes, who went by the name of 'Lizé'. When they revealed that there were only 600 guns to arm the abundant volunteers, the vice president of the CPL, Léo Hamon, stepped in. Hamon was a thirty-six-year-old lawyer, the son of Jewish émigré intellectuals from Poland and Russia. He was also the representative of Ceux de la Résistance, an apolitical organization of middle-class reserve officers, bureaucrats and businessmen. When he heard how few weapons were available he insisted 'that we couldn't yet launch the order' for the uprising.

Although other moderates agreed with him, the argument for delay was steadily losing its force. Patton's troops were less than 40 miles from Paris, the city was paralysed by strikes and the Germans were on the defensive. Appeals to caution now sounded like selfish political calculations – or worse, cowardice. Once again Parodi recognized the futility of holding back. He was supported by a new Gaullist arrival, Charles Luizet, a de Gaulle protégé who had been head of intelligence operations in North Africa, then prefect of Corsica after its liberation in 1943. In early August he was ordered to get to Paris in readiness to succeed the hated prefect of the Paris police, Amédée Bussière.

Once Parodi and Luizet had given their approval the uprising was official. The following day, 18 August, posters bloomed on walls around the city declaring that 'all French men and French women should consider themselves mobilized and immediately join units of the FFI'. They were to 'attack the enemy wherever you find him, in the streets and in their bases'. The text ended with a stirring quotation from de Gaulle urging the French to get 'On your feet and into battle'. It gave the impression that the call to arms had the enthusiastic backing of everyone from the leader of the Free French down. This was far from being the case, but it was now clear among those wrestling for control of events who was leading the charge. It was Rol-Tanguy and the communists at the vanguard, and the Gaullists were trailing in their wake.

With the SS and Gestapo off his back, Choltitz could breathe a little more easily. He had no quarrel with his new Wehrmacht chief, Field Marshal Walther Model, who was about to replace Kluge as supreme commander in the west. But the collapse of the Vichy government brought fresh problems. He badly needed the goodwill of local interlocutors if he was to have any hope of convincing Parisians of his good intentions and of persuading them to behave. At 6 p.m. on 16 August he called a meeting of senior French officials at the Meurice. They included the police commissioner Bussière and the prefect of the

Seine department, René Bouffet. He began by addressing them in
halting French but after a while gave up and allowed Madame Fontanille from the Paris city hall to translate.

Choltitz seemed to want to dissociate himself from the Nazi way
of doing things and to give the impression that he was a stern but reasonable man. His main objective was to 'ensure the safety of his
troops'. However, in the event of continuing attacks and unrest he
would act on the proclamation issued the day before, promising 'the
most severe and brutal repression'. Such threats from the Germans
had by now become almost ritualistic and the visitors formed the
impression that Choltitz was above all trying to calm things down.
He also made a serious gesture of goodwill, saying he was prepared to
distribute German military rations to Parisians to help with the food
crisis. At the end of the fifteen-minute meeting Bouffet concluded
that the new military governor 'seemed like a good fellow'.

The following day Choltitz had a visit from the president of the
Paris municipal council. Pierre Taittinger was a rich man and the owner
of the famous champagne house that bore his name. Before the war
he was a leading figure of the far right, the founder of the violently
anti-communist Jeunesses Patriotes youth movement and a parliamentary deputy for the 1st arrondissement in Paris. He had fully
supported Pétain and the National Revolution, but he was also a businessman and a realist and he cared about Paris. As early as September
the previous year, he had written to Laval asking him to declare the
capital an open city as the government had done in June 1940, to spare
it when the inevitable battle for France began. Later he tried to persuade General Franco and the Portuguese dictator António de Oliveira
Salazar to intervene with Hitler on the city's behalf. He had no reason
to like Germans. His twenty-year-old son Jean had died fighting at
the head of his mostly African troops in the Battle of France after
holding up a German armoured unit for five hours.

Taittinger went to the Meurice after hearing reports that houses on
either side of the city's bridges were to be evacuated, presumably as a
preliminary to blowing them up. He was there to ask Choltitz to spare
them. Taittinger was tall and stout with imperious dark eyes, a full
mouth and a glossy moustache. He looked like he drank plenty of the

wine he produced and he radiated self-regard. Choltitz led him on to the balcony of his suite overlooking the Tuileries from where you could see most of the city's great monuments. The scene seemed placid enough and Choltitz insisted that he wanted to keep it that way, but if attacks on his men continued he would freeze normal activity and turn Paris into an armed camp. Taittinger was as eager as he was to preserve the peace and had no sympathy for those now threatening it.

With the beauties of Paris spread out before them, he launched into his appeal. He sounded like an upmarket tourist guide as he gave a *tour d'horizon* of the sights. 'On the left you can see Perrault's colonnade and our magnificent Louvre palace, on the right . . . the place de la Concorde, unique in the world, and between these two marvels so many buildings, loaded with history . . .' Choltitz understood only some of the torrent of French but seemed impressed, muttering 'Es ist ja sehr schön' ('It's really very lovely') before taking up Madame Fontanille's offer to translate. Finally, the Frenchman got to the point. Destroying the bridges would violate the city and wouldn't slow the Allied advance by a single hour. 'If I was General von Choltitz,' he finished boldly, 'I would very much want to leave Paris in the same state as I found it in.' Choltitz replied neutrally. Blowing up the bridges was not his idea. He would pass Taittinger's appeal up the line but he was 'only a little general. I receive orders. I execute them.'

Nonetheless, it seemed that Choltitz had found a Frenchman with whom he could at least discuss matters, even though it was clear that Taittinger had no control over the insurrectionary elements in the city. He had also met another figure who would prove a very useful ally.

Raoul Nordling was Sweden's long-serving consul general, a businessman and chairman of the French branch of a Swedish ball-bearing company that sold its wares to the Germans. He was born and brought up in Paris, an old boy of the Lycée Janson de Sailly, was married to a Frenchwoman and spoke French better than he did Swedish. He was short, heavy-set and sixty-one, though his grey hair, smudge of greying moustache and mournful eyes made him look older. His unheroic appearance belied a strong streak of courage and decency that both Choltitz and the people of Paris would come to thank him for.

Nordling had first approached Choltitz to ask for his help in obtaining the release of political prisoners. Some, held under French control in the Santé, the Roquette and the Tourelles prisons, had already been freed by the police prefect Bussière in a vain attempt to chalk up some credit with whoever took over from the Germans. However, there were thousands more captives in the hands of the Nazis and Nordling feared that the SS would take them with them on departure or kill them on the spot. There was good reason to worry. On leaving Caen a few weeks previously, the Germans had murdered Resistance prisoners while letting ordinary criminals go free. He had already approached the German ambassador Otto Abetz to try to place political prisoners under the protection of the Red Cross, but the initiative had come to nothing. He then teamed up with a German counter-espionage officer called Emil Bender, who was willing to help broker a deal. When Nordling and Bender met Choltitz at the Meurice he seemed uninterested in the proposal at first, playing the bluff soldier and claiming not to recognize the category of 'political prisoner'. In his eyes there were only combatants in uniform, who would be treated according to the Geneva Conventions, and gunmen in civilian clothing who would be shot according to the laws of war.

'The Gentleman of Paris'

But while they were talking, the SS commander in France, Carl Oberg, turned up to say his farewells. Oberg confirmed that orders had been issued a few days before to empty the prisons and send the inmates east in cattle trucks, to a fate that did not need to be spelled out. As he confirmed later, Choltitz already had the thought of post-war legal proceedings weighing on his mind, and like his fellow senior commanders lived with the certainty that 'their adversaries would be looking to condemn them for war crimes'. Once Oberg had departed he changed his tune. Nordling and Bender got their authorization and within a few days the shadow of death lifted from some 3,000 prisoners.

In his first week as military governor of Paris Choltitz had proved himself pragmatic and adaptable. His future depended on him convincing his superiors that he was loyally carrying out orders while, at the same time, signalling to the French and the advancing Allies that he was a decent human being and not a Nazi brute. Such a balancing act had never been required of him to date. Now it was a matter of survival.

As his fellow generals noted, Choltitz was a good judge of his audience. He flattered Taittinger ('noble and dignified, a valiant defender of Paris') with the respect the champagne magnate clearly felt was his due, and gave Nordling ('defender of human rights, "the Gentleman of Paris" as we called him') the impression that he shared his values. His message was that they were all civilized Europeans and essentially on the same side, 'men who in these hours of danger moved to defend the interests of their fellow citizens . . . real patriots'. Their sense of responsibility was a shining contrast with the 'many others in the town who were calling the people to a battle that would do them no good and only hurl them into who knew what misery'.

Choltitz's schmoozing of Vichy holdovers would do him little good, however. Nordling potentially had value as a neutral intermediary. But the likes of Taittinger, Bouffet and particularly Bussière were traitors in the eyes of the insurgents. On the early evening of Friday 18 August, Choltitz again met Taittinger and Paris officials to discuss an alarming escalation of the crisis. That morning, armed men had taken over the *mairie* at Montreuil in the eastern suburbs and raised the tricolour. Infantry, supported by tanks, had then attacked the building and two German soldiers had been killed in the fighting. It felt like the start of the uprising.

10. *Flics* and Fifis

Saturday 19 August was another sultry morning and the sun was already pressing down on the all but deserted streets as Rol-Tanguy mounted his bicycle outside his temporary base in Montrouge and set off to meet his staff on the other side of town. As he crossed the bridge by Notre-Dame at about 9 a.m., he heard male voices. It sounded as if there were hundreds of them and they were singing the 'Marseillaise'. Bizarrely, the noise seemed to be emanating from the nearby police prefecture which had been deserted since the start of the strike. 'Very intrigued', he pedalled over, parked the bike and announced his identity to the policemen guarding the grandiose main gates.

They had never heard of him and he was turned away. He went back and fetched his knapsack. Inside was a submachine gun and his old International Brigades tunic from Spain, the epaulettes gleaming with five gold bands sewn on by Cécile and denoting his new rank of colonel. This seemed to impress the guards for when he returned they let him in. He found the courtyard 'in a state of extraordinary agitation', crammed with about 2,000 officers. It seemed they had taken over the building about an hour earlier.

His first thought was to wonder who had ordered the police to escalate their strike to full-scale defiance of the Germans. He, for sure, 'knew absolutely nothing about it' and Parodi and Chaban-Delmas had not mentioned any such move. The startling new development appeared to make another item in his knapsack redundant. The sheaf of papers, typed up neatly by Cécile, giving Rol-Tanguy's orders for how the newly declared uprising should develop appeared to have been overtaken by events.

Under his 'General Order of 19 August 1944' the FFI together with any police volunteers were to start patrolling using requisitioned vehicles and wearing FFI armbands marked with the Cross of Lorraine. It also urged the population to take over public buildings, factories and railway stations. Their joint mission was 'to open the route to Paris to the victorious Allied armies and welcome them here'. The directive sounded as if it came from the headquarters of a red-tabbed general who enjoyed total control of the situation and whose wishes would be obeyed to the letter. It was a common communist delusion that by forcefully stating an objective you were halfway to accomplishing it. In theory Rol-Tanguy's authority as the FFI's Paris regional commander was accepted by all, from General Koenig to the distrustful communist hardliners of the FTP. The scene at the prefecture revealed the more fractious reality.

Rol-Tanguy thought fast. The police initiative was actually very welcome. It could potentially boost the number of trained men at his disposal and, more importantly, the number of weapons. He asked to be taken to the 'liberation committee' representing the three police resistance movements. They gave him an enthusiastic welcome. There were no objections to their men patrolling jointly with the FFI, as per his 'General Order', and attacking the Germans when the odds were favourable. Rol-Tanguy insisted that the *flics* should dress as civilians. The sight of uniforms would create a 'very real risk of clashes with the resisters' and particularly with the communist hot-bloods of the FTP who regarded the change of heart with justified scepticism. One activist, André Calvès, the Breton who had come to Paris to join the fight, recalled a story about his comrade Guy Dramard. A few weeks before, when the tide was already turning against the Germans, his room near the Bastille was raided by the police, weapons were found and he was arrested. The inspector in charge told him he was an idiot for not making a run for it. Dramard replied, 'Well, if you're for the Resistance why don't you just let me go?' He was told: 'It's too late now,' and he was handed over to the Milice who beat him up and threw him in prison. 'This was completely typical of the behaviour of thousands of *flics* who were still hunting down resisters until the minute before they put on the Cross of Lorraine,' concluded Calvès.

Rol-Tanguy left feeling pleased with the turn of events: the police had 'tilted finally on to the side of the insurrection'. As he departed, the police told him not to bother getting back on his bike. A Citroën

7CV *traction avant*, whose raked lines and flared front mudguards would become an enduring image of the uprising, the vehicle generally crammed with gun-toting young men, was at his disposal along with a driver and bodyguard.

What had prompted the police to abandon their long complicity with the enemy and wholeheartedly join the insurgency? The immediate suspicion in communist minds was that this was a manoeuvre by the Gaullists, who had indeed been planning a takeover for some time. Eight days before, Algiers had received a telegram from Parodi outlining a scheme by which 'the police themselves and elements of the Resistance would carry out the occupation of the prefecture . . . which will immediately be put under the control of the new commissioner'. That was Charles Luizet, sent in expressly to take over from the Vichy loyalist Bussière. It soon transpired that the occupation had been the idea of the Gaullists of the Honneur de la Police faction. That morning one of their leaders, Yves Bayet, had decided to seize the initiative before he was beaten to it by the communist Front National de la Police. He walked into Bussière's office and announced that he was taking over in the name of the provisional government of the French republic. One way or another, the Gaullists' plan had been executed and they now controlled a key citadel from which they could capture other strategic heights of the institutional landscape. It was the first step in de Gaulle's campaign to take over as many state functions as possible and establish facts on the ground that the Allied powers – or the communists – would find it very hard to overturn.

With the occupation of the prefecture, the smouldering insurrection became a roaring blaze. All over the city groups of young men and sometimes women, with a handful of small arms between them and identified as fighters only by an improvised FFI armband, were making their entrance. Their first act was typically to take over the local *mairie* and run up the tricolour. The buildings were invariably large and imposing and the military wisdom of gathering in one location and identifying your presence to the enemy was doubtful. By doing so the insurgents were showing their defiance and declaring the cause they were fighting for: the republican values of liberty, equality and democracy enshrined in the bust of Marianne which before the Germans came was displayed in every *mairie* in the land. By the end of the day, forty-three of the capital's eighty districts were in the hands of the Resistance.

That Saturday, the police prefecture was the beating heart of the uprising. For the first time in the history of the city, the *flics* were on the same side of the barricades as the revolutionaries. They seemed determined now to atone for their years of shame serving the oppressor and crushing the forces of freedom. That morning many *agents* returned to their home stations and teamed up with the local FFI. A hard core of several hundred remained at the prefecture. Someone climbed on the roof and hoisted the tricolour. Claude Roy, a twenty-eight-year-old writer who had flirted with the right before the war and written for *Je Suis Partout* but had since turned communist, was alerted to the sight by shouting outside his apartment window. 'The concierge called up to me: "The flag is on the prefecture!" I run down to the street. It's true. On the rooftop of the prefecture is a little dark shape, some fellow who has just run up the flag. The flag floats in the breeze. One flag, two flags. A flag on the towers of Notre Dame. A flag on a balcony . . .'

Inside, the defenders were turning the huge, seven-storey grey stone hulk looming the length of the quai des Orfèvres on the south bank of the Île de la Cité into a fortress. Fortunately there were materials to hand. In the tumultuous years before the war, tens of thousands of sandbags had been stored in the cellars for protection in case of attack by an insurgent mob. They were now packed around windows and doors to create firing points. The building commanded clear fields of fire over a large swathe of the Left Bank. There were no heavy weapons to make maximum use of these advantages, just rifles and seven machine guns. Around mid-morning Luizet was cheered by the defenders when he arrived to take up his new appointment in the name of de Gaulle and the provisional government.

Luizet was careful to respect the agreed chain of command. He contacted Rol-Tanguy and asked him to come straight away to meet Parodi. The rendezvous was in an apartment in the avenue de Lowendal near the Invalides. He advised Rol-Tanguy to wear civvies. Rol-Tanguy was reluctant. Having ceremoniously put on his old uniform, it might look rather cowardly if he now took it off. Luizet was insistent. The streets around the meeting place were swarming with Germans and if they spotted him they might all end up in the bag. Rol-Tanguy complied. It was a small, but symbolic, indication of how power was starting to shift from the soldiers who had kept the flame of resistance alive through the war years to the sophisticated new arrivals.

It was the first time that Parodi and Rol-Tanguy had met. At the outset, Parodi made it clear who was in overall charge. It was the provisional government of the French republic, led by General de Gaulle. At the same time he was careful to say that every combatant, be they policeman or resister, was under Rol-Tanguy's orders. This was a politeness rather than a statement of fact. The Paris police were always going to answer to their new prefect Luizet rather than the FFI chief. But the need to maintain unity was paramount and at that moment it suited everyone to swallow the fiction.

By the time the meeting was over, so many bullets were flying around the prefecture that Luizet had to delay his return. Tension had been building for a showdown with the Germans all morning. The journalist Claude Roy saw 'little by little, the streets emptying, except for the FFI with brassards on their arms . . . in front of the cafés the tables and chairs were all stacked up and the steel shutters pulled down'. Two big cars passed by with tricolour markings, one of them the former property of Cardinal Suhard. The windows had been knocked out to made shooting easier. The Germans in the back of speeding trucks seemed 'like hunted animals' and opened up at random on passers-by.

The streets around the prefecture had become a firing range with those inside shooting at any German vehicle that passed. When Choltitz first heard of the takeover he held back from launching an immediate counter-attack for fear of triggering a major clash. The situation inside and outside the city was changing constantly and his instinct for self-preservation warned against any hasty moves. His method throughout the crises ahead was to bluster threateningly while trying to calm the situation and play for time. But by early afternoon the challenge to his authority could no longer be ignored. At 2 p.m. the Germans launched their riposte. The assault opened when a truck crammed with troops screeched along the boulevard du Palais, pouring fire into the east façade of the prefecture. Then a squad of infantrymen crept across the Petit Pont, a few hundred yards to the east. Sharpshooters in their sandbagged eyries knocked them down 'like clay pipes in a shooting gallery'. A convoy of troop carriers attempted to cross to the Île from the Left Bank by the same route. They came under fire, this time from FFI fighters in the place Saint-Michel and were driven back.

The Germans tried to seal off the bridge with lorries but soon gave up, abandoning a burning truck. A snatch squad darted from the prefecture to grab discarded weapons then hurried back to await the next assault. It came at 2.45. Three more lorries carrying about fifty soldiers made it on to the boulevard du Palais and tried to storm the main entrance, only to be beaten back leaving several dead behind.

Claude Roy managed to sneak into the prefecture by a back door. Inside the main courtyard were stacks of seized German weaponry, a few captured enemy vehicles and some nervous prisoners. In the first flush of battle the 'Fifis', as everyone was starting to call the FFI fighters, were anxious to show that although they might be irregulars

Defending the prefecture

they fought more cleanly than their enemies in uniform. He saw a fighter 'offer a cigarette to a prisoner. [The German] was trembling, convinced he was going to be shot. Another [Fifi], dark with sweat and dust, gave a shot of alcohol to a young, exhausted SS officer.' Roy was touched by the gesture then remembered 'the twenty-year-old lads, the Maquis members killed by the Germans, the FFI prisoners in German hands who even now they might well be putting up against a wall and machine-gunned' and his heart hardened.

The prefecture echoed to the 'incredible racket of the gunfire, bouncing around the walls, the corridors and staircases'. During the rare moments of calm, the big doors opened to let in ambulances and stretcher bearers waving Red Cross flags. Roy went up to the prefect's office to make a call and found a secretary serenely manning the phones. She wore 'a short, immaculately white, rayon dress', and a bouquet of roses – a little faded – sat on the desk. 'Doesn't look like I'll be making it to the Piscine Deligny today,' she remarked with a wry smile. Men came and went carrying cases of explosives and detonators. A Fifi arrived to call a friend. 'You'd better get a move on, Nini!' he boasted. 'I've already notched up five Frisés. We'll have the bastards!'

The high spirits dipped when three German tanks were seen grinding into the forecourt of Notre-Dame a few hundred yards to the east. A couple of shells slammed into the barricaded main entrance, tearing one of the heavy doors off its hinges. Some of the men in the courtyard ran for the safety of the steps connecting the building to the next-door Métro station. The others stayed put, blocking the gaping door with trucks and sandbags. Soon afterwards the tanks moved off, apparently on the orders of Choltitz, keen once again it seemed to avoid further escalation. The defenders were unappeased. They shot up a convoy of lorries that wandered into the boulevard du Palais, knocking out three of them and making off with a haul of guns. At 5 p.m. the Germans attempted another infiltration up the steps below the quai des Orfèvres but after taking a number of casualties were forced to retreat.

The fighting had by now spread well beyond the prefecture and small battles were raging all over Paris and in the suburbs. Just opposite the prefecture on the Left Bank a combined force of FFI and local police had turned the boulevard Saint-Michel into a killing zone.

Young men in shirtsleeves planted a machine-gun post in the Café du Départ overlooking the fountain in the place Saint-Michel and blasted away at any German truck or car that showed itself. During a mad few hours they shot up twenty-five vehicles, hauling the dead away and stacking them up on the river embankment, out of sight of the next unsuspecting Germans to wander into their view. Shedding German blood felt like an act of redemption. From his fifth-floor apartment on the place Saint-Michel a fifty-nine-year-old veteran of the last war called Gustave-Jean Reybaz watched the carnage below and trembled with pride. Four years before, he had looked down on the same square and seen the Germans 'invading the café terraces . . . spreading themselves out through the little streets, the cosmopolitan hotels, the dives and dodgy little bars' of the Latin Quarter, 'getting a loud welcome from the collaborators and congratulating each other as they drank all night'. Now 'Paris was liberating itself and the lads of Saint-Michel were wiping away the stain that was inflicted on our souls those first days.'

By the standards of the day Reybaz was an old man, but he could not resist going down for a closer look. In the place Saint-Michel he heard 'a noise of grinding metal' and saw the Fifis ducking into doorways. 'A German lorry swept in from the pont Saint-Michel, with a soldier in green lying on the bonnet.' It had not yet passed the Rotisserie Périgourdine restaurant when the man was hit. 'He dropped his rifle, slid off, rolled along the ground . . .' The lorry halted. 'A great cry went up across the square. Hooray! We've got them! And from everywhere the FFI threw themselves at the truck. These men, armed only with revolvers, were attacking a nest of automatic rifles and carbines . . . the first fell but those following climbed over them in a hellish rattle of gunfire until at last it stopped and the square rang with cries of victory.'

The desperate need for weapons produced acts of extraordinary bravery. The only way to get them was to physically take them off the Germans. One simple but very dangerous method was to scatter nails on the road to burst the tyres of any passing lorries. When a convoy ground to a halt in the rue Saint-André-des-Arts near the place Saint-Michel that afternoon, a forty-three-year-old police inspector called Louis Desnos ran out and jumped on to the footplate of a lorry, pistol in hand. He killed the driver and wounded another

German before being shot dead by the third man in the cab. His comrades swarmed in to grab their guns. It was a terrible price to pay, but three more rifles had been added to the armoury – and every weapon counted.

The battle was taking place just round the corner from Picasso's studio on the rue des Grands-Augustins. As the situation deteriorated, he had decided to break his rule of non-cohabitation with Marie-Thérèse and had temporarily moved in with her and their daughter Maya in the flat he paid for across the river in the boulevard Henri-IV near the Bastille. Dora Maar was left behind in the rue de Savoie. As there were no cars to drive him and the Métro had long ago stopped running, he was forced to cross the city on foot. According to family legend, on the way he was 'grazed by a sniper's bullet'. Maya was approaching her ninth birthday. He holed up with her and her mother, recounting to his daughter some of the myths and legends that had helped shape his artistic imagination. There he would stay until it was safe to return home.

By early evening the situation inside police HQ was getting desperate. Léo Hamon, the cautious Ceux de la Résistance leader, made a visit to liaise with contacts inside. When he asked how long they could hold out he was told: 'If we don't shoot too much, maybe until five or six in the morning.' After that they would have to give in and Hamon feared that surrender could easily be followed by a massacre. The defenders held their fire and he crept out and raced off on his bicycle to find Parodi. He eventually tracked him down in a nearby apartment where he was huddled with Chaban-Delmas. The atmosphere was strained. Chaban-Delmas was still angry at his colleague's decision to give official backing to the uprising. He told Parodi it was in direct contradiction of the orders he had received from London to hold back the insurrection until the Allies were at the city gates. The information he was receiving from across the front lines suggested it would be Wednesday at the very earliest before they could get there – even if they could be persuaded to do so. That left four more days, by which time every building now held by the Resistance would probably have been recaptured and many of those inside dead. In his messages back to the Free French he said that he dreaded the possibility of a 'new Warsaw' and he made it clear to Parodi that he would hold him responsible for what happened. 'When you've done something stupid, you shouldn't be surprised at the consequences,' he snapped. The older man was philosophical. 'If I was wrong to agree to it, I will have the rest of my life to repent,' he replied.

None of this was helping the men in the prefecture. Hamon's report on the situation only deepened the delegation's anxiety. They had no guns or ammunition to offer the defenders. After a short debate they decided that the only option was to wait until it was dark and then attempt to evacuate the building. Hamon set off to tell the police the decision. As he approached, he saw that the Germans had taken over the surrounding streets. He retreated to an apartment in the rue Saint-Jacques. He had not been there long when the firing outside slackened. Though the city was without gas, electricity or transport, by some miracle the telephones still worked. Hamon called the prefecture to find out what was going on. The policeman who picked up the phone told him: 'It looks like there's a ceasefire.'

The story of how the ceasefire at the prefecture – and the patchy and very short-lived wider truce that followed – came about would be told in many forms and no account would ever be agreed. The left and right of the Resistance each had their own version, and memories were shaped accordingly in the post-liberation scramble to gain maximum credit for their role in events. As it turned out, the brief cessation of hostilities did little to alter the course of the uprising, merely bringing a short respite that at the time suited Choltitz on one side and the Gaullists on the other, as well as the beleaguered *flics* at the prefecture.

Choltitz always maintained that his first priority was the safety of his men. All day they had come under attack by gunmen who wore no uniform. In the eyes of a conventional German officer, the correct response was to treat them as criminals and shoot them out of hand along with a salutary number of civilians. But Choltitz had no desire for a bloodbath. Massacres and reprisals would divert resources from the defence of the city. They might also lead him to the gallows after Paris inevitably fell. His second concern was to show his superiors he was doing his best to facilitate the great German retreat. The Battle of Normandy was over. The German armies were falling back across the Seine and troops would be routing through the Paris region on their way east. He saw his job as subduing the area until the withdrawal was over. He still believed he had sufficient resources – in particular the Panther and Tiger tanks that would be coming from the west – to crush an uprising. If he wanted to, he could have ended the occupation of the prefecture in a couple of hours. Instead he had acted with caution and his preference was to try and persuade the population that he would leave them alone if they co-operated. But how was he going to communicate his intentions?

The arrival of Raoul Nordling, 'the gentleman of Paris', that Saturday afternoon offered at least a sympathetic ear. The Swedish consul general had already had a very busy day. Early that morning, he went to a camp at Romainville outside Paris to speed up the prisoner releases arranged with Choltitz. Then he set off to the prefecture in response to an urgent message from Bussière. It was not yet noon and still reasonably quiet. When he arrived, he found Bussière gone and Luizet and the police liberation committee in charge. When Nordling had offered his services as a neutral intermediary with the Germans he was rebuffed.

That afternoon Nordling got a call from Parodi's team alerting him to the arrival of the tanks in the forecourt of Notre-Dame and the likelihood that the Germans were about to assault the prefecture. He rushed to the Meurice to try and intercede. When he got there he found that Choltitz was getting angry at the apparent failure of his softly-softly approach. He had demonstrated his good faith by freeing political prisoners but 'a bunch of terrorists' had now repaid him by capturing the prefecture and 'are shooting right below my windows'. Nordling feared Choltitz was about to order an all-out attack on the police HQ and tried to talk him down. 'If you destroy the prefecture,' he told him, 'you'll also destroy Notre-Dame and La Chapelle,' the luminously beautiful thirteenth-century church which stood next door.

Choltitz seemed to be listening. If order was to be restored, though, he needed 'someone in authority' with whom he could do business. Nordling told him it was no use looking to Bussière and Taittinger or any other members of the old Vichy establishment for help. To reach a deal he would have to negotiate directly with the Resistance. Choltitz objected that he would 'never talk to criminals, terrorists, communists'. Nordling persisted, however, pointing out that at their head were 'the men of Algiers', representatives of the provisional government. 'You ought to have more respect for them than for the men of Vichy,' he told him. 'If you had been French, you would have been one of them.' The flattery worked. Choltitz accepted Nordling's offer to be an intermediary, as long as it didn't involve Choltitz himself talking to the enemy. Nordling returned to his consulate and shortly afterwards, at 6.30 p.m., the telephone rang. It was Luizet's people in the prefecture. Things were looking very bad for the defenders and they needed his help.

In the discussions between the prefecture, the consulate and the Meurice that followed, a clear deal emerged. A communiqué was drawn up in the name of 'the patriots of Paris and the German command'. It called on all combatants to suspend operations 'while awaiting the hour of Liberation' and allow the Germans to carry on evacuating Paris unmolested. The agreement left captured public buildings in the hands of the resisters. It also stipulated that the laws of war would be respected and Fifis taken prisoner would be treated as regular soldiers.

By the next morning, Léo Hamon had taken advantage of the lull to extend the authority of the state. There was a storm overnight and the air was clean and fresh when, at daybreak, he crossed the river to the Right Bank accompanied by a gaggle of officials and helpers, including some women 'auxiliaries'. Their destination was the vast, châteauesque neo-Renaissance concoction of the Hôtel de Ville, which looked as if it had been uprooted from the Loire valley and plonked down beside the Seine. The building was only seventy years old. The previous one had been burned down in the days of the Commune. Practically, and symbolically, it was the seat of power in the capital, housing the offices of the prefect of the Seine and the municipal council. Whoever held it could claim to possess the city.

The team marched in and up to the sumptuous marble- and

wood-lined office of the prefect, where the incumbent René Bouffet looked on, outraged. Striking the desk with his fist, Hamon cried out: 'In the name of the Provisional Government of the French Republic and on behalf of the Paris Liberation Committee, I am taking possession of the Hôtel de Ville.' Seeing a bust of Pétain, he ordered it to be taken down. Bouffet blustered for a while, accusing them of 'acting like children'. Then he asked nervously, 'I hope you're not going to do anything stupid.' Bouffet's reign was over. He was arrested and led away, to await whatever justice would emerge from the chaos. Hamon's day had got off to an excellent start. Both city hall and police HQ were now in the hands of the respectable wing of the Resistance.

Before the communiqué could be issued it would have to be approved by a plethora of Resistance chiefs. A group including the Gaullist delegation of Parodi and Chaban-Delmas and members of the CNR and the CPL, including the communist representatives André Tollet and Pierre Villon, were summoned to the Hôtel de Ville. To the Gaullists, the truce made perfect sense. The Germans had more or less signalled that they were leaving. The Resistance anyway lacked the arms to drive them out, and with the police prefecture and city hall in their hands the moderates had a firm grasp on the vital administrative organs of Paris. To Tollet and Villon, the truce was a betrayal. The people were on their feet, reclaiming their fate. It was unthinkable that they should now be told to lie down again. The militants were outnumbered and outvoted. The communiqué went back to Choltitz, who added an appeal to the population to stay calm. He emphasized the need for the streets to be kept clear so that German traffic could move freely. There were to be no roadblocks or barricades. The news of the truce could now be broadcast to the population via loudspeakers mounted on cars.

There was one glaring absentee from the Hôtel de Ville meeting. Parodi had not thought it necessary to invite the man commanding those who were now being told to lay down their arms. He excused Rol-Tanguy's non-invitation on the flimsy grounds that the matter under discussion was political rather than military. The truth was, the decision had been taken by a small and barely representative cabal, and it was bound to be challenged by the militants.

Rol-Tanguy had shifted headquarters again, this time to a bunker deep under the streets of Paris. It had been built before the war, 85 feet below street level, as a shelter for the Paris water and sewage systems in case of an enemy poison-gas attack, just next to the major street junction at Denfert-Rochereau in the 14th arrondissement. It came equipped with its own telephone network, accommodation, air-conditioning system and bicycle generators to provide electricity. The new command post was certainly secure but hardly very practical. Each trip to the surface to survey the situation on the ground meant Rol-Tanguy had to climb 118 steps.

He first heard of the truce at 7.30 on Sunday morning, 20 August. A message arrived from the headquarters of the Paris FFI commander Colonel Lizé in the rue Guénégaud near the Paris Mint on the Left Bank reporting that they had been instructed by Chaban-Delmas to 'avoid all combat and bloodletting in Paris'. Rol-Tanguy phoned Lizé and told him to ignore the intervention, which was a 'flagrant contradiction' of the insurrection order of the day before. Lizé had already come to the same conclusion and his men were fighting on. Other FFI commanders in the city had also decided to ignore the truce.

Even so, Sunday started off quieter than Saturday. There were tanks on the streets but the muzzles of their main guns were covered with leather caps. It was hot, a real August scorcher, and many Parisians ignored the distant patter of gunfire to follow their usual summer city routines. The bars were open. The smell of beer and Caporal tobacco, the click of billiard balls and the sound of the latest hits on the radio drifted out over the pavements. Down by the pont d'Iéna, on the artificial beach created for the great exhibition of 1937, old men sat in deckchairs, bald heads protected from the throbbing sun by hats made from folded newsprint, the young sunbathed on airbeds and anglers sat staring at floats bobbing in the milky-green river. Sometimes a burst of fire near by disturbed their composure briefly before they resumed wallowing in the simple pleasure of doing nothing on a sunny Paris Sunday.

As the day passed, a new sound was heard around the city. Cars with FFI markings, fitted with loudspeakers and loaded with young men, toured the streets broadcasting the message that 'As a result of promises made by the German commander not to attack public buildings occupied by French troops and to treat all prisoners according to the laws of war, the Provisional Government . . . and the National Resistance Council ask you to hold fire against the occupants until the total evacuation of Paris . . .' Behind them cruised German field police escorts.

The announcement was met by the civilian population with relief and even rejoicing. Many seemed to believe that it indicated the end of the war, at least in France. Walter Dreizner, whose signals duties meant he would be staying in Paris until the end, was now installed in a hotel in the rue du Mont Thabor behind the Meurice. That afternoon he heard cries of 'La guerre est finie!' and saw 'everywhere joy, mass gatherings and tricolours'. It was as if they were celebrating a victory. The German masters may not have been defeated but they had been forced to come to terms with the Resistance, and that, after the years of oppression and humiliation, for the ordinary inhabitants felt like a sort of triumph.

The frequent rattle of unexplained gunfire cautioned against too much optimism. The Germans were jumpy and unpredictable, as Parodi discovered that afternoon. He was being driven to a meeting with two other members of the Gaullist delegation when they were arrested and taken to the Meurice. Before they could be seen by Choltitz, one of the last remaining Gestapo officers in the city spotted them and they were handcuffed and hauled to an office in the 16th arrondissement where it seemed for a time that they might be shot. Parodi's cool authority persuaded the Nazi he had better check before having him killed and he was taken back to the Meurice where, this time, Choltitz saw him. Choltitz had accepted Nordling's advice to make a distinction between the communists and the FFI, whom he continued to deplore as 'hooligans' and 'terrorists', and the 'gentlemen' representing the provisional government.

The well-dressed, assured figures standing before him with the confidence of equals were clearly 'gentlemen'. He 'felt for the first time that I was dealing with . . . real spokesmen for the population', and after a few stiff exchanges he treated them as such. He asked first if they intended to abide by the truce and whether they were able to

exercise real control over the insurgents. Parodi's replies were eva-
sive. Choltitz had to realize that 'a population in arms' couldn't be
ordered about like a conventional army. The Resistance was made up
of different groups, with different tendencies. Boldly, he now sought
his own assurances from the general: that the occupation of public
buildings would be 'respected' and that the Resistance newspapers
which were now springing up everywhere would be left alone.

Choltitz replied that he was concerned only with military matters.
Ministries and newspapers 'were all about politics' and didn't interest
him. The important thing 'was to maintain the suspension of hostilities. I will give the order not to fire on [occupied] buildings. But you
must see that you don't shoot at my troops. And there must be no
barricades.' The gentlemen had reached an agreement. When Choltitz told them they were free to go, he offered his hand to Parodi, who
declined it but courteously lowered his head.

For the arrangement to work the assent of the 'hooligans' was
needed. It was immediately clear that this was not forthcoming. While
the ceasefire was being broadcast, posters authorized by Rol-Tanguy
went up declaring that no truce had been agreed and threatening
reprisals against German prisoners if any violence was done to civilians. Many FFI units had anyway made their own decision to fight on,
clashing with SS escapees from Normandy who did not take their
orders from Choltitz.

That Sunday morning, Raymond Ruffin was holed up in the
family apartment in the east of the city eating a meagre breakfast.
The apartment overlooked the German base in the medieval fortress
of the Château de Vincennes. Looking down over the cours des
Maréchaux he saw a tank appear, surrounded by ten or so helmeted
soldiers. There was a knocking on the door. It was the concierge, out
of breath, telling his mother, 'Don't let your son go out! The Germans are shooting at every man and boy they see in the street.'
Women were apparently allowed free passage and, risky though it
was, Madame Ruffin left to try and find bread. Raymond tried to
read but his concentration was shattered by a burst of automatic fire.
He went to the window but could not see who, or what, the Germans were shooting at. He ran downstairs to go and find his mother,

but the concierge stopped him and ordered him back to the flat. Shortly afterwards his mother returned. She was pale and her legs were shaking. 'The dirty Boches stopped me and slapped my cheek,' she told him. The Germans were shooting at pedestrians in the boulevard de Paris and she thought they had hit an old man walking behind her, 'but I wasn't brave enough to turn round and look'.

The pair could not resist crawling to the bay window and looking down. The concierge joined them. The walls of the fort were lined with chestnut trees under which stood a handful of soldiers. They wore SS uniforms and clearly were taking no notice of the supposed truce. From time to time they pointed their rifles towards the apartment block, sending the three of them sprawling on their bellies. When no shots came, Raymond raised his head again. There was movement under the trees. A gang of men in civilian clothes appeared with spades over their shoulders, escorted by the SS. They began digging furiously in the earth until only their shoulders were visible. Then they were ordered out of the ditch to line up with their backs to the trench and the Germans levelled their rifles. 'I lowered my head,' Raymond wrote. 'I didn't want to look. I was quivering, waiting for the shots. Ten seconds passed. Nothing.' When he looked again, the men were being marched away at the double, up the stone staircase that led to the fort's inner courtyard.

They re-emerged, now carrying makeshift stretchers loaded with corpses. They tipped them into the ditch and then set off again, speeded by blows to the kidneys from German rifle butts. They came back with another load of bodies, this time dragging them by their shoulders and legs. Raymond couldn't keep track of the numbers of dead as each time the guards glanced his way he dived to the floor, but he counted at least ten. When he raised his head for the last time the corpse bearers were lined up again along the ditch. Having completed their task, was it their turn to die? But no. They began shovelling dirt over the bodies then were marched back into the fort. It was over. The concierge was weeping and Raymond and his mother sat in stunned silence. It was still only early afternoon.

The dead were captured Fifis and policemen and their killers were SS troops fleeing Normandy. The gravediggers were *flics* arrested when

SS victims at the Château de Vincennes

SS troops raided the police post in the rue de Lyon in the 12th arrondissement the previous afternoon. When an FFI brassard was discovered, about twenty officers were herded on to buses and driven off to the fort. The station chief, Inspector Silvestri, had stepped forward to accept responsibility for the armband. He was taken away and shot. The others were told their lives would be spared if they disposed of the bodies. There would be more executions the following day.

Similar atrocities were committed elsewhere in the city. Within a few hours of the ceasefire beginning, it was clear that it was a truce in name only. At Vitry, six FFI men who left the telephone exchange they had occupied in search of food were arrested and shot in cold blood. Germans stormed a police station in the 20th arrondissement and freed *miliciens* being held there. At the Porte d'Orléans, an FFI position was attacked by forty SS, supported by an armoured car, and overwhelmed. In the face of these acts the moderates' calls for restraint and warnings about reprisals sounded very like cowardice and many FFI foot soldiers, especially the old guard who had joined before the Allied landings, were in no mood to lay down their guns. That Sunday afternoon, a loudspeaker car broadcasting the news of the truce was stopped in the rue de Laborde near Saint-Lazare station by Fifi militants who told the broadcasters they would shoot them if they did not stop.

Neither Choltitz nor the Resistance leaders had complete authority over the forces they were supposed to control. It nonetheless suited both the German commander and the Parodi faction to keep at least the pretence of a truce in place for the time being. Both were buying time: Choltitz for an orderly withdrawal of his men; the moderates to stave off a full-scale uprising until the Allies were on the doorstep. This 'synchronicity' – a favourite word of Hamon's – would allow the city to claim to have played a major part in its own liberation without risking too much disorder, bloodshed or kudos for the communists.

Parodi's agreement was, however, conditional. The respite was welcome but it could not be allowed to threaten a much greater consideration. Since Jean Moulin had forged the National Resistance Council in May 1943, communists, socialists, radicals, Christian democrats, rightists and trade unionists had been united under the same banner. The alliance had often been ragged and fractious, but it sustained the hope that the cohesion that France had spent its modern history trying to achieve could at last be realized and even carried into peacetime. The truce had driven a wedge into the ranks. A schism now would be catastrophic, wrecking the Resistance narrative of duty and patriotism over self-interest, and blighting the prospect of a more harmonious future.

In an effort to limit damage, Parodi called a meeting of the CNR, the National Resistance Council, for Monday afternoon. The cracks were widening. The communist-dominated Paris Liberation Committee had already issued a call for the truce to be abandoned. At 5 p.m. the CNR leaders gathered in a house near Denfert-Rochereau station. The little drawing room, furnished in bourgeois style with Louis XVI armchairs, was barely big enough to fit everyone in and some had to sit on the floor. It was stiflingly hot and the windows were left open, only to be hurriedly shut again for fear of attracting the Germans' attention, as tempers and voices rose. Pierre Villon, communist, founder of the National Front resistance group and member of the COMAC military committee, led the charge. The decision to enter the truce had been taken by only five CNR members and was therefore illegal, he declared. Parodi defended himself, saying that the population of Paris had been at risk and there was no time to follow the formalities. Villon and his allies were unappeased.

The language got harsher and tempers shorter until Chaban-Delmas intervened, convinced apparently that his eloquence could save the day. The heat seemed to have no effect on him. He was cool and measured, every inch the cerebral inspector of finances. He went on for thirty-five minutes, laying out the background to the negotiations and emphasizing the dangers. They had very few weapons and there was no sign that the Allied arrival was imminent. It was therefore necessary to stick to the truce until the moment was ripe. At one point he unwisely referred to the deal with Choltitz as a 'gentleman's agreement', which provoked some growls from the militants, who wondered out loud how it was possible to consider a German general a man of honour. When he had finished his speech, Villon remarked loudly, 'It's the first time I've heard such cowardice from a French general.' In the uproar that followed, Chaban-Delmas maintained his sangfroid, smiling as Parodi stepped in to pay tribute to his courage and call on Villon to retract, which he quickly did.

In the end it was Parodi who broke the deadlock. While agreeing with the Chaban-Delmas analysis, he also understood the necessity of taking the fight to the Germans if Paris was to have any plausible claim to have liberated itself, as well as the vital importance of unity. He proposed a compromise. The truce would be broken – but not until 16.00 hours the following day. It was an absurd suggestion that no one could take seriously but it allowed both sides to claim victory. They were all exhausted and overheated and their nerves were stretched as tight as guitar strings. Parodi's compromise was put to the vote and unanimously approved. As they trooped out on to the burning pavements, Parodi could feel reassured that things might yet turn out for the best. His mission to establish de Gaulle's authority was going well and his men had taken advantage of the lull to tighten their grip on the organs of government. The previous day they had occupied not only the Hôtel de Ville and prefecture but also the Hôtel Matignon, official residence of the French prime minister, as well as the ministries of the Interior, Finance, Health and Public Works. The prospect of the Allies setting up their own military government was receding by the hour.

The threat of a bloodbath remained. Whatever the councils of the Resistance might decide, the uprising was taking on a life of its own. The FFI bands, many of them new arrivals with years of humiliation to avenge, seemed deaf to the communiqués that flowed from Resistance HQs. That morning, the first barricades appeared around the city as Parisians felt the tingle of revolt in their blood. Choltitz had specifically warned against this, and for every placatory word he had uttered there had always been a corresponding threat. How would he react to an outbreak of mass disobedience?

It was this uncertainty that persuaded all elements of the Resistance to agree on at least one thing: the paramount necessity for the Allied armies to go hell for leather for Paris. The previous day, Rol-Tanguy had received a message from a leading Paris physician called Robert Monod. His Red Cross doctor's pass allowed him to travel relatively freely in the region and he was also entitled to coupons to obtain petrol, now in very short supply. He was offering his services as a guide to help an envoy to make contact with the advancing Americans. Rol-Tanguy's chief of staff was Roger Cocteau, a cousin of Jean Cocteau and a former professional soldier who was better known by his code-name 'Gallois'. He happened to know Monod and spoke fluent English. Rol-Tanguy ordered him to contact the doctor. The two met and that same evening set off to cross the lines.

11. Volte-face

For all its mystique and heady symbolism, the American and British generals chasing the Germans back across the Rhine saw Paris as an irrelevance, merely an 'ink spot on the map' according to the commander of the 12th Army Group, Omar Bradley. Pausing to liberate it would only waste time and soldiers' lives and land the Allies with the huge logistical burden of feeding and caring for millions of hungry inhabitants. Since long before D-Day, the intention had been to bypass the city and deal with the garrison later. But Dwight D. Eisenhower, the man in charge of the enterprise, knew the fragility of plans when they collided with reality. The situation was changing fast and pressure was mounting for Allied tactics to change with them.

On the morning of Sunday 20 August, a Lockheed Lodestar passenger plane arrived at Maupertus airfield east of Cherbourg. The wheels threw up a curtain of spray as it touched down on the landing strip, sodden from a night of torrential rain. The plane stopped and the rear door opened. A very tall man stooped to squeeze through and with ponderous dignity descended the ladder. Then Charles de Gaulle mounted the jeep waiting to whisk him away to Eisenhower's forward HQ, a 'tent and trailer' camp set up in fields near Tournières, 50 miles to the south-east.

De Gaulle had shown uncharacteristic restraint since his visit to Bayeux in June and had left the Allies to get on with winning the Battle of Normandy. He stayed in Algiers, preparing the ground for his accession to power, taking time out to visit Roosevelt in Washington. On hearing of the growing unrest in Paris he decided it was time to intervene. On 14 August he told the British he wanted to return to France. They were all in favour. De Gaulle's authority might impose some order on the unravelling situation in the capital, and the Foreign Office were as concerned as he was at the prospect of the communists exploiting the growing chaos to launch a coup. Eisenhower had no objection, nor did the US chiefs of staff.

The arrangements for the journey from Algiers had been fraught with arguments, with de Gaulle, in the words of the British representative to the Free French Duff Cooper, 'giving trouble about this as he does about everything'. The Americans offered to fly him in a B-17 Flying Fortress, but he refused unless the bomber carried French blue, white and red markings and ended up using his own aeroplane. The Fortress was good enough for his staff, however, and the two aircraft set off from Algiers on the afternoon of 18 August. At a stopover in Casablanca, the B-17 developed engine trouble. There were more mechanical problems at Gibraltar. An exasperated de Gaulle announced they would fly on alone in the unarmed Lodestar, leaving on the 19th. It was night and a storm was raging as they flew along the Normandy coast. De Gaulle's pilot, Colonel de Marmier, lost his bearings and ended up crossing the English Channel. The fuel needle was dipping alarmingly and de Marmier proposed landing to refuel. De Gaulle refused. They were going to France, or would die trying, and the plane swung back across the Channel, touching down at Maupertus with the gauge on empty.

De Gaulle's perpetual prickliness was a defence mechanism, the armour he put up to shield his pride. It had received many dents during the years of exile, due to his lowly position in the Allied hierarchy. He was the eternal supplicant with much to ask and very little to give. Now he was on his way to seek another favour, this time a huge one. When he arrived at the muddy field that was the supreme commander's forward base, he could not afford to show the unbending haughtiness with which he habitually treated the British.

To impose his authority on France he had to control Paris. As well as being the heart and soul of the nation, it was the cerebral cortex, directing all the essential functions of the state. Parodi and Chaban-Delmas had made progress establishing his authority, but to his suspicious mind the dangers of a collapse into chaos and the threat of a Red putsch were still very real. He also detected trouble from another direction, also aimed at denying him power. Word had reached him of Laval's manoeuvre to win over Herriot and form a transitional government. De Gaulle was nervous that the White House and State Department were in on it and would be happy to see him sidelined. His fears were groundless, and Laval's deluded initiative had already failed, but de Gaulle couldn't shake the view that there was a conspiracy against him. To thwart any fait accompli, the Allies had to march on the city immediately. And Eisenhower was the only man who could make the decision and hand him the keys to his kingdom.

On the general's arrival at 10 a.m., Eisenhower was there to greet him, along with an American honour guard. De Gaulle responded graciously, congratulating his host on the crushing defeat that he had just inflicted on the Germans. A photographer snapped them standing together in a field in the Normandy sunshine, Eisenhower smiling with evident sincerity at the stiff Frenchman in a heavy serge uniform that must have felt stifling in the humid heat of the morning. Ike's affection for de Gaulle endured, and he felt a fundamental sympathy with his difficulties and respect for his achievement in conjuring a virtual France out of almost nothing. Nonetheless, when he told his visitor his plans, there was no deviation from the original intention to bypass Paris.

The scheme was not his. It had been drawn up in London by Allied staff well before the invasion. The planners had thought it likely that the Germans would hold on firmly to Paris. Attacking it directly would therefore probably mean prolonged street fighting, considerable losses and delay. The city would be badly knocked about in the process, and there was a strong possibility that the challenge might push the enemy to destroy as much of it as they could. The best option was to leave Paris alone, swinging around it to the north and south, cutting it off and leaving the isolated defenders to eventually accept their fate and surrender. If the Allies did occupy the city they would immediately become responsible for the welfare of the four and a half million living in the greater Paris area. Eisenhower's instructions were that he was to distribute relief only if it did not conflict with the logistical needs of his own forces. Getting sucked into a major humanitarian operation could only benefit the enemy and put off the day of victory.

The plan, as he explained to de Gaulle, was that Patton's Third Army would cross the Seine at two points, Mantes to the north of Paris and Melun to the south. Meanwhile, Montgomery's 21st Army Group were to strike through Rouen, to hound the Germans to the Belgian border. De Gaulle listened, then responded politely that of course 'the conduct of operations must proceed from you'. But, however logical the plan might be in military terms, 'the fate of Paris' was involved and that was 'of fundamental concern' to the French government, in the person of himself. He therefore 'felt obliged to intervene and to ask you to send French troops there'. The obvious choice to liberate the city was Leclerc's 2ème Division Blindée, as had been agreed eight months before in North Africa.

De Gaulle developed his case, which he later put in writing, telling Eisenhower that everything he was hearing 'leads me to believe that . . . serious trouble must be foreseen in the capital'. He claimed that the German forces had almost completely disappeared – a considerable and potentially dangerous exaggeration. Also that the police were no longer on duty to impose order and there was an 'extreme shortage of food', both of which were true enough. It was therefore 'really necessary to occupy Paris with French and Allied forces, even if it should produce some fighting and some damage within the City'. When they parted, Eisenhower assured him that he would keep his promise to send Leclerc's division to Paris, but he could not say exactly when. De Gaulle left somewhat consoled. But time was pressing and every minute counted if he was to pull off his grab for power and save the capital from prolonged suffering.

The GIs converging on the Seine had no idea where they were going next. With the signposts telling them that Paris was just down the road, they dared to hope that they might soon be marching through the streets of the fabled city. Very few of them had ever set foot in the place. Some had fathers and uncles who had fought in the last war. They had heard from them about the delights of Paris and the sort of reception they could expect if they got there. Everyone knew that, before you died, you had to have seen the City of Light. And death, these days, was never very far away.

The same thought had occurred to Ernest Hemingway. With the Battle of Normandy all but over, he had left the care of his hosts in the Ivy Division and was hanging around the front lines with Private 'Red' Pelkey, his faithful driver and now adoring acolyte. He soon picked up the buzz that the next objective might be the city where he had made his name. War was rejuvenating him and a triumphant return to Paris would feel like a dip in the fountain of youth. It was where he had first flexed his muscles as an artist, mixing with the resident literary greats and starting to imagine that one day he might stand among them. The streets swam with good memories. He was already feeling extraordinarily exuberant. The melancholy sense of waning powers that had plagued him in Cuba had gone, driven out by the 'tough times and . . . wonderful times' on the road with the Ivy. The strife and jealousy that poisoned his marriage with Martha were pushed aside by the excitement of his headlong new adventure with Mary Welsh. He felt like the fighter he had always wanted to be, a participant rather than a scribbling onlooker. His thirst for action was interfering with his duties as a war correspondent and he filed to *Collier's* only infrequently.

Pushing forward with Red Pelkey on a reconnaissance trip on the road to Épernon, less than 50 miles south-west of Paris, he started to realize his warrior fantasy. The Allied advance acted like rain on the desert in the liberated towns and villages. Young men who had lain low throughout the occupation now sprang into action, eager to redeem their mortgaged manhood. Somewhere near Épernon, Hemingway came across a bunch of French *maquisards*, stripped to the waist and toting Sten guns and captured German Luger pistols. They took him to a crossroads where it seemed an American patrol had run into a German ambush. There were wrecked jeeps and a truck and freshly turned earth where the *maquisards* had apparently buried the dead GIs.

None of them had heard of Ernest Hemingway, but they recognized the middle-aged American as a kindred spirit who despite his years brimmed with restless bravado. He now looked suitably soldierly, dressed in helmet and fatigues, with a moustache replacing the London beard. Like them, he saw the war as a sort of carnival with bloodshed, where norms were junked and violent appetites satisfied. They told him that Rambouillet, the next town along, was free of Germans. Hemingway returned to the American lines and after several rebuffs managed to scrounge some weapons for his new companions, with which they advanced to Rambouillet. By now an American reconnaissance unit had arrived and the enemy had indeed departed. Hemingway had the place to himself. Looking for somewhere to set up camp he discovered the perfect base. Rambouillet was the site of a famous château, used as a royal hunting lodge, which had subsequently become the summer residence of presidents of the Third Republic. The Hôtel du Grand Veneur in town was suitably classy, elegantly built of grey stone and with a good restaurant and abundant rooms. Hemingway installed himself in style, then set off with his 'irregulars' to patrol the area as the hotel began to fill up with assorted soldiers, spies and the rest of the press corps who had now caught up with Papa and, like him, were desperate to get to Paris.

The day after his meeting with de Gaulle, 21 August, Eisenhower received a letter from him repeating his arguments for an immediate march on Paris. It was delivered by General Koenig, who arrived armed with updates from the city which suggested it was on the point of meltdown. One of Eisenhower's strengths was his flexibility and willingness to adjust to new realities. In his memoirs he makes no mention of de Gaulle's lobbying but states that he was ready to review the bypass plan if he 'received evidence of starvation or distress among its citizens'. That had now arrived, and he knew enough about French history and politics from his spell in Paris to realize that the threat of revolutionary chaos was real. He also accepted that the best chance of avoiding it was for de Gaulle to stamp his authority on the place as quickly as possible. He was inclined to believe that 'no great battle would take place' and that 'the entry of one or two Allied divisions would accomplish the liberation of the city'.

This was a momentous shift in thinking, but Eisenhower could not make the decision alone and there were several steps that needed to be taken before the order to divert to Paris could be given. They would require some of the diplomatic dexterity for which he was renowned. The first was to get the assent of the Combined Chiefs of Staff, his superiors back in Washington. The cable he composed was a masterpiece of subtlety. He hid his intention in a cloak of detail concerning the next phase of the operation. The question of Paris took up only five of the thirty-five sentences. He started off by acknowledging that the burden of feeding and supplying power to the civilian population meant that it would be much better to 'defer the capture of the city until the important matter of destroying the remaining enemy forces up to . . . the Pas de Calais area' had been dealt with. However, he did 'not believe this is possible'.

If the enemy remained in Paris in any strength 'he would be a constant menace to our flank'. But 'If he largely concedes the place, it falls into our hands whether we like it or not,' leaving the Allies responsible for the inhabitants. The upshot was that they had no real choice but to take the city, with or without a fight. He therefore proposed to send Leclerc's 2DB 'accompanied by token units of British and American forces'. Then, 'some days thereafter, General DE GAULLE will be allowed to make his formal entry . . .' Ike had no plans to go there to share the triumph unless military circumstances required it.

Eisenhower's argument presented only part of the picture and made no reference to crucial elements shaping his thinking. The main point – the supposed threat to the Allied flank from the German garrison – was the least significant, for Choltitz was in no position to mount a serious counter-offensive. The crucial development was the uprising. The Resistance had forced his hand. He had formed a good opinion of them during the post-D-Day fighting and later paid them a very generous compliment, claiming in his memoirs that 'without their assistance the liberation of France and the defeat of the enemy in Western Europe would have consumed a much longer time and meant greater losses to ourselves'. Now that the FFI had risen up inside the capital 'it was necessary to move rapidly to their support'.

The fighting in the city greatly increased the danger of massacres and destruction. But, if the information the French had given him was correct, the Germans were too feeble to resist an Allied attack, even though they had the means to crush the rebels. The likelihood was there would be no Battle of Paris, but the decision was still a gamble.

Ike's cable presented the Chiefs with what was in effect a done deal, leaving little room for further debate on the matter. He was also handing de Gaulle Paris on a plate. With Free French troops in the vanguard and the Free French leader heading the triumphal entry, de Gaulle's claim to incarnate legitimate France would be all but unanswerable. It would also give substance to the idea that it was the French themselves, both inside and outside the city, who had liberated the capital.

Eisenhower could have simply ordered his subordinates to execute the new plan, but he preferred to lead by persuasion and would rather that Omar Bradley was on side. Bradley commanded the 12th Army Group and Paris fell right in the middle of his area of operations. The modest Missourian was happy with the existing arrangement. He recorded later that everyone wanted to liberate Paris: 'Everybody, that is, except me. In a tactical sense, Paris was meaningless. We were in pursuit of the fleeing German army which was leaving Paris behind . . . pausing to liberate Paris would not only needlessly slow our eastward drive, but also require the diversion of transport and gasoline.' On top of that came the 4,000 tons of food and supplies that would be needed to sustain the population. After despatching the long cable, Eisenhower sent a message to Bradley asking him to come and see him in Tournières.

That same evening, Rol-Tanguy's envoy Major Roger Cocteau, aka 'Gallois', finally crossed the enemy lines twenty-four hours after he had set off from Paris with his friend Dr Monod. The doctor was armed with his Red Cross pass and Gallois had papers identifying him as his male nurse assistant. Monod's speciality was tuberculosis and their story was they were on their way to a children's sanatorium close to the American lines. The Germans they ran into were unimpressed by their credentials. At one checkpoint they were told they would be shot if they went another yard. After hours of wandering, they made contact with a local Resistance leader in the Corbeil area, Commandant Desnoues, who hatched a plan for getting Gallois across the line while Monod returned to Paris. Moving from one zone to another was a potentially fatal business. Three days before, Rol-Tanguy had sent a member of his staff, André Trutié de Varreux, to try to make contact with the Allies and inform them of the situation. He had been killed near Étampes, not by the Germans but by bullets from an American aircraft.

Desnoues seemed to know everyone, and every field and back road of his domain. He summoned a van from a pork butcher friend and led Gallois off down winding lanes with two gendarmes as bodyguards. It was starting to get dark when they stopped at a farmhouse and Desnoues went inside. When he emerged, he pointed down a track and passed on what the farmer had told him: 'The Americans are three hundred metres away. They haven't budged in forty-eight hours.' It wasn't that simple. First they had to bypass five Germans holed up in a hayfield, armed with a machine gun and 'ready to shoot at anything that moves'. They set off at a crouch. Gallois was certain that the Germans had seen them but had held their fire, apparently for fear of giving away their position. Reaching the bottom of a slope they saw a bunch of Americans, quietly eating their rations.

When Gallois announced himself in his perfect English, no one spoke. To allay suspicions that he might be a spy he told them about the Germans in the field behind. 'Why the hell are you bothering me?' replied the NCO in charge. It was not a good start, but the sergeant soon relented and had him driven to a camp near Chartres, which turned out to be Patton's field headquarters. After five hours of being passed from officer to officer, Gallois finally met the general. By now it was the early hours of the morning and Patton appeared in his shirtsleeves, dishevelled and unshaven, and not happy at being woken up. He asked brusquely, 'OK, what is it you have to tell me?' For the umpteenth time Gallois recited his story. Patton replied with the standard objections, finishing by telling Gallois, 'There is nothing I can do for you, nor for Paris,' and wishing him good luck. Gallois was exhausted and 'in a state of emotional collapse'. Patton had a heart, however. A few minutes later he returned, holding a bottle of champagne. 'You're not too tired to make another long journey, are you?' he asked. The Frenchman's spirits rose. Patton popped the cork on the bottle and they drank a toast to victory. Then Gallois climbed into yet another jeep. It was 3.30 on the morning of 22 August and he was on his way to Bradley's HQ.

Bradley's base was at Laval, 120 miles to the south-west. That morning, the general was about to board a plane to Tournières in answer to his summons from Eisenhower. Gallois arrived with just enough time to tell his story all over again to Bradley's staff. This time he threw in an appeal to conscience, telling them, 'The French will never forgive America if it does not save the capital which has already been half liberated by its own inhabitants.'

After Bradley's departure Gallois was approached by a Free French liaison officer who told him that Leclerc was about to arrive by air. They drove out to the airfield where the 2DB commander landed half an hour later.

Le Patron was also there to agitate for an immediate march on the capital but had arrived too late to bend Bradley's ear. He had little time for politics, and even found some of de Gaulle's endless manoeuvrings distasteful. But he understood the huge symbolic necessity for his division to be the one to liberate Paris. The 2DB was the only French armoured division in the invasion force and he the most senior fighting French officer. The honour of France was on their shoulders, but his men were now kicking their heels some 125 miles to the west of the capital near Argentan.

Leclerc's chronic impatience ensured he had let his feelings be known and he had made a nuisance of himself at the headquarters of his American superiors with increasingly impertinent demands for the 2DB to be unleashed. In return, with maddening condescension, the Yanks had told him to calm down and be patient. Leclerc's immediate superior was General Leonard Gerow, commander of V Corps, a precise, efficient man who did not take kindly to being disobeyed. Two days before, Leclerc had been driven to outright insubordination. Without telling Gerow, he sent a small reconnaissance force ahead under Major Jacques de Guillebon to scout the approaches to Paris. When the American forces in the area reported Guillebon's presence, an angry Gerow ordered Leclerc to call them back. Leclerc ignored him and had decided to fly in his Piper Cub air taxi to appeal over Gerow's head to Bradley.

Finding him gone, Leclerc was now in a 'black fury', viciously decapitating wild flowers with his trademark cane. As they waited for Bradley to return, Leclerc vented his feelings to Gallois. The Americans were 'bastards'. He was entirely dependent on them for the fuel and supplies he needed to get to Paris, but they were refusing to let him have them, suspecting correctly that if they obliged he would set off, with or without American permission.

Just as dusk was falling Leclerc heard the sound of an aircraft. He ambushed Bradley as soon as he got off the plane, volubly pleading his case. There was no need. His staff's account of Gallois' report had impressed him and he had raised no objection when Eisenhower informed him of the change of plan. Bradley told Leclerc: 'You have the authorization to set off for Paris.' According to Gallois, the 2DB commander 'jumped for joy'. Bradley then gave his orders. Leclerc was only to enter the city if confident that his relatively light forces would be enough to overcome the opposition. If he ran into serious resistance he was to retreat immediately and await reinforcements. Once inside the city he was to relieve the FFI and take over responsibility for security. On the walk back, Leclerc beheaded more flowers, but this time in jubilation.

He arrived at his open-air HQ at Fleuré later that evening. His staff were sitting in an orchard, smoking and chatting amid the scent of ripening apples. 'Gribius!' he called out to his chief staff officer. 'Mouvement immédiat sur Paris!' There were shouts of relief and excitement, but they were a long way short of the capital. They were going to have to move at record speed if they were to get to there before it was too late.

Raymond Dronne and the Spanish republicans of La Nueve were still in Écouché recovering after the Battle of the Falaise Pocket. They had spent the previous few days burying their dead and catching their breath. Dronne had been talking to the locals and hearing about their war. He learned that for most of the time life under occupation had been easier there than it had been in Paris. Liberation was much more painful. Much of the southern half of the town had been destroyed and forty inhabitants had been killed when American bombs missed the railway station. There had been a second raid in July, but by then most people had fled. The ground fighting left many more homes damaged by shellfire. No one was complaining. The inhabitants of Écouché had been on the same journey as the rest of France. In June 1940 'Everyone believed in Marshal Pétain and was grateful to him for stopping the war,' and 'all thought that those who left for England were crazy'. As the months passed, little by little the humiliations of the occupation, Vichy's craven behaviour and their increasing faith in what they heard on the BBC from London had eaten away at their loyalty. Now 'Most people were more or less Gaullists and there are as many of them now as there were Pétainists in 1940.'

With the Battle of Normandy over, visitors from Free French headquarters in London began to appear. They were from the civil affairs department and announced that they were there to take over the local administration with a mission to 'cleanse and purify'. Like most of the old sweats of the fighting Free French, Dronne 'felt little sympathy for that odd species of Frenchman who had seen out the war in London'. He told them he had no need of political commissars and advised them to make themselves useful by joining a combat unit.

By now there was no shortage of manpower. La Nueve were

inundated with volunteers, all of whom were turned away. Some were genuine, but many seemed more concerned with obtaining testimonials from Dronne. One young man, 'in a lovely brand-new uniform, adorned with many stripes, came to tell me he was a hero of the Resistance and asked me to authenticate the fact'. He took down his details, then wrote out a document stating: 'I, Captain Raymond Dronne, commander of the 9th Company of the Third Battalion of the Infantry Regiment of Chad, certify that Mr X has come to see me so that I can officially attest that he is a hero of the Resistance. I confirm that I saw him for the first time this day at my command post at Écouché after the departure of the last German.' He folded it, sealed it carefully and handed it to the newly minted *maquisard*, who left well satisfied.

On the morning of Tuesday 22 August the company received an order to get ready to move. The order did not say where to. They and the rest of the division were about 125 miles from Paris and it appeared unlikely that this was their next destination. The day passed and there were no further instructions. It seemed like the sort of stop–start routine that every soldier was familiar with.

Then that night, around midnight, came another signal. They were to leave at dawn, they were bound for Paris and they were to go at full throttle.

At about 1 p.m. on Wednesday 23 August Leclerc and his headquarters staff arrived at Rambouillet, about 40 miles south-west of Paris, ahead of the bulk of his division. They set up camp in the park of the château to plan the approach to the city. The town was swarming with journalists. In the space of a few days, Hemingway had turned the Hôtel du Grand Veneur into his fiefdom and command post for his French 'irregulars'. He swaggered around with a pistol on his hip, and was now addressed as 'mon capitaine' and even 'mon colonel' by his fifteen or so *maquisards*. Among the new arrivals was a real colonel, David Bruce, head of the European section of the recently formed US Office of Strategic Services intelligence agency, the forerunner of the CIA. Bruce was from an old Maryland family, sophisticated and elegant, but he could not help admiring Papa's pantomime warrior performance.

Not everyone at the hotel was so indulgent. William Randolph Hearst, son of the famous press magnate, who was there to represent the newspaper group, found Hemingway 'a pain in the ass all round'. When a tall, no-nonsense reporter from the *Chicago Times*, Bruce Grant, turned up to find there was no room at the inn he began mocking the pretensions of 'General Hemingway' who, when he heard of this *lèse-majesté*, knocked him down in front of everyone in the hotel dining room. Grant hit him back and the fight was broken up only when a small photographer interposed himself between the two middle-aged brawlers. Hemingway went outside and called on Grant to come and finish it, a challenge he sensibly declined.

Hemingway was drunk, not only on the endless supplies of liberated booze but on his own grandiosity. When his old comrade Robert Capa turned up at Rambouillet, he found 'every international typewriter was assembled . . . and every accredited war correspondent wrangling and conspiring to be the first to enter Paris'. He was amused to see the 'irregulars' aping Papa, 'copying his sailor bear walk, spitting short sentences from the corners of their mouths'. When Capa tried to team up with them he found that 'Papa had no place in his army for Hungarian experts any more'. Hemingway had apparently not forgiven him for failing to come to his rescue when he was pinned down for hours by German fire in Normandy a few weeks before, and still harboured the suspicion that Capa had held back in order to snap 'the first picture of the famous writer's dead body'.

Capa was content to travel on in the jeep of his *Time* magazine colleague Charlie Wertenbaker, with whom he had met up in Rambouillet. On his journey from Normandy he had achieved far more with his camera than Hemingway had with his typewriter. Among the pictures he took was a series that would sear themselves in the memory of all who saw them. Arriving in Chartres on 18 August he witnessed the humiliation of women accused of consorting with the enemy. The sequence includes one of the great images of the war. A shaven-headed woman, cradling a baby and dressed in a thin, shapeless frock, is being paraded through the crowded streets, escorted by three policemen. Her mother, whose head is also shaved, walks behind and her father in front. The faces of the onlookers are contorted with savage joy as they shout abuse at the trio. The photograph is full of movement and violent energy. The only point of calm is the loving look that the mother gives to her serene-looking baby. Her name was Simone Touseau and her three-month-old daughter Catherine was the result of a long and serious relationship with a German soldier who, though she did not know it, had just been killed on the Eastern Front. The family had owned a fish shop before it went bust in the 1930s and had become keen supporters of the far right. Simone learned German and worked as a translator in the local German HQ. She and her mother were later accused of having denounced to the German security police five local men who were subsequently deported to Mauthausen concentration camp in Austria where two of them died. Given the circumstances, the fury of the mob was perhaps understandable. But the images became an instant symbol of the *épuration sauvage*, the savage cleansing that followed in the wake of liberation and which did not bother itself too much with the niceties of justice.

Hemingway was now far more interested in participating in the war than chronicling it. When he heard that Leclerc was at the Rambouillet château, he set off to see him, accompanied by David Bruce, sure that the general would be grateful for the intelligence his men had gleaned on their patrols around the area. Leclerc though was unimpressed by Hemingway's fame and even less interested in his offer of help. Since arrival he had received reports from his own recce units and had been visited by several bona fide Resistance figures whose information was likely to be far more accurate than the scraps picked up by Papa's crew. Even so, it was far from complete, as he would learn to his cost the following day. With a curt 'Bugger off' Hemingway was sent on his way. He never forgot the slight and thereafter the French hero would always be 'that jerk Leclerc'.

Leclerc gave orders that his men were to give no help to the foreign press. But whether he liked it or not they were determined to tag along anyway and there was little that could be done to stop them. When the first units moved out in heavy rain on the morning of Thursday 24 August, their columns were threaded with the jeeps of reporters, photographers and camp followers, all determined to see history being made.

12.   Days of Rage

Tuesday 22 August would turn out to be the most violent day of the uprising, when a new generation of Parisians earned their place in the national pantheon of strugglers against tyranny and established August 1944 as a battle honour to stand alongside the revolutions of 1789, 1830, 1848 and 1871. It was the time of the barricades, with 600 of them springing up around the city. Ever since Delacroix's painting *Liberty Leading the People* showing a bare-breasted Amazon standing atop a corpse-strewn barricade, waving the tricolour and urging on the citizenry, these makeshift fortifications had become an emblem of popular defiance. The picture commemorated the 1830 overthrow of King Charles X. Liberty holds a rifle with bayonet fixed. She is flanked by a young man gripping a musket and a street urchin brandishing an outsize pistol in each small hand, and is followed by a horde of enraged Parisians. Their twentieth-century descendants were now out in force.

The barricades went up mostly in the centre and in the north and east of the city, where the poor and lower-middle classes lived. There were few blocking the pompous boulevards of the affluent districts in the west. To the wealthy bourgeoisie, their appearance was a portent of bloody chaos and only deepened their yearning for the swift arrival of the Allies before their compatriots became more of a threat to them than the Germans.

The inhabitants of the 16th arrondissement were anyway unsuited by temperament and physique for the work required. Barricade building was a task for the people. It involved the communal effort of every able-bodied citizen regardless of sex. The men cut down trees and dragged them across the roads and dug up the *pavé*. The women and children formed chains to pass along the railings, sandbags, mattresses and anything else that came to hand to stuff into the gaps. Often the barricades were adorned with portraits of Hitler for the Germans to shoot at. Old ladies cheered the workers on and young girls carried *demis* of beer and glasses of wine to slake the men's thirst. Some barricades never amounted to more than a few layers of paving stones, piled two or three feet high. Others, 'like an illustration out of *Les Misérables*', climbed up to first-storey level. The activity felt self-consciously heroic. One delirious spectator described watching a working-class man hard at work and feeling that 'the look of him was like a historic revelation'. He seemed to 'embody every insurrection' since France became a nation. He had 'broad shoulders and a narrow upper body, lively eyes under thick lashes, a cigarette butt glued to his lip, a real Parisian guy, hardened against suffering, booze and illness . . .' And having finished his task, with rifle in hand he took his place behind the piled-up wood and stone, ready to defend to the death 'his house, his street, his friends, his family, his independence and his ideas'.

Streets that the Germans had once traversed without hindrance were now a maze of ripped-up cobbles, felled trees and burned-out vehicles. The quarters of the central arrondissements bristled with mini-fortresses, and convoys trying to cross from one strongpoint to another had to make constant detours into unknown territory. The

barricades were partly a response to calls like that issued by Rol-Tanguy on 18 August to 'stay faithful to your glorious past!', and the transformation signified that this was now a popular and not just a Resistance uprising.

Many – perhaps most – who took to the streets that day were answering their own impulses rather than acting on the specific orders of the Resistance leadership. Some of the defenders of the barricades had some formal connection to one of the FFI groups. Others had come on to the streets of their own accord, driven by a simple urge to strike their blow for freedom. Groups of schoolfriends, united by a loose determination to do something, overnight transformed themselves into ad hoc fighting units. They might have no training, though there was no real preparation for this sort of street fighting, nor did they have any weapons, but as hours passed, one way or another firearms fell into their hands. This was the experience of Gilles de Boisgelin, a well-born Sciences Po student who had teamed up with his mates in an informal fighting unit. His operational career started on Saturday 19 August delivering petrol for FFI vehicles. By Monday morning he was hunting down SS men on the rooftops of the 6th arrondissement and shooting up German lorries. By the evening he was in hospital, hit in the leg during another ambush.

Unexpected leaders emerged, whose only qualification was their natural authority. When Lieutenant Sarran, a local FFI commander in the Saint-Michel area, went on a tour of the barricades he was initially told to mind his own business by Madame Béatrice Briand, a baker by trade who was in undisputed command of the barricade at the corner of the rue de la Huchette. When Sarran proved his worth leading an attack on an armoured car, she graciously agreed to listen to any military advice he had to offer.

The message to the Germans was that Parisians were taking back Paris. For the first time in four years citizens could read something like the truth in the uncensored newspapers now pouring out of the giant presses of the big Paris dailies. The street sellers were swamped with customers grabbing copies of *Combat*, *Le Populaire*, *Le Franc Tireur* and *L'Humanité* to read the latest updates on the whereabouts of the Allies and despatches from the city front lines. There was a new boldness in the air. Gustave-Jean Reybaz was impressed by the sight of young women on bikes, determined to go about their business despite the fact that it meant pedalling through a war zone. 'I saw many of them in the first days,' he wrote, 'cruising unconcernedly around despite the whistling bullets . . . taking no notice of the fighters' warnings.'

The young warriors, he noted, were 'almost all of them, the sons of the people'. The innate patriotism of the French working class had been proved throughout the nation's modern history, but there were others now in the fight who had little reason to risk their lives for the honour of France. Photographs and movie footage as well as the testimony of numerous observers record the presence of young Black and Arab men in the ranks of the uprising. Most of them were poor. The liberation saga would be built on the testimony of the educated and the well-connected and the contributions of those without a voice were pushed to the edges of the story. One Frenchman did try to give the Arabs their due. 'Resourceful, active, agile, vigorous, you saw these North African muslims everywhere,' wrote Charles René-Leclerc, a colonial administrator, 'building barricades [and] ambushing tanks and armoured cars and trucks with all the wile of their old ancestral instincts . . . and volunteering for the most dangerous missions.' Among them was Bouras Bou Médiène, a nurse at the Val-de-Grâce hospital who formed a section from among his least incapacitated patients, and 'for six days we fought the Germans alongside our Parisian comrades, FFI, policemen, Republican Guards, all manner of French patriots'. René-Leclerc regretted that the names of many of those who died would not be inscribed on any monument for 'these modest heroes weren't really known to anyone or didn't have any papers on them'.

As a result of ambushes and weapons seizures, by Tuesday the insurgents had added about 450 rifles to their armoury as well as ammunition, grenades and machine guns. Tactics were evolving all the time, meaning fewer pointless casualties and better results. Jean Amidieu du Clos, a thirty-seven-year-old engineer who was in the thick of the fighting, watched 'comrade V . . . stop a truck with two

15. Soaking up the sun at the Piscine Deligny floating swimming pool on the Seine.

16. Raymond Dronne plans a clearing operation fortified with local intel – and a bottle of champagne.

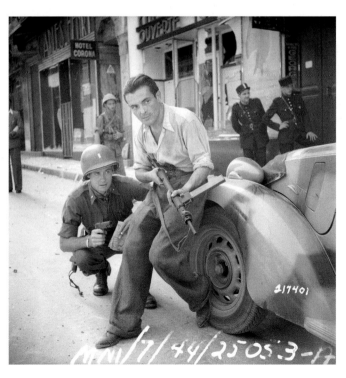

17. Brothers in arms: an American officer and photogenic FFI man prepare to engage *les Chleuhs*. Note the British-supplied Sten submachine gun.

18. Welcome to Paris. US troops on the happiest day of their war.

19. Resistance thoroughbreds: Henri Rol-Tanguy, reviewing his men at the Reuilly barracks after the fighting.

20. And – immaculate as ever – Jacques Chaban-Delmas.

21. Vengeful Parisians taunt their former masters as they are led away under protective escort.

22. . . . and vent their shame on scapegoats like this *femme tondue*.

23. 'A canyon of ecstatic humanity.' The 26 August victory parade sets off down the Champs-Élysées.

24. The partisan and the painter: Madeleine Riffaud and Pablo Picasso.

25. A toast to victory before getting back to the war.

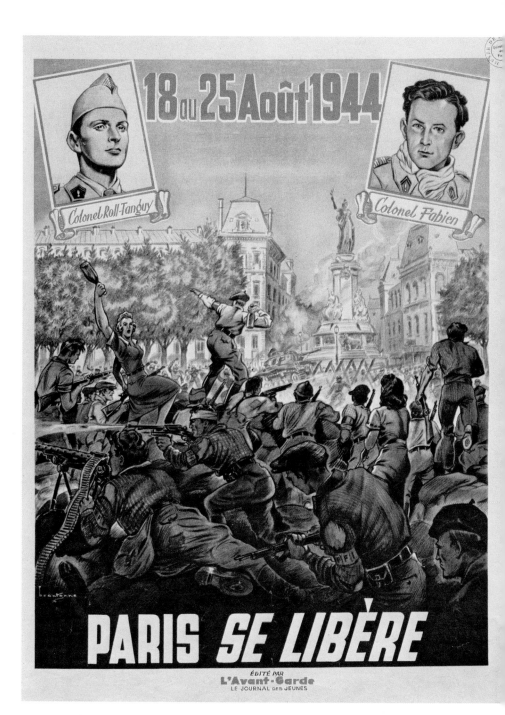

26. A myth is born.

grenades. Result: one German killed, five prisoners, one truck seized along with its contents including a heavy machine gun which was immediately installed at the Saint-Germain barricade . . .'

At Batignolles in the 17th arrondissement the journalist Claude Roy was astonished to see a French tank enter the fray in the colours of the FFI. 'My throat tightened,' he wrote. 'I had not seen one since the last days of fighting, in June 1940.' It came from the Somua factory in the nearby suburb of Saint-Ouen and had been handed over to the Resistance by the workers. At one o'clock that afternoon it nosed out of the rue Puteaux and on to the boulevard des Batignolles to beat back a German attempt to retake the *mairie*, which had been in FFI hands since Saturday. The fighters crouched around the hull as the enemy 'sprayed the boulevard with grenades and bursts of machine-gun fire'. One was hit and 'the blood ran, red on the white shirt and the black skin'. The man was Georges Dukson, a twenty-two-year-old from French Equatorial Africa who had joined the French army and been captured by the Germans in 1940, before escaping and returning to Paris where he was a leading figure in the local Resistance, earning the nickname 'The Lion of the Seventeenth'. A team of Red Cross stretcher bearers ran through the bullets to retrieve him and movie footage shows him being led away for treatment. Such acts of selfless bravery by medics were repeated hundreds of times around the city.

The liberation would be more extensively filmed and photo-graphed than any great historical event to date and some of the outstanding photographers of the age, the likes of Henri Cartier-Bresson and Robert Doisneau, were now out on the ground creating images that would stick in the world's imagination for ever. The man who recorded the Batignolles fighting was a newsreel cameraman called Georges Méjat whom Roy watched darting from doorway to doorway. He was one of a team from the Comité de Libération du Cinéma (Cinema Liberation Committee), which had set up shop in an office in the Champs-Élysées to direct coverage.

The Batignolles action ended with the Germans surrendering, but such successes were a rarity. There was only one French tank. To take the fight to the Germans the FFI needed many more, or at least anti-tank guns of which they had hardly any. The German defences had been boosted by a number of heavy Tiger and medium Panther tanks – the exact quantity would never be established, but fewer than the hundred claimed by excitable contemporary accounts – diverted from the Panzer units heading east. The barricades presented no real obstacle to them, as they could be bulldozed or blasted apart by their 88mm and 75mm main guns. Nor did they have much to fear from the petrol bombs which makeshift factories were now turning out by the thousand. On 17 August Rol-Tanguy issued a notice publicizing a refinement of the Molotov cocktail recipe. You filled a bottle three-quarters full with petrol, topped it up with sulphuric acid, a supply of which was available from the chemistry labs of the Sorbonne, and wrapped it with paper soaked in potassium chlorate, on sale at pharmacies to treat sore throats. When the bottle shattered, the mixture ignited, producing 'an enormous flame'.

The one-sided nature of the combat was recorded by Amidieu du Clos. He was one of the defenders at a barricade on the corner of the boulevards Saint-Michel and Saint-Germain, which the resisters called the 'crossroads of death'. They had been told to expect a tank attack and had orders to pull back into neighbouring buildings and leave it to petrol bombers stationed in the upper storeys to drive it off. An armoured column of two Tigers and three light tanks appeared. The Tiger was a monster, clad in thick armour and weighing 57 tons and alongside its main 88mm cannon it carried two death-spitting 7.92mm machine guns. The lead Tiger turned sharply into the boulevard Saint-Germain, crush-ing a plane tree on the corner. The first Molotov cocktail was hurled and the tank's machine guns opened up. Despite their orders Amidieu and his comrades had stayed put and opened fire, hitting some infantrymen riding on the hull. 'Petrol bombs showered down from the upper floors, grenades exploded, the tanks fired, the noise was incredible.' Teenage boys crept up under cover of the wall of the Cluny Garden on the east side of the junction to lob their bottles. A petrol bomb from somewhere set the last tank in the line afire. The lid of the turret opened and a soldier jumped out with an extinguisher and while putting out the fire was shot dead. The column decided to call it a day and pulled back.

It was magnificent but it wasn't war. The spectacle of insurgents confronting tanks seemed to the writer Jean-Paul Sartre, who roamed the city observing the fighting, like 'prehistoric hunters, attacking a mammoth with sharpened stones'. A Molotov cocktail bursting on the side of a tank enveloped it in flames but only scorched the paintwork, though the spectacle fooled combatants into thinking they must have knocked it out and the numbers reported destroyed would turn out to be greatly exaggerated. To do real damage required an artillery shell or bazooka and there were hardly any of either. The day before, at the same barricade, Amidieu and his comrades did briefly get hold of an anti-tank gun seized from a captured truck and brought it into action effectively, hitting and apparently badly damaging a Tiger. It had been in their hands for only a few hours when a lorry turned up with a party of policemen who insisted it was needed for the defence of the prefecture.

The street fighting had the intimacy of a battle of antiquity. The killing was at close quarters and warriors saw their enemies die before their eyes. Sartre witnessed a grisly incident when the FFI ambushed a German saloon car, 'black and powerful like an Andalusian bull', as it drove up the boulevard Saint-Michel. Coming under fire, it swerved into the metal shutters of a bookshop. 'Enormous flames spurted out of the broken windows and a voice screamed "Kamerad!" and "Mercy! Mercy!"' A group of Fifis approached cautiously. 'We're not your comrades,' said one of them. 'Let him roast like a pig.' But another, 'tall, thin and brown haired', had seen enough. He levelled his pistol and with the 'slow, careful grace of a *torero* calculating the moment for the last fatal plunge of the sword' pulled the trigger. The shot rang out. The screaming stopped. The car burned for hours.

Gustave-Jean Reybaz witnessed a similar scene a few hundred yards down the road in the place Saint-Michel when a German lorry got trapped between the barricades. This time it was the FFI who called out 'Kamerad!' because 'rather than kill these men they had at their mercy, they preferred to take them prisoner'. Reybaz got the impression that the Germans had been told by their commanders that they were fighting 'terrorists' and if captured they should expect the worst. Some of them made a run for it. The others opened fire. Grenades rained down killing three, who lay 'in large pools of blood. One of them was staring upwards at the sky and his face had ceased to be human. Bits of brain and other debris were scattered far and wide.' The lorry caught fire and those inside were incinerated.

The FFI were under orders to obey the rules of war and demonstrate that far from being 'terrorists' they occupied the moral high ground. In the first days stretcher bearers took the same risks to pick up enemy wounded as they did their own, and once in hospital the Germans were treated well. Most Fifis tried to follow their instructions, though inevitably in the heat of the moment there were beatings and executions. Even so, Germans taken prisoner were in far less danger of being killed than captured resisters. There were numerous cases of insurgents being gunned down in cold blood. Anyone found carrying weapons at the checkpoints set up around the zones into which the Germans had retreated was liable to be shot on the spot. At one crossroads in the 12th arrondissement, where the rue de Lyon met the rue Traversière, twenty-five people were murdered between 19 and 25 August, including some who were unarmed and wearing Red Cross armbands. The pointless bloodshed would continue to the end.

Alongside the new recruits to the Fifi ranks was a veteran who, miraculously, was returning to the fray. Madeleine Riffaud had killed her first German in July when she shot down an off-duty non-commissioned officer as he strolled along the Seine. After arrest she claimed she had no connection with the Resistance and was avenging the death of her lover. Over the days that followed, her story unravelled. She was interrogated, beaten and forced to watch other prisoners being tortured. While held at the police prefecture, she witnessed a pregnant Jewish woman being kicked repeatedly in the stomach. She used her midwifery skills to staunch the bleeding, but failed to save the baby. Madeleine ended up in Fresnes prison. On 15 August she was put on a bus with other prisoners for deportation to Buchenwald on what would be the last train to carry French men and women to the camps. She was saved when a Red Cross team intervened to win a reprieve for the sick and young and was taken back to jail. Three days later, thanks to the deal brokered by Raoul Nordling, the prison gates opened. She spent the next few days recovering in a Red Cross centre near the Gare de l'Est, but then left to make contact with her old Resistance comrades. She was assigned to the Saint-Just Compagny of the FTP – André Calvès' outfit – operating in the north-east of the city.

On Wednesday 23 August they received intelligence from Rol-Tanguy's headquarters that a train was about to leave Paris carrying troops and materiel. It would be travelling along a local line that passed through Belleville and La Villette. Madeleine was put in command of four men, the youngest of whom was only seventeen. They were armed with machine pistols, grenades and petrol bombs. They took up position on two bridges that spanned the tracks and when the locomotive emerged slowly from a tunnel opened fire, forcing the driver to retreat. The racket attracted resisters. A local railway worker appeared who descended the embankment, switched the points to immobilize the train and, after exchanges of fire in which five Fifis were killed, the resisters finally got the German soldiers to surrender.

More than a hundred were led away from the tunnel, and the resisters had to protect them from an angry mob. Despite everything she had suffered, Madeleine had a powerful need to restrain the desire for vengeance. 'We protected our prisoners,' she said later. 'We did not strike them and we gave them food to eat . . . we felt strongly that if we acted otherwise, we would ourselves have become beasts.' And those 'who felt this way most strongly were those who like me had undergone torture'.

After their victory there was a party. It was Madeleine's birthday. She was twenty years old. When word got around, the people in the neighbourhood produced hoarded treats and wine. After weeks in captivity, Madeleine was unused to the rich food and it made her sick. But she felt joy. The impromptu party was one of many moments of wild happiness that broke out amid the violence, for despite the risks and the bloodshed Madeleine felt Paris in those days 'was in love with itself, you loved everyone you saw'.

But darker feelings were bubbling under the gaiety. After stopping the train, Madeleine and her men got caught up in a commotion near by. A *milicien* was holed up in the upper storey of an apartment block and had been shooting into the street below. One of his bullets killed a child. He was captured and dragged down to the pavement where an angry crowd had gathered. Madeleine's unit tried to intervene but the mob was in no mood for mercy. Rather than leave him to be torn to pieces the resisters felt they had no choice but to shoot him on the spot.

The incident was a rare case where one of the mysterious shooters who featured in the memories of so many Parisians was actually captured and identified. Almost every account of the times makes reference to the sharpshooters who perched in upper-storey windows or on rooftops firing at random at Fifis and civilians alike with no other apparent purpose than to kill. Who they were was a subject of much debate, and soon everyone was calling them simply the *salopards* – the bastards. Most were assumed to be diehards from the Milice indulging in a last act of nihilistic violence before justice caught up with them. Others were said to be Germans who for unknown reasons had decided to make a lone stand. The shooting points were hard to identify and the unexplained crack of a rifle would lead to Fifis pounding up the stairs of the nearest apartment building hunting for the culprit.

Everyone was suspect. One *Figaro* journalist solemnly recorded that he had heard from several sources of a seventy-two-year-old woman who had been caught shooting down from a building in the avenue d'Orléans. When the first stories began to circulate, sober witnesses like Reybaz 'were tempted to believe that the "roof shooters" existed only in the rather overheated imaginations of some young Fifis' but concluded that 'you had to look at the evidence and there were several men wounded by bullets that could only have been fired from on high'. Whatever the truth, the presence of mysterious snipers would be an enduring thread in the liberation story.

They were another sign of the surreal, dreamlike atmosphere that sometimes seemed to float over events. The tough Breton FTP activist André Calvès was with Saint-Just Compagnie comrades in the avenue de Laumière in the north of the city, watching from a side street as a German patrol approached. One young soldier 'had his rifle pointing upwards and was scanning the rooftops. Suddenly he saw me. I could swear he smiled. The situation was almost funny. We were three metres away from each other. He lowered his rifle. I fired. He fell in the road. We couldn't even get his weapon as his comrades were behind him.'

Beneath the apparent chaos, the machinery of the insurrection functioned with increasing smoothness. There was now an efficient system of casualty evacuation with 150 first-aid posts around the city which, at the height of the fighting, were coping with a thousand cases a day. Casualties were then taken for proper treatment to a hospital. Claude Roy spent a morning at the Hôtel-Dieu hospital on the Île de la Cité and found it bursting with French and German wounded being tended by the staff and an army of volunteers. 'They talked about their work as if it was something unremarkable and unheroic, these civilians who had left the counter of their bank, their office, their workshop, their shop, their schoolbooks to live day and night in the storm of insurrection.' Roy was humbled by the sight. 'I will admit that from time to time I have had doubts about my comrades and indeed about the whole of the youth of France,' he wrote in his report. 'But today I know I was wrong. Anyone who has witnessed that weary, smiling joy has looked on the face of hope. These are the fighters and stretcher bearers of the Parisian uprising; heroes in their white blouses and heroes in their FFI brassards. We shall never forget them.'

The corpses that the hospital mortuaries could not accommodate were taken to makeshift morgues where they lay decomposing in the August heat until they could be decently buried: the Catholics in Notre-Dame des Victoires in the 2nd arrondissement and the Protestants in the Oratory in the 1st. Those of no religion or who remained unidentified were buried in a special plot in the cemetery at Pantin.

To feed the fighters, canteens sprang up in the back of bistrots and restaurants and in private kitchens. Food was still in desperately short supply. On 19 August there was only enough flour to last the city a week, and the stocks coming from the giant mills at Pantin were much reduced when the Germans decided to set them on fire. There was some relief from stores left behind by the departing troops. The FFI seized a sizeable stock of frozen meat from refrigerated warehouses around the city; it was then moved to distribution centres, which needed guarding to protect them from looters. It was something, but it was never going to meet the needs of a famished city.

On Wednesday 23 August Walter Dreizner was working inside the Meurice, fitting a new accumulator to ensure that headquarters could stay in contact with the outlying posts. The atmosphere was 'nervous', though the hotel felt relatively safe despite the odd incoming rifle round from the direction of the Louvre, half a mile down the rue de Rivoli to the east. Those doing the shooting were the same Parisians whom he had once looked upon with affection. When he wrote his diary, there were no more kindly references to the French. Everyone who was not a German soldier was a 'terrorist' and he used his camera now to record the marks of war on the city.

During a break he went up to the observation post on the hotel roof to take pictures of the black pall of smoke rising up from the direction of the Champs-Élysées. The fire was coming from the Grand Palais where a fierce fight had broken out. At nine o'clock that morning an armoured column arrived from outside the city and descended the Champs. It came under fire from a police post at the side of the Palais and a soldier was killed. The Germans responded with a hail of fire and despatched several Goliaths, small tracked vehicles carrying mines that they used to blow up buildings and bridges. The blasts set the huge glass and steel exhibition hall built for the 1900 Universal Exposition ablaze. When the *pompiers* arrived with their fire hoses they were shot at, and by the time the conflagration was under control the roof space of the great Paris landmark was destroyed and the pillars in the nave warped by the intense heat. A Swedish circus had been giving shows at the Palais and the performing animals stampeded to freedom in the chaos. A horse was killed by a stray bullet. It was a measure of the hunger felt even in this most privileged *quartier* that, once the shooting had died down, the inhabitants emerged knives in hand and soon all that remained of the horse was a skeleton.

Choltitz was never formally told that the truce was over. As a result of his Sunday afternoon meeting with Parodi he had little faith in the ability of de Gaulle's representatives to impose order on the situation and concluded that 'the agreement negotiated by M. Nordling would not be respected by the opposition'. The proof was there in the hundreds of barricades that had sprung up in defiance of his demand that German traffic should be allowed to move freely.

However, he still controlled the centre and most of the west, where his forces had a firm grip on a number of strongholds close to strategic crossroads and thoroughfares. From the Hôtel Majestic and some neighbouring buildings they could dominate the place de l'Étoile and access the avenues that radiated from its hub. Troops occupying the Tuileries and the Meurice and Continental hotels and various apartments opposite secured the east–west axis of the rue de Rivoli. The Jeu de Paume, tucked into the north-west corner of the garden, had become an important part of their defensive architecture. The main galleries were empty now after the looters of the Einsatzstab Reichsleiter Rosenberg had carried off the great trove of contemporary masters at the beginning of August.

During the stormy early morning of Sunday 20 August, Rose Valland recorded, 'about fifty men arrived on the terrace on the rue de Rivoli side and despite the beating rain . . . rolled out lines of barbed wire and spiked barriers between the museum and the garden railings. By the morning the terrace was completely covered in them. It was impossible to get round the museum or to take the defenders from behind . . . when everything was finished we found ourselves entrenched!' Despite the glaring dangers, Rose decided not to leave and very soon would have a ringside seat for the final battle for Paris.

Garrison troops were also installed in the Naval Ministry and the Hôtel Crillon on the north side of the place de la Concorde. Across the river on the Left Bank, they held the Ministry of Foreign Affairs on the quai d'Orsay, the Bourbon Palace and the École Militaire.

These were all reasonably close to each other and could provide over-lapping support. There were a few more isolated outposts like the large barracks in the place de la République and in the Luxembourg Palace, formerly the home of the French Senate. Since 1940 it had been the HQ of the Luftwaffe in France and the opulent personal quarters of Field Marshal Hugo Sperrle, its supreme commander in the west. Sperrle was corpulent and luxury-loving and lived in sybaritic splendour, eating copiously, sweating off the fat in a steam bath and overseeing squads of gardeners who kept the roses blooming in the gardens. The failure of the severely depleted Luftwaffe to pose any real threat to the Allied armies in the Battle of Normandy had set the seal on his career, and that day he received news of his recall.

Over the years of occupation, the Luxembourg Palace and surrounding gardens had been turned into a bastion. The perimeter and grounds were studded with massive concrete blockhouses and strung with barbed wire. The palace sat above an old quarry, now a network of tunnels where the defenders could shelter and move from location to location in safety. The compound was also used as a tank park for the Tigers and Panthers. The 1,500 Luftwaffe headquarters staff had departed with their chief and their place was taken by a mixed force of 300 garrison soldiers, a company of military police and SS troops from Normandy, about 600 men in all, spread around the palace, the gardens and the neighbouring École des Mines and Lycée Montaigne. It would prove a very tough nut to crack if Choltitz chose it as the place to make a stand.

Choltitz's early confidence that he could handle the situation was dwindling. He was unable to make up his mind whether it was better to run or to fight. When, on Model's orders, an officer from the 6th Parachute Division contacted him to discuss the situation, Choltitz told him that it was 'untenable' as he had insufficient forces to defend the city. The priority now should be to get as many men and as much materiel as possible out of the city before the enemy arrived. But in his memoirs he claimed that he was simultaneously wondering whether the time had come 'to send in the tanks and the bombers' against the main Resistance redoubts: the police HQ, the Hôtel de Ville and the various occupied ministries. That was what Hitler would have expected him to do, and what his fellow generals had done in Warsaw. The Luftwaffe could still bomb the city, though for fear of Allied fighters they would have to operate at night. He decided that, although it would be easy enough to reduce the Resistance bases to rubble, it would 'be impossible to achieve a tangible success' and the fighters would just spring up elsewhere. As for calling for an air raid, 'it was obvious that the bombers would kill far more innocent women and children than they would resisters'. Choltitz was already constructing a version of events that made him the victim of a situation forced on him by the 'fanatics' of the Resistance who were 'ready to sacrifice the wellbeing of people for an ideology'. For all their lofty talk, he was the humanitarian here and they were the bloodthirsty zealots.

But this new narrative would need careful handling. Restraint could easily be presented by the hardliners back in Berlin as defeatism and a cowardly manoeuvre to wait for the Allies to come to the rescue. He had been warned that rumours of his negotiations with the insurgents were circulating among senior officers in the retreating army and that he 'had already aroused suspicions'.

At 11 a.m. on Wednesday 23 August, an encrypted signal arrived from army headquarters in Berlin to add to his distress. He knew from his meeting with the Führer at the Wolf's Lair that, if it came to the worst, he was expected to mount a suicidal last stand in the ruins of Paris. If he had dared to hope that that order might have been forgotten or abandoned as militarily senseless, the message made it clear that Hitler was entirely serious. It stated that it was of vital symbolic importance that he clung on to the capital for 'throughout history, the loss of Paris has meant the loss of France'. The Paris region was also important for the 'long-range war against England', being fought with flying bombs and soon with rockets. He was urged to take the 'strongest possible measures' to crush any uprising (headquarters clearly did not know the extent of the insurgency) with demolitions of entire city blocks, just as was happening in Warsaw, and the public executions of ringleaders. The Seine bridges were to be made ready for demolition. In the last resort Paris was 'to be turned into a field of ruins' (*Trümmerfeld*).

It was a little over four years since Hitler had stood below

Sacré-Coeur with his artist companions, looking out over his prize, 'this great city which has always fascinated me', and decreed that it was 'absolutely essential that this marvel of western culture that flourishes below us should be preserved intact for posterity'. The words had been spoken when it seemed that not just Paris but all of Europe would soon be at his feet. That dream had vanished and the only glory now was in death and destruction. At the end of the tour he had confided to Albert Speer that 'in the past I have often wondered whether we would not have to destroy' the city. He concluded that the grandiose plans he had for Berlin would make Paris 'only a shadow' and not worth the trouble of annihilation. But the new Berlin of his dreams would never be built and the old one had been battered terribly by British and American bombers. Why then should Paris be spared?

Choltitz thought Hitler's order 'a piece of paper devoid of any military value'. Field Marshal Model faced an impossible task in cobbling together a defensive line that was capable of stopping the Allies from crossing the Seine. He had lost touch with large elements of his surviving force. The Luftwaffe had nothing like the aircraft it needed to slow the armour flooding eastwards. The plan had always been to try to stop the Allies before they reached Paris. A stand within the walls would end in certain defeat, heavy losses and humiliation. Model had assigned General von Aulock to defend the approaches of the city using the 48th Infantry Division and the First Army. It sounded impressive. The truth, as Choltitz knew all too well, was that after the losses suffered in the Battle of Normandy this was essentially a phantom force.

Choltitz decided not to share the 'field of ruins' order with his wider staff, but he did show it to a trusted aide, Colonel Hans Jay, a forty-eight-year-old cavalry officer. Jay was later described by his British captors as 'a defeatist who deplores the Führer's institutions' as well as a 'very keen horseman [who] seems to have spent his time in Paris in contacting French racehorse owners'. He was as alarmed as his chief and they stood on the balcony of Choltitz's office overlooking the Tuileries and the monuments they had been ordered to destroy, bewailing 'the madness of the medieval command'.

Choltitz also confided in another man he trusted. Later that day he called an old friend, Lieutenant-General Hans Speidel, the first commandant of Paris and now chief of staff at Model's headquarters currently situated in Cambrai. Security considerations necessitated some caution when talking to anyone and Choltitz used heavy irony to convey his message. 'Thank you for your beautiful order,' he told him, and went on to detail how he proposed to raze Paris with three tons of explosive in Notre-Dame, two in the dome of the Invalides and one in the Chamber of Deputies. It was when he told him his plan to blow up the Eiffel Tower to block the passage of enemy tanks that Speidel realized he was not serious and murmured conspiratorially: 'We're happy to have you in Paris, General.'

By now German commanders had got used to receiving deranged and unexecutable orders. One of Choltitz's fellow captives at Trent Park, General Heinrich Eberbach, told how he had received a 'ridiculous' Hitler order demanding that all young French men capable of bearing arms should be abducted on the withdrawal from Normandy and all property that could not be carried away should be destroyed.

Disobedience did not necessarily require a bold moral decision. The truth was that they were being ordered to do the impossible. Choltitz had shown himself willing to carry out whatever instructions he was given. He had not hesitated to play his part in the destruction of Sebastopol and if he had been in Warsaw there is no reason to suppose he would not have executed the orders to lay waste to everything as best he could.

But he was in Paris and the calculus was very different. Choltitz had no intention of going down in flames with the Führer. But even if he had, did he have the means to carry out the order? Was it really possible to reduce Paris to a field of ruins? In his memoirs Choltitz claimed that everything had been prepared 'with quite commendable zeal'. It would emerge many years later that although bridges and major buildings had been readied for demolition in what was clearly a programme of mass destruction, the work had not yet been completed.

A French TV enquiry in 2019 discovered documents detailing the de-mining work done by the explosives department of the Paris police prefecture after the liberation. They revealed that in his call to

Speidel, Choltitz had only been half joking. A report by the department's director, who had the very unFrench name of Henry Moore,
stated that the Luxembourg Palace had been extensively rigged with
explosives. So too had a huge ammunition storage dump at Fort
Charenton in the south-east of the city. The most heavily mined
building was the Bourbon Palace, the parliament of the Third Republic before the war, where the investigators found nearly 2,500 kilos of
explosives. All three sites were primed for detonation.

Mines were found at telephone exchanges, the Naval Ministry, Le
Bourget station and the Porte de Saint-Cloud. Preparations to plant
charges had also been made at several key bridges – the pont de
Neuilly, the pont de Joinville, the pont de Saint-Cloud and the pont
Alexandre III as well as the Invalides. The most famous Paris landmark had been spared and, despite rumours, nothing sinister was
discovered at the Eiffel Tower.

Choltitz's claim to be the saviour of Paris hung on the assumption
that he was in a position to blow up the city but had chosen instead
to defy Hitler and side with the forces of civilization. But the evidence suggests that the decision had been made for him. A massive
wrecking operation required manpower, time and calm conditions.
By Tuesday 22 August, Paris was in chaos and there was no possibility
of demolition squads reaching the sites and carrying out their work
unmolested. It is hard to disagree with the verdict of Director Moore
in his report of 9 September 1944 that 'it is probably due to lack of
time . . . the immediate consequence of the effective harassment carried out by the FFI, that the explosive charges were not detonated
everywhere'.

Self-interest had in all likelihood persuaded Choltitz from the beginning that there was nothing to be gained by blowing up Paris. Instead
he was coming to the conclusion that the best hope of salvation now
lay in the hands of his enemies. On Tuesday evening, he summoned
Nordling and proposed a mission across the front lines to try to make
contact with de Gaulle, in the hope that he might be able to rein in
the Resistance. He was careful to make it clear that this was an initiative to protect his men, and not an attempt to parley with the Allies.

The distinction would fool no one. As soon as Eisenhower heard of the approach, it would tell him that Choltitz had no intention of putting up a serious fight. Before Nordling could depart he suffered a minor heart attack and his brother Rolf went in his place. In the end it would make no difference. The decision to march on Paris had already been taken and Choltitz's fate would now be decided by who got to Paris first: the Allied forces or nemesis, in the form of a summons from Berlin.

13.   Chimes of Freedom

On the first day of their march eastwards, Wednesday 23 August, Leclerc's men covered 130 miles. It was a huge distance for an unwieldy force of 16,000 men travelling in 4,000 vehicles – tanks, half-tracks, lorries and jeeps. The division approached Paris from the north and south. La Nueve were at the head of the southern column. The Germans gave them no trouble en route. The main problems were breakdowns, diversions and the weather. The storm that threatened all morning broke in the afternoon, soaking their dusty khakis and coating them in grey, sticky grime. The company stopped for the night in a field at Limours. Raymond Dronne was too busy sorting out repairs to a half-track and trying to find a section of his men who had gone astray to get much sleep. When they woke at dawn, they were still 25 miles south-west of the capital and no one knew for sure the strength of the German defences ahead. The information reaching the Allies about German dispositions was patchy and contradictory. Eisenhower suspected Leclerc's troops might walk into Paris without much of a fight. The only way to find out was to go up the road and see what happened.

The Americans' experience of working alongside the French in Normandy had taught them that their Gallic comrades had 'a casual manner of doing almost exactly what they please, regardless of orders'. General Gerow, commander of V Corps, which included the 2DB, nonetheless tried to hold Leclerc to a tight set of instructions. His division was to spearhead the drive on Paris, with American troops in reserve. The main support would come from the now much battered Ivy. The French were to enter Paris from two directions, with the northern force delivering the main punch through Versailles. The Ivy would be following the southern column.

Unless things went badly wrong and the opposition was stronger than expected, the French would have the honour of marching into the city first. But they would have to share the glory with the

Americans and other Allied troops, including a British contingent. Gerow specified that the American 38th Cavalry Squadron was to accompany Leclerc to 'display the [American] flag upon entering Paris'. It would be some compensation for the 29,000 US soldiers who had so far lost their lives in the Normandy campaign.

Leclerc had his own ideas. He disagreed with Gerow on where the main thrust should come. He ordered some of his troops, led by Colonel Paul de Langlade, to head as instructed towards Versailles, but they were to skirt round it to enter Paris via the western suburb of Sèvres. The bulk of the force, led by Colonel Pierre Billotte with Colonel Louis Dio's men in support, were to attack Paris from the south, where Leclerc believed the German defences to be weaker.

La Nueve were at the head of Billotte's column. On Thursday 24 August, they set off eastwards from Limours to the small town of Arpajon, then turned north towards Paris. The first stage passed smoothly. At 8 a.m., at Longjumeau, about 10 miles from the southern gates of the city, they ran into the first resistance. The Germans had had plenty of time to prepare strongpoints equipped with heavy machine guns and above all 88mm anti-aircraft artillery which was highly effective against both armour or infantry. The German defenders were determined but not fanatical and, after a short fight, most were ready to surrender. It still took time to outflank and suppress each outpost, and momentum slackened alarmingly.

Leclerc's men were slowed down further by the civilian population, who poured out of their homes to greet them. In every town La Nueve were met by 'an immense crowd invading the street and the pavements, surrounding and submerging our vehicles, kissing everyone on board and holding out precious food and bottles they had been saving up in anticipation of the great day'. They scattered 'like a swarm of grasshoppers' when a machine-gun burst or the blast of a cannon sounded too close by, only to rush back when the shooting died down. Sometimes they lingered too long. Dronne would never forget 'the vision of a beautiful young woman, her breasts covered in blood, sliding along the side of a tank, clutching at the turret' after being caught in a gust of fire.

The people looked much thinner and hungrier than the folk in Normandy, which made their generosity all the more touching. In

Antony, in the southern suburbs a butcher set up a table in front of his shop, piled with snacks. When they stopped to help themselves, a hidden German 88 opened up, wounding one of Dronne's section leaders, Lieutenant Vicente Montoya.

Near the town they had been approached by a convoy of jeeps carrying some of the many war correspondents who had infiltrated the vehicles. Among them was Bob Capa, travelling with the *Time* correspondent Charlie Wertenbaker. The reporter's story appeared a few days later, noting the Spanish republican flags on display and the 'very telling names painted on the fronts and sides' of La Nueve's half-tracks – 'Ebro', 'Guadalajara', 'Belchite' and other battles of a war that was now a memory. Leclerc had ordered that no assistance be given to foreign pressmen, but when the Spanish, with some embarrassment, explained the situation, Capa piped up. Pointing to a half-track named 'Teruel', he told them that he had been present at the battle. It was true. He had been there with Hemingway in December 1937 to cover the fighting. The Spaniards welcomed him as a comrade and Capa and Wertenbaker were invited to follow behind them.

Some soldiers of La Nueve with a half-track

The Americans watched Billotte's progress with mounting concern and irritation. Leclerc's arrival in Paris was scheduled for noon that day. The target time had been set before the level of German determination had been revealed, but it still seemed to Gerow that the French were showing too much caution as well as being seduced by the rapturous reception they were getting from the locals. He signalled to Bradley that he could not wait for the French to 'dance their way to Paris' and asked for permission to order the Ivy to take the lead, in the hope that it would shame Leclerc into getting a move on. Bradley was equally exasperated. 'To hell with prestige,' he messaged back. 'Tell the Fourth to slam on in and take the liberation.' But Leclerc was going as fast as he could. He, more than any American, understood the importance of his men reaching Paris first. The honour of France depended on it. Yet he was constantly frustrated by the skill and measured tenacity of the Germans, and the need for repeated detours to get round their strongpoints.

As they slogged through the outer suburbs, the fighting got heavier. At La Croix-de-Berny the path was blocked by a stubbornly firing 88 planted at the main crossroads. Dronne ordered Sergeant Chef Federico Moreno's section to deal with it. An elderly civilian with medals from the last war pinned proudly to his chest offered to guide them down a side street to the gun's unprotected flank. They crept along, preceded by a Sherman tank. A single round was enough to knock out the 88 and kill and wound some of the crew and the rest came out with their hands up. A mile further on at Fresnes, the notorious jail was now a fortress. The Resistance prisoners were gone but it still held German military felons who joined their guards to mount a fierce defence, and it was not until late afternoon that they were routed. Another obstacle had fallen, but the fighting was taking its toll. The day's French losses would total ninety-two killed or missing, 225 wounded, and thirty-five armoured vehicles and six self-propelled guns destroyed. It was a heavy price to overcome what had been hoped would be only token resistance. Fighting in the dark would only bring confusion and more casualties, and as the sun started to set it seemed unlikely that any French troops would enter Paris that night.

★

Inside the city hopes were soaring that salvation was only hours away. That afternoon, morale was boosted when Leclerc's personal Piper Cub appeared over the Île de la Cité and a shower of leaflets tumbled out. They read, 'Hold tight, we're coming,' and the message was soon leading the communiqués on the radio, which had belatedly started to broadcast uncensored news. The FFI maintained the pressure throughout the day. No German vehicles dared venture out unless escorted by armour, and streets like the boulevard Saint-Germain were now considered too dangerous to use. Armed only with petrol bombs and a captured enemy 77mm cannon, the FFI fought off an attempt to break through the barricades in the faubourg du Temple and the rue d'Angoulême. Rol-Tanguy now decided that the time had come for concentrated attacks on enemy outposts, with the proviso that frontal assaults should be avoided.

The toughest objective was the enemy compound in the Luxembourg Palace and gardens. The operation was commanded by Pierre Georges, now known as 'Colonel Fabien', the communist whose assassination of a German naval officer at the Barbès Métro station almost exactly three years before had marked the start of the armed struggle. Georges escaped the fate of many of his comrades killed in the crackdown that followed. He had never given up the fight. Moving to the eastern region of Franche-Comté he organized an FTP network of communists, escaped Soviet prisoners of war, Catholic peasants and local patriots. He had narrowly escaped capture when someone betrayed him to the police. He was wounded in the operation to grab him but managed to make it back to Paris. It was not long before he was picked up again. A few days later his wife Andrée was also arrested and deported to Germany. Georges was tortured by the Gestapo then imprisoned in the Fort de Romainville, from where he escaped in March 1943. After months recovering he returned to the struggle, moving around the country recruiting and organizing. In August he was back in the capital, commanding FTP operations in the southern Paris area. Fabien had nothing like the scale of weaponry needed to take the Luxembourg, but the FTP had been swamped by last-minute recruits and there was no shortage of men, women or enthusiasm. All the suffering and danger had cloaked Fabien in an aura of indestructibility as he prepared the attack in his headquarters in a large modern dental clinic in the 13th arrondissement, watched by a reporter from *Ce Soir*. 'The twenty-five-year-old colonel dictated careful and precise orders with impressive ease,' he wrote. 'He paused to take off his jacket and looked very thin in his blue shirt.' The confidence was infectious. 'Tomorrow we're going to take the Luxembourg!' exclaimed a young fighter as they filed out. It was not that easy. With grenades, rifles and Sten guns they managed to drive the Germans and their Milice allies out of some positions beneath the arcades behind the Odéon theatre which faced the compound. But lacking mortars or artillery they were forced to break off the attack. The Allies were on their way with their tanks, and the capture of the Luxembourg would have to await their arrival.

From midday, the Germans began their own offensive, targeting the provisional government strongholds in the Hôtel de Ville and the prefecture, but they were held off by the police and the Republican Guard. Once again, Choltitz decided against a full-scale assault with the tanks at his disposal, which within a few hours could probably have captured the buildings and wiped out much of the Gaullist leadership. His direction of the defence was now largely a performance designed to ensure that he emerged from a complicated and dangerous situation with his skin and his reputation intact.

A call from the Luftwaffe presented another dilemma which threatened to wreck his strategy and land him in the role of the Butcher of Paris. General Otto Dessloch, the commander of Luftflotte 3 which covered France, phoned to tell him he had been instructed to assist Choltitz's struggle with the insurgents by bombing the city. Choltitz had to think fast. He feigned enthusiasm then, through careful questioning, got Dessloch to admit that the raid would have to take place at night. As it would be impossible to pinpoint precise targets, the bombs were as likely to fall on Choltitz and his men as they were on the enemy. If that was the case, Choltitz went on, he would have to disobey Hitler's order to stand and fight, and instead evacuate the city. Was that what Dessloch wanted? Dessloch did not. When Choltitz put down the phone, he sensed that the Luftwaffe chief was as relieved as he was by the outcome of their conversation. Paris had been spared a battering from the air for which he would get the blame and there was nothing in the conversation for the ears of the Gestapo to seize on.

To further promote his image as an honourable man, Choltitz decided to appeal to the population in a leaflet dropped by air. It called for the 'immediate and unconditional cessation of acts of violence' and urged the citizens to 'defend themselves against the terrorists' of the Resistance. Under German protection, he claimed, Paris had known four years of relative peace and 'for us it continues to be one of the beautiful cities of Europe'. It would be easy for the Germans to pull out after first blowing up all the warehouses, factories, railway stations and utilities, bringing about 'a terrible catastrophe in less than forty-eight hours'. But this would happen only if the fighting continued. If it stopped, 'you may rely on our love for this marvellous centre of European culture [and] on our sympathy for all reasonable Frenchmen, for the women and children of Paris'. Choltitz's message was strictly for the record, a useful piece of evidence to show his captors. The conventional homage paid to the beauty of Paris added a finishing touch to the picture: the sentiments of a civilized man who shared the same values as his enemies.

Another performance was needed if he was to preserve his self-esteem and the respect of his fellow officers when the war was over and normal life resumed. The situation was clearly hopeless, but a premature surrender was out of the question. On Wednesday night a meeting took place at the Swedish consulate which significantly increased his chances of staying alive. It was organized by Raoul Nordling and brought together the Abwehr military intelligence agent Emil Bender and Lorrain Cruse, sent by Chaban-Delmas. The aim was to explore arrangements for a possible German surrender. Bender was there to represent Choltitz. He explained that when the Allies reached Paris it would not do for the general to capitulate immediately. There would have to be what the French called a *baroud d'honneur*, a token stand for form's sake that would save Choltitz's face. Furthermore, there could be no question of a German commander giving in to a bunch of rebels and he would surrender only to representatives of the French army. The message was clear. An attack aimed at the Meurice would be resisted for a while, after which Choltitz would accept defeat. Cruse hurried off to report to Chaban-Delmas, who immediately passed the news by radio to Leclerc.

By early evening, Dronne and La Nueve were still at Fresnes, about 10 miles from the centre of Paris. Dusk was falling and an order came over the radio for the company to pull back and rejoin the main column, halted more than a mile away near Antony. Dronne raged against being reined in when Paris seemed tantalizingly close, though he had no choice but to obey. On arrival, he ran into Leclerc, who was standing alone at the side of the road, tapping his cane on the pavement and 'clearly impatient and dissatisfied'. 'Dronne, what the hell are you doing here?' he demanded. Dronne told him about the recall signal and felt bold enough to offer his opinion that they were through the worst of the fighting and there was little serious resistance ahead. Leclerc murmured that there was 'no requirement to execute stupid orders'. Then he grabbed him by the arm and pointed his stick northwards: 'Dronne, head straight for Paris!'

Despite his optimistic assessment of the strength of the German defences, Dronne thought it wise to request some armoured support and three Sherman tanks came up to join his fifteen M2 half-tracks and assorted jeeps and trucks. Before they left, Leclerc told him he must enter the city that night. He was to tell everyone that 'the entire division will be in Paris tomorrow morning'. Dronne grasped that Leclerc was anxious to lift the spirits of the city. 'It was all about boosting the morale of the Resistance and the people . . . they were hanging on for the entry of the Allies and every hour that passed increased their fears and anguish and our presence, even if it was just symbolic, was needed to give them courage.'

It was 8 p.m. when the 130-strong company set off in a cacophony of roaring engines, clattering tracks and clouds of dust and exhaust fumes. A young man from Antony called Georges Chevallier volunteered to show them the way and hopped into Dronne's jeep. They wound down side roads through the modest suburbs, L'Haÿ-les-Roses, Cachan, Arcueil, avoiding any crossroads where the Germans might be waiting. Some streets were blocked by trees, felled to form barricades, but helpers rushed to clear the way. They approached the fort at Bicêtre cautiously, worried that the enemy would be waiting, but no shots came, and at 8.45 p.m. they reached the Porte d'Italie, the south-eastern gate to the city. A mile further on they arrived in the circular expanse of the place d'Italie, which was quite crowded despite the hour.

A panicky cry went up: 'The Boches are coming!' Then others shouted: 'The Americans! They're Americans!' It was only when the crowd surged forward to greet their saviours that they learned the truth. The column was 'surrounded, crushed, submerged in a sea of humanity'. A woman bizarrely dressed in the traditional costume of Alsace jumped on Dronne's jeep, fell forward and smashed the windscreen. For a few minutes the path was blocked. In the midst of the hysterical joy Dronne managed to stay calm. Leclerc had not specified a final objective when ordering him to Paris. He decided suddenly that only one destination would do. 'It was the Hôtel de Ville, which since the distant past was the symbol of Paris liberty and the beating heart of every uprising.'

To get there quickly and safely meant avoiding Germans and barricades, but when Dronne asked the rejoicing civilians to tell him a safe route nobody seemed to know one. Then a man appeared, pushing a moped, who offered to lead the way. He was, it turned out, an Armenian called Dikran Lorénian and he took up position at the front of the column and drove off, taking them on a meandering passage northwards down the narrow streets of the 13th arrondissement towards the river. They crossed the Seine at the pont d'Austerlitz and hurried along the Right Bank by way of the quai de la Rapée, the quai Henri IV, the quai des Célestins, and at last reached the quai de l'Hôtel de Ville. Dronne glanced up at the great clock above the city hall, set for the last four years to Berlin time. It was 9.22 p.m. and the last glimmers of light were fading over the exhausted city.

The square was almost deserted. Dronne reported his arrival by radio to Leclerc's HQ, then ordered the column to take up defensive positions. He handed command to Lieutenant Granell and walked over to the Hôtel de Ville. The FFI guards on the door were expecting him. The news of La Nueve's entry had swept across the city and the radio which had been broadcasting all evening from a studio in the rue de Grenelle had already announced their imminent arrival at the city hall. Dronne climbed the great staircase. The power had been switched on specially and he entered the brilliantly lit Grand Salon to a roar of jubilation. A small, thin grey-faced man stepped forward. It was Georges Bidault, the president of the National Resistance Council, who welcomed him in a voice shaking with emotion. Dronne mumbled a few words in return, expressing 'the joy of the outside Resistance at meeting up with the leaders of the inside Resistance'. The hall rang with cries of 'Vive de Gaulle!' and 'Vive la France!' and endless, overlapping choruses of the 'Marseillaise'. Dronne suddenly felt very alone and acutely self-conscious. It dawned on him how he must appear to the drab but neatly dressed men and women before him. He felt 'monstrously dirty, even disgusting. The dust, the mud, the exhaust fumes sticking to my clothes and skin had combined with the rain and the sun to coat me in a repulsive carapace.' Then the celebrations were interrupted by the sound of gunfire and shattering glass. There was a scramble to switch off the lights and everyone dropped to the floor. When the shooting stopped, every non-combatant was ordered to leave the building.

Dronne was led off to the police prefecture to report to Parodi, Luizet and Chaban-Delmas. A radio reporter had set up his microphone and Parodi announced Dronne's arrival over the airwaves. 'I have before me a French captain who is the first to enter Paris,' he declared. 'His

Dronne at the prefecture with Chaban-Delmas (*right*)

face is red, he's dirty and unshaven but none the less I want to kiss him.' He looked like a vagrant compared to Chaban-Delmas, who had somehow managed to be measured for a 'beautiful brand-new khaki uniform' and seemed to Dronne 'very young, smooth and elegant'. He was grateful when he was led away to the prefect's opulent private bathroom to soak away the grime of the road. Dronne's night was not yet over and he returned to check on his men.

All over the city that night, Parisians allowed themselves an hour of anticipatory rejoicing. When Cécile heard the news at Rol-Tanguy's underground headquarters, 'We had a party and the women celebrated with a pillow fight.' Windows were thrown open and neighbours filled the stairwells of the apartment blocks, swapping the scraps of news they heard by telephone or over the radio, which had abandoned professional standards and was spreading a constant stream of rumours and fabrications. The hot, still air was flooded with the sound of bells. It had started just as Dronne arrived at the Hôtel de Ville, a few timid notes at first, 'but then it widened and amplified, so that soon all the bells of Paris were ringing at the same time, and the last to join in the dance was the great voice of the big bell of Notre-Dame which since the Middle Ages had rung out at the great moments in the history of Paris and it filled our ears and our hearts'. This was not his men's city nor even their country, but they heard the bells and felt the same thrill of emotion. 'Our hearts had not been so hardened by the fighting that they were not gripped by the sound,' remembered Lieutenant Amado Granell. 'The shouts, the singing of the Marseillaise mingled with the chimes. We all had tears in our eyes and lumps in our throats . . . This was the sound of freedom, the sound of victory.'

The Germans heard the bells too and felt a different emotion. Walter Dreizner was on guard duty above the rue de Rivoli, pacing the roofs in rubber-soled boots, when the bells started up, 'chasing one another into the dark summer's night'. He felt a 'shiver go down my spine. I wanted them to stop but they went on without respite, mercilessly pounding in my ears.' After an hour the ringing ceased. The windows closed again and the lights went out. Silence and darkness settled over the city, broken only by isolated gunshots and mysterious fires springing up and then dying away on the distant heights.

14. The Day the War Should Have Ended

On Friday 25 August 1944, Paris lived out the greatest day of its modern history. All its multiple personalities fused in an immortal spectacle that rekindled humanity's love affair with the city. The streets throbbed with relief, joy and love, all emotions sharpened by the danger still hanging in the air. When the Germans marched into Paris in June 1940 it felt as though Europe had fallen into darkness. Now the land was bright again and the path to total victory seemed that much shorter and clearer. The war had swept away all that was predictable, normal and comforting. A Paris filled with grey uniforms and swathed in swastika flags was not – could never be – Paris. At last the City of Light, the city of love, still fully recognizable, was restored to the world's imagination in all its clichéd but hugely reassuring familiarity.

The first French and American troops to enter the city that morning encountered little or no enemy opposition. Instead they were met by ecstatic crowds, whose conformity to popular notions of Frenchness was so complete that it sometimes seemed the extravaganza was being orchestrated by Hollywood. The impression was strengthened by the ubiquitous teams of cameramen and photographers whose work would stamp the delight of the day indelibly in the memory of the century and beyond. The moment when the relieving force joined with the insurgents created a cinematic feast of contrasting but complementary imagery. Trundling along the great avenues and boulevards came lines of tanks, armoured cars and jeeps, topped by the warriors of the 2DB, whose helmets, sun-bronzed faces and dust-stained khakis made them look like statues on a monument. Alongside them slid the low-slung Citroën *traction avant* saloons of the FFI, loaded with young fighters in summer shirts and high-waisted *zazou* trousers, long hair in careful disarray and rifles ported at theatrical angles. They seemed to have been chosen by central casting for their looks, their dash and their insouciance, and many displayed an actorish awareness of every camera turned their way. The liberation of Paris was momentous history but it was also a performance, and everyone, soldiers and civilians, French, Americans and Germans, played their part to perfection.

Billotte's force had spent the night near La Croix-de-Berny. They set off at 7.15 in a morning mist that promised a glorious day, aiming for the police prefecture and following Dronne's route of the night before. Colonel Dio's men, held in reserve on Thursday, were split in two, with one column heading to secure Montparnasse station where de Gaulle had told Leclerc to set up his headquarters and other objectives near by. The second column was ordered to take control of the city bridges over the Seine. It was still early as the steel tracks ground over the cobbles and the clattering brought everyone, some still in their nightclothes, out of their apartments and into the streets.

The northerly formations of the 2DB under Colonel Paul de Langlade had penetrated the city from the direction of Versailles via the pont de Sèvres the previous evening but bivouacked on the southern edge of the 16th arrondissement. There was a delay while fuel trucks were brought up to replenish the vehicles. Then the main column, led by a detachment under Major Jacques Massu, a gruff veteran who had been with Leclerc from the beginning, processed through the pompous thoroughfares of western Paris – the rue Michel-Ange, the rue de la Pompe and the avenue Victor Hugo, at the top of which reared the great, sombre hulk of the Arc de Triomphe, whose grey stones embodied all the glory and all the hubris of France.

The crowd lining the route, two and three deep, pressed forward with outstretched arms and incoherent shouts of welcome, all reserve dissolved by the relief bursting inside them. There were old people. There were children, and a large number of youngish women, dressed in their best, in blue, white and red, hair washed, curled and coiffed, their lips rouged and their figures svelte from four years of enforced dieting. Many of their husbands were far away, and had been for the past four years, stuck in prisoner-of-war camps or labouring on German farms and factory floors, and it would be a long time before

they returned. Some of the lucky ones would be reunited that night with their men, coming home with the 2DB.

All the stored-up love and frustration broke like a wave over the anonymous saviours. Respectable matrons who had flinched at the sight of a Wehrmacht uniform pulled any soldier within reach to their bosoms, pinioning them in hot arms inside a cloud of scent and plastering them with kisses so that even the tall, elegant and aristocratic de Langlade arrived at the place de l'Étoile smothered in lipstick. Younger women climbed on to the hulls of the tanks and the bonnets of the jeeps, their dresses splashing the drab green-brown steel with vivid colour like flowers in a muddy field.

There were women in the convoy too, from the Rochambelles' ambulance unit and a company of British Quaker volunteers. Leclerc had been opposed to females serving in the 2DB but had eventually relented, and they had been with the division all the way since they landed. 'They were gay, they were young, they were charming and they joined in the spirit of that joy that felt like it would never end,' reported Jean-Jacques Gautier of the *Figaro* breathlessly.

Eighteen-year-old Françoise Bratt had been working all night in a Resistance first-aid post in the avenue de la Grande-Armée off the place de l'Étoile when she heard a 'roaring clanking noise coming nearer and nearer'. On the street she saw a mass of 'madly enthusiastic' Parisians, some 'weeping with joy'. Soon she was boiling salted water to treat the many soldiers whose eyes were red and swollen with conjunctivitis from the dust of the road. Some were Parisians and asked to use the phone, calling parents and siblings. All outside communication with France being cut, it was the first time they were hearing their voices since 1940. Then there was a new wave of casualties, most of them civilians wounded by random gunfire which would be heard sporadically and whose source was often mysterious.

At the Étoile the celebrations were interrupted by shooting from the German positions clustered around the Hôtel Majestic, on the avenue Kléber, just down from the Arc de Triomphe. The headquarters was heavily defended and Massu had come expecting a fight. As they approached the Arc, over which a giant tricolour now stirred in the breeze, 'a squall of machine-gun fire swept the street in front of us'. It came from a blockhouse in the rue de Presbourg behind the hotel. A tank in the lead column 'moved forward, slowly, very slowly ... Its turret swung right, two metres, one metre.' A burst from the Sherman's .50 calibre machine gun killed the German gunner. The rest of the crew watched, 'terrified by the appearance only twenty metres away of this steel monster which points its 75mm cannon towards them ... everyone holds their breath. Then the cannon fires. The shot and the exploding shell combine in a deafening din with the shattering of glass as the windows of a shop blow in. Two rounds from the cannon and all the defenders are dead.'

Those inside the Majestic realized their situation was hopeless and an officer emerged, waving a white table napkin in lieu of a flag. He was escorted to Colonel de Langlade's command post next to the Arc de Triomphe, where a crowd of civilians who had taken shelter shouted abuse at him. De Langlade saw before him 'a lieutenant-colonel, thin, haggard, eyes burning in his pale face'. The German asked what terms were on offer for the garrison to surrender. De Langlade, as he recalled, 'replied sharply that they were very simple. They had thirty minutes to give themselves up or the hotel would be stormed and everyone killed.'

The officer returned under escort and half an hour later Massu went forward to take the surrender. As he approached, a sergeant at his shoulder was shot dead by a rooftop sniper, but he pressed on and found gathered in the Majestic lobby fifty officers and 300 men, whom he led back to the place de l'Étoile.

The Majestic had been designated the centre for the defence of western Paris and with its capitulation one of the main German citadels had fallen. Some Germans tried to salvage their dignity as they were taken off into captivity. When Sergeant Michel Chauvet of the 2DB saw an officer, 'small, round and chubby', ordering his men to march in step he could not contain his anger and 'jumped on him to remind him that dignity is not the same as arrogance', wrenching from his neck the binoculars that 'were his last symbol of authority'. Many of the Germans were frightened that the crowds pressing around them would tear them to pieces or that the FFI 'terrorists' who had now sprung up everywhere would treat them with the same merciless cruelty as the SS and Gestapo had shown the Resistance.

Everyone was jumpy. Many of the liberating troops had been drinking since their arrival from the endless bottles and glasses pressed into their hands by the crowds. When a soldier escorting some of the Majestic prisoners accidentally detonated a phosphorus grenade – used for clearing bunkers – which instantly generated a cloud of choking gas, his comrades opened up indiscriminately. After the smoke had cleared, another soldier in the escort, Jacques Desbordes, saw 'about ten dead Germans, their bodies riddled with bullets', and 'puddles of blood which coagulated very rapidly in the heat'.

Dreamlike scenes of swift, ugly violence punctuated the rejoicing. Four German soldiers were pulled out of a house near the place de l'Étoile, from where they had apparently been firing on the crowds, killing a woman and child and wounding three others. They were taken to the Arc de Triomphe and shot dead by a 2DB soldier in front of hundreds of onlookers. The execution was filmed but understandably did not feature in the footage that the French showed to the world.

With the Majestic neutralized, the next objective was Choltitz's headquarters at the Meurice. Choltitz had given the impression via intermediaries that he was prepared to give up after a token fight.

Leclerc's men were about to find out whether he really meant it and, if so, what this would entail.

On arrival at the police prefecture at 8.30 a.m. Billotte held a quick conference with Parodi and Chaban-Delmas. They set about issuing Choltitz with an ultimatum to pave the way for his capitulation. It announced the 2DB's arrival in the city and warned that a much bigger Allied force was on its way. The German position was hopeless and to 'avoid any useless bloodletting, it remains to you to cease resistance immediately'. The letter was typed up, timed at 10.30 a.m., and delivered to the Swedish consulate in the rue d'Anjou for the now recovered Raoul Nordling, who had once again agreed to act as go-between.

Choltitz's situation had become even more delicate. The day before, he had heard that Model was sending help in the shape of a scratch division patched together from units falling back from Normandy. It was the last thing he wanted, but for appearance's sake he had called his staff together in the afternoon to deliver a spine-stiffening address urging them to fight to the last man. Billotte's ultimatum was carried to the German HQ by Nordling's Abwehr agent ally Emil Bender. When he handed it over to Choltitz's assistant, Lieutenant von Arnim, the aide told him that the general would refuse to accept it. Honour demanded that he be taken prisoner before he could surrender. Upstairs Choltitz maintained his sang-froid, taking lunch as usual with his staff while they waited for the *baroud d'honneur* to commence.

At 1.30 p.m. the operation to take the Meurice began. The plan was for a three-pronged attack. The main thrust by about fifty men supported by five tanks would come down the rue de Rivoli from the east. They would be supported by other units charged with crushing the formidable defences and tanks in the Tuileries, facing the hotel to the south. Another force would infiltrate the streets behind the Meurice from the north and west.

Lieutenant Henri Karcher was waiting with his men at the Tour Saint-Jacques on the rue de Rivoli about a mile east of Choltitz's HQ when he got the order to move. He took the north side of the street with his twenty-five men. Lieutenant Jacques Franjoux led a similar force along the south pavement. Falling in behind them came a motley band of FFI fighters, and cheering them on was a crowd of civilians, who had to be prevented by a cordon of police from accompanying the attack. Karcher was nearly thirty-six and rather old for his rank, but like many of the 2DB he had not started out intending to be a soldier. He was studying at the Paris faculty of medicine when the war intervened. He escaped to England in 1940, joined the Free French and campaigned through Africa and Syria before returning to France with the 2DB in August. He was lean, cheerful and despite being badly wounded in Tunisia and again in Normandy was still full of fight.

It was soon clear that they would be facing more than token resistance. As they advanced westwards machine-gun fire swept down the rue de Rivoli from marines barricaded inside the Navy Ministry in the place de la Concorde, killing and wounding several of Franjoux's men. The rest scurried over to join Karcher's section, who were moving under the protection of the stone-pillared arcade that ran along the north side of the street. Tanks moved forward to suppress the fire from the Concorde, but at each intersection the foot soldiers came under attack from Germans holed up in the upper storeys firing down and tossing grenades, as well as from the strongpoints planted in the Tuileries. One grenade fell into the open turret of a French tank, badly burning three of the four-man crew.

It was 2.35 p.m. before they reached the revolving door of the Meurice. Karcher and Franjoux stormed in, submachine guns stuttering. In the grand marble lobby Karcher noticed a 'fine portrait of the Führer' nestling incongruously in a display cabinet surrounded by expensive handbags and face powder. A machine gunner was posted behind sandbags on the staircase, but Karcher disposed of him with a burst from his *mitraillette*. They threw phosphorus grenades and a line of coughing, spluttering troops emerged, tears pouring down their faces. Karcher demanded to know the whereabouts of General von Choltitz and was told he was on the first floor. He sent a German officer upstairs with a machine pistol poking into his back with a message that he was on his way. A minute later he was standing in a salon overlooking the hotel courtyard.

There was Choltitz, neck bulging over the collar of his field-grey uniform, monocle clamped into his red, angry face. He was leaning forward with his hands planted on the table in front of him, as if demanding the meaning of this impertinent intrusion. The visitor announced himself as 'Lieutenant Karcher, officer of General de Gaulle', and asked one of the staff if Choltitz spoke French, to be told that he understood it well enough.

'I then said, General, do you surrender?'

'Ja.'

'Then lay down your arms.'

Choltitz and his aides placed their pistols on the table. It was over, and Karcher felt a flood of emotions rising inside him. This was the moment he and all his comrades had dreamed of since June 1940 when they had refused to accept France's defeat and had begun the long, lonely fight back under the banner of General de Gaulle. 'I thought of all my companions who had died along the way,' he remembered. 'But at this moment Paris was officially liberated. We had taken back Paris!'

Just then Colonel Billotte's chief of staff, Commandant Jean Fanneau de La Horie, arrived to take over. He demanded that Choltitz now order his men occupying the remaining strongpoints around the city to cease firing. Choltitz agreed, but insisted first that he and his men 'be treated as soldiers', fearful, it seemed, that they might be handed over to the Resistance. De la Horie assented and Choltitz was led down through the back entrance of the hotel on the narrow rue du Mont Thabor and driven off in the commandant's jeep. Karcher found himself with a gaggle of Choltitz's staff. Someone produced a bottle of champagne which had been cooling in an adjoining bathroom. Another brought him a glass. He poured the wine and raised it in a toast. 'Gentlemen. To the health of General de Gaulle and to victorious France!'

The jeep carrying Choltitz turned right down the rue d'Alger and on to the rue de Rivoli, heading for the Île de la Cité and the police prefecture. Stricken vehicles pouring smoke and flames littered the streets, but the shooting was fading and civilians were edging back on to the pavements. En route, Choltitz's escort saw Billotte's personal scout car heading their way and handed over the prisoner.

When Choltitz was delivered to police headquarters the place was crowded with Free French officers, FFI commanders, Resistance figures and journalists. Leclerc had already arrived and after a quick lunch was waiting with some of his staff and Chaban-Delmas in the first-floor salon of the prefect of police's private quarters. Light streamed in from two tall windows, a Gobelins tapestry adorned one end of the room and a large white marble fireplace stood at the other. Much of the space was taken up by a full-sized billiard table, around which, down the years, many a delicate matter had been settled. Leclerc was sitting on a sofa next to Chaban-Delmas beneath the tapestry when the door opened and Billotte walked in. 'Here he is,' he said. A minute seemed to pass before Choltitz entered warily, eyes darting around the company to assure himself that he was safely among fellow officers. His face was still an unhealthy red and the buttons of his tunic strained to contain his bulk, a squat, unsoldierly figure compared to the lean warriors before him fresh from the battlefield. He advanced towards Leclerc, hand outstretched. Leclerc ignored it, introduced himself in German which he spoke fluently and asked Choltitz to confirm his identity. Then he invited him to sit down at a table installed between the sofa and the billiard table.

Before they got down to business the sounds of a commotion drifted from the room next door. Chaban-Delmas went to see what was going on. Henri Rol-Tanguy had just arrived with his chief of staff, another veteran communist, Maurice Kriegel-Valrimont. They were arguing fiercely with Luizet, insisting that the FFI, who had been fighting the Germans long before the 2DB arrived, had the right to be present at the moment of capitulation. Luizet and Chaban-Delmas could only agree, and Leclerc, who knew little or nothing about Rol-Tanguy, summoned them in.

Choltitz was read the surrender agreement, first in its entirety, then paragraph by paragraph, translated into German by a 2DB staff officer called Captain Betz. It was issued under the authority of Leclerc as commander of the French forces in Paris, in the name of the provisional government of the French republic. It called on Choltitz to order his men to cease fire immediately, run up the white flag, lay down their arms and hand over all their supplies. The first objection

came not from the German but from Rol-Tanguy. Strongly supported by Kriegel-Valrimont, he wanted to know why his name was
not attached to the document. Leclerc was taken aback, but replied
calmly that as *he* was his overall commander Rol-Tanguy was represented by his signature. Then Choltitz raised his objections. He
pointed out that he could be held responsible only for the Paris garrison and had no control over German soldiers passing through the
city from Normandy who might chose to fight on. The text was
altered accordingly and, breathing heavily and struggling to preserve
his dignity, Choltitz took the pen offered by Leclerc and signed.

The company then departed for Leclerc's headquarters at Montparnasse station, taking Choltitz with them. Immediately, the squabble
over signatures reignited. Kriegel-Valrimont was still indignant at
that absence of his chief's name on the document. He cornered
Chaban-Delmas and argued forcefully that Rol-Tanguy and his forces
had played at least an equal part with the 2DB in the victory and
deserved to share the credit. Excluding him meant they were playing
the enemy's game as the Germans had always refused to treat directly
with the 'terrorists' of the FFI. For all his respect for form and convention, Chaban-Delmas acknowledged the justice of the demand.
Together they approached Leclerc who, without fuss, agreed to an
amendment. In the new surrender agreement, he even put the name
of 'Colonel Rol, commander of the FFI of the Île de France', first.

At Montparnasse, Choltitz was told to sign a sheaf of papers ordering his men to lay down their arms. Teams of two officers, one
French, one German, set off to the twenty or so German positions
around the city to deliver them by hand. When they arrived at the
heavily fortified compound of the Luxembourg the fighting was still
going on. Colonel Fabien had joined forces with the 2DB and
together they were besieging the 600 men within. At around 5 p.m. a
French officer was allowed to enter to deliver the surrender order,
but it took two and a half hours of parleying before the shooting
stopped. Once disarmed the Germans seemed instantly deflated and
officers and men sprawled listlessly in the courtyard. Reports had
suggested there were sixty tanks in the compound, but there turned
out to be only a handful – four Panthers, three flamethrower tanks

and three old French light tanks. The French were shocked by the scene inside the palace, which hardly matched the Germans' projected image of order and efficiency. A reporter from *Défense de la France* saw 'ripped-up papers strewn everywhere as if a tornado had passed through, bowls full of mouldy food, brimming glasses of kummel, broken plates and tattered clothing and bottles and bottles of champagne'. The Luxembourg was the last bastion to fall. By 7.35 p.m. all the other major strongpoints including the Bourbon Palace, the Foreign Ministry, the École Militaire, the Naval Ministry and the barracks in the place de la République had surrendered.

The masses on the streets were now relishing the delicious spectacle of their former masters being led away, defeated and humiliated, hands clasped behind their heads, some weeping, many of them wild-eyed and quivering with fear. They strained to get at them, jeering, spitting and screaming their hatred. Sometimes they managed to break through the protective cordon to throw punches and pull hair. At the place de l'Étoile, a woman darted into a column and drove a hat pin into the eye of a German officer.

When the Meurice fell, Walter Dreizner was captured with the rest of the headquarters staff and marched towards the rue de Rivoli. As they turned into the street 'the man in front of me was knocked down by an uppercut to the chin. A few metres further on a Frenchman lifted up a bicycle and threw it at us. We were driven like animals towards the Louvre. A flood of curses deafened us from all sides: "assassins", "bunch of pigs", "thieves" . . . Blows rained down on us, people were spitting, there were no restraints . . . the people of Paris were in their element.' Dreizner felt he was the victim of a terrible injustice. They were 'being hounded through the streets as no animal would be hounded'. Some of his comrades mumbled in broken French, 'Allemands pas méchants,' seemingly incapable of understanding that after four years of repression, exploitation and constant humiliation Paris should have turned on them like this. Fearing that they were about to be lynched, some prisoners broke away and ran into the Louvre looking for sanctuary. One by one they were winkled out, some of them discovered hiding inside the tombs in the Egyptian section. Dreizner was likewise sure he was going to be killed. They were herded into a metal cage in the courtyard of the Palais-Royal, which gave them some protection from the mob. The FFI guards went through their pockets and Dreizner was relieved of 1,400 francs. The guards threw some of the loot over the wire to the crowd in an effort to appease them. The sight of the ugly face of victory left some Parisians feeling queasy and ashamed. In the place de la Concorde, in front of the Hôtel Crillon, a male civilian who had slapped the face of a German prisoner was challenged by an elderly man with the rosette of the Légion d'Honneur in his buttonhole: 'Have you no shame? He's a prisoner who should be treated according to the laws of war.' The man snarled back: 'I was a prisoner too. Do you want to know how they treated me?' The older man persisted: 'Just because the Boches behave brutally, does that mean we do the same?' The crowd began to murmur their agreement. 'He's right, we're not the Boches.' But the events of the next few days revealed how easily joy could give way to the spirit of revenge, and many scores would be settled before the fever ran its course.

Ernest Hemingway arrived in Paris just behind de Langlade's troops. He crossed the bridge at Sèvres on the morning of 25 August in a jeep driven by the faithful Red Pelkey and in the company of David Bruce of the OSS, leading his French 'irregulars'. At his first sight of the old place, he told his *Collier's* readers later, he 'had a funny choke in my voice and I had to clean my glasses because there now, below us grey and always beautiful, was spread the city I love best in all the world'.

There were several adventures before they reached the Arc de Triomphe. Bruce recorded that 'As we drove into a large square near the Bois de Boulogne, we were suddenly halted in front of a café, and it was said that snipers were firing from some of the upstairs windows of a large apartment house.' They sheltered in a doorway until 'finally a tank sent a few shells into the unfortunate house and we were told to move on'. Thereafter 'we were surrounded continually by surging masses of cheering people. Kissing and shouting were general and indiscriminate.' They reached the Arc in the early afternoon and climbed to the top, from where they watched columns of smoke rising from the fighting in the Tuileries and the Luxembourg. When they descended Bruce saw 'seven or eight Germans . . . dead in a heap on the street' – probably the corpses from the phosphorus-grenade episode. The direct route to the centre of town was down the Champs-Élysées, but as they moved forward there was a rattle of gunfire and they took shelter in the lee of a tank. A man dived in beside them and when the shooting died down he had little trouble persuading them to come back to his apartment in the avenue Foch near by to drink several bottles of champagne. Thus fortified they felt ready to risk the journey down the Champs and ripped 'at racing speed' over the cobbles, stopping outside the Travellers Club, housed in the former mansion of a famous Second Empire courtesan. In the cavernous marble and gilt bar, the club president was hosting a small party and they were plied with more champagne. From there they made another dash to the Café de la Paix on the place de l'Opéra which was filled with 'a solid mass of cheering people and, after kissing several thousand men women and babies . . . we escaped to the Ritz'.

The hotel stood at the north-east corner of the place Vendôme and for the last four years had been where the Luftwaffe brass and VIP visitors from the Reich lodged, as well as the likes of Coco Chanel who moved there at the start of the occupation. It seemed empty but the manager Claude Auzello, who had run the hotel with his wife since the 1920s, soon appeared and asked Hemingway what he could do for him. He replied that he would like forty-seven martini cocktails for himself, Bruce and his entourage. The drinks duly appeared, a satisfying flourish with which to begin a new chapter of the Hemingway legend.

That evening he met up again with Bob Capa, who had arrived mid-morning with Charlie Wertenbaker and the Billotte column via the Porte d'Orléans. Capa made light of everything, but his description of that day was full of fresh and childlike wonder and for the years that were left to him it would always be 'the most unforgettable day in the world'. It seemed to him as they drove through the cheering, weeping, singing throng that 'Never were there so many who were so happy so early in the morning.' Paris was the city where he'd 'learned to eat, drink and love' and he felt as if the spectacle 'had been made especially for me'. There were too many pictures to take and he found that 'the thousands of faces in the finder of my camera became more and more blurred' with tears. The route took them through Denfert-Rochereau, past an apartment block where he had lodged before the war. The concierge was on the pavement waving, and as Capa swept by he yelled, 'C'est moi! C'est moi!' They stopped at his favourite café, the Dôme in the boulevard Montparnasse. Then it was on to cover the fighting around the Bourbon Palace before crossing the river and bagging a large room in the Hôtel Scribe next to the Opéra, which became for a while *Time* magazine's Paris headquarters. Word soon reached him that Hemingway was at the Ritz, and when he went round to visit, 'He made up with me and gave me a party.' Their tiff at Rambouillet was forgotten and Papa and Capa were friends again.

The Ivy entered the city from the south that morning with the 12th Regiment in the lead, arriving at Notre-Dame at noon. Jerry Salinger and his counter-intelligence buddy John Keenan were with them. As Salinger's jeep – spade and entrenching tool strapped to the side – pushed through the throng, women held out babies for the victors to kiss and men thrust bottles into their hands. After all they had been through, the welcome, Salinger told Whit Burnett, 'made things seem more worthwhile'. They 'cried, they laughed, they besieged us, brought barrels of cognac out to the jeep . . . it was really fine. There was still shooting in the streets but nobody seemed to care. All the girls looked elegant, put on their best August dresses.' He felt that 'If we had stood on the hood of the jeep and taken a leak, Paris would have said "Ah the darling Americans! What a charming custom!"'

It seemed to Captain Fernand Auberjonois, a Swiss officer serving with the Americans, that the crowds could not quite believe their eyes and needed physical evidence that this was not all a dream. 'They felt the need to touch – they touched our uniforms as if to reassure themselves that those wearing them truly existed.'

The scene was now set for the entrance of the man whose name the throng was chanting and which adorned the FFI cars and trucks. Charles de Gaulle drove in from Rambouillet through rapturous crowds in an open-topped black Hotchkiss convertible. He had planned every step, every gesture, with the greatest care, and every utterance too, each charged with meaning and purpose. All had the same aim: to ensure that it was his vision of the new France that emerged from the confusion and that he would be at its head. Bidault and the rest of the CNR were waiting for him at the Hôtel de Ville, but rather than do them the honour of going there first he went to Montparnasse station, where he arrived at 4.30 p.m. He greeted Leclerc and congratulated him on having taken Paris intact. He was introduced for the first time to Chaban-Delmas, who seemed to him astonishingly young for his exalted position. Rol-Tanguy was also waiting and de Gaulle praised him and the FFI for 'having driven the enemy from our streets'.

But when Leclerc showed him the surrender document, de Gaulle bristled. What was Rol-Tanguy's name doing on it? Leclerc explained that Chaban-Delmas had pushed for his inclusion and, for the moment, de Gaulle left it at that. He was already determined that credit for the victory would be apportioned according to his version of the liberation legend, which would be shaped to suit his plans for the future of France. Even now he was still fearful of an attempted communist takeover, and was determined to allow Rol-Tanguy and his men only a minimum share of the spoils. He had time to embrace his son, Philippe, serving as a lieutenant with a marine unit of the 2DB, who was just about to leave to negotiate the surrender of the German outpost at the Bourbon Palace. His next destination was the Ministry of War in the rue Dominique. He had been its chief when he quit Paris on 10 June 1940 and, by stopping there, he sought to plant a sense of continuity, immutability and legitimacy.

He decided to make the ministry his headquarters for the time being. Even de Gaulle realized that a move to the presidential Élysée Palace might seem presumptuous given that he had never been elected to anything. Very soon he received his first visitors, his loyal lieutenants Parodi and Luizet, who pressed him to show some respect to the Resistance leaders waiting at the Hôtel de Ville by going to see them next. De Gaulle at first refused, stating that they were simply municipal representatives, whereas he embodied the government of France. He eventually relented, but only after he had taken two further measures to tighten his authority. The first was to arrange for a victory parade to be held the following day down the Champs-Élysées, led by himself in the role of conquering hero. The second was to insist that before calling on the CNR he would go to police headquarters. On his arrival at the prefecture, the police welcomed him, as if they had always been his loyal liegemen. He responded in kind, thanking them for having initiated the actions which had helped to end the years of humiliation and restored the pride of Paris. It was a cynical piece of flattery and historical distortion, designed to bind the forces of law and order to him and create a bulwark against potential challenges from the communists.

De Gaulle chose to walk the short distance to the Hôtel de Ville, arriving at 7.15 p.m. A multitude was waiting for their first sight of this quasi-mythological being, known to the masses primarily by the sound of his voice. He looked appropriately otherworldly, at 6 feet 5 inches nearly a foot taller than most around him, and wore a plain khaki uniform almost devoid of decoration. In someone else his size, stiff, ponderous bearing and self-consciously frozen features might have seemed ludicrously pompous. Instead he radiated majesty. If he was displeased that it was a communist from the Paris Liberation Committee called Georges Marrane who was the first to speak, he did not show it. The next to welcome him was the CNR president, Georges Bidault, whose address, full of warmth and admiration, pointed out the happy symbolism of the day, celebrated so close to the Île Saint-Louis named for the holiest king of France.

Now it was de Gaulle's turn. The speech was delivered in a passionate growl, full of stabbing emphases and carried over the host packed into the first-floor salon and into the microphones of several

radio reporters. The audience were hearing the greatest speech of de Gaulle's life:

How can one hide the emotion that grips all of us who are here, *chez nous*, in Paris which has risen up to defend itself and which has done so by itself. No! We will not hide this sacred and profound emotion. There are moments which go beyond each of our own poor lives.

Paris! Paris outraged! Paris broken! Paris martyred . . . But Paris liberated! Liberated by itself, liberated by its people with the help of the armies of France, with the help and assistance of the whole of France, of that France which fights, of the only France, of the true France, of the eternal France!

When he had finished, de Gaulle seemed as moved by his own words as was the watching crowd. He looked around him, swallowing hard and blinking as if on the point of subsiding into tears.

It was brilliant oratory, but only lightly anchored in the reality that those who heard him had lived through. There were no thanks to those present, who had kept the spirit of France burning, no specific mention of the Resistance except a sketchy reference to our 'brave and dear forces of the interior'. As to the Allies, without whom there would have been no liberation and indeed no de Gaulle, there was only a passing acknowledgement of their 'help'. When he finished, Bidault asked timidly if he was now going to go on to the balcony and announce to the crowds outside the restoration of the Republic. De Gaulle replied curtly that he was not. The suggestion was illogical as the old Republic had never ceased to exist.

As evening fell, bottles stashed *derrière les fagots* for the great day were recovered and uncorked and neighbours sat in their apartment-block courtyards toasting their deliverance and remembering those who were not there to enjoy it. In the Ritz and the Scribe the old Dorchester crowd appeared to have arrived en masse from London and were drinking champagne, which seemed to flow from a magic fountain that would never run dry. At the Étoile, Jacques Massu was asked to dinner at the grand apartment of some wealthy residents of the avenue Foch, perhaps the same ones who had hosted Hemingway earlier. He felt out of place, 'as dirty as a pig, having not washed for days'. He was relieved when a message came from Leclerc inviting him to join him at a celebration at the Invalides. He made the journey in his jeep, taking side roads to avoid the bullets fired by German snipers – or perhaps by the FFI, who David Bruce observed were 'well out of hand and draw on anybody whom they consider suspicious'. At the party were all the senior officers of the 2DB as well as General Koenig and Chaban-Delmas. When it finished, Massu returned to check on his men, stretched out on the tarmac around the Étoile, many with a woman to keep them warm. Everywhere around town Parisiennes were making sure the liberators did not spend the night alone. As the veteran American war reporter Ernie Pyle joked: 'Anybody who does not sleep with a woman tonight is just an exhibitionist.'

In the early hours it started raining. On the other side of the city in the Bois de Vincennes, the Ivy were bedded down in bivouac tents. They were damp and dirty but, lying there with the raindrops pattering on the canvas, they felt secure and glowing with the joy of existence. It seemed to Irwin Shaw, former lover of Mary Welsh, and now in Paris with the army film unit, that this 'was the day when the war should have ended'.

15. Awakening

On the first day of freedom, the outside world was told that despite everything that had happened in the preceding four years, the soul of the city had emerged blessedly unchanged. Every Parisian cliché got an airing in a typical despatch by an American network radio reporter, Herbert Clarke, relayed to fifteen million listeners via the BBC's nightly *War Report*. 'Paris is still Paris,' he announced. 'Her heart is still warm and young and gay. Nothing the Nazis have done has penetrated into the spirit of the city. There are bicycles in the streets instead of taxis, but they only add to the charm of the picture, because many of them are ridden by girls in summer dresses.' The women might not be quite as chic as in the days before the war, but 'Every one of them has that old "je-ne-sais-quoi", that certain something that sets them aside.' Many other journalists echoed Clarke's positive and sentimental tone. 'Paris seems to have all the beautiful girls we have always been told it had,' the American war correspondent Ernie Pyle told his readers. 'The liberation is the loveliest, brightest story of our time.'

That morning, hangovers notwithstanding, the journalists had work to do. The city was bursting with a thousand stories and they made a start on collecting them before moving on to cover the great setpiece of the day. De Gaulle had intended his official entrance into Paris as the moment when he was confirmed in power by mass acclamation. It was to be a deliberately informal affair and he would walk not ride, from the place de l'Étoile down the Champs-Élysées to the place de la Concorde, then travel on by car to Notre-Dame for a service of celebration.

The population of Paris was drawn to the parade as if by some organic force. A cameraman looking down from an aeroplane saw the city as 'a human body with all the blood flowing like a black river' towards the arteries of the procession route. The afternoon began with the relighting of the eternal flame at the Tomb of the

Unknown Warrior beneath the Arc de Triomphe, spitefully extinguished by the Germans in 1940. The procession was led by four Sherman tanks of the 2DB, with the Régiment de Marche du Tchad tucked in behind the first ranks to provide protection. Their presence was a deliberate snub to Leclerc's American commander, General Gerow, who wanted the 2DB to continue mopping-up operations once it had entered Paris. De Gaulle rejected the order and was backed by Eisenhower, who had decided it was best that his protégé establish his authority in the city as swiftly as possible.

At 3 p.m. de Gaulle stepped down the Champs and into a canyon of ecstatic humanity. A wall of policemen locked arms to pin back the enormous crowd. The pavements, the streets leading off the grand avenue, the balconies, the lamp posts, the trees, were crammed with flag-waving, chanting Parisians. He strode along, looking around him and swivelling his arms upwards from the elbows in a curious gesture that he seemed to have invented for the occasion, as if pumping up the roaring acclaim. Flanking him were his generals and a selection of the men who had prepared the ground for his return, Parodi, Chaban-Delmas and Luizet, while the leaders of the left were relegated to the ranks behind.

Having suppressed the after-effects of the night before with a restorative 'Suffering Bastard' cocktail, Capa was in action, perched on the bonnet of a car and concentrating on the crowd rather than the notables, filling his lens from the vast, pure reservoir of human happiness. Then, as they reached the place de la Concorde, everything changed. Raymond Dronne was in his La Nueve command half-track right behind the first ranks of the procession, positioned there 'because we always feared that some *salopards* or Germans would fire on de Gaulle and the parade'. Capa's pictures captured what happened next. The rattle of shots, coming it seemed from the rooftops along the north side of the square, sent many of the crowd diving or scuttling for cover. But others stood their ground, pointing out to the soldiers and the FFI men in the column where they thought the fire was coming from.

De Gaulle did not appear to notice, striding stiffly on to the open-topped saloon waiting to drive him the rest of the way. The car stopped at the Hôtel de Ville. He walked across the pont d'Arcole with his entourage to the *parvis* in front of Notre-Dame, where a Resistance guard of honour was waiting, along with BBC correspondent Robert Reid. Radio despatches sounded much more dramatic and urgent these days as reporters were now equipped with portable recording machines that captured sound effects and the journalists' emotional reactions to what they were seeing.

'They're a variegated set of boys and girls,' Reid told listeners that evening. 'Some of the men are dressed in dungarees, overalls. Some look rather smart, the bank-clerk type. Some are in very shabby suits but they've all got their red, white and blue armlets with the blue Cross of Lorraine, and they're all armed . . .' Just as de Gaulle arrived, the recording was interrupted by the sound of machine-gun fire and shouts of alarm from the crowd. As they rushed for cover, the microphone cable was ripped from Reid's machine and he resumed his despatch from inside the cathedral. When de Gaulle entered, there was more shooting and it seemed to Reid that it came from the galleries high up in the nave.

Once again, it had no effect on de Gaulle. Reid told his listeners admiringly how the general 'walked straight ahead into what appeared to me to be a hail of fire . . . straight ahead without hesitation, his shoulders flung back, and walked right down the central aisle, even while the bullets were pouring around him. It was the most extraordinary example of courage that I've ever seen.' Police, soldiers and FFI men opened up and the cathedral was filled with the deafening crack of rifle rounds and the stink of cordite. A man next to Reid was shot in the neck, but despite all the commotion there seemed to be few casualties and even while the firing continued the congregation rose and began chanting the *Te Deum*. The mass was celebrated by a Monsignor Brot, rather than by Cardinal-Archbishop Suhard. Having presided over the mass attended by Pétain in April and the requiem for the ultra-collaborator Philippe Henriot in July, Suhard had been told his services were not required.

When mass ended, Reid resumed reporting. There was yet more gunfire as de Gaulle left the cathedral, and shortly afterwards the sound of shouting. Reid explained that the 'cheering you can hear is four prisoners just being taken away. These are four of the snipers who've been caught inside the church. They were all in civilian clothing – grey flannel trousers and simply [sic] white singlets. They've got their hands above their heads, and they look very obvious Germans.' The actual identity of the prisoners, and what happened to them next, remains a mystery. Nor was it ever discovered who was behind any of the various attacks. Suspicious as ever, de Gaulle believed that the culprits were neither diehard *miliciens* nor German holdouts, but FFI extremists who 'by shooting a few bullets into the air at the agreed hour' hoped to 'create the impression that certain threats were still lurking in the shadows' and that 'the resistance organisations must remain armed and vigilant'.

Raymond Ruffin was at the cathedral with a group of his friends, keen to get their first sight of de Gaulle. When they arrived, Raymond remarked that the crowd was bigger than the one that had turned out to greet Pétain in the spring. 'Perhaps they're the same people,' his friend Claude replied cynically. When the shooting broke out, they fled, returning to their homes near the Château de Vincennes. At 9.30 p.m. the air-raid sirens sounded. Raymond and his mother decided not to bother going down to the shelter: with Paris liberated, they had nothing more to fear. 'How wrong we were,' he wrote in his diary, 'because soon we were subjected to a violent bombardment that shook the surrounding buildings and we rushed down to the shelter.' When the all-clear sounded they went back upstairs to see 'an immense red glow lighting up the east of Paris'.

The Luftwaffe attack, launched from bases in Belgium and eastern France, killed 214 people, including a number of Leclerc Division soldiers, wounded nearly a thousand and damaged hundreds of buildings. It was an act of pure revenge. Hitler had responded to the news that Paris had fallen with vindictive fury. As well as the bombing raid, on 26 August he also ordered V-1 flying bombs to batter the city. The launch platforms in the Pas de Calais were all aimed at London, however, and to reconfigure them was a huge task, though weeks later he would order Paris to be briefly bombarded by V-2 rockets.

With the end of the battle for the city, the Germans who had escaped capture hurried to join other Wehrmacht units at Le Bourget and

Montmorency to the north-east, where in the following days they battled the 2DB. Accurate figures for casualties on all sides are impossible to establish as there was no formal official reckoning by the relevant military or civil authorities, but it would seem that about 3,000 Germans were killed in front of and inside the city and nearly 13,000 taken prisoner. Allied casualties were much lower but still painful. Philippe de Gaulle calculated the 2DB's losses at ninety-seven dead and 283 wounded inside the boundaries of the city and twice as many in the fighting in the surrounding area, which made the liberation of Paris more costly for the division than the Battle of Normandy. The Resistance and the civilians suffered most, with between 1,500 and 2,000 losing their lives. Even so, in the arithmetic of the war it counted as a skirmish.

Since the start of the uprising the ranks of the FFI had been hugely expanded with new recruits. Its estimated strength nationwide was 100,000 in January, 200,000 in June and 400,000 by October. Some were opportunistic latecomers to the cause, out for adventure and a share of the glory. In Paris it seemed that almost every young man was wearing a Fifi armband. With the influx, the relative discipline exercised by the old guard started to unravel. Two days after the liberation, Eisenhower was driven to the capital by his chauffeur, Kay Summersby. She noted that 'The only cars were those operated by the mad-eyed FFI men who careened through the streets, firing their guns whenever the spirit (or a new bottle) moved them.' These latecomers became known ironically as the 'FFS' – Forces Françaises de Septembre – or 'Resisters of the 25th Hour'. Leclerc too had a low opinion of many of the Fifis. He reckoned that 10 per cent were 'very good, brave and real fighters', while 20 to 25 per cent were 'acceptable and prepared to follow'. The remainder he dismissed as 'riff-raff and con-artists'.

A number of newly minted patriots had begun making trouble as soon as they felt it was safe, confronting anyone who aroused their suspicions. Even Rose Valland had attracted their attention. When the victory parade came under fire in the place de la Concorde, 'a human torrent' of panicked spectators rushed to the Jeu de Paume near by, forcing the doors and windows to seek shelter. One of the museum guards who had climbed to the roof to get a grandstand view of the parade was mistaken for a sniper and Rose had to shout at the soldiers and FFI not to shoot him. The crowd then turned on her, until a Free French officer intervened to calm things down. But later, when she tried to stop the mob going down into the basement where paintings were still stored, 'I was accused of hiding enemy soldiers down there and I was forced to lead a search party into the cellars with a machine pistol poking in my back.' She was extremely relieved to find there was no one there, though that very morning she had come across a German survivor of the previous day's fighting in the Tuileries, lying low until the coast was clear.

Jubilation, the liberators were finding, could easily slide into mob hysteria. After the ecstatic welcome given to the 12th Infantry when they entered Paris, they were given the job of securing the city. There was plenty of work for the counter-intelligence unit, interviewing captured Germans and their French associates. Jerry Salinger and John Keenan were told to go and pick up a suspected collaborator, a medic

Rough justice

who worked at one of the hospitals, and they set off with a fellow sergeant in his jeep. Years later Jerry told his son Matt what happened next: 'They got there and there was a real mob . . . This collective, primal ugly thing took over.' There was no question of drawing their weapons as the only way to stop the savagery was to shoot. In Matt's words, Salinger was 'really scared, just seeing these faces close, and seeing what they were capable of'. Shortly before, he and his comrades had been 'met with so much joy and relief and gratitude'. Now they were seeing the dark face of liberation and it 'really rocked him . . . for the rest of his life'.

There were many in the city with something to fear. Robert Brasillach had gone into hiding a week before the Allies arrived. The events of the 24th, 25th and 26th were relayed to him as a soundtrack, drifting up to the window of his attic hideout in the rue de Tournon: first the chimes of the Paris bells announcing the arrival of the 2DB, then the shooting, then the gusts of cheering and choruses of the 'Marseillaise'. He did not dare go down to the street to witness the spectacle but was already working on his own caustic interpretation of what was happening. The story under construction, he decided, was a dishonest, self-serving myth, starting with the claim that Paris had liberated itself. 'I knew very well that although there were only a few thousand Germans in Paris, without the American advance, the FFI would never have been able to dislodge them,' he wrote. 'I never believed in the deception of a heroic Paris uprising.' He felt sorry for the masses now gripped by 'naive joy'. He told himself 'that the poor folk who were now so glad to see the back of the Germans would be disillusioned soon enough when they saw that the war was far from over and the misery, the cold and the bloodshed remained'. For all that, he envied them their happiness and, although he knew it was absurd, he felt 'unjustly punished' for not being able to share in it.

On the day of the victory parade, Brasillach was startled by a fusillade coming from nearby rooftops. Then a search party arrived, hunting for the mysterious gunman. He heard boots thumping on the staircase as they went from door to door. The footsteps faded and he breathed again. He learned later that the concierge had vouched for him as a 'nice young man who was not to be disturbed'. After three more days, the loneliness and gnawing fear got too much and he slipped out to find his brother-in-law, Maurice Bardèche, who was being sheltered in the apartment of some mutual friends, removing his trademark round, heavy-framed glasses to make himself less recognizable. From Bardèche he learned that 'danger was all around'. A witch hunt was under way, led by the communists, and his own brother Henri had already been arrested. Brasillach slunk back to his room. It was another week before he dared to try to contact Bardèche again, phoning from a nearby café. He was not there. Maurice, he learned, had been arrested on the evening of 1 September and taken off to Drancy.

Only a few weeks before, Drancy had been a staging post for Jews and resisters on their way to the death camps. Now it was a holding centre for suspected collaborators. Bardèche's friends told Brasillach that it was 'because of me' that he had been picked up. He thought 'that this was highly probable. I was dismayed. What was the point of me going into hiding if they came instead for my friends?' And not just his friends. Next, Brasillach heard that his mother Marguerite and stepfather had been arrested at gunpoint at their home in Sens, 75 miles south-east of Paris. It was clear that the avenging forces of the liberation would not rest until they found him. Brasillach 'thought of my courageous, philosophical mother, thrown into some vile prison, all because of me'. Nonetheless, he hesitated before giving himself up. The news of his mother was old by the time it reached him. Perhaps the situation had changed for the better in the meantime and she had been freed. He thought of asking for information from people he knew in Sens, but the post wasn't working properly.

On Thursday 14 September he decided he could delay no longer. He packed a washbag, underwear and a snack into a small rucksack and left his hideaway for the last time to walk to the police prefecture. He stopped to get his hair cut then set off on the same journey in reverse that he had made in the spring of 1941 on his return to Paris after his release from prisoner-of-war camp. He 'crossed the boulevard Saint-Germain . . . and followed the river bank for a while, offering a salute to Notre-Dame and Saint-Michel, the grey and charming backdrop of my youth'. He paused by the Seine for a few moments to drink in the grace and beauty of the scene. 'How long would it be before I found

myself here again?' he wondered. 'Would I ever, in fact, return?' Whatever happened, 'What I saw was beautiful, and I had loved it well.'

For most, liberation brought a rush of optimism. But Brasillach
was right; the euphoria could not last, though for a little while no one
wanted to dim the dream of a fresh start and a better future. 'A new
era is beginning,' wrote Raymond Ruffin a week after the great day,
'an era of liberty, the most important thing in the world. But will it
succeed in sweeping away all the harsh memories of what we have just
been through? I really want to hope that it does. Men must understand that we only have one life and that it must be lived in peace and
brotherhood.'

For those arriving in Paris the joy of return was mingled with fear
of what they might find. Most had not seen or heard from their families and friends since their departure. They had no idea if they were
dead or alive and their first thought when the fighting stopped was to
track them down. Lieutenant Alexandre Rosenberg, the scholarly
son of the famous Jewish art dealer Paul and now a lieutenant of the
2DB's Régiment d'Artillerie Coloniale, went first to the address of
his uncle Léonce, who was also a dealer and had chosen to stay behind
when his brother Paul departed in 1940 to start a new life in New
York. To his huge relief Léonce was there, reading a book of philosophy, apparently oblivious to the great drama that had been playing
out around him and uninterested in enlightening Alexandre as to
how he had managed to stay free and alive.

As soon as he had a few hours to spare, Raymond Dronne contacted
an old friend called Roger Gérard, who invited him to dinner at a restaurant they had known as students, a timeless Latin Quarter bistrot
called Polidor in the rue Monsieur-le-Prince. He was pleased to see
that it was still in the hands of its old *patron* Albert Bony, who greeted
him rapturously along with his wife Léa and daughter Antoinette.
Gérard had put the word out that Dronne was in town and before long
a gang from the old days had gathered. The 'setting and the people
brought back to me the radiant times of our youth', Dronne recalled.
They passed an evening of good wine and the best food available, nostalgia and reminiscing, and mourning absent friends. 'Not everybody
was able to come,' he wrote. 'Some were dead, like the lawyer Bouin,

taken prisoner in 1940 and died in Germany. Still more had been arrested by the Gestapo and deported, like the Penez brothers, doctors at Montfermeil. Others had left Paris for the provinces . . .' The absences told the story of the occupation. Leaving the restaurant and strolling down the rue Monsieur-le-Prince at the end of the evening he saw Ernest Hemingway, 'already three sheets to the wind, followed by an escort of drunks. I would have loved to have introduced myself to this *monstre sacré* but in the state he was in, what was the point?' Instead he set off to the Hôtel de Ville to rejoin his La Nueve comrades.

The diversion to Paris had been a disruption to the Allied plan and Leclerc's men and the Ivy were needed back in the line to resume the pursuit of the Germans. De Gaulle nonetheless asked Eisenhower if he could loan him two US divisions, saying he needed them for a show of force and to strengthen his hold on the capital. Once again, Ike showed an extraordinary willingness to oblige, and while he could not spare troops to linger long in the city he was prepared to divert two units to march through the centre on their way to the front in a demonstration of Allied solidarity. On Tuesday 29 August, the 28th Infantry Division and 5th Armoured Division duly paraded down the Champs-Élysées, with de Gaulle and General Bradley side by side to take the salute.

Alexandre Rosenberg

The 2DB was soon back in action after the delirium of liberation day, chasing the retreating Germans out of north-east Paris. On Sunday

27 August, Lieutenant Rosenberg noted 'numerous [enemy concentrations] around Le Bourget, Gonesse, Saint-Denis. Very tough infantry battles at Le Bourget.' As the 2DB advanced, an urgent message was received from railway workers asking for troops to be sent to the commune of Aulnay-sous-Bois to capture a train which was sitting in the sidings under German guard. The task was given to Rosenberg, who set off with a platoon of about thirty men. They found the train where they were told it would be and blew up the tracks in front and behind. There was no resistance when they launched their attack. As Alexandre told his daughter Marianne, the guards were mainly elderly and jumped out with their hands up. The real surprise came when they opened the wagon doors. The cars were 'full of all the stuff the Germans wanted to bring back . . . furniture and books and pots and pans and furs and clothing . . . then there was art'. The train was number 4044 – the same one that railway Resistance workers had tracked down after learning from Rose Valland the identifying marks of the packing cases containing the last cargo of looted paintings from the Jeu de Paume.

Alexandre had no idea that they were on board, still less that many of them belonged to his father. The trove included sixty-four pictures by Picasso, twenty-nine by Braque, twenty-four by Dufy, four by Degas, as well as works by Cézanne, Gauguin, Modigliani and Toulouse-Lautrec. Among them were what Rose described as 'some of the most authentic masterpieces of modern art'. A guard was put on the train to prevent looting and lorries arrived to carry the paintings off to the safety of the Louvre.

Before Jerry Salinger moved on, he wanted to call on Hemingway, who as everybody in Paris now knew was holding court at the Ritz. He had got hold of a copy of the 15 July issue of the *Saturday Evening Post* featuring 'Last Day of the Last Furlough', which he wanted to show Hemingway. Papa received him warmly in Room 31, a large, plush suite which was his Paris command post. The reunion strengthened the spark of mutual affection kindled at their first meeting in Normandy. Salinger was sure of his own talent and believed he had found his voice, but Hemingway's approval meant much to him, and although he was not his favourite writer he admired his dedication and craft. Not long afterwards he received a handwritten letter to 'Dear Jerry'. According to Salinger's long-time friend the *New Yorker* writer Lillian Ross, to whom Jerry showed the letter, it told him: 'First you have a marvelous ear and you write tenderly and lovingly without getting wet.' Hemingway finished: 'How happy it makes me to read the stories [sic] and what a god-damned fine writer I think you are.'

By showing his gentle side to Salinger, Hemingway was taking a break from the roistering persona dominating the never-ending party that had begun the moment he hit town. For the time being he set aside his journalistic duties for *Collier's*. His first despatch, 'Battle for Paris', did not appear until 30 September, and took the story only as far as the gates of the city. As he told Mary Welsh in a letter shortly after arriving, he had spent the first days visiting 'all the old places I ever lived in Paris and everything is fine. But it is all so improbable that you feel like you have died and it is all a dream.'

While the fighting was still raging he called on someone he had first met twenty-two years before when he was a young nobody struggling to make his name in the city. Sylvia Beach, the American Presbyterian minister's daughter whose Shakespeare and Company bookshop was a magnet for expatriate writers, had stayed in Paris and been arrested and interned by the Germans for six months before being released on health grounds. She was in her apartment in the rue de l'Odéon on the Left Bank with her friend Adrienne Monnier when she 'heard a noise out in the street and looked out of the window and saw a string of jeeps'. Next she heard 'a deep voice calling Sylvia! Sylvia! and it was Ernest Hemingway and his men'. She 'rushed down the stairs and he picked me up and swung me around'. When he asked if there was anything he could do for the women 'we said oh liberate us, liberate us!' There was still much firing on the surrounding rooftops, and Hemingway ordered his followers to come up and deal with it. 'We heard a great deal of shooting going on for a few minutes,' she recalled, 'and then the shooting stopped forever.'

In his letter to Mary he suggested interceding with his fellow war correspondent Charlie Wertenbaker to see if he could arrange for her to come and join him. But she was already in town, turning up that night at the Ritz, which would be her base for the next seven months.

Hemingway was still unsure of his hold on her and was on his best behaviour, though she was already aware that if they stayed together she was in for a bumpy ride. He expected her to stick by his side throughout the drink-fuelled day, which started mid-morning with champagne in the Ritz bar. Mary was a working journalist but 'Ernest kept forgetting that I lived by deadlines.' More ominously, she 'was beginning to feel that I was being swallowed by him . . . he seemed to me to melt away my identity'.

Hemingway soothed her anxieties by plying her with expensive gifts and taking her to meet celebrity friends. One night they dined in a black-market restaurant with Picasso and his new mistress, Françoise Gilot. Hemingway asked him if would paint a portrait of Mary, naked from the waist up. 'Picasso's enormous black radar eyes turned onto me . . . for a moment, [then he] smiled and said, "*Bien sûr*. Have her come to my studio."' The project went no further.

Picasso had spent the days of the liberation with Marie-Thérèse and Maya in the flat in the boulevard Henri-IV, painting a copy of Nicolas Poussin's *The Triumph of Pan* with watercolours and gouache. It shows a woodland scene with nymphs frolicking in the arms of lascivious satyrs and seemed an appropriate subject, anticipating the revelry to follow. As soon as he returned to the rue des Grands-Augustins he was besieged with visitors, from VIPs to humble GIs, and he received them all gracefully and with a fetching show of humility. When word got around of his hospitality, a line of US soldiers formed outside the door for their moment with him. They brought gifts of chocolate, coffee and tins of fruit. Picasso went along with the callers' assumption that life had been very tough for him under the German boot.

One visitor was John Pudney, the RAF public relations officer who had escorted Hemingway on a press visit to an airbase a few months earlier. He came across Picasso in the street ('his hand was warm, his greeting was quick, the great dark eyes as vivid as ever') and was invited back to his home. There he was given a tour of the studio, the bedroom with its Spanish tiled floor and even the bathroom, equipped with two hand basins, which Picasso remarked allowed for 'either a hand in each or an intelligent conversation with a friend while you wash'.

He showed Pudney some collaborationist magazines with articles denouncing him as 'Picasso the Jew', the 'obscene pornographer'. Even though he had been denied the right to exhibit his art during the occupation, he had 'worked on, and all my work is here'. Pudney had brought a gift of cigarettes and asked if there was anything else he needed. 'His only request was modest enough. He showed me the worn wafer of soap which was the butt of his shaving stick.' Perhaps Picasso had given some of his stock of Marseilles soap to Marie-Thérèse after all. Pudney came away 'enriched by the powerful serenity of the man, the glorious indifference'. He also believed him to be a seer, 'the prophet painter of Guernica' who had glimpsed the horrors that would afterwards be visited on much of the world. This was an early indication of the awe in which Picasso would be held when the war was over, not only a great painter but a symbol of liberty and defiance in the face of tyranny, and in his own quiet, stoical way a resister.

Bob Capa also came to see Picasso. Surprisingly, the two had never met, but on 2 September he shot a photo story on the daily visitations, which had already been formalized into an 11 a.m. open house. In the first days of freedom, Capa rocketed around his old haunts, the Flore, the Dôme, the Deux Magots, creating an instant party wherever he landed, looking up old friends and bumping into new ones. As ever, some were dead, some departed and some, to his relief and slight amazement, still alive. Among them was his fellow Hungarian Anton Prinner. He had been living on the brink of destitution during the occupation, but managed to keep working and even to show some of his sculptures at a 1942 exhibition in the Montparnasse gallery of the pioneering art dealer Jeanne Bucher. It was there that he first met Picasso, and a long friendship began. Picasso admired Prinner and Prinner adored Picasso. Born a woman but living and looking like a man, Prinner felt 'a certain homosexual drive in me . . . I'm attracted to men.' Picasso called him 'Monsieur Madame'. He was also kind to him and on his frequent visits to Prinner's studio in the rue Pernety would discreetly leave behind money.

Prinner had a generous spirit. During the occupation he had risked his life to shelter a fellow Hungarian, the Jewish painter Sándor Heimovits, and his children in his flat. His compassion was now aroused by the fate of the victims of the vengeful mood gripping the city. The ugly scenes of women accused of sleeping with the Germans having their heads shaved and being paraded through the streets to be jeered and spat upon, which Capa had recorded in Chartres, were taking place all over France. Prinner responded with a prose poem, *La Femme tondue* ('The Shaven-Headed Woman'), written in the language of the streets, which conveyed the savage hypocrisy of the spectacle. It opened with a volley of insults as the mob lays hands on one of the wretched *horizontales*: 'Slag! Whore! Bitch! Slut! Disgusting. Look at her. Piece of shit. Do you see her eyes? Christ almighty. Look! Look at her eyes! She's been giving me that look since the moment we caught her. No shame at all. Go on, say something then for Christ's sake! Give her a smack in the gob. Let's make her cry, shout out, shit herself . . .'

At least 20,000 French women were treated like this. Some were prostitutes, some women who had simply fallen for a German. By mid-1943 about 80,000 had brought a baby into the world after a liaison with one of the occupiers, and mother and child would have to live with sideways glances and whispered remarks for years to come, perhaps for the rest of their lives.

Others were simply the victims of malign stupidity. Two sisters sharing a flat in Saint-Germain-des-Prés were dragged out and shorn because their 'judges' went to the wrong floor. None of the other tenants intervened to protect them. The punishment was carried out in a grotesque carnival atmosphere. The many photographs taken of these events show that those doing the shearing and pinioning the victims are invariably men, casually smoking as they go about their work and smirking gleefully at the humiliation they are inflicting, while women and children look on. Few of the persecutors had done much to be proud of during the occupation and the Americans who witnessed such scenes found it hard not to interpret them as an attempt to wipe out the shame of years of supine acceptance in an orgy of phoney righteousness. Many wore FFI armbands and carried weapons. The old guard of the Resistance abhorred the practice, and as soon as he heard what was going on Rol-Tanguy ordered posters to be issued promising stern action against those involved.

He was powerless to stop the bloody score settling that began even before the fighting was over. The methods employed in the *épuration sauvage* sometimes resembled those of the Nazis. The writer and British intelligence officer Malcolm Muggeridge arrived in Paris in the first days of the liberation to be received with 'friendly smiles, embraces, bed-fellows even, as and when required, as well as limitless hospitality', with even Maxim's refusing to present a bill when he ate there. At night the city seemed a different place, sinister and lawless. 'It was when darkness began to fall that one became aware of the breakdown,' he wrote; 'with no street lighting and the tall houses all silent and locked and boarded up, like sightless eyes. Inside them I imagined cowering figures, hopeful of surviving if they remained perfectly still and hidden. Then, as night came on, sounds of scurrying feet, sudden cries, shots, shrieks, but no one available, or caring to investigate.'

On 10 September a corpse tied to a paving stone was fished out of the Seine at the Passerelle de l'Avre at Saint-Cloud. It was semi-clothed, the hands were tied and it had a bullet hole in the back of the head. Over the next few days, twenty-seven more were recovered from the river, all in the same condition. A piece of clothing bore the name of the 'Institut George-Eastman'. This was the large dental clinic in the 13th arrondissement, built in the early 1930s by the American philanthropist and founder of the Eastman Kodak photographic company. The Germans had requisitioned it for their own needs on arrival. On 20 August 1944 it was taken over by the FTP and became Colonel Fabien's command post. Very soon it was functioning as prison, court, and torture and execution centre for suspected collaborators. Presiding over it was Fabien's deputy, 'Captain Bernard', a forty-four-year-old Parisian taxi driver and communist trade unionist before the war whose real name was René Sentuc. In three weeks around the time of the liberation about 140 men and women were imprisoned there, of whom up to forty-four were put to death. Some were collaborators. Others were completely innocent, arrested simply because a neighbour had denounced them. The victims included Madeleine Goa, who was beaten, shot multiple times and her body thrown in the street. Her husband was already dead. He had gone on to their balcony with his telescope to watch the arrival of the Leclerc Division, was mistaken for a sniper, dragged down to the street and thrown under a tank. It turned out later that the couple were supporters of the Resistance and had sheltered Jews and escaped Allied airmen. Was Fabien aware of what was going on at his head-quarters? A few months later he was dead, and he left nothing behind to shed any light on the matter.

Such revolutionary tribunals sprang up all over France. The number of those who died has never been accurately established, but police investigations in 1948 and 1952 suggested 6,000 executions took place during the liberation period and 4,000 thereafter, though some claimed the figure was considerably higher. It was not until mid-October that a proper legal reckoning began when the government announced the establishment of three new courts to deal with crimes of collaboration. De Gaulle's primary aims were to restore French unity and self-respect. His contention all along was that the Pétain government was an illegal aberration that had nothing to do with 'the real France'. In that case, the sooner Vichy and collaboration were forgotten the better. There was nothing to be gained from a systematic programme of investigation and retribution. There had to be some period of reckoning before France could move on, but it would be short, limited and selective. This would be the *épuration légale*, a formal purge, properly conducted with due process.

De Gaulle's immediate concern was to establish political control and imprint on the consciousness of the French people and the world at large his version of what had just happened. To do that it was necessary to start bulldozing away the landscape of recent memory to make way for the France of the future. That meant an immediate realloca-tion of the communists, and the Resistance in general, to what he saw as their rightful place in the story. He saw no point in delaying. 'The iron was hot,' he said later. 'I struck.' On 28 August, just two days after his triumphal march down the Champs-Élysées, he summoned to the War Ministry 'twenty leaders of the Paris partisans to meet them, to congratulate them and to let them know of my decision to fold the FFI into the regular army'. Twelve thousand resisters would put on uniform and continue the fight against the Germans. He told them that now that the provisional government had arrived, there was no more need for the National Resistance Council nor for the Committee for the Liberation of Paris. To soften the blow he handed out some choice appointments. The CNR head Georges Bidault became foreign minister and Charles Tillon, communist former FTP chief and president of the CPL, head of the Air Ministry.

Before making the announcements, de Gaulle was as friendly and relaxed as his temperament allowed. Chatting to Rol-Tanguy he asked him what he had been doing in 1940. He replied that he had been serving with his regiment. 'And before that?' 'I was fighting in the International Brigades in Spain.' 'Bon,' said the general, shaking his hand, and that was that. The only woman present was Cécile Tanguy. She felt conspicuous among all the men and was unimpressed by the general's hospitality. 'There wasn't much warmth to it and it was a pretty small affair. There wasn't even a glass of wine at the end.'

16. *Mise en scène*

Among the first things to be tidied up once the party was over was the history of what had just happened. Early in September cinemas screened a thirty-one-minute documentary called *La Libération de Paris* which used footage shot by Resistance cameramen. It was followed in November by an exhibition in the Musée Carnavalet dedicated to the history of the city, which displayed photographs, written testimony, sketches, posters and other ephemera to celebrate the great days of August. Bookshops and news kiosks were stacked with illustrated commemorative albums and pamphlets. For a while there was a huge market for everything to do with the liberation. When the film was first shown, 6,000 people crammed into a theatre designed to hold 2,000.

The enthusiasm was understandable. If this was the first draft of history, then Paris and Parisians came out of it very well. Events were presented overwhelmingly in visual terms and the imagery was both flattering and reassuring. Commentary on the documentary is sparse and not very informative and the editing is disjointed, with little attempt to string together a narrative. Instead it creates an impression – a powerful one – of a people united in defiance of their oppressors with all differences of class and politics forgotten, at least for the time being.

The anonymous stars are the men of the FFI – mostly, but not all, young, virile and vigorous in shirtsleeves and singlets, often with a bandana knotted at the throat to add a touch of desperado chic. Some carried captured German carbines or submachine guns supplied by the Allies. Others clutched only small-calibre pistols which, though they might do little damage to the enemy, established the carrier's credentials as a bona fide resister.

In the documentary and the thousands of photos taken by professionals and amateurs that covered the walls of the Carnavalet *expo* and appeared in the multitude of publications there are plenty of shots of real fighting recording the undoubted courage of those who engaged

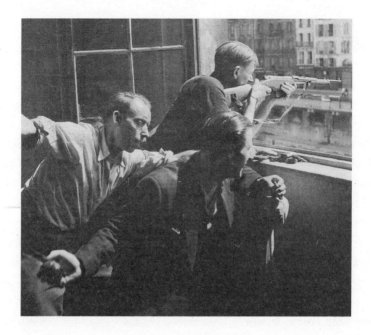

the Germans and the civilians who risked death to cheer them on. But the pictures often have the feel of a performance, and some are definitely posed. A photograph by Serge de Sazo shows three fighters framed theatrically at a window of the police prefecture looking across the river to the Left Bank. One is pointing a rifle and the others have grenades in their outstretched hands. It is certainly dramatic but bears no resemblance to how the men would behave in real combat. The FFI men pictured at the barricades are often conscious of the camera, arranging themselves to appear suitably grim and determined. Overall the images seem like an assertion of masculinity. Despite everything the Germans had done to us, the pictures say, we never stopped being men.

French male pride had suffered dreadfully in the war. The debacle of defeat and surrender had been an entirely male affair because in 1940 there were no French women politicians, soldiers or even voters. The occupation heaped even more humiliation on French manhood. In 1944 about a million soldiers were still captive in Germany, where they laboured in the enemy war economy alongside hundreds of thousands of compatriots forced there by the Service du Travail Obligatoire work scheme. The photographers and cameramen of the liberation did French men a favour by helping to erase the memory of dishonour. The images, transmitted globally, of the days of rage recast them as dashing guerrillas, heedless of death, and this picture would stick for ever in the world's imagination.

Women also got a share of the kudos. Stills and movie footage recorded the cool bravery of the nurses, running out in the midst of a firefight to tend to a young body sprawled on the cobbles, and of female Fifis relieving a dead German of his weapon. In some cases there seems to be a conscious attempt to associate the subject with revolutionary heroines of the past. A favourite with the photographers was Béatrice Briand, the baker who commanded the barricade at the corner of the rue Saint-Jacques and the rue de la Huchette, a narrow old Latin Quarter street. She was captured in her cotton dress, pistol on her hip, wearing a twentieth-century German steel helmet rather than a 1789 Phrygian bonnet, like a homely reincarnation of Delacroix's *Liberty Leading the People*. In the Carnavalet exhibition her picture hung in close proximity to a portrait of de Gaulle, thus linking working-class *boulangère* and lofty general as partners in the same great enterprise.

The notion of national solidarity was a common theme of all the post-liberation instant history. To sustain it required some radical editing of the photographic record. In *La Libération de Paris*, two male collaborators make only a glancing appearance and there is just one image of a woman accused of *collaboration horizontale*, though with her head as yet unshaven. There is no footage of the Milice and the police are portrayed as doughty patriots. The side of France that aided and abetted the Nazis was also almost completely absent from the celebratory *expo* and the outpourings of the publishing houses – several of which had carried on business happily under the occupation. There is no recognition that Vichy and Germany were in many cases partners in crime. Instead, the torture, killings and incarcerations were presented, as in another photographic exhibition, as *Crimes Hitlériens*, which opened in the Grand Palais in June 1945 before touring the country and attracting large, horrified crowds.

The limited scope of the *épuration légale* and the need to maintain order and keep the economy functioning meant that many policemen, officials and businessmen stayed in place. Between 1944 and 1951, special courts investigated about 300,000 cases. This was a ritual of justice rather than a serious attempt at retribution and the process was less rigorous than in countries with much smaller populations like Belgium (400,000 cases) and the Netherlands (110,000). About half of the proceedings were dropped. The cases that came to court resulted in around 6,700 death sentences. The vast majority were commuted by de Gaulle himself and fewer than 800 were actually carried out.

Among those executed were Pierre Laval, the Milice leader Joseph Darnand and Fernand de Brinon, Vichy's ambassador to the German high command in Paris. Pétain was found guilty of treason at a short trial in August 1945 and sentenced to death, reduced on account of his great age to life imprisonment in comfortable circumstances on the Île d'Yeu off the Atlantic coast, where he died in July 1951. Thanks to de Gaulle's policy of reconciliation and official amnesia, many of Vichy's most egregious collaborators had a respite lasting decades during which their careers prospered. It was only when, following the student and worker upheavals of 1968, the suspicions of the rising generation forced a re-examination of the past that the likes of Vichy police chief René Bousquet faced any sort of justice.

Robert Brasillach's mistake was to have stayed in Paris rather than heading to Sigmaringen like Lucien Rebatet and Louis-Ferdinand Céline. After turning himself in he was charged under article 75 of the penal code, covering the crime of treason. It proposed the death penalty for anyone who in wartime had 'dealings with a foreign power . . . in order to promote the actions of that power against France'. He went on trial in the Palais de Justice on 19 January 1945, a bitterly cold day. Brasillach had lost some of his puppy fat and his dark suit hung off him, offset by a bright red tie which sounded a note of defiance. He was the first collaborator who had so far been tried not to apologize for his actions. He told the court he felt a responsibility 'not to abandon people who might have believed in me' and claimed that much of what he was accused of could be said of many who were now walking free.

Brasillach ran rings around the presiding judge, and some of his sallies went down well in the packed public seats. He met his match in the prosecutor, Marcel Reboul, who zeroed in on the erotic

Judgement Day

phrasing of Brasillach's articles expressing love for Germany, and his metaphorical description of the occupation as a sexual act. The French had 'more or less slept with Germany – not without quarrels – and the memory of it will remain sweet for them'. As the historian Alice Kaplan wrote later, Reboul's message was 'we were dominated, humiliated, we were forced into submission. We were buggered . . . and this man liked it.' Brasillach's own invective was turned against him. The prosecution cited his calls for the deaths of Third Republic leaders and the execution of the communist deputies: 'Let them croak. We won't lift an eyebrow.' Then there were the attacks on the Jews and the *Je Suis Partout* denunciations of opponents of collaboration, printed in the full knowledge of the consequences for those named. Brasillach had been keen on deadly vengeance for his enemies; Reboul demanded it should now be applied to him.

Brasillach was defended by Jacques Isorni, a young star of the pre-war bar and an Action Française supporter who would go on to represent Pétain. His high-flown arguments and praise for Brasillach's literary gifts went over the heads of the four-man jury and were summed up in his closing appeal: 'Do civilized people shoot their poets?' The answer was 'yes' and Brasillach was condemned to death. The trial had lasted only six hours. The verdict triggered protests from intellectuals of the left and the right. The matter went up to de

Gaulle. The dossier included a letter from Brasillach asking for clemency to spare the feelings of his mother, whose soldier husband had died for France. De Gaulle's recipe of selective justice required that some examples be made: Brasillach would do for the traitors of word and pen. He was executed at Montrouge on 6 February 1945. As he reminded his lawyers, it was the eleventh anniversary of the Concorde riots, where the ideological journey that had taken him to this place had properly begun.

Other German stooges were luckier. Rebatet was arrested in Austria, tried in November 1946 and sentenced to death, but reprieved and released in 1952, and soon afterwards he was making a living as a journalist once more, having repented nothing. Céline spent the postwar years in Denmark and was tried *in absentia* in 1950. The sentence of a year in prison was never served. Before he died in 1961 the process of literary rehabilitation was well under way. Non-ideological artists and entertainers who had performed for, and socialized with, the occupiers, such as Jean Cocteau, Sacha Guitry, Maurice Chevalier and Arletty, had a sticky time for a few months, but public memory and the appetite for punishment eventually faded. No one suffered lasting damage to their careers and stage, screen and radio were soon filled with familiar voices. As for the Germans, Otto Abetz was brought back to France and put on trial in 1949 on charges including complicity in the deportation of 40,000 Jews to death camps in Poland and responsibility for the looting of Jewish property. He was sentenced to twenty years in prison but released after five.

The different elements of the Resistance had been fighting for competing visions of the future. It was a struggle that nobody won. The communists' wartime contribution enhanced their political stature when voters – at last including women – went to the polls in October 1945. The PCF entered the contest in a 'Three-Party Alliance' with the Socialists and Christian Democrats. The communists gained the most seats and the alliance overwhelmingly dominated the new chamber. De Gaulle was appointed president and it was then that the trouble began. It was plain by now that the PCF had no intention of taking advantage of their popularity to launch a putsch and Moscow had ordained a 'non-revolutionary path to power'.

De Gaulle remained suspicious and gave them only four ministries in the new government, none of them key posts. He seemed unable to adapt to peacetime politics. After failing to impose his preferred constitution, he resigned in January 1946 and withdrew to Colombey-les-Deux-Églises, 160 miles south-east of Paris, where he would remain brooding until the collapse of the Fourth Republic and the crisis in Algeria returned him to power in 1958.

The joy of the liberation soon felt like a distant fantasy for the men of the Ivy and the 2DB. For the Americans, the last phase of the war was the hardest, and the worst battle took place in the Hürtgen Forest, fifty square miles of conifer-covered hills east of the Belgian–German border. It would be remembered as the 'Death Factory', a nightmare series of costly and often futile operations fought out between September and December 1944. No one who survived it could ever forget it. Jerry Salinger retreated to a hospital to recover 'physically, mentally and spiritually', as his son Matt put it, before the war was finished. Alexandre Rosenberg, who was attached to the American forces as an artillery spotter, was similarly hospitalized for a spell.

Salinger never described the war directly in the books that followed and any mention he made to his family of the horrors he had seen and endured were brief and elliptical. His son Matt says that as a result of what he went through that winter 'He would keep his house at seventy-two degrees because in the Hürtgen Forest he was so cold for so long.' His war experiences did inspire one much loved story. 'For Esmé – with Love and Squalor' describes a brief meeting shortly before D-Day between an American soldier and a thirteen-year-old girl and her young brother in a tea room in a small Devon town very like Tiverton. Esmé is posh and educated but sweet, innocent and slightly unsure of herself under the surface sophistication. Her mother is dead and her father was killed in North Africa. She wears his outsize watch as a memento. They talk for the time it takes to drink a pot of tea. When her governess drags her away Esmé asks him if he minds her writing to him overseas and tells him, 'I hope you return from the war with all your faculties intact.' The story then switches to Germany. The war has just ended and Staff Sergeant X has 'not come through ... with his faculties intact'. He chainsmokes, his hands shake and a loutish roommate can't stop pointing out that his face is twitching. Sifting through his mail he finds a package, much re-addressed. Inside is a note from Esmé written just after D-Day and her wristwatch which she hopes will be a 'lucky talisman'. The reconnection lifts his spirits. Perhaps he 'stands a chance of again becoming a man with all his fac- with all his f-a-c-u-l-t-i-e-s intact.' The story appeared in the *New Yorker* in April 1950 and was very popular with readers. It heralded the huge success he would have the following year when *The Catcher in the Rye* established Holden Caulfield as a character that generations of readers would identify with.

Ernest Hemingway quit Paris in early September to cover the Allied advance. He ran into Salinger several more times and both men enjoyed the encounters. Between reporting trips he returned to the Ritz to roister and pursue his affair with Mary Welsh. At Christmas he was at the front near Luxembourg when Martha Gellhorn showed up. The altercations that followed removed any chance of either party harbouring any fond memories of the other. A few months later when passing through London they had one last, bitter meeting, and Hemingway agreed to give her a divorce. He then left for the US and Cuba, where he saw out the end of the war, making preparations for life with Mary.

Papa's adventures since landing in France provided much potential material for his fiction. His experiences in Italy in the Great War and then in Spain had inspired two of his best novels, *A Farewell to Arms* and *For Whom the Bell Tolls*. The 1950 novel that emerged from this war was by almost unanimous consent a dud. In *Across the River and into the Trees* an American officer, Colonel Richard Cantwell, fifty years old and terminally ill, sits in the Gritti Palace hotel in Venice and looks back over his life and experiences in two world wars in the company of his implausible eighteen-year-old aristocratic Italian girlfriend Renata – based on a real-life infatuation. Cantwell is an outstanding soldier but his career has unjustly stalled due to unspecified events. He is hard-bodied, sexually potent, multilingual, steeped in literature and history, a fine shot and universally adored by everyone from the hotel waiters to the Venetian nobility. Hemingway would later suggest that Cantwell had been inspired by Brigadier Charles 'Buck' Lanham, his old Ivy comrade. Lanham was far from flattered. He 'couldn't abide the book' and rejected Hemingway's suggestion that he was the hero, telling him: 'You damn well know I'm not, Ernesto. You know *you* are the hero of every book you've written.'

If Cantwell is Hemingway then Papa's feelings about the liberation of Paris had been revised somewhat since his *Collier's* despatch. 'The taking of Paris was nothing,' he tells Renata. 'It was only an emotional experience. Not a military operation. We killed a number of typists . . . I suppose [the Germans] figured they were not going to need a hell of lot of them any more and they left them as soldiers.' The 2DB had been engaged in a performance rather than a battle and 'shot a great number of rounds to make it seem important'. Certainly Cantwell's scathing judgements on combatants and commanders chimed with Hemingway's own loudly expressed views. The British 'could not fight their way out of a wet tissue towel' and General Leclerc was 'another jerk of the third or fourth water whose death I celebrated with a magnum of Perrier-Jouet Brut'.

Only Hemingway's most devoted fans found any merit in the book. Most reviewers saw it as evidence of the shocking collapse of his literary powers. An influential critic, Philip Rahv, wrote in *Commentary* magazine that it 'reads like parody by the author of his own manner . . . so biting that it virtually destroys the mixed social and literary legend of Hemingway that has now endured for nearly three decades'. Hemingway was wounded but defiant, though it was clear that his brand of masculinity was passé and that the future belonged to Holden Caulfield and his ilk.

Hemingway did write at least one more book that added something to his reputation. *A Moveable Feast* was a rhapsody about his early years in Paris with his first wife Hadley and first child Jack, a time when they were 'very poor and very happy'. The poverty was an exaggeration but the happiness probably not. The city he describes is a place of beginnings, fresh and full of hope and possibility. It was a remarkable feat of evocation. He finished it in the autumn of 1959. Less than two years later he killed himself with his favourite shotgun.

The death of Leclerc that Cantwell/Hemingway celebrated was a tragedy for France. He died, mundanely, in a plane crash in Algeria in

November 1947 while serving as inspector of French land forces in North Africa. His body was taken to Paris along the same route followed by the 2DB on its famous march and was buried in the Invalides. Three months after liberating Paris he and his men had had the satisfaction of fulfilling the oath sworn at Kufra, when they took Strasbourg and on 23 November 1944 the tricolour's 'beautiful colours floated over the cathedral'. But there were many more months of fighting before they could rest and many more lives to be lost. Among the dead was Colonel Fabien, killed by a mine on the Alsace front two days after Christmas. Raymond Dronne survived to go on to fight in Indo-China before leaving the army to become a politician, serving as a senator and deputy in the French parliament. The La Nueve survivors were ready to fight their own war of liberation, to free Spain from Franco, but they never got the chance. Some would die in exile, though others were able to return home after Franco's death.

The veterans of the communist Resistance soon found that their service was no guarantee of reward. When Maurice Thorez returned from wartime exile in Moscow to resume command of the party he began a purge of the old guard who had stayed behind. Henri Rol-Tanguy escaped the cull as he had joined the French First Army immediately after the liberation, fought in the battles in Germany and had been decorated for bravery. He remained a professional soldier, retiring as a lieutenant-colonel in 1962. He died an old man in 2002, laden with honours and saluted on all sides as one of the great heroes of the liberation. Despite the strains and clashes of those days, he remained on good terms with the Gaullist leaders. Many of them did well after the war. Alexandre Parodi ended up as France's permanent representative to the UN Security Council. Jacques Chaban-Delmas pursued his political and sporting career with his usual enthusiasm, winning a rugby cap for France in 1945. He stayed a de Gaulle loyalist, helping to engineer his return to power in 1958. From 1969 to 1972 he served as prime minister under President Pompidou. He died in 2000, optimistic and energetic to the end.

Nearly a third of voters supported the communists in the post-war period, but this popularity never translated into real political power. As a cultural force they were more successful. The most unlikely people were turning Red. Even Maurice Chevalier was spotted at a communist demonstration. In October 1944, Picasso had come out as a communist, telling the world that 'My joining the [PCF] is the logical outcome of my whole life and my whole body of work . . . by my painting I have always fought as a revolutionary.' The announcement boosted his credentials as an authentic resister, a man of great moral weight as well as an artist of genius. Madeleine Riffaud, who had fought the Germans with guns and bombs, got to know him and he once sketched her, capturing wonderfully her passion, youth and beauty. Her commitment to progress lasted longer than Picasso's. After the war she became a journalist, covering France's wars in Indo-China and Algeria and bringing the same passionate indignation to what she saw as burned within her during her years in the Resistance.

As long as Picasso remained in Paris the city could make some claim to still be the modern-art capital of the world. In reality the centre of gravity had shifted to the United States. Paul Rosenberg never reopened the rue La Boétie gallery and carried on his business in New York, which Alexandre later took over. From 1946 Picasso began spending more and more time in the South of France and eventually moved there permanently, living in a succession of houses on the Côte d'Azur, where Anton Prinner also shifted his studio. The orbital pull of Paris on writers was fading and, though big names continued to live and work there, they lacked the stature of the inter-war giants. Robert Capa and a group of his friends and fellow photographers set up the Magnum picture agency co-operative in Paris in 1948, and the city was nominally his home although he never stopped travelling. Capa swore off war photography after one close shave too many in the 1948 Arab–Israeli conflict. In the spring of 1954, short of money as ever despite his huge success, he took up a last-minute assignment to go to Indo-China for *Life*. On 25 May, he was with a column of French troops under fire from Vietminh insurgents. For all his reluctance to return to the front he was as cool and fearless as ever. After announcing he was walking up to the head of the column to get closer to the action he stepped on a landmine and died of his wounds.

The fading cultural power of Paris scarcely affected its international image. The Paris of the imagination flourished as vigorously as ever, its surface given another gleaming coat of lacquer by the story of the liberation. The euphoric scenes of the newsreels were followed by a succession of movies that reinforced the narrative of stylish heroism. *The Train*, released in 1964, told the story of the rescue of the last great hoard of loot to leave Paris and was inspired by the story of Rose Valland, who by now was herself a French national treasure. It was followed by the 1966 epic *Is Paris Burning?*, based on the book by Larry Collins and Dominique Lapierre of the same name. The title was the English translation of Choltitz's book *Brennt Paris?* The words were allegedly Hitler's, sent in a telegram which Choltitz admitted he only heard about later and which probably never existed.

The movie was directed by René Clément, whose post-war film *La Bataille du rail* had celebrated the role of the *cheminots* in the Resistance. The storyline sticks fairly faithfully to actual events and the use of genuine footage adds to the sense of documentary realism. Several of the actors looked remarkably like the people they represented, with Alain Delon as Chaban-Delmas, Bruno Cremer as Rol-Tanguy and Pierre Dux as Alexandre Parodi. Some of them had lived through the history they were portraying. Leslie Caron, who played a young *résistante*, was a teenager in Paris during the occupation, and Gert Fröbe – General von Choltitz – had been drafted into the German army. Fröbe played him as an honest soldier and fundamentally a decent man, and the script perpetuates the idea that he had defied Hitler by refusing to blow up the city.

Choltitz's self-mythologizing as 'the Man Who Saved Paris' began almost immediately and his interrogators at Trent Park recorded how, under questioning, he had 'launched into a long and dramatic story about his noble efforts' to protect the population from communists. He was released from the US in 1947 and two years later continued burnishing his image in a series of articles in the *Figaro* followed by two books. Despite regular authoritative challenges, Choltitz's version of events proved remarkably durable. The truth was that he had had no means of carrying out the 'field of ruins' order even if he had wanted to. With the mining preparations only partially completed and the city engulfed in the uprising there was no possibility of launching a systematic demolition programme.

If any one person deserved the title of the 'saviour of Paris' it was Dwight D. Eisenhower. His unilateral decision to alter the Allied plan prevented a meltdown into anarchy and starvation. Characteristically, he never made the claim himself. Paris also owed a great debt to the insurgents in all their forms. Not only did the uprising force the Allies to divert, it also restored the city's self-respect and allowed France to go forward buoyed with pride instead of sunk in doubt and shame.

Venal and self-serving though he was, Choltitz deserved some credit. A different German commander might have responded to the uprising with unrestrained ferocity, killing tens of thousands. He had the decency to express remorse for the crimes he and the Wehrmacht had committed, telling his fellow generals in Trent Park, 'We all share the guilt. We went along with everything, and we half took the Nazis seriously, instead of saying "To hell with you and your stupid nonsense."' Before his death in 1966 he returned to the Hôtel Meurice incognito for a nostalgic look around, refusing an offer of champagne from the manager who took a while to recognize the frail old man as the once mighty military governor of Paris.

The myth that *Is Paris Burning?* perpetuates had never been swallowed wholesale and communists and Gaullists did not wait long before struggling to impose their own version of events as historical truth. It would later come under sustained attack by French and American historians, and by films like the Marcel Ophuls documentary *Le Chagrin et la pitié* (1969). It scarcely seemed to matter. Perception was as powerful as established fact and there was enough truth in the story to preserve for ever the memory of the liberation as a shining hour in the nation's history and a foundation legend for post-war France. There was shame but there was also glory. Catholic, communist, bourgeois and worker could treasure it as a moment which the French should never forget, when all stood together on the same side of the barricade and the people of Paris showed what they were worth.

Clément chose to shoot *Is Paris Burning?* in black and white, but as the credits come up it switches to colour for a panoramic view of the city with all the familiar landmarks. In one of the last scenes, a bookish, innocent US infantryman called Sergeant Warren, played by Anthony Perkins, teams up with an FFI fighter to knock out a German tank. They celebrate with a glass of wine in a corner bistrot. 'You know this is exactly the way I thought Paris would be,' says the sergeant. 'A little place like this. Chequered table cloths. Red wine.' Then a hidden German shoots him. It is a bittersweet moment. All along the way poor Warren has been studying maps and trying to fix in his mind the geography of the fabled city which he never thought he would visit. At least he got to see it before he died.

Epilogue: The Ghosts of Paris

I had been in Paris a while when I noticed a small marble plaque, set unobtrusively in the wall of a busy street. After seeing one I saw them everywhere. They were all slightly different in size and there were minor variations in the lettering and wording. The information was the same: *Ici est tombé X . . . Mort pour la France* – a gentle reminder to passers-by that on this spot, during the hot days of August 1944, some FFI fighter, Leclerc Division soldier, Red Cross stretcher bearer or civilian onlooker had been killed – and they had died for the liberation of Paris and France.

ICI EST TOMBÉ
LE 24 AOÛT 1944
...CHEL de BRETAGNE
...RT POUR LA FRANCE

The plaques, I learned, began to go up in the autumn of 1944, paid for by the family, friends, comrades and colleagues of the 'fallen'. Somehow they carry a much stronger emotional charge than a pompous lump of stone or bronze. In the rue de Rivoli where I lived and worked for a few years there were lots of them and walking around the neighbourhood, there was always a ghost at your shoulder.

My newspaper's office was at number 242, above the arcades and opposite the Tuileries where, on the afternoon of Friday 25 August, the battle to capture Choltitz's headquarters at the Meurice was fought. The hotel itself was fifty yards away, its revolving front door the same one that Lieutenant Karcher had burst through to demand the general's surrender.

The office was on the sixth floor and came with a large flat attached and a panoramic view across the city. A few floors below was a club for Swedish expatriates, the Cercle Suédois, where 'the gentleman of Paris', Raoul Nordling, had once socialized. The building appeared in a famous colour photograph taken during the occupation showing enormous swastika flags hanging from the façade. It was not difficult to half close your eyes and imagine the click of jackboots on the pavements and the sound of loud and confident German voices ordering drinks on the café terraces. The apartment itself was said to have been requisitioned, but whether by the Wehrmacht or some more sinister outfit was unclear. I lived there alone and do not mind admitting that sometimes at night I felt spooked, though that may have been because the long main corridor reminded me – and virtually every visitor – of the creepy hotel in *The Shining*, rather than the presence of Nazi phantoms.

Even now, eighty years on, it is easy to summon up the memory of wartime and occupation from the stones of Paris. One reason is that the heart of the city is so intact. The Luftwaffe extensively remodelled the centre of London, Warsaw, Rotterdam and many other European cities. The RAF and the US Army Air Forces did the same for Berlin and virtually every town of any size in Germany. By comparison, Paris emerged from the war a bit chipped at the edges, but the grand boulevards and the narrow streets of the Latin Quarter look much the same today as they did when the bullets were flying.

Paris, anyway, doesn't much like change. For all its sophistication and historic links with the artistic avant-garde, it remains a conservative city. Parisians show a loyalty to old ways of doing things that Londoners and New Yorkers long ago abandoned. At midday, an impressive number of workers, high and low, head off to a neighbourhood bistrot for the *pièce du boucher* washed down with a near-obligatory carafe of *rouge*. Some of the restaurants haven't changed since 1944.

Lunch at Chez Georges near the place des Victoires is not cheap but included in the bill is a journey on a time machine. For the price of a glass of Sancerre you can experience the same vibe in Le Rubis, a wine bar in the rue du Marché-Saint-Honoré.

Political life also resists innovation. The Parti Communiste Français is still a presence, with seventeen deputies, sixteen senators and only a few thousand fewer members than the French Socialist Party. The lanky figure of General de Gaulle continues to cast a long shadow, with President Emmanuel Macron frequently citing him as an inspiration. The old impulse to go down into the streets to make your point is as strong as ever, and there have been many reruns of the 6 February 1934 place de la Concorde riots. In the autumn of 2018 my wife Henrietta, daughter Honor and I were living in bourgeois splendour in the rue de Miromesnil in the 8th arrondissement. Each Saturday, for months, the hi-vis-jacketed *gilets jaunes* protesters took over the quarter to vent their anger at the cost of living. When they departed at the end of the afternoon to take the Métro home, they left behind burned-out cars and smashed shop windows. As the placards they carried depicting Macron as Louis XVI and his wife Brigitte as Marie-Antoinette made clear, they were consciously following a tradition of popular disturbances that ran from 1789 and before, and would keep going until that never-to-be-realized day when every French man, woman and teenager was happy with their lot.

Our prosperous neighbours didn't like it but they didn't complain too much, treating it as a fact of life that must be lived with, like the weather. We decided then that the spirit of Paris is made up of one part conservatism, one part rebelliousness and one part pride, derived from the Parisians' universal conviction that they live in the best city in the world. This was the spirit that sustained the uprising, and it would have survived even if Choltitz had blown the place to smithereens. After all, Paris had been laid waste before, peaceably, by Baron Haussmann when in 1853 he began demolishing the crooked streets of old central Paris to clear the way for the broad, interlocking avenues and neat parks and squares of today. The city was transformed but the people remained the same. Maurice Chevalier was right: 'Paris sera toujours Paris'.

Source Notes

Introduction

'The maternity wards of Paris': For example in the 15th arrondissement, the birth rate more than doubled, with 163 births recorded
between 22 May and 30 June 1945 compared with 79 for the same
period the previous year. There were also significant rises in the 17th
arrondissement for the same period (68 births compared to 47 in 1944)
and the 12th arrondissement (129 compared to 96). In some arrondissements, however, the numbers flatlined and in a few there was a
slight decrease. For the data see www.actedenaissance.fr.

'The American war reporter Ernie Pyle': Ernest Taylor Pyle was
the son of poor Indiana farmers and recorded the war brilliantly from
the perspective of the ordinary GI. He was hugely popular with the
'mud-rain-frost-and-wind boys' of the infantry, and became a
national figure praised by generals and presidents. He was killed in
action in the Pacific in April 1945. Even Ernest Hemingway admired
him. On encountering troops in the field he would sometimes intro-
duce himself as 'Ernie Hemorrhoid – the poor man's Pyle'. For more
see *Ernie's War: The Best of Ernie Pyle's World War II Dispatches*, ed.
David Nichols, Random House, 1986, pp. 42–4.

Gustave-Jean Reybaz was a Swiss-born French army veteran of
the 1914–18 war and an acute observer whose eyewitness testimony to
the uprising will feature later. Maurice Chevalier was vilified by
some in France and Britain after the war as a collaborator. He did
indeed perform for the Germans during the occupation, but his marriage to a Jewish woman made his situation precarious. The translation
of 'Paris sera toujours Paris' is mine, as is the case with other French
texts unless otherwise stated. I try to convey the spirit of the words
rather than go for verbatim accuracy. The African-American vaude-
ville star Josephine Baker made her name as a singer, dancer and

actress in France, performing to mostly white audiences. One of her biggest hits was 'J'ai deux amours' – her love song to Paris. When the war came, she carried on her career in the Unoccupied Zone, while spying for the Allies. In 2021, forty-six years after her death, she was installed in the Panthéon, France's mausoleum to its great men – and, belatedly, women. The contrasting wartime careers of Chevalier and Baker are among many stories showing how the entertainment and artistic worlds dealt with the occupation recorded in Alan Riding's erudite, entertaining and enlightening *And the Show Went On: Cultural Life in Occupied Paris*, Duckworth, 2011.

De Gaulle's speech at the Hôtel de Ville is taken from Julian Jackson's superb and unbeatable *De Gaulle*, Belknap Harvard, 2018, and the translations here and in Chapter 14 are his. The campsite in the Bois de Boulogne is still there, though considerably classier than in 1969 when the restaurant seemed to serve only frankfurters and chips while the soft-porn strains of Serge Gainsbourg and Jane Birkin's 'Je t'aime . . . moi non plus' drifted endlessly from the jukebox.

Prologue: The Diabolical Tourist

Arno Breker provided a long account of the visit in *Paris, Hitler et moi*, Presses de la Cité, 1970, his exculpatory biography charting his journey from expat German artist in 1920s bohemian Paris to official sculptor of the Nazi state. Albert Speer also covered the trip in *Inside the Third Reich*, Weidenfeld & Nicolson, 1990. Hans Baur left behind a memoir, *J'étais le pilote de Hitler*, Perrin, 1990. He became Hitler's personal pilot in 1932 and stayed at his side to the end in the Führerbunker, where he was captured by the Soviets; he spent the next ten years in captivity.

The identity of 'Glouglou', the Opéra's dignified caretaker, comes from *Paris in the Third Reich*, Collins, 1981, by David Pryce-Jones, an excellent illustrated account with many shrewd observations. For another fine illustrated history see *Paris under the Occupation*, The Vendome Press, 1989, which combines fascinating pictures with commentary by the journalist and historian Gilles Perrault and

Jean-Pierre Azéma, a leading French historian of the period. Unauthorized photography of sensitive areas was banned by the French authorities in May 1940, and when the Germans arrived the restriction was applied to the whole of France. Thus all the photographs we have of the period up to the liberation were taken by either German- or Vichy-approved French photographers, or by the multitude of camera-toting German occupiers.

1. City of Darkness, City of Light

Carlos Baker's *Ernest Hemingway: A Life Story*, Collins, 1969, provides most of the biographical details for the early part of Papa's war, supplemented by his own commentary in *Ernest Hemingway: Selected Letters, 1917–1961*, ed. Carlos Baker, Charles Scribner's Sons, 1981. There are too many books on J. D. Salinger to list here. Kenneth Slawenski's *J. D. Salinger: A Life Raised High*, Pomona, 2010, and *Salinger* by David Shields and Shane Salerno, Simon & Schuster, 2013, are as thorough as they could be given their subject's fierce defence of his privacy. The difficulties for the biographer were explored in Ian Hamilton's light-hearted *In Search of Salinger*, Heinemann, 1988. Inevitably the picture is less than complete or reliable. I benefited greatly from the help given to me by the author's son Matt, which is detailed in the Acknowledgements. There are two excellent Capa biographies, Robert Whelan's *Robert Capa: A Biography*, Alfred A. Knopf, 1985, and *Blood and Champagne: The Life and Times of Robert Capa* by Alex Kershaw, Macmillan, 2002. Capa wrote his own wonderful memoir – *Slightly Out of Focus*, Modern Library, 2001, which while not to be treated as strictly factual gives an idea of what it must have been like to be at his table in some bar or restaurant, the booze flowing and the air thick with cigarette smoke, basking in the glow of his warmth and charisma.

I stumbled on the fascinating figure of Anton Prinner in the catalogue of the Charles Chadwyck-Healey Liberation Collection 1944–6, a treasure trove of more than 3,200 books and pamphlets held at Cambridge University Library. Its purpose is to 'show how the

French used the medium of the book to express what had happened to them over the previous five years' and includes a rare copy of Prinner's *La Femme tondue*, published privately in a limited edition of 600 in 1946. Intrigued, I tracked down the Prinner expert Júlia Cserba, who introduced to me to the artist's long-time friend Monique Tanazacq. The three of us had a very enjoyable lunch on Midsummer's Day 2022 in the appropriately nostalgic Le Select brasserie in Montparnasse. Material on Prinner is sparse. The most substantial source is *Anton Prinner*, Éditions du Panama, 2006, a collection of essays and photographs of the work.

Robert Brasillach's story has been studied extensively. A sympathetic view is offered by Pascal Louvrier in *Brasillach: L'illusion fasciste*, Perrin, 1989. Brasillach's brother-in-law Maurice Bardèche defended his old friend faithfully in essays such as 'Une autre image de Brasillach' (in *Robert Brasillach et la génération perdue*, Les Cahiers du Rocher, 1987) which claimed that their circle had no knowledge of the Nazi extermination programme. The best judgement on Brasillach's character and beliefs is in Alice Kaplan's excellent *The Collaborator: The Trial and Execution of Robert Brasillach*, University of Chicago Press, 2000.

Judith Warner gives a good account of the Violette Nozière affair in 'The Murder That Transfixed 1930s Paris', *New York Times*, 3 June 2011. The story inspired the 1978 film *Violette Nozière* directed by Claude Chabrol with Isabelle Huppert in the title role. Roger Bourderon's *Rol-Tanguy: Des Brigades internationales à la libération de Paris*, Tallandier, 2004, provides most of the biographical details cited here. Bourderon had the full co-operation of his subject. He was a communist himself and the tone is respectful. Some comrades had issues with Rol-Tanguy's actions, particularly in Spain, but in general his reputation has weathered well. 'He looked a bit like Jean Gabin': Unlike some of his fellow showbiz contemporaries the great actor had an admirable war, abandoning filming to report for duty in the navy on the first day of mobilization, leaving France to make propaganda movies in Hollywood after the German invasion and returning to Europe as a tank commander with the 2DB.

2. The Black Rain

David Drake's *Paris at War, 1939–1944*, Belknap Harvard, 2015, provides an excellent account of the occupation in the capital. *France: The Dark Years, 1940–1944*, by Julian Jackson, Oxford University Press, 2001, does the same for the whole country. Also see *Occupation: The Ordeal of France, 1940–1944*, Pimlico, 1999, a very readable account by the late Ian Ousby, an often overlooked British historian of France. *Vichy et les Français*, Fayard, 1992, is a monumental collection of essays covering every aspect of the period, under the direction of Jean-Pierre Azéma and François Bédarida. It opens with an account of how historians inside and outside France have treated the subject since the end of the war, a prime example of how historiography can be as interesting and revealing as history. The reality of existence is examined in rich detail in *La Vie des Français sous l'Occupation*, Fayard, 1990, by Henri Amouroux. The debacle is dealt with well in Herbert Lottman's *The Fall of Paris, June 1940*, Sinclair-Stevenson, 1992. The opening quote is from *Paris pendant la guerre (juin 1940–août 1944)*, Hachette, 1946, by Pierre Audiat.

Roger Langeron as prefect of police had a ringside seat at the German takeover and recorded events in his diary, reprinted as *Paris, Juin 1940*, Flammarion, 1946. He was sacked in February 1941 by Vichy for his republican sympathies and retired, to re-emerge after the war as a historian. The Némirovsky quote from *Suite Française* is from the Sandra Smith translation (Vintage Canada, 2007). The success of *Suite Française* and the tragic story behind it have overshadowed Némirovsky's earlier novels, which as well as being works of art provide an invaluable contemporary commentary on the history of the time. The detail about her daughter is from Olivier Philipponnat and Patrick Lienhardt, *The Life of Irène Némirovsky*, Vintage, 2011. Elliot Paul's lament for Paris comes from *A Narrow Street*, The Cresset Press, 1942, also published as *The Last Time I Saw Paris*. Paul was the quintessential American expat writer in inter-war Paris, and a friend of James Joyce and Gertrude Stein. The words of the refugee on the road to Tours come from Roderick Kedward, 'La Crise française vue d'outre-Manche', in *Vichy et les Français*, ed. Azéma and Bédarida.

Of all the books on Picasso the one I leaned on most was Arianna Stassinopoulos Huffington's *Picasso: Creator and Destroyer*, Weidenfeld & Nicolson, 1988. While never denying her subject's genius, Huffington is unflinching in confronting his flaws. Some of the details of Paul Rosenberg's Bordeaux period and back story come from Anne Sinclair, *My Grandfather's Gallery*, Profile Books, 2014. They were supplemented by interviews by phone and in person with Marianne Rosenberg, daughter of Alexandre Rosenberg and granddaughter of Paul, who runs the family's modern and contemporary art gallery on East 66th Street, New York. More details are given in the Acknowledgements.

The life and character of the marshal are examined fairly in Herbert Lottmann's *Pétain: Hero or Traitor*, William Morrow, 1985. The details of his daily routines come from the 'Royaume de Vichy' chapter in Amouroux, *La Vie des Français sous l'Occupation*. In the 1993 documentary *The Eye of Vichy*, Claude Chabrol used official newsreels screened in cinemas throughout the occupation to show how Vichy tried to sell itself to the French people. You can find it on YouTube.

3. *Deutsches Paris*

The description of Brasillach's return come from Louvrier, *Brasillach* and Kaplan, *The Collaborator*. Drake's *Paris at War*, Riding's *And the Show Went On*, Pryce-Jones's *Paris in the Third Reich* and Perrault and Azéma's *Paris under the Occupation* all have a wealth of testimony as well as photographs of the Germans in Paris. The 2020 documentary *When Paris Was German*, available on YouTube, combines fascinating footage with interviews of German men and women who were posted there. The Ernst Jünger diary entries are from *A German Officer in Occupied Paris: The War Journals, 1941–1945*, Columbia University Press, 2019, which has a good biographical foreword by Elliot Neaman. See also Allan Mitchell's *The Devil's Captain: Ernst Jünger in Nazi Paris, 1941–1944*, Berghahn Books, 2011.

The wonderful observation about Picasso's sycophantic visitors was made by an art dealer, Pierre Berès, in an interview with Arianna Huffington, *Picasso*. An account of the activities of the Einsatzstab

Reichsleiter Rosenberg can be found in *Göring's Man in Paris: The Story of a Nazi Art Plunderer and His World* by Jonathan Petropoulos, Yale University Press, 2021. The whole story of the despoliation of French art treasures is told in depth in Michel Rayssac's *L'Exode des musées*, Payot, 2007.

The quote from Ursula von Collenberg comes from a remarkably unreflective but nonetheless revealing interview she gave to David Pryce-Jones. Walter Dreizner's diary entries come from the long article on him by Stefan Martens and Friedrich-Rudolf Nagel, 'Walter Dreizner: Ein deutscher Soldat erlebt die Befreiung von Paris im August 1944', *Militärgeschichtliche Zeitschrift*, vol. 65, issue 2 (2006); Robin Gedye translated. See also Françoise Denoyelle, 'Walter Dreizner: Un Amateur sous influence: *Des télécommunications à la photographic*, in *Francia*, vol. 33, no. 3 (2006), which has a selection of Dreizner's photographs.

The scenes of underfed women at the hospital come from Madeleine Riffaud's *On l'appelait Rainer*, Julliard, 1994. I came across Françoise Bratt, née Girardet, through Mike Kelleher, who kindly arranged for us to meet in March 2022 at Denham Golf Club, where until recently she had been playing regularly. We had a delightful talk, and I supplement her memories with details from her book *Out of Conflict*, Pro-Print, 2003. After the war she married a British diplomat and had many subsequent adventures around the world.

4. First Blood

The French Resistance by Olivier Wievorka, Belknap Harvard, 2016, and *The Resistance: The French Fight against the Nazis* by Matthew Cobb, Simon & Schuster, 2009, are excellent histories of the origins, structure, operations and significance of the movement. The Musée de la Résistance provides full biographies of many of the participants on its website, https://museedelaresistanceenligne.org/. For the relationship between the PCF and Moscow see David Wingeate Pike, 'Between the Junes: The French Communist Party from the Collapse of France to the Invasion of Russia', *Journal of Contemporary*

History, vol. 28, no. 3 (July 1993). Alain Monchablon's 'La Manifestation à l'Étoile du 11 Novembre 1940: Histoire et mémoires', *Vingtième Siècle: Revue d'histoire*, no. 110 (2011/12), gives a full account of the first big anti-German demonstration.

Jacques Chaban-Delmas wrote about his life and motivations in two books, *L'Ardeur*, Stock, 1975, and *Mémoires pour demain*, Flammarion, 1997. Rose Valland described her part in saving art treasures in France from the Nazi industrial-scale looting operation in *Le Front de l'art: Défense des collections françaises 1939–1945*, RMN, 2014, while revealing hardly anything about herself. Madeleine Riffaud wrote her own idiosyncratic autobiography, *On l'appelait Rainer*. Her extraordinary life is the subject of Keren Chiaroni's *Resistance Heroism and the End of Empire: The Life and Times of Madeleine Riffaud*, Routledge, 2017, which also chronicles her subsequent career as a war correspondent. At the other end of the publishing spectrum but equally enjoyable is a graphic treatment of her life on which Madeleine collaborated, by Dominique Bertail and J. D. Morvan: *Madeleine, Résistante*, vol. 1: *La Rose dégoupillée*, Dupuis, 2021. *Dégoupiller* means to unpin, as in hand grenade, and is a nice way of summing up Madeleine's Resistance period.

5. Countdown

Matt Salinger kindly provided additional details and corrected information gleaned from elsewhere about J. D. Salinger's wartime career. He also shared a recording of a lunch he had with his father's friend and counter-intelligence comrade John Keenan in which Keenan reminisced about their service together. I am grateful to the Keenan family for allowing me to use the material. The letters to Whit Burnett are held in the Special Collections department of the Firestone Library at Princeton University, in the Story Magazine and Story Press Records (CO 104) along with unpublished J. D. Salinger story manuscripts, including 'The Magic Foxhole'.

The campaign is chronicled in *History of the Twelfth Infantry Regiment in World War II* by Colonel Gerden F. Johnson, National Fourth

Division Association, 1947. The details of Hemingway's pre-invasion roistering in London come mainly from Capa's *Slightly Out of Focus* and Charles Whiting's *Papa Goes to War: Ernest Hemingway in Europe, 1944–45*, The Crowood Press, 1990, which is entertaining and well researched, though in my view a little too hard on its subject. The *Spanish Earth* documentary is available on YouTube. The commentary was supplied by Hemingway and his rather grating voice comes as a surprise. For the story of La Nueve I have relied largely on Raymond Dronne's account of his war, *Carnets de route d'un croisé de la France libre*, Éditions France-Empire, 1984, supplemented by Evelyn Mesquida's very useful *La Nueve: 24 août 1944*, Cherche Midi, 2014. There are several major biographies of Philippe Leclerc de Haute-clocque in French but only one that I know of in English and it is a very good one. As the title suggests, *Free France's Lion: The Life of Philippe Leclerc, de Gaulle's Greatest General* by William Mortimer Moore, Casemate, 2011, is an unashamed celebration of *le Patron* but is far from hagiography. The details of the last days before embarkation are from Stephen E. Ambrose's superb *D-Day: June 6, 1944*, Simon & Schuster, 2014.

6. Bouillon

The damage done to occupied Europe by Allied bombers is often overlooked. Eddie Florentin revealed the human and material cost to France in *Quand les Alliés bombardaient la France, 1940–1945*, Perrin, 1997. Charles Rist was an old-school economist and French government adviser whose thoughtful wartime journal was republished in translation as *A Season of Infamy: A Diary of War and Occupation, 1939–1945* by the Indiana University Press in 2016. Raymond Ruffin provided another perceptive account from the viewpoint of an adventurous and questioning adolescent in *Journal d'un J3*, Presses de la Cité, 1979. The title refers to the category he was assigned to as a thirteen- to twenty-one-year-old for the allocation of rations. Jean Galtier-Boissière's shrewd and sceptical observations first appeared just after the war as *Mon journal pendant l'Occupation, 1940–1944* and were republished in 2016 by Libretto. Some of the details of the marshal's visit to Paris were taken from Robert Aron's massive *Histoire des années 40*, which first appeared in 1954. Before the war he was a proponent of economic and social reform along corporatist lines and an enthusiast for a European federation. He was arrested in 1941 as a Jew but freed and later escaped to North Africa. I bought my set of the ten volumes, published by Librairie Jules Tallandier in 1976 and beautifully bound in blue leather, from the antiquarian bookstore which used to sit under the arcades of the rue de Castiglione on the corner with the rue du Mont Thabor. A regular customer was the then president of France, François Mitterrand, who liked to browse there anonymously.

The 'Manouchian Affair' generated much bitter debate inside communist ranks which smouldered on long after the end of the war, bursting into flames again in 1983 with the appearance of the documentary *Des terroristes à la retraite* ('Terrorists in Retirement'). Written and directed by Mosco Boucault it sought to win the FTP–MOI their rightful place in the history of the Resistance as well as to reanimate the controversy over the arrests of Manouchian and the rest of the group. France finally acknowledged its debt to them in June 2023 when President Macron announced that Manouchian would be entered into the Panthéon the following February. Some friends of Picasso disputed his apparently flippant response to Max Jacob's arrest, recorded in Pierre Andreu's *Vie et mort de Max Jacob*, La Table Ronde, 1982. Whatever the truth, it seems clear that this was not the artist's finest hour. The story of Lecompte-Boinet's sobering evening with the general comes from Julian Jackson's monumental *De Gaulle*, cited above.

7. Ashore

The sources for the Salinger material are detailed in the notes for Chapter 5 above. The battery at Azeville is now a museum where visitors can explore the tunnels connecting the casemates and reflect on what a cushy life the German garrison enjoyed compared to the hellish existence of their comrades on the Eastern Front. See www.batterie-azeville.manche.fr for more details. 'Voyage to Victory', Ernest Hemingway's D-Day despatch for *Collier's*, is included along with those covering the liberation of Paris on the www.billdownscbs.com site. Eisenhower's relationship with de Gaulle is set out very fully in Jean Edward Smith's *The Liberation of Paris: How Eisenhower, de Gaulle, and von Choltitz Saved the City of Light*, Simon & Schuster, 2019. Smith is a distinguished biographer of Ike and this short account is commendable for its clarity and handling of the overlapping narratives.

8. Reveille

A key work in chronicling the progress of the uprising remains Adrien Dansette's *Histoire de la libération de Paris*, first published by Fayard in 1946 and, as the historian Henri Amouroux noted, 'a book made to last'. Dansette was in his mid-forties and had already established a reputation as a historian of the nineteenth century. He seized the opportunity to record history almost as it happened through the testimony of many participants gathered while memories were still fresh. Nearly eighty years on, the book still conveys the excitement of the time. It remains a key resource and much of the information that follows derives from there. André Calvès wrote a remarkable memoir, *Sans bottes ni médailles: Un trotskyste breton dans la guerre* ('No Boots, No Medals: A Trotskyist Breton in the War'), Éditions La Brèche, 1984, which sets out in unromantic detail the brutal ad hoc nature of much Resistance activity.

We are lucky to be able to assess Choltitz from several angles. He was voluble on the subject of his career and his time in Paris, starting with a series of articles in the *Figaro* newspaper in October 1949 ('Pourquoi, en 1944, je n'ai pas détruit Paris') and including a memoir which appeared in France as *Un Soldat parmi des soldats* – roughly 'A Soldier's Soldier' – Aubanel, 1962. Naturally, all showed him in a sympathetic light. Thanks to the brilliant bugging operation carried out by British intelligence at Trent Park where high-ranking German captives were held, we also have the opinions of Choltitz's fellow officers on his character which are sometimes far from flattering, supplemented by the assessments of his captors. The entire transcripts, which provide a fascinating insight into the German and Nazi military mindset, can be found at the British National Archives in WO 208/3504, WO 208/4363 and WO 208/5018. The story of Trent Park is excellently told in Helen Fry's *The Walls Have Ears*, Yale University Press, 2019. Details on Choltitz's service in the east come from *The Holocaust in the Crimea and the North Caucasus* by Kiril Feferman, Yad Vashem Publications, 2016, and *War of Extermination: The German Military in World War II*, ed. Hannes Heer and Klaus Maumann, trans. Roy Shelton, Berghahn Books, 2004.

9. *Chacun son Boche!*

For the best account of the day-to-day progress of the uprising and liberation see Matthew Cobb's *Eleven Days in August: The Liberation of Paris in 1944*, Simon & Schuster, 2013. Some of the Chaban-Delmas details in this chapter are taken from Philippe Ragueneau and Eddy Florentin's *Paris libéré: Ils étaient là!*, France-Empire, 1994. This is a collection of interviews with key participants dating from the late 1980s.

'The police were a byword for cynicism': The role of the *flics* in the uprising and liberation is one of the most fascinating aspects of the story. See Simon Kitson's 'The Police in the Liberation of Paris', in *The Liberation of France: Image and Event*, ed. H. R. Kedward and Nancy Wood, Berg, 1995. The description of Brasillach's farewell dinner in the garden of the Deutsches Institut comes from his *Journal d'un homme occupé* ('Diary of an Occupied Man'), a memoir of wartime, put together from his writings after his death and republished in 2019 by Pardès.

10. *Flics* and Fifis

'The Vichy loyalist Bussière': The story of Amédée Bussière, prefect of the Paris police from June 1942 until his arrest and imprisonment on 20 August 1944, is an illustration of how even ostensibly enthusiastic collaborators took care to keep at least a toe in the opposite camp. Bussière was present at the meeting to organize the great round-up of Paris Jews in July 1942 and threw police resources into the struggle against the 'communo-terroristes' of the Resistance. But he also appears to have given help to certain of its members and to have done something to hinder German anti-Jewish operations, all of which helped to get the death sentence he was handed after his trial in the summer of 1946 commuted to one of forced labour. He was freed in 1951 to the fury of the communists. For further biographical details on him and many other characters featured in this book see the very useful *Dictionnaire historique de la France sous l'Occupation*, ed. Michèle and Jean-Paul Cointet, Tallandier, 2000.

Claude Roy's report comes from a despatch he wrote for *Les Lettres Françaises*. It appeared along with a number of other eyewitness accounts in *La Libération de Paris (19–26 août 1944)*, collated by Suzanne Campaux and republished in 2019 by Éditions Glyphe. Campaux is an interesting figure who translated literary works from Russian, Italian and English into French and worked with Adrien Dansette interviewing participants. In his own book, *Histoire de la libération de Paris*, Dansette issued a health warning about the strict veracity of the details and counselled against reading too much into individual testimony, asking, 'Does having spent one day tossed by the waves mean one knows the sea and the mystery of its depths?' Perhaps not, but it must give you a pretty good idea. Images of the fighting in and around the prefecture can be seen in *La Libération de Paris*, the documentary put together from footage shot by Resistance cameramen and released in September 1944. It is available on YouTube.

11. Volte-face

Normandy is well stocked with memorials marking the progress of the Allies, and there is a modest monument at Eisenhower's rural advance command post on the D15 just outside the village of Tournières. Allied strategy is explained clearly and entertainingly in

Martin Blumenson's *United States Army in World War II: The European Theater of Operations: Breakout and Pursuit*, Whitman, 2012. Jean Edward Smith, *The Liberation of Paris*, gives a definitive account of the process by which Ike came to change the plan. The epic journey across the lines by Roger Cocteau-Gallois may have had little effect on the decision but it made for a great story and featured in the 1966 movie *Is Paris Burning?* David Bruce's journals were published as *OSS against the Reich: The World War II Diaries of Colonel David K. E. Bruce*, edited by Nelson Douglas Lankford, The Kent State University Press, 1991. Bruce went on to be US ambassador to France and the United Kingdom. Capa's brilliant photograph of Simone Touseau inspired many French journalistic enquiries into the story behind it, such as 'La Véritable Histoire de la tondue de Chartres', *Paris Match*, 22 August 2014. Touseau's fascinating back story was also the subject of a 2017 documentary, *La Tondue de Chartres*, and the basis for a novel by Julie Héraclès, *Vous ne connaissez rien de moi*, which appeared in 2023.

12. Days of Rage

The descriptions of the heroic defenders of the barricades come from Dansette, *Histoire de la libération de Paris*. The barricades were a natural subject for the professional and amateur photographers out in force during the uprising, who sometimes seemed to frame their images in conscious reference to Delacroix and to photographs taken during the 1871 Paris Commune. For a fascinating discussion of the subject with illustrations see Catherine E. Clark, 'Capturing the Moment, Picturing History: Photographs of the Liberation of Paris', *American Historical Review*, vol. 121, no. 3 (June 2016). Georges Dukson appears in several shots in the 1944 *Libération de Paris* documentary and was pictured a few feet away from de Gaulle as he set off down the Champs-Élysées on 26 August. After the liberation he became a minor celebrity but got involved in the black market, was arrested and then shot while trying to escape; he died in hospital of his wounds on 11 November 1944. There is an interesting article on him by Éric Lafon, 'Photographie de Dukson, "un oublié de l'histoire" de la Libération', on the www.fondationresistance.org website. The extent to which Choltitz was capable of carrying out the 'field of ruins' order had he so wished was investigated in the thorough and convincing 2019 French documentary, written and directed by Françoise Cros de Fabrique, *Détruire Paris: Les plans secrets d'Hitler* ('Destroy Paris: Hitler's Secret Plans').

13. Chimes of Freedom

'The Americans watched Billotte's progress with mounting alarm': Their exasperation with the French continued throughout the liberation and often with good reason. Martin Blumenson in *Breakout and Pursuit* records how Leclerc seemed irritated when the 4th Infantry Division's commander Major-General Raymond O. Barton interrupted his lunch at the police prefecture. The sentiment was not confined to the brass and some in the ranks of the Ivy felt that the French had hogged the glory for what had been a joint effort.

'The radio which had belatedly started to broadcast uncensored news': French broadcasters reacted cautiously to the fast-changing circumstances and on 22 August initially limited their defiance of the Germans to broadcasting music by composers and artists banned by the authorities on account of their Jewishness. At 10.30 that evening they joined the fray, broadcasting Rol-Tanguy's call to arms.

14. The Day the War Should Have Ended

The Leclerc Division's operations before and inside Paris are chronicled in forensic detail in Laurent Fournier and Alain Eymard's *La 2ᵉ DB dans la libération de Paris et de sa région*, vol. 1: *De Trappes à l'Hôtel de Ville*, Histoire et Collections, 2009; vol. 2: *De l'attaque de l'hôtel Majestic aux combats du Bourget*, Histoire et Collections, 2010 – a gorgeous ensemble of photographs, movie stills, graphics, maps and personal testimony. Several 'Rochambelles' wrote their own memoirs, and their exploits produced a history, Ellen Hampton's *Women of Valor:*

The Rochambelles on the World War II Front, McFarland, 2021. The story of the British Quaker volunteers is waiting to be written. Lieutenant Henri Karcher's recorded account of taking the Meurice was considered exciting enough to be put on sale as a 33⅓ rpm disc, *La Capitulation du Général von Choltitz*. It can be heard online on the Bibliothèque Nationale de France website www.gallica.bnf.fr.

If Ernest Hemingway returned to the Travellers Club today he would find it much the same as it was on 25 August 1944, possibly with some of the same members at the bar. The Ritz would be his base on his frequent post-war visits to Paris and his loyalty was rewarded when the staff recovered two suitcases of his notes dating back to the 1920s which he thought had been lost. They were restored to him in August 1957 and must have helped jog his memory when he began writing *A Moveable Feast* later that year. He would surely be delighted that Le Petit Bar at the rear of the hotel on the rue Cambon side was in 1979 renamed the Bar Hemingway.

'When he had finished, de Gaulle seemed as moved by his own words': De Gaulle's emotions are movingly displayed in a clip of the speech at the Hôtel de Ville available on YouTube. Jacques Massu, who took the surrender at the Majestic, went on to fight in Indo-China and Suez. In 1957 he led the campaign against Algerian FLN fighters rebelling against French rule in the Battle of Algiers and became notorious after admitting that captured insurgents were tortured to gain information. He later expressed regret and his wife Suzanne, a former Rochambelle, adopted two Algerian children.

15. Awakening

Robert Reid's dramatic radio report of de Gaulle's arrival at Notre-Dame features in the 'History of the BBC' section of the Corporation's website www.bbc.co.uk, complete with gunfire which at points is continuous. Sylvia Beach gave a delightful account of her reunion with Hemingway in a 1962 interview also available on YouTube. It was more than sixty years before the story of torture and murder at the Eastman Institute began to circulate widely, thanks to books and articles by historians like Jean-Marc Berlière. A documentary on Berlière's findings, *Règlement de comptes à l'Institut*, appeared in 2021. When he began his research many files were still closed under the terms of the amnesties that followed the *épuration légale*. René Sentuc was never brought to justice and ended up as deputy mayor of the Paris suburb of Malakoff.

16. *Mise en scène*

The way in which the post-liberation authorities moved to shape the narrative of the events of August 1944 is laid out in Catherine E. Clark's article 'Capturing the Moment'. Robert Brasillach continued until recently to be an inspirational figure to the French far right, quoted approvingly by Jean-Marie Le Pen, founder of the National Front, since renamed National Rally. J. D. Salinger's stay in Tiverton which inspired 'For Esmé with Love and Squalor' was the subject of a BBC Radio documentary, *J. D. Salinger, Made in England: How 3 Months in Rural Devon Influenced One of the Greatest Chroniclers of Urban New York*. That is not perhaps how he would like to be described but it is a charming exploration of a geographical footnote of literary history and, though first broadcast in 2016, was still available at the time of writing on BBC Sounds.

Epilogue: The Ghosts of Paris

The locations of the memorial plaques can be mapped by Googling 'Les Plaques commémoratives de la Libération de Paris'. There are 282 listed, which is far fewer than the number of French men and women who died. Nearly eighty of them memorialize policemen. As the monuments were put up privately, this may have been an attempt by the *flics* to repair their image by reminding the public that they too had shed their blood. Readers should also check out Paris historian Gilles Primout's website, https://liberation-de-paris-gilles-primout.fr

which recounts the stories of the events and personalities of the liberation from street level.

The office where I worked as the Paris bureau chief of the London *Daily Telegraph* at the turn of the century was at 242 rue de Rivoli. In those days the area still had local shops and restaurants, most of which have now been turned into designer outlets. There are nonetheless a healthy number of reminders of old Paris like Le Rubis, our office watering hole in the rue du Marché-Saint-Honoré. The old owners have long gone but the young new *patron* is pledged to keeping it as it always has been.

Patrick Bishop is happy to be contacted by readers on paddybishop2001@gmail.com.

Acknowledgements

Research is fun. Writing, not so much. Amassing the material for *Paris '44* was a labour of love, but the task was made easier by the expert help offered by archivists and librarians in France, the United States and Britain. In Paris, I would like to thank Sylvie Zaidman, director of the Musée de la Libération, and Catherine Castéra, head of the documentation department; Evelyne Gredin, head of archives at the Ville d'Aulnay-sous-Bois, and the staff of the Bibliothèque Nationale de France. In the US, I am grateful to Emma Sarconi, Taylor Madison and AnnaLee Pauls for guiding me through the J. D. Salinger material in Princeton University's Firestone Library Special Collections department. In the UK, my thanks to the ever-obliging staffs of the London Library and the National Archives as well as to Claire Welford-Elkin of Cambridge University Library for her help accessing the wonderful Chadwyck-Healey Liberation Collection.

Very few of those who were there at the liberation are still with us. As a result of a generous intervention by Mike Kelleher, I was privileged to meet Françoise Bratt, née Girardet, at Denham Golf Club in Buckinghamshire, where she played until recently, to hear her memories of wartime Paris. All the other characters who feature in the story are dead, apart from Madeleine Riffaud, ninety-nine years old at the time of writing. We spoke on the phone a few times but given the richness of her recorded testimony I didn't want to burden her with the bother of an interview.

My researches into other players were supplemented by the help I got from their family and friends. I am particularly grateful to Matt Salinger for his great generosity in helping me understand this period in his father's life. Matt answered all my questions patiently and thoroughly by email, following up with an enjoyable lunch in Westport, Connecticut. He also shared a fascinating tape of a conversation with

J. D. Salinger's wartime comrade and lifelong friend John Keenan, which the Keenan family have kindly allowed me to make use of.

Some of the many gaps in the largely unrecorded life of Anton Prinner were filled in for me by longtime friend Monique Tanazacq and art historian Julia Cserba. We met at a place Prinner would have known well, Le Select in Montparnasse which, though on the tourist trail, still retains a touch of old bohemian Paris – a memorable encounter which greatly enriched my understanding of this fascinating figure. *Merci mille fois, mesdames.*

I would also like to thank Marianne Rosenberg for taking the time to talk to me over the phone and in person in her New York gallery about the quiet heroism of her father Alexandre.

On my travels I was looked after and kept company by old friends Askold Krushelnycky and Irka Chalupa in Washington and Pirate Irwin and Florence Biedermann in Paris. There will always be a bed, a bite and a bottle for you in Brook Green. I would also like to acknowledge the running support I got from colleagues and pals who chipped in their thoughts and suggestions. In particular my agent, counsellor and buddy Annabel Merullo, who as usual was always there to encourage and commiserate. Richard Foreman's wisdom and humour lightened the load and Jonathan Ford, Robin Gedye and Lesley Hall were always on hand for a pint in the BGH.

Book writing is a team effort. I am very grateful to the professionalism and skill of Daniel Crewe, Greg Clowes, Alexandra Mulholland, Emma Brown and the rest of the team at Penguin Viking. My greatest thanks go to Peter James. Peter is the king of copy-editors, enormously knowledgeable and ever alert to the dud fact or sloppy sentence. His creative rigour has benefited *Paris '44* enormously. So too have the very helpful comments of Professor Julian Jackson who kindly read the manuscript.

The last word, as always, goes to Hen and Honor. It's over now. All my love and thanks for putting up with me.

Index

Page references in *italics* indicate images.